The English Country House Chapel

Building a Protestant Tradition

For Theo and Katie

The English Country House Chapel

Building a Protestant Tradition

Annabel Ricketts

Edited by Simon Ricketts

Spire Books Ltd

PO Box 2336. Reading RG4 5WJ
www.spirebooks.com

Spire Books Ltd
PO Box 2336
Reading RG4 5WJ
www.spirebooks.com

CIP data:
A catalogue record for this book is available
from the British Library
ISBN 978-1-904965-05-3

Designed and produced by John Elliott
Text set in Adobe Bembo

Printed by Latimer Trend & Company Ltd
Estover Road, Plymouth PL6 7PY

The publisher and editor gratefully acknowledge financial assistance from the
Paul Mellon Centre for Studies in British Art, the Marc Fitch Foundation and a
Dorothy Stroud Bursary awarded by the Society of Architectural Historians of
Great Britain

CONTENTS

THE AUTHOR AND EDITOR

Before her early death in 2003, Annabel Ricketts had made the study of the 16th and 17th- century private chapel very much her own. She was educated at St Mary's, Wantage, and London University (where she read English and, later, Art History). She worked initially for the National Trust and, while bringing up a family, as a freelance/visiting lecturer in Architectural History for, among others, London University (Birkbeck and University Colleges, and the Courtauld Institute), the Department for Continuing Education at Oxford University, the Study Centre, Renaissance Art Studies, the Victoria and Albert Museum, and the Royal Academy. She also reviewed for the arts pages of *The Spectator*, and contributed to the *Dictionary of National Biography* and the *Grove Dictionary of Art*. From 1995 to 2003 she was Head of the Fine & Performing Arts Department at Regent's College, London. She submitted her Ph.D thesis on the development of the English Protestant country house chapel to Birkbeck College in 2003 and was awarded a posthumous degree in 2004. Her publications include *Michelangelo* (with Lucinda Collinge: London, 1991); 'The Country House Chapel in the Seventeenth Century' in *The Seventeenth Century Great House* (M. Airs, editor), (Oxford, 1995); '"All the Pride of Prayer": the Purpose of the Private Chapel at Chatsworth' in *Baroque and Palladian: the Early 18th- Century Great House* (M. Airs, editor), (Oxford, 1996); 'Hatfield: a House for the Lord Treasurer' (with J. Newman and C. Gapper) in *Patronage, Culture and Power: the Early Cecils* (P. Croft, editor), (New Haven and London, 2002); 'Designing for Protestant Worship: The Private Chapels of the Cecil Family' (C. Gapper and C. Knight, editors) in *Defining the Holy: Sacred Spaces in Medieval and Early Modern Europe* (A. Spicer and S. Hamilton, editors), (Aldershot and Burlington, 2005).

Simon Ricketts was educated at Ampleforth, and Magdalen College, Oxford, where he read History. He is a Civil Servant and was appointed CB in 2000.

Annabel photographed in 2001.

ACKNOWLEDGEMENTS BY THE AUTHOR

(from her Ph.D thesis)

My greatest debt is to the owners, trustees and curators of the chapels covered in this thesis, for without their help it could not have been written. I am particularly grateful to all those who spent valuable time discussing their chapels with me and who provided much appreciated sustenance.

Thanks too are due to the archivists, and here I owe much to Robin Harcourt Williams of Hatfield, who has been unfailingly helpful and patient, and to Peter Gray at Chatsworth. At National Trust houses my task was considerably eased by being able to benefit from unpublished research, particularly at Petworth. At The Vyne, I benefited greatly from the knowledge of Kevin Rogers and the archaeologist Ed Wilson, both of whom have given much time to the numerous problems this chapel poses.

Many friends and colleagues contributed information that I would otherwise have missed, such as the 17th-century chapel at Woburn brought to my attention by Dianne Duggan. Claire Gapper and Caroline Knight were informed and congenial travelling companions, while Nicholas Cooper had an uncanny knack of making discoveries that solved seemingly intractable problems. I owe a great debt to Margaret Aston who both helped me to understand the context in which the chapels developed and commented on a draft chapter with erudition, patience and humour.

Countless people had me to stay. Particularly hospitable were Alice Fremantle and Lavinia Marsden Smedley who, being so perfectly placed off the A1 and M5 respectively, found themselves seeing more of me than they had bargained for. My family bore the tribulations of chapel visiting with (mostly) good-humoured resignation, and my husband, Simon, patiently read and bravely commented on the draft.

Finally, my supervisor Peter Draper was wise enough not to try to hurry me, but in the final rush to get the text finished, with Laura Jacobus, did everything that could possibly be done to help. This included giving me vital encouragement and assistance at the end, and setting up an expert team at Birkbeck – under Hazel Gardiner, with Anna Bentkowska, Francis Ware and others – to help with reproducing the illustrations. Without all that kindness the thesis would not have been finished.

Annabel Ricketts

ACKNOWLEDGEMENTS BY THE EDITOR

This book is a slight reworking of my wife, Annabel's Ph.D thesis on the development of the English country house chapel after the Reformation. The thoughts and words are hers, and the primary acknowledgement is therefore to her for leaving such a lucid and well-written work. She died before she could make a start on the book, and she would have made it more punchy and amusing than I have dared (or would have been able) to do. But I hope she will approve of it in a small way, not be too cross that I have had the courage to modify one or two of her sentences, and be pleased that her very special and original work has been brought to a wider audience.

Academic friends and colleagues have helped me to adapt Annabel's thesis for the more general reader without, it is hoped, diluting the scholarly value of her discoveries. My deepest thanks go to Claire Gapper and Caroline Knight who made numerous wise comments as the book developed, as well as giving emotional support. I am also extremely grateful to Maurice Howard and Margaret Aston, both of whom found time to read the revised text at an early stage, for their advice and suggestions.

Julia Brown generously discussed the illustrations, and taught me to negotiate reproduction rights and other related pitfalls; Dorothy Girouard patiently explained how books are put together and helped choose and lay out the colour plates; and Robert Gray conducted diligent and fruitful researches in the British Library. Thanks also to Melissa Beasley who, assisted by James Boatright, has drawn some wonderfully clear and accessible plans, and to the Sir John Soane Museum for allowing her to examine their collection of John Thorpe's drawings. Thanks too to the many organisations which, almost without exception, waived or reduced reproduction fees on illustrations; to Geoff Brandwood, John Elliott and Chris Webster at Spire Books; and to the Paul Mellon Centre, Marc Fitch Foundation, and the Society of Architectural Historians of Great Britain for their generous donations, without which there would have been no plans, no illustrations, and no colour. Thanks, finally, to Trevor Dannatt, and to John and Virginia Murray, for their support before and during the project, and to many other friends for their sustained interest and encouragement.

Any author's royalties will go to the Society of Architectural Historians of Great Britain Annabel Ricketts Memorial Fund.

Simon Ricketts

PICTURE CREDITS

KEY TO PLANS

A = Chapel (A1 = Chancel, Inner Chapel or East Cell; A2 = Nave, Outer Chapel, Ante-chapel, West Cell or Narthex)

B = Chapel Closet

C = Upper Chapel or Chapel Gallery

D = Other Peripheral Chapel Space (Chapel Chamber, Vestry, Dual Purpose Space, etc.)

E = Great Hall

F = Great Chamber

G = Dining Room

H = Parlour

I = Library

J = Bedroom or Other Private Chamber

K = Nursery

L = Kitchen

M = Service Rooms and Accommodation

N = Great or Main Stair

O = Long Gallery

P = Courtyard

Q = Building Entrance

INTRODUCTION

Those of us who think of the English country house chapel may well call to mind a vision rooted in the late 17th century. With the architecture neatly and logically ordered after the manner of Christopher Wren, the chaplain officiates from the east end, the family presides from a first-floor gallery at the west end, and the respectful household is gathered obediently in the body of the chapel beneath. But this dignified and serene picture represents the Protestant chapel at a fully developed stage. The reality is that it evolved tortuously over 150 years following the Reformation, undergoing numerous transformations as patrons sought to achieve a definitively Protestant design. Time has a tendency to tidy away extreme and idiosyncratic examples of architectural experimentation, and private chapels, with the added pressure of changes in patrons' religious affiliations, were more susceptible to alteration or destruction than any other area of the house. And makeshift arrangements were once common, both before and after the Reformation, especially in gentry houses. In the early Tudor extension at Gurney Street Manor in Somerset, for example, there is a hatch in the floor of an upper chamber which can be lifted to establish a direct connection with the tiny chapel below.[1] Over one hundred years later, the now lost chapel of Hunstanton Hall in Norfolk was located 'within the turn of the (great oak) staircase'. It 'was open on all sides through the banisters, and to the gallery above; so that the domestics might be present at the offices there performed: for the chapel itself is more like a large pew for the family.'[2] Ironically, it took the return of Roman Catholicism to the centre of power with the accession of James II in 1685 to prompt the creation of a fully Protestant solution. In this the humble, single-cell chapel was transformed into a grand and dignified space, and Protestant decoration found an independent voice.

The Form of the Pre and Post-Reformation Chapel

Like the parish church, the typical pre-Reformation private chapel consisted of two cells: the nave (or outer or ante-chapel), where the congregation gathered, and the chancel (or inner chapel), where Mass was celebrated and the chapel staff (and in some cases important lay people) were accommodated. Access to the chancel from the nave was impeded by the chancel screen. During the lengthy period of experimentation that followed the Reformation, different types of chapel evolved as patrons struggled to conform to the developing (and often competing) practices and beliefs of the reformed religion and changes in decorative and architectural fashion. Patrons also had to track the changing fortunes of the monarchy and episcopate, where the penalty for getting it wrong could lead not just to financial ruin, but also to arrest, imprisonment and even death. At some periods during this evolution the chapel comprised an important, and sometimes contrasting, element in the architectural hierarchy of the house, while at others it was reduced to a room with no independent facade or external differentiation. Variations in the way in which patrons and architects approached the design of the chapel derived not just from the demands of fashion and competing ideas about religious practice and decorum, but also from the need to resolve the sometimes conflicting pressures of expressing both piety and social status.

Four main types of private chapel evolved in the course of this experimentation. They can be defined by the differing architecture of their inner and outer spaces, and the position of a screen (if any). They ranged from the single-cell chapel; through the narthex type (where a screen or other partition was installed west of the main seating area); to the assembly chapel (which possessed dual function spaces separated by openwork screens); and the double-cell, two-centred chapel. In the latter, which superficially resembled the pre-Reformation chapel, the screen created two areas with different liturgical functions. In the eastern section the congregation gathered when celebrating communion, while the western cell was used for other services such as those centring on prayer and preaching.[3]

The Rooms and Spaces around the Chapel (the Peripheral Spaces)

Two types of peripheral space were associated with the chapel, often increasing its capacity for worship. The first comprised subsidiary household rooms known as chapel chambers. They were associated with the chapel by function, by architectural features such as squints or, in some cases, by proximity alone. Like so many 16th-century rooms, they could fulfil a variety of uses, the most frequent being that of a bedchamber. Often they were used in conjunction with the chapel for religious purposes, for example as a vestry, but some had no obvious religious use. And, confusingly, some chapel-less houses possessed chapel chambers that had no discernible religious function. Whatever the case, the term was becoming old-fashioned by the start of the 17th century.[4]

The second type of peripheral space was more closely linked to the main chapel and occurred in the form of galleries and closets at ground-floor and first-floor or mezzanine level. Over a period spanning some 200 years chapel terminology changed. For example, the word 'gallery' was rarely used to refer to any chapel space in the early Tudor period. The relatively neutral term 'upper chapel' will be used here to refer to this type of space before the Restoration, although it was in fact an early 17th-century term, first appearing in the 1601 inventories for Chatsworth and Hardwick Hall in Derbyshire.[5] Its gradual spread can be followed in microcosm at Hatfield House in Hertfordshire: the 1611 inventory lists this space as 'the closett above the chappell', but there were already references to the 'upper chapel' in the building accounts, and the 1621 inventory describes it as the 'upper chapel'.[6] An inventory was often the final record of a generation's tenure and likely to be backward looking in its terminology. Evidence taken from inventories, therefore, is at best conservative and at times positively old-fashioned.

The character of the upper chapel spaces changed after the Restoration. Formerly, many were in effect rooms and often included fireplaces, but after 1660 they were usually relatively narrow, lost the shape and character of a room and migrated to the west end.[7] It is interesting that the name of the space also changed, perhaps heralded by the use of the term 'chapel gallery' in the 1660 inventory of Temple Newsam in West Yorkshire to denote the upper level space at the west end of the chapel there.[8] Accordingly, the term 'gallery' will be used for upper chapels created after the Restoration.

Private Closets

Before the Reformation, aristocratic patrons might follow the practice of early Tudor royal households of attending Mass in a private closet near the bedchamber, while appearances in the chapel proper would often serve a symbolic rather than a spiritual purpose. The celebration of services in a private closet or oratory appears to have continued into the 17th century.[9] Maintaining the pre-Reformation separation of public and private religious life could have been in part an attempt to solve the problem of worship in households made up of Roman Catholics and Protestants. Mixed households certainly existed during the 17th century. Henry Percy, 9th Earl of Northumberland, keen to affirm his Protestant credentials, wrote 'I am no supporter of recusants, neither is my house pestered with them, some one or two old servants of my house excepted'.[10] And in the 1640s, Thomas Bayly, the chaplain at Raglan Castle in Monmouthshire, where the patron, the Marquess of Worcester, was a Roman Catholic, wrote 'that which is most wonderful unto me was the servants of his house (being half papists and half Protestants) were never at variance in the point of Religion, which has been brought about by prohibiting disputations'.[11]

Chapel Fittings

Information about chapel fittings is sparse.[12] No surviving chapel retains a complete set of original fittings and, given the ease with which woodwork can be altered or re-used, and the zeal with which patrons in the 19th century used old woodwork when altering or creating chapels, it is unwise to accept too trustingly what remains today. It is clearly unlikely that fittings from a pre-Reformation chapel would survive unaltered for many generations in a family that had transferred its loyalties to the Protestant religion; equally, since attitudes to Protestant worship did not remain static, further changes were to be expected as generation succeeded generation. The problems are at their most intractable in the 16th century, but the 17th century also poses difficulties because, although the amount of surviving fittings increases considerably, it is often difficult to identify later alterations and insertions.

Unfortunately, the two major documentary sources for the 16th and 17th centuries – inventories and plans – are in most cases of little use in determining how private chapels were fitted out. Some types of fitting, such as screens, never appear in inventories whilst others, such as altar rails, do so only sporadically. Hence the absence of a particular element cannot be taken as evidence that it did not exist. Similarly, plans often do not record altars, let alone pews, screens and pulpits. Written descriptions are relatively rare and, where they do exist, do not usually focus on fittings.

Chapel Decoration

Similar difficulties arise when considering the decoration of private chapels.[13] No chapels retain their decoration unaltered: indeed, as with fittings, those that appear to do so should be viewed with suspicion. Successive patrons used decorative forms and iconographic schemes in different ways to express their personal beliefs and respond to regulatory Injunctions and Acts. As perhaps the most personal, and therefore most revealing, decorative scheme in the house, it was also the most vulnerable to change. Those chapels whose form and decoration expressed a clearly defined religious position were particularly likely to have been altered to accommodate the views of a new patron, or destroyed during the turmoil of religious upheaval. The levels of destruction experienced during the Civil War, for example, are well demonstrated at Compton Wynyates in Warwickshire. Unusually, the house, owned by the royalist Earl of Northampton but garrisoned by Parliamentarians, had two chapels, one in the house (Compton Wynyates I), and a detached chapel a few hundred yards away (Compton Wynyates II) which was largely razed to the ground.[14] Although the house chapel survives, the pre-Reformation stained glass in the east window was shattered, and it is probable that other contentious decorative elements were also destroyed, leaving only the shell of the original interior.[15] Nor was such destruction the preserve of Cromwell's garrisoning troops alone, for it is clear from the journal of William Dowsing, the Commissioner responsible for cleansing 'superstitious' imagery in Suffolk and Cambridgeshire, that private chapels did not escape the destructive attentions of zealous officials.[16]

Any overview of decorative preoccupations based on surviving fabric risks being coloured, therefore, by the likelihood that it is the blander, less controversial (and on occasion, deliberately censored) elements that have survived. It relies on fragments rather than complete schemes, augmented by a piecemeal assemblage of inventories, building accounts and personal descriptions. This can produce a distorted view. For instance, there is more information about tapestry hangings than wall paintings. This is because the latter were never included in inventories whilst tapestries usually were, often with their subject matter described. Moreover, tapestries were a flexible form of decoration since their size could be altered, and they could be rehung elsewhere, or rolled up and stored. In contrast, wall paintings could not, of course, be moved or stored, and were also at risk from damp, the use of inferior materials and changes to the fabric of the house. And whitewash was cheap and easy to apply.

Decoration in a private chapel had a much more complex function than in the country house as a whole. In the latter the purpose was to provide a setting suitable to the status of the patron, demonstrating aspects such as lineage, political loyalties or intellectual and connoisseurial interests. But the chapel should, in theory, provide a decorous and suitable setting in which the household could gather for worship, and so represent spirituality as well as status. However, as we shall see, striking a proper balance between secular and religious functions was not always part of the agenda and, particularly in the later 17th century, the glorification of the patron could be the overriding aim. On the other hand, the decorative scheme could become the means of conveying to the household (at times with some danger to the patron) the religious beliefs and mores of the extended family to which they belonged. The didactic role of chapel decoration, and the importance of the religious lead given by the family to its servants, are emphasised in numerous documents (again especially in the 17th century), and in many cases decoration was carefully chosen to promote specific beliefs and attitudes. The problem for the 21st-century commentator is to distinguish between a worldly display of magnificence, and a decorative scheme conceived to convey a deeper spiritual meaning.

1

STATUS OR SPIRITUALITY:
WHY HAVE A PRIVATE CHAPEL?

After Henry VIII's young illegitimate son, Henry Fitzroy, had been created Duke of Richmond in 1525, Cardinal Wolsey wrote that the King wanted him to have a private chapel because Lords Darcy and Latymer each had one.[1] Except during the reign of Elizabeth, a similar competitive drive existed throughout the 16th and 17th centuries. An aristocratic house would often, but not always, contain a chapel, while an ambitious member of the gentry aiming for ennoblement would see the inclusion of one at his new seat as a shrewd, career-enhancing move. And patrons were naturally subject to the contradictory pressures imposed by the need to emphasise in their chapels the importance of worship by a show of pious splendour, while at the same time underlining their status and power by a magnificent secular display. In 1614, John Bowle (former chaplain to Robert Cecil, Earl of Salisbury, and future Bishop of Rochester) gave expression to this dilemma when he pronounced that God much preferred a public 'temple' to a private chapel. He excoriated the latter as being designed more for the ease of the worshippers 'as though we cannot adore the God of heaven except we be attended like Berenice with pomp on earth'.[2] The same tension between piety and power is highlighted in Alexander Pope's lines written some hundred years later:

> And now the Chapel's silver bell you hear
> That summons you to all the Pride of Pray'r:
> Light quirks of Musick, broken and uneven,
> Make the soul dance upon a Jig to Heaven.
> On painted Ceilings you devoutly stare,
> Where sprawl the Saints of Verrio or Laguerre,
> On gilded clouds in fair expansion lie,
> And bring all Paradise before your eye.
> To rest, the Cushion and soft Dean invite,
> Who never mentions Hell to ears polite.[3]

In the 21st century the challenge is to recognise which motive provided the greater driving force. And because a private chapel can be constructed and fitted out to satisfy both the materialistic demands of a secular world and the spiritual needs of the household, the study of its development during the political and religious turbulence which followed the Reformation gives a unique insight into major concerns of the 16th and 17th centuries. Unlike the parish church, which was encumbered for the most part with buildings designed for Roman Catholic worship and fettered by ecclesiastical law, patrons were relatively free to create and explore new types of space and decoration suitable for distinctly Protestant forms of devotion. The results can be unexpected, and provide new insights into secular attitudes to magnificence and Protestant thinking about the relationship between religious buildings and worship.

Status and piety may have been the major reasons for having a chapel but, especially in respect of local gentry houses, there could also be practical considerations such as the distance local people needed to travel to the parish church. At Chantemarle House in Dorset, Sir John Strode noted that the old chapel (which he started to replace in 1612) existed because the house was more than a mile from the parish church at Caystock.[4] In 1632, at the consecration of the chapel of All Saints near Risley Hall in Derbyshire, Sir Henry Willoughby underlined the practical difficulties of attending the parish church, explaining that in winter pregnant women, young children and the old and sick had to negotiate dangerous floods to reach it.[5] Nor were aristocratic patrons unmindful of such considerations. In the 1670s, the Duke of Lauderdale was planning a modest house in Edinburgh, and did not include a chapel in early designs. However, he changed his mind after building had started because the house was so far from the church.[6] Where practicable, it was the duty of the patron to bring his household to the parish church at least on special holy days, and preferably every Sunday. Failure to do so was an offence. Sir Henry Rosewell of Forde Abbey in Dorset was excommunicated for failing to attend his parish church, having given the excuse that he could not get on with the new incumbent who had arrived in 1628.[7]

Patrons often financed and built chapels of ease for those who could not attend their parish church. Indeed the existence of parochial free chapels was a long-standing means of providing religious essentials in large parishes. Many were similar to private chapels in that, to an extent, they were beyond the close attention of ecclesiastical superiors. For this reason, a number of such chapels with a high level of patron involvement (both financial and aesthetic) may be counted as private chapels. A good example is Rug in Clwyd, built in 1637 by Sir William 'Old Blue Stockings' Salesbury to fill a gap after two parishes were amalgamated and the local church pulled down, and where the Church authorities exercised little control over what went on.

The Reformation profoundly affected the creation of private chapels in that after about 1540 there was a marked decrease in their status and number. The effects of what Margaret Aston has called 'the switchback upheaval of the first generation of England's reform' are sometimes difficult to track in detail because of its changeable nature.[8] However, Elizabethan inventories for older houses provide vivid examples of this decline, often referring to 'former' chapels, or listing contents indicating that the chapel was no longer being used for its original purpose. Particularly in smaller gentry houses, chapels were often put to new uses, or just fell into disuse. Some served a productive purpose (at Wood Hall in Worcestershire the chapel seems to have become a still[9]), while others degenerated into storerooms (at Ripley Castle in North Yorkshire, the chapel in the early 17th century contained a long table, two old bedsteads, and various other pieces of timber[10]). A number were converted into living space. At the early 16th-century Woodsome Hall in West Yorkshire, the chapel was divided into two parlours in the late 16th century, while at Ledston Hall, also in West Yorkshire, the results of the conversion of the medieval chapel into a parlour in 1588, can still be seen.[11] Similarly, at Woodlands Manor in Wiltshire the 14th-century chapel was converted into one of the principal chambers in about 1570.[12] These changes are almost certainly attributable to new attitudes to worship, in which readings and sermons supplanted divine service, and converting a chapel for secular use could be seen as an indication of conformity.

In low-church houses, worship often took the form of an assembly, with all members of the household gathering in a large room, usually the great hall or the great chamber.[13] Lady Margaret Hoby's 1599-1605 diaries, which record the religious life of a North Yorkshire baronet's wife in painstaking detail, make it clear that the family often did not use the chapel at Hackness Hall, their impressive Elizabethan house, but assembled with their retainers for prayers in the great chamber or the parish church near by.[14] Higher up the social scale, it is very unlikely that, during the occupancy of the Lord Protector, Somerset House on The Strand in London had a chapel.[15] That the absence of chapels in aristocratic houses was relatively widespread is indicated by certain household regulations of the early 17th century. Those for an earl in the opening years of James I's reign, for example, draw no distinction between chapel and chamber when instructing the preacher or chaplain.[16] But no generalisations can be made, and it is certainly not correct to assume that all low-church patrons used a chamber rather than a chapel for prayer. For instance, the 1609 household book of the Puritan Henry Hastings, 5th Earl of Huntingdon, enjoined the gentleman usher to set a good example by being present in the chapel 'in prayer and preaching tyme'.[17]

Many of the larger, newly-built, Elizabethan houses, such as Montacute House in Somerset, do not appear to have possessed a chapel, and it is notable that of the four great surviving 'prodigy' houses only Hardwick had a functioning chapel throughout the period.[18] At Longleat House in Wiltshire, the chapel was not fitted out until the second half of the 17th century; at Wollaton Hall in Nottingham, no convincing position for a chapel can be identified (despite the presence of a chapel chamber); and at Burghley House in Lincolnshire, a makeshift chapel was hurriedly created as an afterthought in the 1570s.

18

Interest in chapels revived following the accession of James I in 1603. Many aristocratic Jacobean houses included them, some richly decorated, and the gentry followed their example. Moreover, patrons were adding chapels to earlier, often Elizabethan, houses which had been built without chapels. Examples include Childerley Hall (Cambridgeshire), Easton Lodge (Essex) and Water Eaton (Oxfordshire). In some cases, such as at Chantemarle, an earlier chapel was deemed too small and replaced. Also indicative of a change in attitude is that between 1617 and the onset of the Civil War few, if any, chapels were abandoned or converted to other uses.

Puritan chapels most probably existed during the Elizabethan period. However, it is not until the reign of James I, when the Puritan nobility, and especially the gentry, strove to promote their religion by supporting nonconformist divines and influencing their retainers and other local people, that there is firm evidence of the creation of recognisably Puritan chapels. In the 1640s and during the Interregnum following the execution of Charles I in 1649 it was, for obvious reasons, Puritan patrons who were the main builders of private chapels. Detached chapels were built near existing houses such as Bramhope Hall (1649) and Great Houghton in West Yorkshire (c.1655), both of which were designed to accommodate the immediate household and fellow worshippers living locally. Other Puritan patrons, such as Sir George Booth at Dunham Massey in Cheshire, converted rooms within the house into chapel (c.1655) or, as in the case of Robert Dukinfield at Dukinfield Hall (also in Cheshire), pressed existing chapels into use as gathering places for nonconformists (from 1653). However, it is noteworthy that two of the most splendid, high-church, detached chapels, those at Cholmondeley Castle in Cheshire and Staunton Harold Hall in Leicestershire, were also built during this period.

The Restoration of the Stuarts in 1660 saw the imposition of curbs on the provision of chapels for services by Puritan patrons, but for Anglicans, the situation was very different. Bishops set about rebuilding their palaces and repairing the damage of the Civil War (even introducing new levels of splendour), and some Oxford Colleges followed suit. It might be thought that private patrons would be inspired by the changed political situation to build rich, highly decorated chapels similar to those seen under the early Stuarts. However, initially at least, they opted for a restrained formality. The pattern of chapel provision during this period appears to have been largely controlled by status. Large houses owned by aristocrats tended to have chapels, whereas smaller houses owned by gentry contained proportionately fewer. Evidently, while it could still be considered appropriate for a nobleman to provide a chapel, in gentry houses chapels were included only as the result of a specific need or ambition on the part of the patron.[19]

Overall, the reasons for providing a chapel changed very little over the period.

While historical events and practical requirements would always play a part, during the early decades of the 16th century and the best part of the 17th century, an aristocratic house was likely to contain a chapel as part of the trappings of high social status. Although different religious groups were at various times vulnerable to persecution, and therefore less likely to create chapels (or more careful about hiding the evidence that they had done so), it was only under Elizabeth that there was a distinct decline in the status and provision of private chapels.

At the same time, spiritual concerns should not be overlooked. Indeed, what remains constant is the patrons' concern for the spiritual well-being of their households. The idea of the servants forming part of an extended family runs through most household regulations. Those of 1652 for John Egerton, 2nd Earl of Bridgewater, are headed 'my orders for the Government of my family' and speak of calling the family together for the performing of their daily duty to God. More ominously for those seeking employment, they also contained the imprecation that all who intended to live in his family must endeavour to live virtuously.[20] Yet more rigorous was the contemporary regime of the (unchapelled) Puritan Barnardiston family of Kedlington in Suffolk. There the servants held readings and prayers every morning and evening, and sang psalms after every meal. Sermons were delivered to them in the buttery, before they were summoned to a repetition in the presence of their master, Sir Nathaniel.[21] Some fifty years later, the Duchess of Devonshire's chaplain, Joseph Williamson, noted that she retained a Minister 'to promote solid Piety and to set home the Influence of Religion upon her own heart and upon the hearts of all about her'.[22]

Similar sentiments can be found carefully spelt out in contemporary guides to behaviour. In 1704, the English Jesuit, William Darrell, published *A Gentleman Instructed*, in which he described a patron's duty to his household:

> your care must not stop at your children, let it reach your menial servants though you are their Master you are also their Father ... Besides as a Christian you are their brother ... all these Relations ... impose an obligation on you to enquire into their behaviour and to provide for their instruction. ... Nor is it sufficient to allow 'em time to look into the Concerns of their Souls, you must see they employ it well: Let 'em meet at Prayers at least once a Day and punish those who neglect this duty.[23]

To some extent the writings of Darrell and others were aimed at curbing licentious behaviour by the land-owning classes. While many might be sincere in providing a chapel to help further the moral rectitude of their household and discharge their pious duty to look after its spiritual needs, for some at least it was also a means of affirming or enhancing their social standing.

2

THE REGULATION AND CONTROL
OF PRIVATE CHAPELS

Between 1500 and 1700 there was no legislation directly controlling the building of a private chapel although, after the Reformation, the regulations of the Anglican Church did provide a framework of law by which they were assessed and governed. Control was exercised in three main areas. First, Injunctions, Visitation Articles and Acts of Parliament had a role to play in governing the way in which private chapels were decorated and licensed, though their influence was variable. Secondly, the gentry, though not the aristocracy, needed a licence from a bishop to appoint a chaplain. Thirdly, the revival of consecration of chapels in the early 17th century, which needed the participation of a bishop, allowed control over the range of services that could be offered. The complexity of historical events and changes within the Protestant Church make it difficult to summarise the regulatory regime, but just as important, and yet more difficult to quantify, were the pre-occupations of individual bishops and the extent to which regulations and conventions were sometimes quietly ignored by both patrons and bishops.

Injunctions, Visitation Articles and Acts of Parliament

Private chapels after the Reformation were, in theory at least, subject to control by the diocesan bishop through his Visitation Articles. However, Henry VIII's Royal Visitation of 1535 was almost exclusively concerned with monastic foundations, and no Henrician Acts associated with the Reformation made specific mention of either the laity or private house chapels. On the other hand, the Injunctions of the 1547 Visitation Act drawn up under Edward VI ranged far wider in that they applied to four sections of society: the bishops, their officials, the chantry priests and the laity. In particular, Injunction 28 considerably extended the Henrician format in ordering that superstitious images and artefacts were to be destroyed in private houses as well as in churches.[1] These Injunctions formed the basis for Archbishop Thomas Cranmer's Visitation Articles a year later which emphasised the importance attached to houses. Injunction 28 was given greater prominence, becoming Injunctions 6 and 7, while a new Injunction 86 concentrating entirely on private houses was added:

> Item, Whether you know any that keep in their houses undefaced, any abused or feigned images, any tables, pictures, paintings or other monuments of feigned miracles, pilgrimages, idolatry, or superstition.[2]

In 1549 the first Act of Uniformity made it clear beyond doubt that private chapels fell within its jurisdiction. It defined the conduct of services as 'prayer which is for others to come unto or hear either in common churches or private chapels or oratories'.[3] Hence legislation was in place, if needed, to control the way in which private chapels were used, furnished and decorated. In 1559, Elizabeth's first Parliament in effect restored the Henrician and Edwardine ecclesiastical legislation, reversed under Mary, with new Acts of Supremacy and of Uniformity.

Overall, there is very little evidence that at this date private chapels were directly targeted by the church authorities. In this context the interest of the regulations of the Edwardine and Elizabethan periods, aimed as they were at returning to what were perceived to be the simple, uncorrupted forms and practices of the early Christians, lies in their influence on the fittings and decoration of the chapel interior. For example, rubrics in the 1559 Prayer Book stressed that a division between the two spaces within the church should be retained. More detailed instructions in respect of screens were set out in the Royal Order of 1561. Although the rood loft, the rood and any flanking figures were to be removed, the screen itself was to be retained. Nor was this to be a passive retention: should the entire screen be removed a replacement was to be erected.

The screen was important because a new role was envisaged for it, emphasised by a matching change in terminology in the Royal Order, where the word 'partition' replaced 'screen'. The Roman Catholic liturgy had treated the laity largely as onlookers, and the pre-Reformation screen had marked the separation of the nave from the chancel, that is, the boundary between the laity, and the preserve of the clergy. However, the rubrics of the Book of Common Prayer required the full involvement of the congregation in both following and contributing to the service. The retention of the screen, which had acted as a symbolic and actual barrier to participation, might therefore seem contradictory. However, the Royal Order, taken with Royal Injunctions of 1559 governing the role and placing of the communion table at the east end, make it clear that a new type of double-cell, or two-centred, chapel, with the two spaces discharging different liturgical functions, was envisaged.[4]

In 1604, a year after coming to the throne, James I called a conference at Hampton Court Palace to promulgate a set of Canons aimed at enforcing religious conformity. To the dismay of the more extreme Puritan elements, what emerged was support for sacramental worship in well-appointed, seemly surroundings. Since the early 17th century saw a new interest in decoration in private chapels, and since there is no record of church intervention in such schemes, it is probable that again private chapels were not singled out for attention.

A real threat to the integrity of private chapels occurred in the mid-17th century. In February 1641 a bill proposing the use of commissioners to 'cleanse' the religious buildings of the country was introduced in Parliament. The result was the Parliamentary Orders and Ordinances of 1641, 1643 and 1644 which required the removal of 'all Monuments of Superstition and idolatry'.[5] Although there are variations between the three sets,[6] they were comprehensive, collectively covering the position of the communion table and ordering the removal of fittings such as rood-lofts, communion rails, and organs, together with crosses and crucifixes, as well as the destruction of images of the Virgin Mary, the Trinity, saints, and angels. Dowsing was in no doubt, as his journal illustrates, that private chapels fell under his jurisdiction. Little Wenham Hall in Suffolk, the only private chapel mentioned by Dowsing still in existence, belonged in 1644 to Lady Brewse. He recorded that 'in her chappel there was a picture of God the Father, of the Trinity, of Christ, and the Holy Ghost, the cloven tongues; which we gave order to take down, and the Lady promised to do it'.[7]

Although no other area endured the thoroughness with which Dowsing went about his work in East Anglia, iconoclasm was a real threat, and it is likely that concerned patrons took action to preserve some of the more controversial elements in their private chapels. Parish records in Hertfordshire tell of iconoclastic activity in the county from 1641, and which reached a peak in 1644-5.[8] It is surely no coincidence that in 1644 the painted ceiling of the chapel at Hatfield was whitewashed, and that in 1645 stained glass was taken down. Moreover, by 1646 a series of paintings of the life of Christ had been removed.[9] Since both the glass (at least for the east window) and the paintings survived, this was most likely done to save controversial elements of the chapel's decorative scheme.

The return to influence of Anglican high-churchmen after the Restoration ensured that, while those of like mind now enjoyed the freedom to run their private chapels with little interference, a distinct line was drawn between office-holders who accepted the Corporation Act of 1661 and signalled their conformity by receiving communion at their parish church, and those who refused to do so. The 1661 Proclamation prohibited all public meetings for religious worship except those in the parish church, while only members of the immediate household could attend services in private chapels. Various Acts of Parliament, known collectively as the Clarendon Code, were designed to hinder nonconformists from gathering for worship, in part by restricting the ability of their chaplains and ministers to take services. The 1662 Act of Uniformity obliged Puritan ministers to quit their livings; in 1664 the First Conventicle Act made it illegal to attend religious meetings that did not conform 'to the liturgy and practice of the Church of England'; and in 1665 the Five Mile Act severely restricted the movements of nonconformist ministers. In 1670 the Second Conventicle Act introduced heavier penalties for such ministers and those who allowed their houses to be used for Puritan worship.[10] The effects were graphically described by the nonconformist divine, Oliver Heywood, who noted that he was obliged to restrict his preaching in private chapels, and whose congregations assembled in a variety of other venues, including a kiln.[11]

Charles II's Declaration of Indulgence of 1672 promised a new period of toleration for nonconformists, and numerous applications for licences for ministers and places of worship were made under it, particularly from gentry families. However, the Declaration was revoked under pressure from the House of Commons less than a year later. It was not until the 1689 Toleration Act that nonconformist congregations were allowed to worship in their own way in meeting houses or private chapels, provided the premises were licensed and the doors left unlocked. However, in the twenty years following the passing of this Act, only four gentry families applied to have their chapels licensed. Among them were the Rodes of Great Houghton and the Dukinfields of Dukinfield (where nonconformist worship had been conducted from at least 1640). Hence the Clarendon Code and ensuing legislation forced the creation of a clear and lasting distinction between those Protestants who accepted the supervision of the Church of England and those who wished to remain independent of it. At the same time, both conforming and non-conforming Protestants were united in supporting the 1673 Test Act which placed new restrictions on the ability of Roman Catholics to hold civil and military office.

Appointment of Chaplains

In the early 16th century the privilege of appointing domestic chaplains as of right was restricted to aristocrats and senior officials, but it was increasingly resented as open to abuse. In 1529, the Pluralities Act regulated the number of domestic chaplains permitted to hold non-resident benefices with, for example, dukes being allowed six pluralist chaplains, marquesses and earls five, viscounts four, barons three and the widows of aristocrats two.[12] The Act was in part intended to restrict chaplain numbers, but Puritan divines increasingly criticised it as too liberal. Something of the animosity attached to non-residence and pluralism in general, and to chaplains in particular, is caught in the Calvinist cleric Thomas Wood's letter of 1576 to the 3rd Earl of Warwick condemning double and triple beneficed chaplains as 'worse than cormorants', and urging the earl to rid himself of them lest he be 'partaker of their sinnes.'[13] However, in the early 17th century the Puritan John Davenport told Lady Mary de Vere that the right to appoint chaplains had been settled upon the nobility and others by Magna Carta, and that it was not in the bishops' power to remove it.[14]

Gentry who wished to have a chaplain needed an episcopal licence, and the ease with which it could be obtained varied according to the climate of the time and the personal inclinations of the bishop. The ability to control the appointment of domestic chaplains at gentry level gave the Church a degree of power to prevent private households from becoming centres for non-orthodox forms of worship. But the preferential treatment of aristocrats established a hierarchy of chapel-building classes, associating the provision of a chapel with high status and making it a focus as much for social ambition as for piety. As William Gibson puts it, 'chaplains, like libraries, [and] chapels... were part of the mental landscape of the land-owning elite'.[15]

Bishops were not alone in acting to control the appointment of domestic chaplains. Worried that they could provide a focus for Puritan opposition, Charles I tried to regulate and restrict their influence. In 1629 he issued Royal Instructions to the Episcopate which required Archbishop Abbott to ensure, among other things, that only 'noblemen, and men qualified by the lawe' were permitted to have private chaplains (Article VII).[16] In fact, while a number of dioceses included the substance of the Instructions in their Visitation Articles, they were carried out very unevenly, their execution depending on the convictions of individual bishops.[17] They do not appear to have greatly influenced the balance of Anglican versus Puritan chaplains.

The fall of the episcopacy obviously affected the regulation of chaplains. Puritan ministers could now act as chaplains, and there was an increase in identifiably Puritan private chapels. From 1655 patrons were forbidden from keeping ejected Anglican clergy or chaplains in their houses, but there was no direct legislation to stop high Anglican patrons building chapels. It was his refusal to contribute to Cromwell's army, and not the building of his flamboyant detached chapel at Staunton Harold, that was the immediate cause of Sir Robert Shirley's imprisonment and early death in the Tower in 1656.

Between the Restoration and the Toleration Act of 1689 there were restrictions on nonconformist chaplains and ministers taking services, and also heavy penalties for those allowing Puritan worship in their houses. Even when the Toleration Act allowed nonconformists their own places of worship, it did not remove their civil disabilities and retained certain restrictions on their meetings. The number of patrons possessing (often unlicensed) chaplains had increased markedly as the 17th century proceeded and received a further boost after the 1662 Act of Uniformity caused ejected Puritan ministers to seek shelter in sympathetic households. Many (particularly Puritan) patrons who employed chaplains did so without possessing a private chapel.[18] They might retain (or share) a chaplain to conduct religious readings, prayers and discourse in their houses (and, on occasion, serve as ministers to the parish church and act as tutors to their children), but such activities did not require a designated chapel.

Consecration

Before the Reformation many private chapels were consecrated as a means of allowing the sacraments to be celebrated. However, although this seems simple enough, the letter of the rule was not always followed. The Vyne in Hampshire, situated well over a mile from the parish church of Sherborne St John, is a case in point. According to the 1541 inventory, the chapel had a font, suggesting that baptisms took place there, while the provision of a Mass book and a splendid set of chapel plates implies that Mass was celebrated.[19] However, there is no record that its 16th century chapel was consecrated or dedicated.[20]

After the Reformation, consecration appears to have ceased for a while, since there are no records of private chapels being consecrated under Elizabeth.[21] Bishop Pilkington's view that 'honest places for Christian services had no need for hallowing' best captures the feeling for simplicity that characterises the period.[22] More practically, no approved Protestant service of consecration existed.

Consecration assumed a growing importance in the early years of the 17th century, and patrons as well as bishops played a major role in devising services. One of the clearest indications of the significance attached to it can be found in the wording of Sir Ranulph Crewe's application in 1635 for his chapel at Crewe Hall in Cheshire to be consecrated. This shows that he saw consecration not simply as enabling the sacraments to be celebrated there, but also as a means of defining the chapel as a separate, sacred space appropriated by God.[23]

But despite the renewed popularity of consecration, the compliance of a bishop could not be taken for granted. It can be surprisingly difficult to unpick the reasons behind some of the refusals handed down by bishops. There was clearly considerable uncertainty about procedure. Canon 71 promulgated after the 1604 Hampton Court Conference stipulated that ministers should not normally preach or administer holy communion in any private chapel that could not lawfully be used for divine services. While there appears to have been no doubt that pre-Reformation consecration remained valid, a radical change of use could cause problems. During the arraignment of Sir Henry Rosewell of Forde Abbey before the Court of High Commission in 1639, members disagreed about the status of his chapel: did it retain its ecclesiastical status from its pre-Dissolution consecration or had its role as a post-Reformation chicken and cattle shed rendered the consecration invalid? The Commission decided that, to be on the safe side, the chapel should be reconsecrated before further services could be held.[24]

Although the usual explanation for the reluctance of bishops to consecrate private chapels — that it would deprive parish churches of custom and revenue — seems straightforward enough, consecration also appears to have been used as a means of control over them. An unconsecrated chapel gave the patron and chaplain greater freedom. At the chapel of ease near Mistley Hall in Essex, for example, the chaplain's failure to wear a surplice was defended on the grounds that, since the sacraments could not be celebrated there, the rules about vestments did not apply.[25] That such quasi-independence rankled was later made very clear at Rug when, after a visitation in 1730, the rector of nearby Corwen complained at his lack of control over the unconsecrated chapel, despite the fact that great numbers of people worshipped there.[26] Nor was it just an 18th-century rector who felt that way. The problem was still there in the 19th century when the Bishop of St Asaph, Thomas Short, lamented: 'you Rug chaplains are my curates and you are not my curates. I have no control over you but as long as you are licensed to me, there's a sort of responsibility'.[27] There is certainly evidence, then, that the authorities were unable to regulate an unconsecrated building, and it could therefore provide greater opportunity for unorthodox behaviour.

But there are also examples of bishops refusing to consecrate for fear of irregularities occurring as a result. When, in the early 1630s, Sir Henry Slingsby II petitioned Richard Neile, Archbishop of York, Neile refused to consecrate his chapel at Red House in North Yorkshire lest the privilege be abused.[28] Neile was reputedly reluctant to consecrate private chapels, reflecting a general high-church concern that consecration, and the related ability to offer a full range of services, might result in irregular celebration of the sacraments. In other words, the efficacy of consecration as a means of control was variable: in one set of circumstances, such as at Red House, consecration could be seen as running the risk of unorthodox celebration of the sacraments, while in another, as at Mistley, the lack of consecration would allow greater excuse for non-conformity. This ambivalence could have had its roots in the recollection that, well before the Reformation, the Lollards had taken advantage of the relative freedom of separate chapels within a parish to assert unorthodox views on decoration and doctrine.[29] It was not unknown for a patron to prevail upon a bishop from another diocese to consecrate his chapel. This was certainly so in the case of the Puritan Sir Thomas Hoby of Hackness Hall who, in 1636 and realising that Archbishop Neile was unlikely to oblige, persuaded the bishop of Sodor and Man to consecrate his detached chapel at Harwood Dale and somehow secured a licensed curate to serve it.[30]

Somewhat surprisingly, the practice of celebrating the sacraments in unconsecrated chapels may have been fairly widespread. Lady Anne Clifford's diary is a good source of information. She describes taking communion in the chapel at Knole in Kent in 1617, and she planned to do so again in 1619. There is no record of the chapel being consecrated (although this may well have been done before the Reformation). More pertinently, on Christmas Day 1661 she received the sacrament at (the unconsecrated) Brougham Castle chapel in Cumbria, and again on 27 July 1662. Moreover, she described taking communion in her chamber at Brougham with her household on 25 January 1676. She also spoke of two marriages in private London chapels: at Thanet House (in Bloomsbury, London) in 1665, and in Sir Charles Littleton's (sic) house in the Minories in 1667.[31] Perhaps a dispensation or licence was obtained, since it seems unlikely that these chapels were consecrated.[32] At Higher Melcombe in Dorset, although Sir Thomas Freke's intention to have his chapel there consecrated was never carried out, the rector still conducted baptisms and marriages.[33] Sir Henry Slingsby II describes christenings in his unconsecrated chapel at Red House in 1636 and in 1638.[34] On the second occasion the preacher refused to preach until he had obtained the permission of the Chancellor of York. Sir Henry's account suggests that preaching rather than baptism was the problem, since he admits that, contrary to the orders of the Church, he continued to have sermons in his chapel now and then despite the danger he would be in should the news get out. This implies that, in parts of the York Archdiocese at least, the requirement of Hampton Court Canon 71 forbidding preaching in unconsecrated private chapels was still observed.[35] That Red House chapel was much larger than was necessary for Slingsby's relatively small household of twenty-four, and easily capable of accommodating people from the surrounding area, may have exacerbated Archbishop Neile's suspicions about the goings-on there.

As if to make up for lost time, numerous consecrations took place in the first decade after the Restoration, but it did not become a formality.[36] When, in 1678, Sir Peter Leycester applied to the Bishop of Chester for a licence for a chaplain and for his chapel at Tabley Hall in Cheshire to be consecrated, pleading distance from the parish church and infirmity, he was only partly successful. His request for a chaplain was granted, but consecration was denied.[37]

3

EARLY TUDOR: A CHAPEL TO BE SEEN

Before the Reformation, the private chapel was often used, like the parish church, for Mass as well as for simpler services. According to *The Northumberland Household Book*, which records the daily arrangements in the households of Henry Percy, 5th Earl of Northumberland during the first decades of the 16th century, four daily services, Matins, Lady Mass, High Mass and Evensong, were held in private chapels belonging to the Percy family.[1] The interior of a private chapel, at least at the aristocratic end of the spectrum, would probably also have looked much like a parish church, that is, with a clear distinction between the chancel, largely the preserve of the chapel staff, and the nave used by the household.

The Chapel in the House: towards Integration

The chapel of the pre-Reformation great house had to be large enough to accommodate the household, as well as visitors and their retainers, and be relatively accessible. This could entail the inclusion of at least three entrances: one near the east end for the chapel staff and to protect the sanctity of the east end, and separate entrances towards the west end for the family and their retainers to preserve the hierarchical distinctions. Seclusion was a third key requirement. In keeping with their sacred character, chapels could not be used as passageways and, since they often rose through two storeys, in a single-pile range overcoming the impediment to circulation routes could be a taxing requirement for planners. Finally, the chapel was usually (but not always) correctly-oriented, that is, with the altar at the east end so that the congregation faced Jerusalem and the rising sun.

Most newly-built country houses of distinction in early Tudor times used the courtyard plan in place of the series of detached blocks or ranges designed for specific purposes that typified the planning of the late medieval period. The new designs deployed a flexible system of, usually, single-pile ranges, loosely grouped into courtyards, which provided access to most interior spaces via adjacent ranges or covered walkways. Moreover, many medieval houses were updated by joining ranges that were originally separate blocks to form one or more courtyards. As a result, the free-standing chapel, common in medieval planning, became relatively rare, with William Smith's Withcote in Leicestershire and Sir James Tyrell's chapel at Gipping in Suffolk, both completed at the start of the Tudor period, being notable exceptions.[2] At Haddon Hall in Derbyshire, for example, centuries of medieval development culminated in the early 16th century with the creation of a courtyard which integrated the sporadic developments of lodgings, kitchens and great hall with the chapel, formerly the parish church, in the south-west corner. Lord de la Warr's remodelling of the medieval Halnaker House in West Sussex included (from 1494) a west range which connected the hall to the 13th-century chapel. At Cotehele in Cornwall, a new hall range, added by Sir Piers Edgcumbe before 1520, connected with the medieval chapel (fig. 3.1). Similar developments can be seen in smaller houses, although the result was not necessarily the formation of a courtyard. The detached 14th-century chapel at Lytes Cary in Somerset was close to the mid-15th-century great hall, but it was not until the construction of the south range by Sir John Lyte in the early 1530s that it became part of the house (fig. 3.2). At North Wyke in Devon, the medieval chapel in the separate gatehouse range was extended by John 'Warrior' Wykes in the 16th century and,

Fig. 3.1: Cotehele, Cornwall: ground plan. An awkward passage connects Sir Piers Edgcumb's new hall range with the east end of the chapel. P1 = the Retainers' Court.

it appears, linked to the main body of the house by an open *loggia* at ground–floor level, with a first–floor walkway giving the Wykes family direct access to the upper chapel. By the end of Henry VIII's reign there were few chapelled country houses that did not have at least one internal or covered entrance to the chapel from the main ranges. However, a good, practical reason for having a detached chapel had been to emphasise the separate and sacred quality

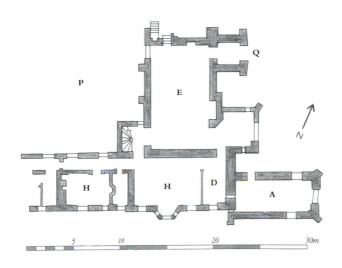

Fig. 3.2: Lytes Cary, Somerset: detail of ground plan. Sir John Lyte's new south range joined the chapel to the house, where a squint connected the 'chapel room' (D) to the chapel proper, while a second overlooked the entrance to the chapel from the oriel of the hall.

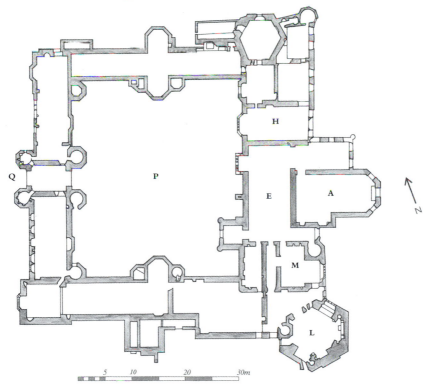

Fig. 3.3: Cowdray House, West Sussex: ground plan. The chapel was unusually close to the great hall.

Fig. 3.4: Cowdray House, West Sussex: detail from Hendrik Frans De Cort's view 'Fountain Court at Cowdray' of c.1793, looking east across the courtyard, and showing the hall (centre) with its Gothic windows. If Gothic forms were intended to convey a feeling of venerable antiquity or expensive display, they were evidently considered more suited to the great hall than the chapel.

Fig. 3.5: Cowdray House, West Sussex: detail of the impressive three-sided chapel apse with its double-height 'Tudor' windows. This dominant feature of the east facade of the house would not have been visible to an approaching visitor.

of this (often consecrated) space, and to address its very specific needs in terms of size, access and orientation. The dilemma for early 16th-century planners was how to integrate the chapel within the courtyard plan while still maintaining it as a sacred entity. The ways in which they tried to solve this complex problem provide insights into the degree of priority they gave to the siting of the chapel when drawing up plans.

The contradictory needs of seclusion and accessibility were best addressed by siting the chapel at the end of a main circulation route, or to one side of it. This apart, its actual position in the new designs appears to have been extremely flexible. It could be found adjoining and directly behind the great hall; at right angles to a range beyond the hall range; in the entrance range; or in a

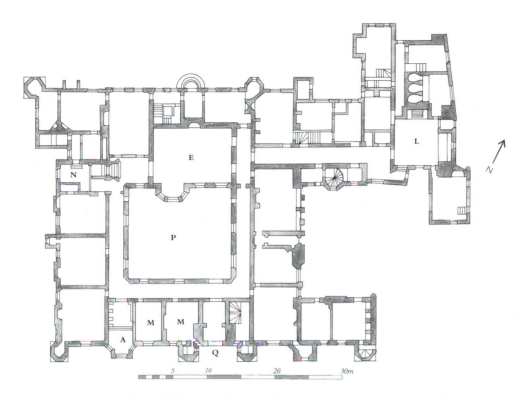

Fig. 3.6: Hengrave Hall, Suffolk: ground plan before 18th-century alterations (after Syndics of the Cambridge University Library Hengrave MS. 27). The position of the cross-range chapel combines ease of access with a degree of seclusion, but the balancing bay to the east contains a small awkward space.

Fig. 3.7: Hengrave Hall, Suffolk: the entrance (south) facade before 18th-century alterations (after Syndics of the Cambridge University Library Hengrave MS. 27). The chapel apse occupies the bay to the left of the main entrance, and was an impressive feature of the entrance range. Note the balancing bay on the right.

side range. At Cowdray House in West Sussex, built between 1492 and 1535, the chapel lay behind the great hall, at right angles to it (fig. 3.3), whilst at Shurland in Kent, it was placed at right angles to the range which appears to incorporate an open *loggia* at ground-floor level (Plate I). The chapel at Ingatestone in Essex

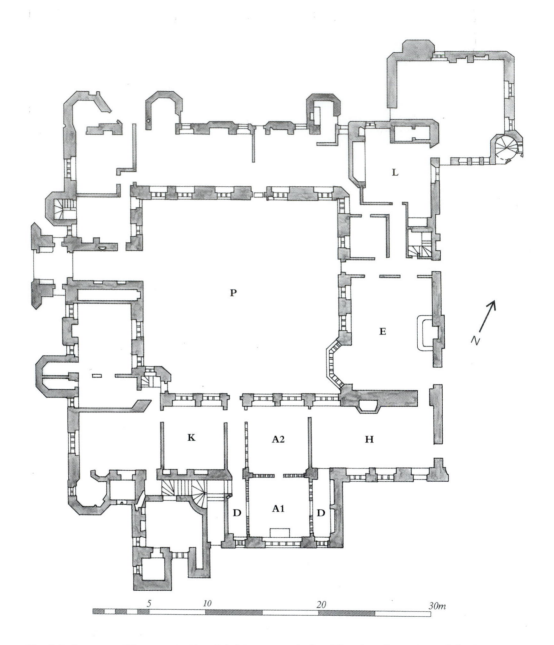

Fig. 3.8: Compton Wynyates I, Warwickshire: ground plan. The chapel terminated the important sequence of staterooms, and possessed a variety of peripheral spaces.

is isolated from the main circulation routes by placing it next to lodgings in a range beyond the hall. The introduction of a passageway round three sides of the courtyard at Hengrave Hall in Suffolk neatly allowed ease of access to be combined with a degree of seclusion (fig. 3.6), while a measure of isolation was achieved at Great Fulford in Devon by placing the chapel in the gatehouse range, where the main entrance terminated the ground-floor circulation route. With relatively

34

Fig. 3.9 (above): Compton Wynyates I, Warwickshire: detail of the east facade, with the magnificent east window of the integrated chapel in the centre.

Fig. 3.10 (right): Compton Wynyates I, Warwickshire: detail of the southern peripheral spaces of the chapel.

low status rooms such as the nursery placed beyond it, Compton Wynyates I lay at the end of the important sequence of staterooms which started from the high end of the great hall (fig. 3.8). At Naworth Castle in Cumbria, although the exact arrangement in the early 16th century is difficult to reconstruct, the chapel was effectively isolated from the rooms which lay to the east of it (fig. 3.11). The lack of a standard position for the chapel reflects the attempts of builders to solve the problems posed by the courtyard plan. It is clear that (with the great hall) the positioning of the chapel was a major influence during the planning process.

Ease of access for the entire household was of great practical importance. The challenge was to ensure that different social groups could enter an appropriate section of the chapel from areas to which they had unconditional access. *The Northumberland Household Book* makes it clear that while some services were intended for the entire household, others were designed for certain sections of it, so allowing normal life in the house to continue uninterrupted.[3] Moreover, since the chapel was always available for private prayer and contemplation, access had to be as simple and undisruptive as possible. Notwithstanding their integration within the overall plan, many chapels possessed an external entrance, usually from a courtyard. This had the advantage of allowing direct access from all parts of the house while avoiding the need for potentially disruptive or socially undesirable access to adjacent rooms.[4]

Wressle Castle in East Yorkshire (fig. 3.13) is a textbook example of good access planning. Very unusually, the early 16th-century plans (fig. 3.14) not only cover both levels of the chapel, but also contain detailed annotations which give an exceptionally clear idea of how the chapel spaces worked.[5] There were a two-

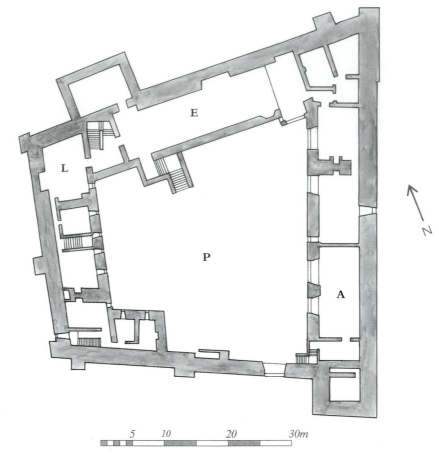

Fig. 3.11: Naworth Castle, Cumbria: main floor plan. The chapel runs along the east range, and was isolated from the rooms beyond it. Lord William Howard's private apartments were in the upper part of the south-east (top right) tower.

storey chancel, and an ante-chapel or nave that was almost certainly separated from it by a screen. There is an entrance from the courtyard into the north-west corner of the antechapel, while in the south-west corner there is a door leading from the dining chamber. At the east end, a door in the north wall close to the altar gives access from the vestry, and finally there are staircases from both the dining chamber and the antechapel to the upper chapel spaces. At Compton Wynyates I, an external doorway gave all members of the household access to the ante-chapel via a passage, while members of the family (and perhaps upper servants) could have reached the chapel either at ground-floor level from the parlour, or at first-floor level from the great chamber (fig. 3.8). A doorway from the south side of the inner chapel to a small staircase most likely provided an entrance for chapel staff. Cotehele (fig. 3.1), on the other hand, highlights what can go wrong when a new building (in this case the hall range) changes the

Fig. 3.12: Naworth Castle, Cumbria: inside the courtyard looking north-east, and showing, on the right, the two great rectangular windows that lit the liturgical north wall of the chapel.

relationship of the chapel to the rest of the house. There is an external entrance in the south wall from the Retainers' Court to the west end of the chapel, while at the east end there is an entrance on the south side for chapel staff. However, the family were obliged to pass along a cramped and awkward passage from the parlour directly into the east end.

Fig. 3.13: Wressle Castle, East Yorkshire: the south range. The chapel chancel occupies the right hand tower, with the ante-chapel to its left.

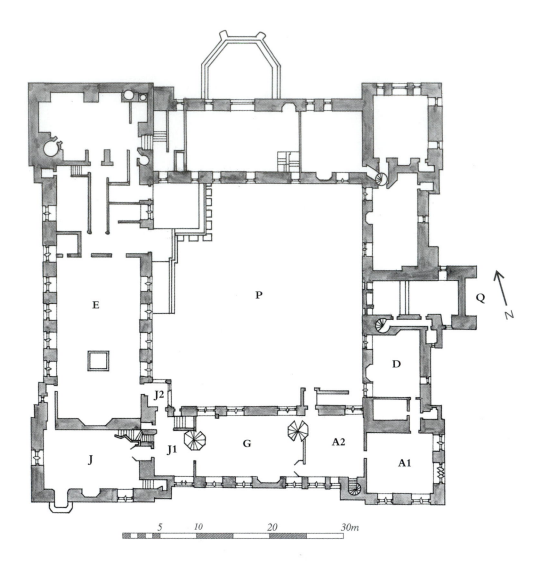

Fig. 3.14: Wressle Castle, East Yorkshire (after a 16th-century plan in West Sussex Record Office, Petworth archives 3538-47, by kind permission of Lord Egremont, the owner of those documents). A textbook example of good access planning that other aristocratic early Tudor chapels probably followed.

a. (above). Principle floor plan: D = Vestry; J = "my Lords chamber"; J1 and J2 = closets, in one of which the 5th Earl of Northumberland may have heard low mass.

b. (opposite). Upper floor plan: C1 = "my Lords pewe or seate"; C2 = "A plac for the gentlmen and servenmen to see servic"; C3 = space possibly reserved for women; J = "my Lords chamber" (upper half).

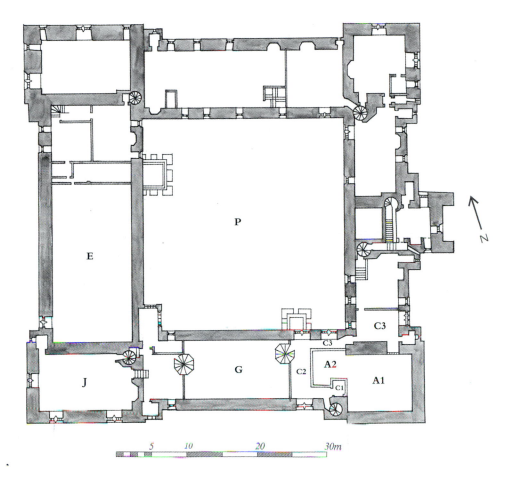

Most new chapels had at least two entrances at ground-floor level and there was often access to upper chapel space. Smaller chapels tended to have only one ground-floor entrance, positioned at, or towards, the west end. This arrangement seems quite practical for a relatively small household where there was internal access to an upper chapel.

There was no hard and fast rule governing which rooms were next to the chapel, though the great hall was usually some distance away (with Cowdray being a notable exception). For two-storey chapels, it is difficult to gather much information about first-floor adjacent spaces, although at Naworth and Ingatestone it appears that there was access to the upper chapel from the long gallery. This relationship appears to derive from French planning ideas, and continued in regular use in England at least until the Restoration.[6]

Correct orientation was an important requirement for a space suitable for worship, but two other features were also desirable: a longer east-west axis, allowing a vista from the entrance to the east end, and a window arrangement that complemented the interior space, with any side windows usually being placed relatively high on the wall to avoid interference with chapel fittings, and shut out distracting views of the outside world. In many cases, the provision of a cross-range chapel space helped achieve the former (Naworth and Wressle were exceptional in having chapels which ran along a range). It also allowed for a west end entrance directly from the courtyard, which emphasised the east-west axis, and meant that the chapel could be independent of the adjacent rooms. Another advantage of siting the chapel axis at 90 degrees to a range was that it facilitated the provision of an apse and large windows to emphasise the liturgical east end.

In his *A Compendyous Regyment* of 1542, Andrew Boorde advises on the ideal arrangement for a courtyard house.[7] He concentrates on the relationship of spaces round the main courtyard, giving precise instructions for the arrangement of the rooms next to the great hall at both the high and low ends, and for the relationship of the great hall to the gatehouse. But it is notable that he makes no specific recommendation for locating the chapel. Also significant is the requirement that 'many of the chambers may have a prospecte into the Chapell'. The implication is that the existence of a chapel was taken for granted, and that it had a pivotal role in relation to the main rooms of state but had no standard position. Up to the accession of Elizabeth the chapel remained an important and individual space within the building, second in importance only to the great hall, and usually immediately recognisable externally and on plan. That the position of the chapel was initially unaffected by the Reformation can be attributed to the innate conservatism of patrons, the uncertain religious climate until the Protestant succession brought relative stability following Mary's death in 1558, and the short time-span involved – less than 30 years. It was to be the next two generations, those educated after the Reformation, who would become instigators of far-reaching change.

Exterior Architecture: Distinction versus Symmetry

At the beginning of the Tudor period, numerous external architectural features were employed to give the chapel a distinctive character, making its position easily identifiable from the outside. While setting the chapel across a single-pile range posed challenges to planners by blocking a circulation route, it did create opportunities for external architectural elaboration. For one thing it allowed the creation of a differentiated roofline, identifying its position in the same way that the roof of the great hall drew attention to the main room of entry. Another advantage was that the chapel gable could be embellished architecturally or sculpturally – a cross placed on the apex of the gable, as at Shurland (Plate I), was the usual motif. Entrances from internal courtyards would often be given a special character. But the two most distinctive architectural features of the chapel, facilitated by the cross-range approach, were an emphasis on the east end, often, as already noted, by means of an apse, and differentiated fenestration, frequently containing stained glass. Neither were innovations. The late 14th-century chapel in the keep at Warkworth Castle in Northumberland and the cross-range chapel at Herstmonceux Castle in East Sussex, where the 15th-century windows survive, are well-known examples of a widespread practice which was continued by many early Tudor patrons.

Often a different architectural form was used for some of or all the chapel windows, and patrons could go to some lengths to ensure that the fenestration had a distinctive character. For instance, in 1509 before starting work on the chapel window, the glazier at Little Saxham Hall, Suffolk, was sent some 30 miles to learn from an example at Horham Hall in Essex.[8] However, there appears to have been little consensus on the form that chapel windows should take. East windows were obviously the most important, and here sheer size often predominated. At Compton Wynyates I, the east end is not apsidal but projects outwards from the eastern range, and is composed of a huge Tudor depressed arch window of double height with cusped lights (fig. 3.9). This is bordered by four rectangular windows, also with cusped lights, which illuminate the spaces flanking the chapel. It is a glittering display of glass, unlike anything else in the house. At The Vyne, three large windows, also with depressed arches and cusped lights, are set into a polygonal apse (Plate III), while at Hengrave, again in an apsidal window, arched lights are set into rectangular frames (fig. 3.7). Almost as impressive must have been the great west chapel window at Shurland (Plate I), also contained within a depressed arch, which towered over the two-storey inner courtyard in the same way that the great hall window looms over the base court at Hampton Court Palace. In contrast, the tiny chapel at Hall Place in Kent also uses a depressed arch, but here the three small lights are separated at the top by simple tracery. At Naworth, the chapel (which runs along the east range) is lit only on the liturgical north side by two great rectangular windows which look onto the courtyard, and which were probably part of the alterations carried out by Thomas, Lord Dacre, in about 1520 (fig. 3.12). They are set relatively low on the wall, an idiosyncratic arrangement that was presumably the result of constraints imposed by the site and the medieval origins of the plan. At the detached chapel of Gipping, which dates from c.1474-1480 with additions before 1502, the large windows – there are five on the south facade alone – feature Perpendicular tracery set below depressed arches and, with their elaborate flushwork and heraldic devices, testify to the expense and craftsmanship devoted to the creation of a chapel of some splendour (Plate II). Withcote is more difficult to assess because of 18th-century renovations, but it shares with Gipping the use of fashionably large windows – which are rectangular with arched lights on the north and south walls.

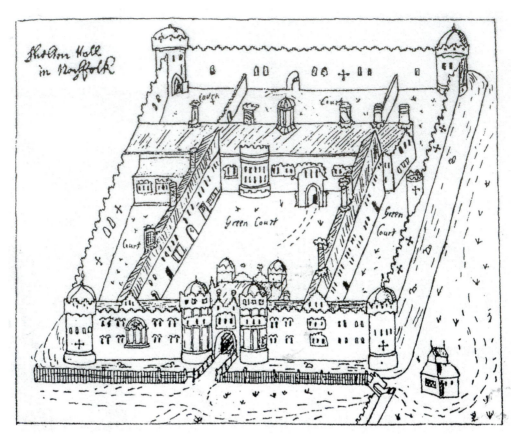

Fig. 3.15: Shelton Hall, Norfolk: 18th-century copy of a 16th-century view. In this late medieval house, there was no need for the chapel window (to the left of the entrance) to be symmetrical with the rest of the facade.

It is often assumed that chapel windows tended to borrow from Gothic ecclesiastical forms – that is using pointed arches and containing elaborate tracery – but there are few, if any, instances of the use of pointed windows (other than Perpendicular) in early Tudor chapels. The most popular forms were depressed arch windows with cusping on the individual lights, or arched lights, either of regular or varying sizes, set in rectangular frames.[9] Equally, tracery is far less common than cusping, and it was normal to use Tudor forms to create distinctive chapel windows. The idea that pointed windows with tracery necessarily conveyed an ecclesiastical character does not apply in the 16th century. At Cowdray, for example, there was no clear link between Gothic forms and ecclesiastical function. Both the hall and the chapel have windows that are differentiated from the standard rectangular mullioned and transomed type, but while the hall windows (fig. 3.4) are Gothic those of the chapel (fig. 3.5) are more Tudor in form. The aura of venerable antiquity or expensive display which

42

Gothic forms were probably intended to convey was evidently considered more suited to Cowdray's great hall than to its chapel. Indeed, as we shall see, Gothic tracery was not used with any regularity for important chapel windows before the 17th century.[10]

Although distinctive windows were an important part of the early Tudor chapel, it is not clear how far their purpose was to confer on it a separate external architectural character. The shape of the east window in the majority of chapels may well have been dictated by the design of the painted glass which most of them contained at least in part, the main purpose being to create an interior of a special character, distinct from the secular rooms of the house. But apses (and perhaps other windows too) could also be valued as imparting an individual character to the outside of the chapel, as well as contributing to the magnificence of the whole house.

There was no consensus among patrons about the role of the apse in the overall design. The chapel at Cowdray has an impressive three-sided ashlar apse lit by large double-height windows which dominate the east facade (fig. 3.5). However, since it did not form part of the entrance (west) front, the visitor's first experience of the chapel would probably have been from the inside. This suggests that its distinctive character derived more from a desire for interior display than to enhance the exterior magnificence of the house. Conversely, at The Vyne, although there are considerable problems with the interpretation of the overall layout, it has been suggested that the east range was originally the entrance range and, if this were correct, the chapel, and especially its apse, would have played an important visual role as the visitor approached the house. Indeed, a family portrait of the 1640s depicted this part of the house in the background, with the chapel apse featuring prominently (Plate IV).[11]

The chapel at Hengrave also has an impressive and highly visible apse, and there is no doubt that it is part of the entrance range. Later than Cowdray and The Vyne (it was built from 1523 to 1538 by Sir Thomas Kytson), it is the last apse known to have been completed in the early Tudor period. By this date another factor – symmetry – had entered the architectural equation. In a late medieval house such as Shelton Hall in Norfolk, built c.1480 (fig. 3.15), there was no need for the large chapel window to conform to a symmetrical design.[12] But as interest in regularity grew, distinctive elements of the facade that could not be easily duplicated began to cause difficulty. It is this problem that is being addressed at Hengrave: the chapel apse projected from the entrance facade and, with its great windows rising through two storeys, was intended to be a highly visible and impressive feature of the entrance range (fig. 3.7). What is new here is the attempt to integrate the apse into the overall symmetry of the facade. The floor plan illustrates the convolutions necessary to achieve this (fig. 3.6).

Fig. 3.16: Ashby-de-la-Zouch Castle, Leicestershire. The pre-Tudor chapel, to the right of the tower, seemed to dissolve into glass above the congregation.

Since the chapel could not form a central feature of the gatehouse range, the only alternative was to construct a balancing apse on the other (eastern) side of the entrance arch. However, an apse is not easily integrated into ordinary room shapes, and at ground-floor level there was a small, awkward space, both illogical and impractical. It is telling, too, that while the west side of the projection was splayed to replicate the chapel apse, its eastern counterpart (less noticeable from the entrance) was set at right angles to the main facade wall, squaring off one corner of this cramped little room. In order to match the apse, the windows of the ground- and first-floor rooms were each positioned as if lighting a double-height space. The unsuitably large lower window followed the normal chapel practice of starting much higher up the wall than was usual in a domestic space, and terminated immediately beneath the ceiling, while the window of the room above started at floor level. Since the chapel is not correctly-oriented, and because the flexible nature, imparted by its internal corridor, of the Hengrave plan allowed Kytson to place the chapel virtually wherever he wanted, it seems likely that he made a conscious decision to site his chapel where it would be most visible. His solution neatly demonstrates the problems of incorporating an architecturally differentiated chapel into a symmetrical design. It had few, if any, followers, not just because of its clumsy nature but also because, within a few years, the temporary demise of the architecturally differentiated chapel caused the problems to disappear.

As the chapel became more tightly integrated into the overall design, the opportunities for distinction were reduced. Sheer size of window, as for example at Ashby-de-la-Zouche Castle in Leicestershire, where three sides of the chapel, built just before the Tudor period, seemed to dissolve into glass above the congregation (fig. 3.16), was no longer practicable as chapels became integral components of the building complex rather than being detached or only loosely linked. However, where possible, large amounts of glass were still used, presumably with the object of enhancing the magnificence of the chapel. Hampton Court Palace chapel was, of course, well provided with windows on all but the west side, and it is likely that the chapel at The Vyne possessed windows on the north and south sides as well as at the east end. At the same time, the desire for symmetry would inevitably influence the handling of chapel windows. Some six years after the completion of the Hengrave apse, Sir John Thynne's mason suggested alterations to the work in progress at Longleat because the chapel window would 'much disvegure' the building. In due course the offending window was 'finally altered or destroyed and the chapel buttresses removed'.[13] The surviving house (and it is known that the exterior was completed before Sir John died in 1580) has no differentiated window marking the proposed position of the chapel. It seems that the architectural features that would have contributed to a differentiated chapel were dismantled because the lack of a balancing feature would have spoiled the overall design.

It is difficult to determine the thinking behind the design of every early Tudor chapel, but the wish to create a distinctive interior set apart for worship may well have influenced the differentiated external design of some of them. Cowdray, Shurland and Ingatestone have their chapels positioned in or behind ranges beyond the hall where any external architectural display would not have made an initial impact. But at Hengrave, and probably The Vyne, the chapel played an important part in contributing to the architectural magnificence of the entrance front. Whatever the reason, differentiated chapels were relatively common, and considerable effort could be expended on providing magnificent exteriors which simultaneously signalled the chapel's importance and could contribute to the overall grandeur of the house. The Reformation did not start to affect the architectural design of chapels to any great degree until after the mid-century. The apsidal glass at Hengrave, for example, was not installed until 1540. It is clear that, as with the positioning of the chapel in the house, major changes in exterior chapel design tended not to be initiated as an immediate result of the Reformation but rather by second and third generation Protestants.

Peripheral Spaces: 'a Prospecte into the Chapell'

When Boorde suggested that as many rooms as possible 'may have a prospecte into the Chapell', he may well in part have been urging the creation of peripheral chapel spaces which increased the range and type of accommodation available to worshippers. Although no pre-Reformation chapel spaces survive intact, a good idea of the complexity and variety of such arrangements can be gained from examining Wressle, The Vyne and Compton Wynyates I.

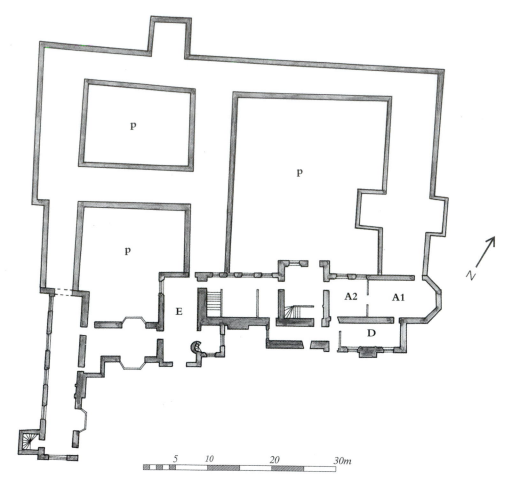

Fig. 3.17: The Vyne, Hampshire in c.1530 (after Howard and Wilson): The northern range was demolished in the 17th century.

a. (above). Ground plan: D = Vestry.
b. (opposite). First floor plan: B1 = Lord Sandys' closet; B2 = Lady Sandys' closet.

At Wressle, as well as a vestry and a smaller unidentified space off the east end of the chapel, at the upper level there were spaces for worship on the south, west and north sides (fig. 3.14b). These comprised, at the east end of the south side, 'My Lords pewe or seate' − a space about 7ft x 6ft immediately over the division between chapel and ante-chapel.[14] Close to the pew is a spiral staircase leading down into the ante-chapel − similar arrangements existed at the royal palaces of Eltham, Hampton Court and Greenwich.[15] The west end is taken up with a space about 10ft deep running the width of the chapel which is described on plan as 'A plac for the gentlmen and servenmen to see servic'. This immediately seems to contradict two major clichés: the upper west end of a chapel was clearly not

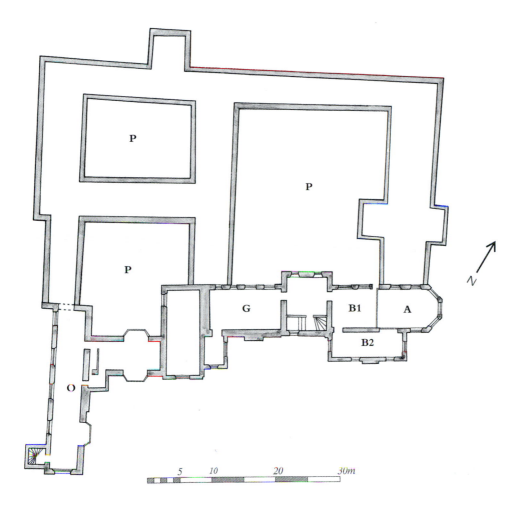

reserved for the family, and there was no hierarchical division between gentry and servants. Both spaces had access to the spiral staircase in the thickness of the south wall, and could also be approached via the staircase from the dining chamber. The fact that they were assigned to men implies that the sexes were segregated, and the narrower north gallery-like space, and the room leading off it which overlooked the east end of the chapel, may have been reserved for women – although in parish churches, where the sexes were usually segregated, the women normally occupied space on the north side of the nave.[16] Interestingly, the staircase which leads from the dining chamber to the upper chapel and its pair at the other end of the dining chamber are octagonal, highly decorated double stairs, apparently smaller versions of the more famous example at Chambord on the Loire. There was clearly a highly elaborate processional route from 'my Lord's Chamber' in the south-west corner, across the dining chamber and up the stair at the east end to his pew and to the upper chapel as a whole. What is not so clear

Fig. 3.18: The Vyne, Hampshire: the interior of the inner chapel looking west (the upper chapel screen is a later addition). A full set of early Tudor stalls is built into the fabric.

is the predominant purpose of the double flight. It might, it is true, have had no specific social function, being simply an object of splendour. Alternatively, it could have served to segregate the sexes or social levels, or perhaps it was simply a device to ease the flow of traffic at busy times.

The Vyne, built by Lord Sandys in the early years of the 16th century, also contained complex peripheral chapel spaces. The interpretation of the surviving parts of the house is problematic, making it difficult to pinpoint even the precise position of the great hall. However, the chapel does survive and has recently been the subject of an archaeological investigation which, together with the inventory of 1541, provides clues to where the peripheral chapel spaces might have been (fig. 3.17). Besides the chapel and the vestry, the inventory also lists 'my lords closet ovr the Chapell' and 'my Ladis closet next the Chapell'. The former probably occupied some or all of the space at the west end, over the ante-chapel, while Lady Sandys' closet could well have been on the south side of the chapel towards the west end. Moreover, the study has revealed that an area of the south wall towards the west end is considerably thinner than elsewhere. This would be consistent with the presence of a blocked-up opening from which Lady Sandys would have viewed the service. Finally, signs of a blocked-up door suggest that there could have been another peripheral chapel space on the north side of the upper chapel.[17]

Compton Wynyates is another early Tudor house where enough of the internal chapel (Compton Wynyates I) survives to confirm the existence of a variety of peripheral chapel spaces. In this case the basic arrangement differs from those at The Vyne and Wressle in that there may have been no peripheral chapel space at the upper west end (fig. 3.8). The liturgical eastern half of the chapel contains peripheral spaces along the north and south sides at ground- and first-floor levels, each with its own external window (fig. 3.10). It is likely that they served different purposes. Of the two at ground-floor level, the southern space was probably used by chapel staff since it was directly linked to the stair leading to rooms traditionally associated with the priest, while the northern space, being accessible only from the parlour, was probably a family pew or space reserved for other high status use. At first-floor level, both spaces seem to have catered for important occupants, since they had fireplaces, and were reached from the great chamber and the chapel chamber respectively. The southern space was also next to the king's bedroom and may, on ceremonial occasions, have been reserved for the king or other important guests.

As already mentioned, the role of another common peripheral space, the chapel chamber, was flexible. The one to the west of the upper chapel at Hengrave was furnished as a bedchamber, but traces of a squint high up on the west wall of the chapel overlooking the altar indicate that a dual function was likely. At Compton Wynyates I, the evidence is less clear. A 1522 inventory describes the room immediately above the ante-chapel as the chapel chamber, and the contents show that it too acted as a bedchamber.[18] Although the inventory lists nothing of a religious nature, its position, with only an internal wall (which now has an opening) separating it from the double-height east end, suggests that it had some direct connection with the chapel. The 1566 survey of Ingatestone refers to 'the chapel chamber over the chapel where the priest in his ministrations can be heard', and the plan shows that this was a relatively standard upper chapel leading off the long gallery. This interpretation is confirmed by a 1600 inventory which lists the space as the closet over the chapel.[19]

A more common use of the term 'closet' was, as we have seen, to denote a room close to the bedchamber where Mass could be heard in private. At Wressle, for example, *The Northumberland Household Book* records that on St Stephen's Day Henry Percy, 5th Earl of Northumberland, attended Low Mass in his closet.[20] Similarly, the will of John de Vere, 13th Earl of Oxford, refers to 'my chapel in my closet' at Castle Hedingham in Essex.[21] This was a richly furnished space which, as his will and the inventory taken on his death show, was provided with everything needed to celebrate Mass. Although it is not now possible to reconstruct this lost arrangement, the closet chapel would certainly have operated independently of the household chapel. Less clear is the purpose of closets at country houses such as The Vyne. Here the inventory refers to an altar in 'my lordes closet over the chapel', raising the possibility that Lord Sandys heard Mass there; there is, however, no mention of an altar in Lady Sandys' closet.

Fittings: Sparse and Simple

It is difficult to be certain what the pivotal chapel fitting – the **screen** – looked like. There are no surviving examples of this date from aristocratic houses. At Cotehele, a gentry house, the screen (with hinged central doors) was restored in the 19th century but is likely to be of early 16th-century origin and, as would be expected, has a solid lower level above which are cusped openings and delicate filigree cresting. Another early Tudor screen is now in Atherington church in Devon where it was probably taken when the private chapel at Umberleigh House was demolished in the 18th century (fig. 3.19). This is similar in form to that at Cotehele, although somewhat more substantial. Unfortunately, the addition of a later cross means that it is not possible to say whether it originally had a rood. Again, information about pre-Reformation roods and rood lofts in private chapels is limited. The best example is at Gipping. The screen no longer survives, but the stairs leading to the rood loft are visible on the south side. At Rycote Park in Oxfordshire, despite subsequent alterations, stairs to the rood loft of the detached chapel mark the position of the original screen, while at Haddon, the position of the rood loft is marked by an otherwise inexplicable opening in the south wall. But both these buildings are medieval in origin, and neither was originally designed as a private chapel.

Fonts and **Easter sepulchres** were not itemised in inventories, but the entry for 'a canabe ... belonging to the sepulchre' in the 1523 Heytesbury House (Wiltshire) inventory suggests that they occurred in private chapels, and a similar entry in The Vyne inventory referring to the font makes it clear that the chapel there was among many that were used for baptism.[22] Liturgical furniture in the form of **choir stalls** and **desks** were provided, but there are no documented examples of **pulpits** at this stage, perhaps because lecterns were preferred.[23] Family **pews** were also an important element, and seating may have been provided for some members of the congregation. The 3rd Duke of Buckingham's accounts for 1509-21 covering the rebuilding of Thornbury Castle in Gloucestershire mention individual pews for the duke and duchess. These were at the upper level of the west end of the chapel looking out towards the altar, and were luxurious constructions, little short of rooms, each having a fireplace. '22 settles of wainscot' were provided for the choir. At Petworth House in West Sussex, 'old' stalls and seats were removed from the 'great chapel' in 1582, implying that there could originally have been seats for some of the household as well as for the chapel staff.[24] Medieval pews (in the modern sense) also survive at Rycote, and possibly at Cotehele, but it is likely that seating, especially for the less important members of the congregation, would have been sparse and that, as in parish churches, many people would have stood.

It is possible to reconstruct the arrangement of the early 16th-century private chapel fittings in only the most general terms, but again Wressle is a good place to start. Here the surviving fabric, in conjunction with information from the 16th-century plans (fig. 3.14) and *The Northumberland Household Book*, conveys an idea of how an early Tudor, double-cell chapel was fitted out. In the chancel it is likely that there were three altars, some form of choir stalls placed college-style and, to their west but still east of the screen, other fittings including a desk. At upper-floor level, the 5th Earl's pew was the most prominent of the peripheral spaces surrounding the ante-chapel on three sides.[25] Given the status of its patron it is likely that Wressle conformed to conventions followed by other aristocratic early Tudor chapels, and surviving fragments of documentation support this. At Petworth, another Percy house and where, as at Wressle, the main chapel had medieval origins, information comes from the 1574 survey of the old house.[26] Petworth had two chapels: the 13th–14th-century 'great chapel' with a large marble altar, and the 'little chapel', next to the parlour and about which little is known, with a smaller altar, also of marble.

Altars were usual (altar furnishings are recorded in the Compton Wynyates I and The Vyne inventories) but, as will be seen, the replacement of the altar by the communion table was very much a feature of second-generation Protestant chapels.

No discussion of early 16th-century chapel fittings would be complete without considering those at The Vyne (fig. 3.18). Here a full set of early Tudor stalls, bearing the heraldic badges of Lord Sandys, is built into the fabric of the north and south walls of the chancel, and in the two west

Fig. 3.19: Atherington church, Devon. The early Tudor screen was probably once part of the private chapel at Umberleigh House. With its solid lower level and cusped openings above, it is one of the few surviving examples of the period. The crucifixion is a later addition.

51

corners adjoining the outer chapel.[27] Although they were there from the chapel's inception, their original form is uncertain due to subsequent alterations and additions. One puzzling element is that the stalls form a very considerable barrier between the outer and the inner chapels, being interrupted by only a central door.[28] In parish churches of this date, the screen's role was to form a visually penetrable (and to a certain extent symbolic) barrier between nave and chancel. But at The Vyne, far from being interconnected spaces, the stalls transform the chancel and ante-chapel into two separate rooms – an arrangement very different in spirit from the much more loosely divided spaces at Wressle. This sense of separation is enhanced by the fact that the upper areas of the chapel overlook only the chancel, further isolating the ante-chapel and increasing the impression that it is a separate room. An ante-chapel that is almost entirely cut off from the rest of the chapel loses the important concept of a sense of a community united in worship which is emphasised in contemporary documents such as Household Regulations and which appears to have been followed elsewhere. The isolation of The Vyne ante-chapel as it now survives suggests that a fundamental change of use occurred at some later stage in its history.

A further puzzle, possibly also indicative of later changes, is the way in which the coving of the stalls fails to integrate with the positioning of Lady Sandy's closet which might be expected to project forward over the stalls. The result is awkward, especially since the planks which form the 'roof' of the stalls canopy immediately below have no decorative finish. There is a similar problem on the north side, although here alterations which are still not fully understood have evidently taken place. Overall there is a surprising amount of rough woodwork visible from the two closet spaces occupied by the patron and his wife.

Finally, there is the question of what the stalls were for. Since it is now generally accepted that Sandys and his wife occupied spaces overlooking the chapel in the same general way as the patrons at Thornbury (and probably also at Wressle), it is reasonable to assume that the stalls were for the chapel staff. However, there appear to have been only three, a priest, a deacon and sub-deacon, whereas the stalls contain seating for about seventeen people. Moreover, unlike other examples, such as at Wressle, Thornbury, and Rushbrooke in Suffolk, there is little to indicate the existence of either gentlemen of the chapel or singing boys.[29] No vestments for them are listed, and there is no reference to lodgings for them.[30] It is therefore possible that Sandys did not have an extensive chapel staff. Instead singers, such as Paul's boys, could have been hired, and senior members of the household rather than chapel staff might have occupied some of the stalls. However, their function remains puzzling, and they might well have undergone more extensive alteration than is at present recognised. Certainly the evident changes in the order of the sections of the small but highly decorated frieze above the stalls and in the stalls themselves need explaining.[31] Although these stalls are the best surviving example of early Tudor chapel fittings, their message is hard to interpret.

Decoration: a Spotlight on the Altar

The purpose of the decorative scheme of the early Tudor chapel was to create perhaps the most colourful and richly appointed area of the house by the use of a rich mix of images, texture and colour. In most cases, the decorative display was carefully graded from the relative austerity of the west end, through the main body of the chapel, and culminating (at least in aristocratic chapels) in a crescendo of colour and texture at the east end. Although there could be other areas of richness, such as the patron's upper chapel, subsidiary altars or the area round the font, the primary function of the decoration was to direct attention to the main altar. The effect was as of a decorative spotlight trained on the most important part of the chapel. This climax was achieved by a combination of highly valuable objects, often of silver or silver gilt, seen against a background of rich textiles, colourful painting and stained glass. Less obvious elements utilising a number of decorative forms were also employed to enhance the emphasis on the altar. An order placed in the 1540s by Sir John Gage for differing types of floor tiles from Antwerp, presumably for his chapel at Firle Place in East Sussex, shows a careful hierarchical gradation between the tiles planned for different areas, with the most expensive and colourful being reserved for the east end.[32] This gradation may well have been echoed by a similar handling of the various sections of roof structure. At The Vyne, the simple, flat construction of the upper chapel ceiling above the outer chapel changes to a shallow pitch over the inner chapel, and then becomes more elaborate in order to encompass the apse.[33] Wall decoration may also have followed the same hierarchical gradation, but unfortunately no complete scheme survives.

Stained or painted glass was the most eye-catching of the decorative media employed, and created an emphasis on the east end through the brightness of its colour and the size, and the clarity of its images. Detached chapels, such as Withcote, and house chapels loosely integrated into the overall plan, could employ a scheme which involved a number of windows arranged to reach a climax at the east end. At Cotehele, for example, there is an early 16th-century glass cycle which includes St Catherine and St Anne in the south window, and a Crucifixion in the east window. Other chapels with a limited expanse of external wall were often organised so that a spectacular display of coloured glass could be set in the east window, as at Hengrave where the great windows of the apse are the only source of light. However, at the end of the period, post-Reformation ideas are becoming apparent for, although heraldic glass continued to be provided, it is notable that no biblical images appear to have been commissioned after the installation of the east window at Hengrave in 1540. Given that stained glass is fragile, that it was targeted for destruction particularly during and after the Civil War, and that it does not appear in inventories, a remarkable amount has survived or is recorded in the private chapels of this period.

Another element that focused attention on the east end was the spectacular quality of the objects on the altar, with the altarpiece often making a highly visual impact. The great gilt triptych on the high altar at Kenninghall in Norfolk measured 12ft x 3ft. [34] More sumptuous still was the silver and gilt altarpiece at Wilton House in Wiltshire.[35] Altarpieces in other chapels were more restrained, possibly because the altar was set below an east window containing painted glass, or because a large quantity of decorative metalwork was already displayed. At Compton Wynyates I with its large east window, one (presumably metal) 'tablet' was listed in the chapel, and at The Vyne, where there was probably painted glass in the apse and certainly a large crucifix, there were two 'large tablettes' valued at 10s.[36] The most frequently recurring image was of Christ, and featured different episodes from his life. Painted altarpieces and pictures were also used and could be large, but they did not come near to rivalling in value the textiles or metalwork.

Sculptural (or graven) images made from painted wood or metal also contributed considerably to the richness of the interior. At the highest level, the 13th Earl of Oxford's chapel at Castle Hedingham is the best documented. Oxford's will of 1509, and the inventory drawn up on his death in 1513, provide a detailed picture of the splendour both of the chapel itself and of his closet.[37] The contents provide a standard against which to judge the decline of the post-Reformation years. Moreover, since the earl's status was similar to that of the 5th Earl of Northumberland, the details, combined with the very different type of information recoverable at Wressle, provide a relatively complete overview of a pre-Reformation chapel belonging to an earl of ancient lineage. Among the metalwork listed on the high altar stood silver statues of Mary and St John (together weighing 138oz). Two crosses were listed: one, of gold decorated with two sapphires which terminated in *fleurs de lys*, stood on a base with twelve pinnacles, contained two fragments of the Holy Cross, and was valued at £30 0s 10d; the other, enamelled on both sides with likenesses of the four evangelists, was valued at £7. There were also silver gilt statues of SS Andrew, Peter and James, and a silver gilt image of the Trinity which included two small angels and a crown decorated with precious stones. This weighed 120.5oz and, at £33 9s 9d, was the most valuable object in the chapel. Other items included two 'great' candlesticks; 'an angel silver and gilt bearing relics', and two monstrances, one of beryl with a foot and covering of silver and gilt depicting St Anne bearing

Our Lady in her arms. Elsewhere, surprisingly little information exists about chapel metalwork, possibly because separate inventories were often compiled for silver and plate. Another factor could be the melting down of chapel plate. For instance, the detailed account of the 3rd Duke of Norfolk's property at the time of his attainder in 1547 does not list the chapel plate, instead noting tersely that it 'was given to be coined'.[38]

Another detailed early Tudor inventory, for The Vyne, comes nowhere near to matching the magnificence of the metalwork at Castle Hedingham, and here the considerable gulf in status should be remembered. As a newly created baron, Sandys could not rival the splendour achieved by one of such lineage and wealth as the 13th Earl of Oxford. However, though relatively simple, the metalwork at The Vyne was by no means insignificant. In particular the 'cross of silver and gilt with Mary and John, with a foot of gilt' weighed 156oz, some 30oz heavier and probably somewhat larger than the cross at Castle Hedingham. In addition, there were three pairs of candlesticks, the richest of which was valued at £3. But nothing else stands out on the comparatively short list of chapel plate.

Tapestry wall hangings were popular, often used, as in domestic spaces, in conjunction with panelling. Altar cloths could be made of rich materials, with the grander ones using cloth-of-gold or being embroidered with gold thread. Many incorporated biblical or heraldic decoration. They were often among the most expensive items in the chapel, and considerably more valuable than the much larger wall hangings.[39] Curtains and hangings, or riddels, specifically associated with the altar would also add colour and richness to the east end. Other options included painted canvas as at Kenninghall, and plain textiles such as the hangings of yellow and red, and yellow and white coarse damask at the Duke of Norfolk's Chesworth in West Sussex.[40]

It is difficult to be certain of the proportion of the different types of decoration used in private chapels because of the variations in survival rates and methods of recording them. Wall and ceiling paintings are not mentioned in inventories, and panelling is only rarely referred to. In spite of this, examples of early Tudor figurative wall painting survive in the chapel of Bramall Hall in Cheshire (Plate VII), and are also known from later depictions of the compartmented chapel ceiling formerly at Kirkoswald Castle in Cumbria (Plates V, VI) and descriptions of the 'Holy History of the Bible ' painted on the ceiling of Sandy's chapel of the Holy Ghost at Basingstoke. The possibilities available to patrons are eloquently illustrated by the cycle of paintings of miracles wrought by the Virgin Mary still to be seen on the walls of Eton College chapel in Berkshire, finished at the start of the early Tudor period, or in the chapel of Durham Deanery, where five surviving scenes from the life of Christ were painted towards the end of the 15th century. Moreover, a number of royal chapels used painted wall decoration. At Whitehall

Palace in London, for example, the chapel walls were painted with saints and prophets as well as stories from the Bible.[41] Rather than an option favoured only by a few, or indeed only by those of limited means, painted decoration was probably more widespread than surviving records imply.

It is clear that, while the main function of decoration was to emphasise and honour the altar as the focal point of the liturgy, other areas played a significant role in the decorative scheme. The variety of methods employed to decorate the side walls of the chapel included wooden panelling, sometimes carved in relief with figurative elements, hangings of tapestry or painted canvas ('counterfeit arras'), and painted decoration applied directly to the plaster. Textiles too highlighted areas of subsidiary importance. In some chapels with more than one altar, such as at Wressle, each would probably have been the centre of a rich decorative scheme. Finally, the apertures giving onto closets and other peripheral chapel spaces would have offered rich glimpses of sumptuous hangings and upholstery, and cushions embroidered with heraldry or biblical imagery.[42]

Decorative Iconography

The biblical subject most frequently depicted in stained glass was Christ's Passion. Side windows could also feature prophets, apostles and other saints as at Withcote and Cotehele. At Compton Wynyates I and The Vyne, donor figures were included in the east window.[43] However, the cycle of glass in the east window at Hengrave, which starts with scenes from the Creation and ends with the Last Judgement, suggests that the range of subject matter was probably far wider.

Tapestry hangings tended to feature biblical events (again, the most popular being scenes from the Passion), or variations on the idea of foliage (or 'verdure' as it is often referred to in inventories).[44] The 'verdure' type was used quite frequently, and was probably not inspired by the Reformation or an indication of Protestant inclinations on the part of the patron. For instance, the (Roman Catholic) Earl of Devon's chapel at Kewe in Cornwall, where an inventory was taken during the reign of Mary, contained hangings 'wrought with flowers and leafs'.[45] In addition, a relatively complete scheme of non-figurative wall painting that may be pre-Reformation survives at The Vyne in a room which probably equates with Lord Sandys' closet. Here black and white stripes (reflecting the Sandys colours) represent hangings complete with looped ties. This is probably an example of secondary decoration – that is, work that was designed to be visible only when tapestry hangings were removed.

Despite the paucity of information, surviving fragments and documents give some insight into the subject matter of figurative wall-painting schemes. One of the most interesting large-scale early Tudor schemes comprised the compartmented ceilings in the great hall and adjacent chapel at Kirkoswald. Each compartment contained a portrait, those in the hall of the descendants of Brutus the Trojan, the mythical first king of Britain, while their ecclesiastical counterparts in the chapel contained fifty-eight portraits of the patriarchs, kings of Israel and Judah and others. The fact that both ceilings followed a similar format introduces the intriguing idea that decorative schemes could run through a number of rooms. However, while there were complex iconographical schemes within a single medium such as glass, cross-media schemes, in which the different media were controlled by an overall concept, were not used at this time.[46] The chapel ceiling was removed to Naworth in the early 17th century by Lord William Howard, and its appearance, is known from later descriptions and two early 19th-century watercolours (Plates V & VI).[47] Another painting of early Tudor date at Naworth was a (1512) Tree of Jesse, shown as 'an old man from whom proceeds a branch, bearing the heads of kings and patriarchs, his descendants'.[48]

The early Tudor decorative scheme at Lord Sandys' Chapel of the Holy Ghost is of particular interest as an example of Sandys' thinking about the decoration of chapels. Known from a later description, the subject was 'the holy history of the Bible ... with living portraits and images representing the Prophets, the Apostles and the Disciples of Christ' on the ceiling.[49] At Bramall, part of an *Ecce Homo* survives on the west wall of the Davenport family chapel, although it was later painted out (Plate VII). The painting may have formed part of a much larger scheme, although it could also have been a single devotional image. Whatever the case, this small fragment poignantly demonstrates the fate of numerous medieval and early Tudor decorative schemes.

Other forms of wall decoration, such as panelling, could be treated figuratively. Great Fulford chapel probably contained panels of Cain and Abel, and Isaac and Esau, dated 1534. Royton in Kent had panels (now at Chilston Park, Kent) depicting the instruments of the Passion and a series of chalices – likely to date from 1520-40.

The predominance of scenes from the Passion – in glass, hangings, wood or paint – together with (in the richer chapels) silver and silver gilt statues of the crucified Christ, Mary, the apostles and other saints, all concentrated attention on the symbolism of the Mass and the place of its celebration. Today, no example survives which even remotely reproduces the level of splendour achieved in the great aristocratic chapels, whose richly distinctive atmosphere rivalled, and often surpassed, the grandest of the secular rooms of parade.

4

ELIZABETHAN: 'HONEST PLACES FOR CHRISTIAN SERVICES'

The well-ordered Protestant country house had fixed times for worship, and the entire household was required to participate. Services centred on prayer, preaching and the Word. These were significant changes from pre-Reformation times, and greatly affected all aspects of chapel design. Most notably, they led to the decisive rejection of the seclusion and other elements that had stemmed from the sacred quality of the (often consecrated) early Tudor chapel, and consequently of the chapel's status as a semi-independent space. A number of new houses did not have a chapel at all, and worship took place in ordinary rooms. Where a chapel was provided, it often became a room of assembly with few distinguishing features. In part this was a reflection of the Elizabethan trend towards more compact, tighter, planning. The decline in popularity of the sprawling yet flexible system of linked single-pile ranges, the continuing fashion for architectural symmetry and an increased emphasis on secular display made planning the country house

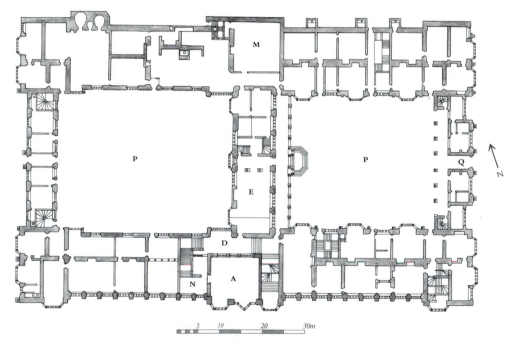

Fig. 4.1: Holdenby House, Northamptonshire: ground plan (after Thorpe T183-4, in which the west entrance to the chapel is concealed in the binding). The main processional route also formed an assembly area for the chapel, whose exciting fenestration merely repeated the rhythms of those for the great chamber above.

Fig. 4.2: Holdenby parish church, Northamptonshire: the screen, probably cut down from the side screen to the chapel at Holdenby House. With its Classical forms, it is an impressive and highly worked object of great dignity and magnificence, and formed an essential ingredient of the so-called 'stately ascent' to the great chamber. The two statues and cross set above it have no known connection with the chapel and were subsequently replaced by an arch with attendant lions – perhaps taken from another part of Holdenby House.

a far greater challenge. But the key issue was the effect that Protestant liturgy and attitudes were having on chapel design. Since few parish churches were built during this period, private patrons were almost alone in attempting to satisfy the demands of a new type of worship when creating or adapting chapels.

The Chapel in the House: Total Integration

Fortunately, considering the poor survival rate of Elizabethan chapels, there is plentiful information about planning in the second half of the 16th century due to the survival of the John Thorpe and Robert Smythson collections of drawings, many of which identify the chapel.[1] Some are surveys of existing houses, others are proposals for alterations, and yet others are plans for new houses which may or may not have been built. It is clear from these that the position of the chapel was becoming more standardised. There was an increasing tendency for it to be close to the high end of the great hall, forming part of a group of spaces – the others being the great stair and the parlour – that, with slight variations, recur together frequently in Elizabethan planning, regardless of whether courtyard or compact plan types were used.[2] The move to standardisation does not in itself carry any intrinsic connotations of a changed status for the chapel, but was a reflection of the new Elizabethan planning priorities. And one advantage of having it close to the centre was that access was normally simple from both low and high ends of the house, while proximity to the great stair could facilitate the provision of a peripheral chapel space at mezzanine level.

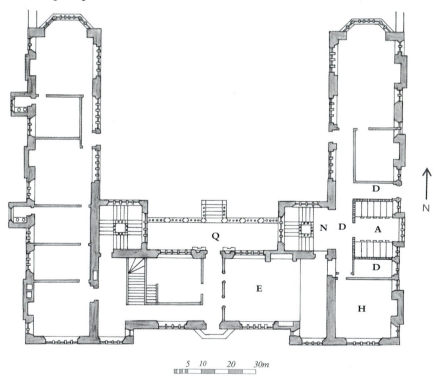

Fig. 4.3: Wimbledon House, London: ground plan (after Thorpe T113). The main circulation route passed through part of this assembly chapel, which is bounded on three sides by open screens. Queen Henrietta Maria's later Roman Catholic chapel, with its three-light Gothic window, replaced the parlour (H) in the south-east corner.

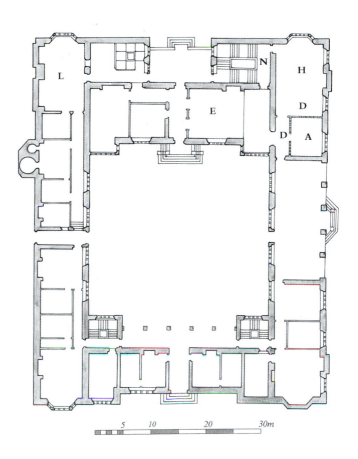

Fig. 4.4: Slaugham Place, East Sussex; ground plan (after Thorpe T239–40, Inset A). The insignificant, probably incorrectly oriented chapel, with its off-centre liturgical east window, was tucked away in a corner and typifies the decline in importance of private chapels under Elizabeth.

With the abandonment of one of the most important pre-requisites for the early Tudor chapel, the need for seclusion, the main circulation route in some houses, such as Holdenby House in Northamptonshire (fig. 4.1) and Wimbledon House in London (fig. 4.3), could pass through a peripheral part of the chapel. This would have been unthinkable for a consecrated chapel, negating as it does the idea of a sacred space set apart from the bustle of the house. Elizabethan chapels tended not to have a direct external entrance, but were usually approached via an internal door towards the liturgical west end, where they often overlapped with the domestic space.[3] Also declining sharply was the provision of an entrance for chapel staff near the liturgical east end, most likely as a result of the drastic reduction in the number of such staff.

Correct orientation also showed a marked decline although, because many plans lack compass points, the evidence is scarce. While Hardwick, Wimbledon and perhaps Holdenby were correctly oriented others, including Slaugham Place in East Sussex (fig. 4.4) and Copthall in Essex, may not have been. Moreover, few new chapels had a strong liturgical east-west axis. Many did not use the standard rectangular shape of the early Tudor period, or did not exploit it as the main axis. At Longleat, for example, the L-shape of the chapel does not appear to have resulted from a considered analysis of the needs of a chapel space, but was probably imposed by the symmetry of the overall plan, and it is notable that the south wall actually cuts into one of the three-light windows. This, coupled with the position of the chapel in the low end of the house some distance from the great hall, indicates that it did not have a high priority in the planning process. In fact, although its position was allocated from the outset, the chapel was not fitted out until the mid-17th century, perhaps reflecting the Elizabethan trend towards using other large rooms for prayer.

The fenestration of the chapel at Longleat is certainly awkward, but this is a

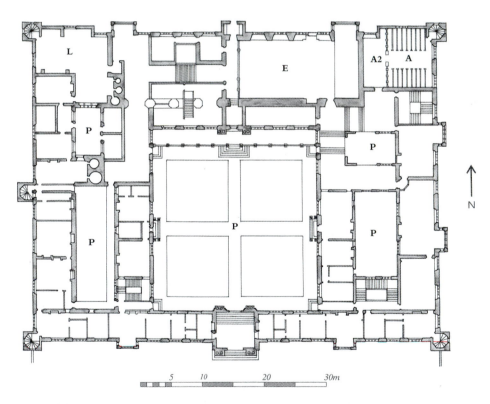

Fig. 4.5: Buckhurst House, East Sussex: unrealised ground plan (after Thorpe T19-20). The screen of the correctly oriented narthex chapel would have formed the prelude to the main area for worship. The most junior members of the household would probably have gathered in the western space. The placing of the windows would have made no concessions to the position of the pews or central aisle.

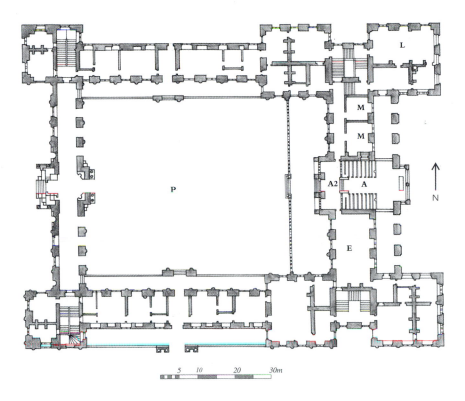

Fig. 4.6: Luxembourg Palace, Paris, France: ground plan (after Thorpe T123-4). The chapel exercised a formative influence on the plan, and probably inspired Thorpe's unexecuted plan for Burley-on-the-Hill at fig. 5.6.

not uncommon characteristic of the Elizabethan chapel. Plans from the Thorpe collection illustrate that, in most cases, fenestration obeyed the needs of the overall symmetry of the façade at the expense of the internal logic of the chapel.[4] At Slaugham (fig. 4.4), the only window is awkwardly positioned well off-centre at the (liturgical) east end, and in Thorpe's unrealised plan for Buckhurst House in East Sussex (fig. 4.5), the windows on the entrance axis are positioned without regard to the proposed pewing arrangement, while the two at the (liturgical) east end relate neither to the pews nor to the central aisle. The absence of a strong liturgical east-west axis at Buckhurst would have been reinforced by the lack of a differentiated east window. In the great majority of houses, the establishment of a pronounced east-west axis within the chapel, with windows designed to emphasise it and provide an appropriate light source, was deemed less important than meeting the needs of the great hall. Indeed, windows were usually adapted to suit the interior design of the great hall rather than the chapel.

Two Thorpe plans demonstrate the difference between a chapel that is an important force in the planning process, and one that has been slotted into a vacant space after the important decisions have been made. Thorpe's variant of a plan for the Palais du Luxembourg in Paris (begun in 1615; fig. 4.6) was French, royal, later in date, and Roman Catholic, but it demonstrates very clearly the way in which the chapel could exercise a formative influence on the plan. Wider and longer than the hall, this double-height chapel formed the focal point of the plan, terminating the main axis, and occupying the most important space in the building. In contrast the plan for Slaugham (fig. 4.4) shows a small chapel with an off-centre east window which is little more than a partitioned-off corner of the parlour. It exemplifies the chapel's decline in importance as a component of the overall plan to the status of an ordinary room.

But it is perhaps Burghley which best illustrates the reducing status of the chapel. In the early work carried out by William Cecil (later Lord Burghley) in the 1560s, a chapel with a distinctive east window following the pre-Reformation tradition was planned. However, when major alterations, including the enlargement of the great hall, were undertaken in the early 1570s the position allocated to the chapel appears to have been given over to the splendid new south-eastern great stair. Nor was it likely that there was a chaplain at the house for, in 1573, there was consternation when Cecil's mother, Jane, moved back to Burghley because 'there is not one that is in the Ministry to do service there ... that she may serve God twice a day'.[5] It appears likely that William's eldest son Thomas (later 1st Earl of Exeter), who was then living in the house, had adopted a more low-church regime, and a chapel had to be hastily formed for Jane out of an empty room. Astonishingly, it seems that this makeshift chapel was not even re-painted. The room had been decorated with grotesque work (of which fragments survive), and Horace Walpole confirmed that the chapel was still decorated in this way in the 18th century.[6] This laid-back attitude of the Cecils – it is possible that William Cecil's London House, Cecil House on The Strand, did not possess a chapel – emphasises the lack of importance attached to chapels by some patrons after the Reformation.[7] Burghley was one of the most splendid houses of the period, but even for the most upwardly mobile, in the new Protestant world the chapel was no longer an essential part of the trappings of status and power, and took second place to the provision of a magnificent processional route.

The new attitudes to worship led to the development of new forms of chapel space in addition to the assembly chapel, and the new two-centred chapel that superficially resembled the traditional pre-Reformation double-cell type (both discussed later). These additional forms comprised the Elizabethan room chapel and the narthex chapel. The former was a reflection of the patrons' need for a space where the entire household could gather and actively engage with the prayer, preaching and readings that were the main components of the new services. This requirement could be fulfilled in a simple room, indistinguishable from the exterior and identifiable from the interior only by its fittings. On plan, therefore, the Elizabethan chapel can often appear as an ordinary room except for the lack of a fireplace.[8] It was only the fittings (and, in a negative sense, the austere decoration) that gave it any distinctive quality.

A good example of the narthex chapel is that proposed by Thorpe at Buckhurst (fig. 4.5). Although the screen acts as a division between two separate areas, it is west of the main seating space, forming an outer area that is much smaller than a normal ante-chapel, and acting as the prelude to the main space for worship. This screen could not be said to be dividing chancel and nave as at Wressle, or marking out two areas designated for different types of service as required in the post-Reformation two-centred parish church. Instead, it defines the beginning of the chapel proper. This change is one logical reaction to post-Reformation changes when household choirs were abolished, the number of chapel staff was sharply reduced and the priority was to provide enough space to allow the whole household to attend the proceedings. And, of course, there was no longer a need for the spacious chancel and conventional screen dividing it from the nave applicable to an altar-centred liturgy.[9] The purpose of the western space, which was often fairly small, is not clear but it could have been where the most junior members of the household gathered.

The Exterior Architecture: the Loss of Distinction

After Hengrave was finished in 1540, and with the exception of Copthall and Little Moreton Hall, it seems that no more architecturally differentiated chapels were built in the 16th century. Although the fashion for symmetry may have played some part in this decline, it was a secondary reason. In the mid-century, second generation Protestant patrons had no interest in what they saw as discredited pre-Reformation practices, and preferred a simpler, more austere, approach. In the midst of Elizabethan secular splendour and magnificence, the chapel was no longer seen as a suitable vehicle for display.

Signs of this change are detectable from the 1550s. Elizabethan Chatsworth was started in 1551. Like Hengrave, it too was a courtyard house composed largely of single-pile ranges and, also like Hengrave, the chapel's liturgical east end was probably part of the entrance facade.[10] But these similarities excepted, the treatment of the two chapels could not have been more different. Significantly, Chatsworth's was not a cross-range chapel, and its liturgical east and north facades most likely continued the general fenestration patterns of the range, resulting in a chapel with no external distinguishing features. Although evidence about the design of the windows of the entrance (west) facade is conflicting, both the needlework view of *c.*1590–1600 (Plate VIII) and a later Richard Wilson copy of a (lost)

Fig. 4.7: Little Moreton Hall, Cheshire: detail of exterior showing the distinctive east window of the cross-range chapel — both attributes were unusual in the 1570s.

slightly later painting show that fenestration patterns were used to emphasise certain rooms. In the needlework view it is the two staterooms, with their large pedimented windows rising through the second and third floors, that are highlighted. While at Hengrave, Kytson was trying to incorporate a differentiated chapel within a symmetrical arrangement, at Chatsworth this approach seems to have been switched to important domestic rooms.

Differentiation may therefore not have been solely a question of architectural fashion, but also of priorities: Kytson (born in 1485) and his family were staunch Roman Catholics, but the builder of Chatsworth, Elizabeth Cavendish (later the Countess of Shrewsbury and better known as Bess of Hardwick), was some 30 years younger with a Protestant upbringing.

As we have seen, the patrons at Longleat and Burghley – two of the great Elizabethan 'prodigy' houses and by-words for architectural magnificence – decided against creating externally differentiated chapels, and the same is probably true of Chatsworth. They are but three examples of a remarkably widespread and consistent development. At only two houses, Copthall and Little Moreton Hall in Cheshire (where an eastern extension was added to the chapel in the late 16th century; fig. 4.7), is there clear evidence of architectural differentiation, both chapels possessing a large, distinctive east window. It is true that the chapel on the ground floor at Holdenby, completed in 1583, made use of some of the most exciting fenestration in the house, but it is clear from inscriptions on Thorpe's plan (fig. 4.1) that it was merely repeating the rhythms needed to provide the great chamber on the floor above with spectacular windows. Indeed, only two-thirds of the central window space at ground-floor level actually affected the chapel, for the remaining bay would have lit what appears to be a service staircase. There is no sign of architectural differentiation at Hardwick, and the chapels at Wimbledon and Buckhurst are, because of the regularity of their windows on plan, unlikely to have been distinguished in any way.

There was also a decline in cross-range chapels, at least in the houses which still used single ranges. Excluding chapels which are set in the angle where two ranges meet, again only Copthall and Little Moreton Hall are the exceptions,

Fig. 4.8: Little Moreton Hall, Cheshire: the east cell of the chapel chancel interior, drawn by James West in 1847. Painted texts within decorative borders covered the cell walls.

being true cross-range examples – a factor facilitating the incorporation of their distinctive east windows.[11]

Patrons of older houses undergoing major renovation or updating did not necessarily sweep away existing differentiated chapels. Examples of medieval (and therefore differentiated) chapels being retained in major 16th-century houses are relatively common. The best documented is at Petworth. In 1574, on his release from prison, Henry Percy, 8th Earl of Northumberland, started to restore his much neglected, largely medieval, house to meet the requirement that he live in the south of England. In 1582-3, the medieval 'great chapel', which was originally set at right angles to the great hall, was thoroughly renovated but, though work was carried out on the windows, no attempt was made to update them.[12] It is difficult to pinpoint precise reasons for decisions such as this, but it is likely that both practicality and a wish to emphasise the family's ancient lineage were factors. The latter motive may well have led that enthusiastic seeker-out of recusants, Thomas Cecil, to retain the pre-Reformation windows in the splendid chapel at Snape Castle in North Yorkshire during a major reconstruction of the house in the 1580s. Cecil's wife, Dorothy Nevill, had inherited Snape in 1577 and he, perhaps conscious of his *arriviste* position in society, may well have

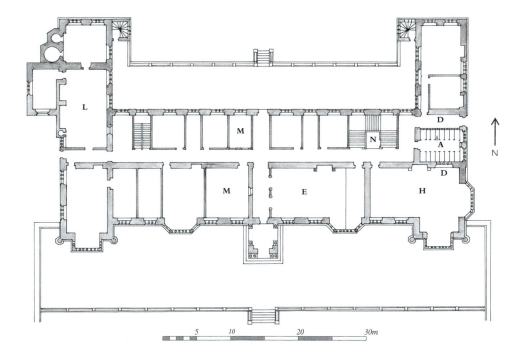

Fig. 4.9: Great House, Chelsea: ground plan (after Thorpe T63-64). An open screen bounds the north side of this assembly chapel, while a four-light window is set into the party wall with the parlour.

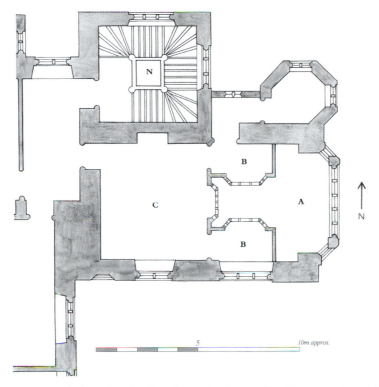

Fig. 4.10: Great House, Chelsea: detail of an alternative layout for the upper chapel (after Hatfield Cecil MSS CPM11/6) showing the complex peripheral spaces of the upper chapel. The design indicates that the screen separating it from the lower chapel may have contained glazed windows.

retained the medieval forms as visible confirmation of his links with the Nevills, one of the most ancient and powerful families of the north.[13]

Peripheral Spaces

The Emergence of the Protestant Assembly Chapel: a Significant Innovation

The most significant innovation of the Elizabethan period, and a hitherto overlooked development, was the way in which peripheral chapel spaces were enlisted to form a new type of chapel designed specifically for Protestant worship. It was distinguished by the way in which it made use of shared space, such as the foot of the great stair, and passages and landings forming part of a main circulation route. The central core of the chapel was still reserved for religious use, but the outer areas shared spaces that had other, secular, functions. In a sense the emergence of this 'assembly' chapel was a compromise between an assembly in a secular room and the traditional chapel.

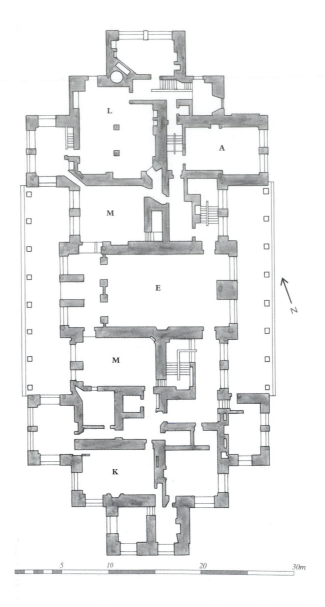

Thorpe's plans are particularly useful in the detection of assembly chapels because they often record the difference between partition walls (thin parallel lines) and screens (alternating black and white squares). It is only through a detailed study of partitions/screens that this new type of chapel can be identified. Holdenby provides a high-profile example.[14] Its chapel, which lay next to the great stair and was separated by a north screen from the main processional route to the great chamber on the floor above, is often misinterpreted because the west wall is concealed in the plan binding. However, the entrance was in fact from the staircase hall through a central opening in this same west wall. It is therefore probable that the chapel was correctly-oriented and that the large

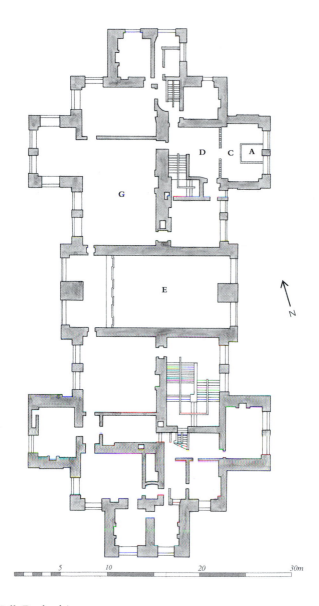

Fig. 4.11: Hardwick Hall, Derbyshire.

a (opposite). Ground plan: positioning the chapel on the low side of the house facilitated access
by the lower servants.
b (above). First floor plan: C = the upper chapel, east of the screen, perhaps for the family; D =
the dual purpose landing west of the screen, perhaps for the upper household. Note the apparent opening in the floor at the east end through which the family and higher servants may have
followed services in the lower chapel.

windows of the south side did not terminate the main axis (fig. 4.1). Although
the exact relationship of the staircase hall and great stair to the chapel is difficult

Fig. 4.12: Hardwick Hall, Derbyshire: a simple, openwork wooden screen separates the upper chapel from the landing to the west.

to determine, it is possible that spaces for the assembled household were provided at the west end or in a mezzanine space off the great stair. Thorpe indicates that the north screen was panelled below with an open balustraded area above. This accords with the imposing example now in the nearby parish church, which is usually accepted as part of the original chapel screen (fig. 4.2).[15] It would not have formed a significant visual barrier between the chapel and the main ceremonial route, so allowing this well-lit passage to double as a spacious outer chapel.[16] The glimpse of the chapel afforded visitors through the screen while processing to the great stair would have added an extra dimension to the 'stately ascent' that was much admired at Holdenby by Lord Burghley.[17]

Other chapels can be identified from Thorpe's plans as assembly chapels. At Thomas Cecil's Wimbledon (built from 1588; fig. 4.3), the single-storey chapel occupied a standard position close to the dais end of the great hall, and was situated in the angle between the great stair and an unidentified room which was probably a parlour. Although the plan appears to show a self-contained chapel, closer examination reveals that it is bounded on three sides by openwork screens giving direct contact with adjacent areas. Those to the north and south of the core chapel area were assembly spaces, enabling people gathered there to see and hear proceedings in the main chapel. The north space, or passage, looked directly into the chapel and linked the garden to the great stairs. The south space, a small room, provided a more secluded space for worship. The openwork screen at the west end has a large central opening, permitting the chapel space to flow uninterrupted into the staircase hall. Smythson's survey of 1609 accords with Thorpe's depiction of the chapel in that both plans show a wide central opening to the west.[18] It is likely that a mezzanine area was provided within the stairs at the west end.[19] The different position and character of the spaces suggests that they were each intended for a different section of the household. The family would occupy a mezzanine-level closet at the west end of the chapel, with perhaps gentlewomen or guests in the south room. Senior members of the household might occupy seats in the chapel itself, lower servants could be accommodated west of the screen, and perhaps outdoor staff would use the northern space leading to the garden.[20]

Another variant of the assembly chapel is shown in Thorpe's plan for another Cecil house, the Great House, Chelsea, London (fig. 4.9). Here the chapel appears to have been entered through a door at the (liturgical) west end. Unlike Wimbledon, there was no west screen, but the entire north wall is shown as screen and, as at Wimbledon, the northern space is a passage between the garden door and the great stair. On the south side a substantial four-light window is set into the party wall between the chapel and the parlour, converting the latter into an extra chapel space when needed. The chapel at Hunstanton may have been another variation on an assembly chapel, centred as it was around the great stair.

One example of an assembly chapel does survive, albeit much altered – Hardwick. Something of the original arrangement can be reconstructed from a combination of surviving fabric and later descriptions. Originally spanning two storeys, in about 1800 the lower chapel was converted into a steward's room by the 5th Duke of Devonshire. The 6th Duke remembered that 'in his boyhood the chapel was open in the middle part to the room below', and Horace Walpole, visiting Hardwick in 1760, described the chapel 'like a well, very indifferent'.[21] It seems that there was an open area in the upper chapel, probably towards the east end, through which the service could be heard (fig. 4.11).[22] It is divided from the staircase landing by a large but simple openwork wooden screen reaching from floor to ceiling (fig. 4.12). This is usually dismissed as a later insertion or the uneasy result of later changes to the staircase. However, it is more likely to have been a contemporary assembly chapel screen.[23] The condition of the surviving fabric indicates that it is in its original position, and forms part of a late change of plan that was nonetheless contemporary with the building work.[24] It was evidently intended as no more than a symbolic barrier, and could not have provided any seclusion for the upper chapel, which is positioned on a busy landing. Perhaps the space west of the screen was used by the upper household, with the area to its east being reserved for the family. Junior servants would probably have congregated in the lower chapel whose entrance was positioned

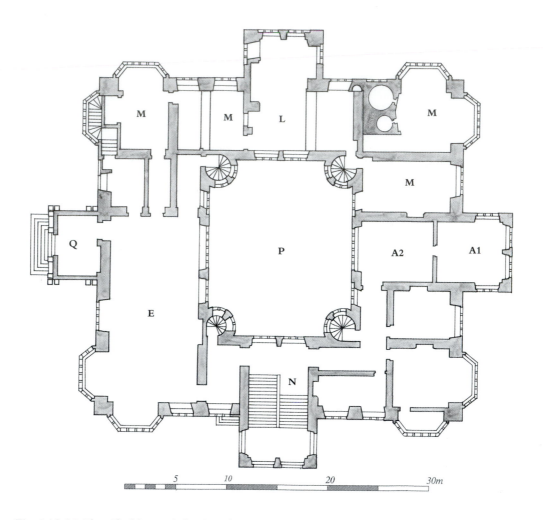

Fig. 4.13: Unidentified house (after Smythson IIa & b): perhaps the earliest 17th-century English design for a country house chapel that occupied an essential and formative part of the planning process.

a. (above). Ground plan: the ante-chapel is approached via an impressive route but undisturbed by passing traffic.
b. (opposite). First floor plan: the bowed central opening of the upper chapel screen may have been glazed.

near the kitchen and service rooms.

Because of the lack of surviving Elizabethan chapels and problems in dating some Thorpe drawings, it is difficult to assess the popularity of the assembly chapel, but the importance and originality of this development cannot be overstated.[25] At a time when parish churches were adapting space originally designed for

74

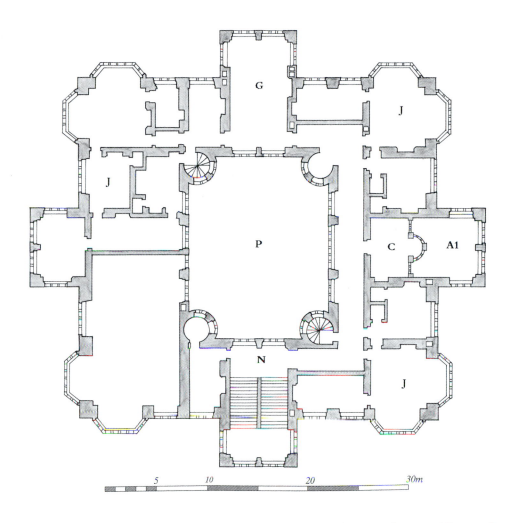

Roman Catholic worship, private patrons were responding to the specific needs of Protestant worship by creating an entirely new type of chapel. As consecration of chapels became more common in the 17th century, its popularity declined.[26] However, during the late 16th and early 17th centuries its features of a relatively small chapel core and linked peripheral spaces, where the entire household could assemble for sermons, prayers and readings, clearly met the needs of a number of Protestant patrons.

Upper Spaces in the Two-Centred Chapel

While the assembly chapel was the most significant innovation of the Elizabethan period, the traditional, double-cell chapel continued in being, albeit in its new, two-centred, guise. As always, the paucity of surviving fabric and first-floor plans makes it difficult to reach firm conclusions about the design and layout of upper chapel spaces in the two-centred chapel, but a series of six designs for the ground and first floors of the Great House, Chelsea, shows that at the end of the 16th century there was a considerable range available to patrons.[27] Of the Chelsea designs, it is likely that two (CPM/II 9, 10) were survey plans of the ground and first floors of the existing house. These show a relatively small chapel with a stacked upper chapel with a small opening approximately 4ft x 6ft immediately over the communion table.[28] The other designs illustrate three different layouts. CPMII/7 shows a small assembly chapel positioned on the main circulation route. The remaining two have a larger chapel (about 31ft x 19ft) and contain different solutions for the upper chapel. One has a standard upper chapel at the west end, while the other (CPMII/ 6, fig. 4.10) shows a much more complex arrangement. Here the upper chapel has a central bay opening, flanked by two doorways leading into projecting closets of approximately 6ft x 4ft, each having bay windows on their internal side walls looking into the body of the chapel below. A further room is shown beyond, and only accessible from the north closet.

This series of designs raises the general question of the physical nature of the contact between upper chapels and the main chapel spaces. It is usual to assume that, apart from some form of low wall at the eastern end, the upper chapel opening was either uninterrupted or sported a woodwork frame or frames. However, the window-like design of CPMII/6 strongly suggests that three glazed internal windows were intended. Smythson's plan of only a few years later of an unnamed house (fig. 4.13b) also shows an upper chapel screen with a bowed central opening which again suggests the use of glass.[29] Some pre-Reformation royal chapels, such as that at Hampton Court, had glazed upper chapels, and it would not be surprising if glass screens were re-introduced.

Another change concerns access to the main body of the chapel from the upper chapel. While some pre-Reformation upper chapels had direct access to the chapel proper, in the Elizabethan period there is rarely direct contact between the two spaces. At Hardwick, for instance, the only possible route between the two areas covered a considerable distance, implying that such access was not of great consequence.

Fittings: Workable for the Protestant Liturgy

The problem for parish churches after the succession of Edward VI had been how to convert space designed for Roman Catholic worship into something that would be workable for the Protestant liturgy as set out in the Prayer Book. As we have seen, the solutions can be followed in some detail through the rubrics of the Prayer Book, and in the Royal Orders and the Royal and Episcopal Injunctions which continued during the reign of Elizabeth. An important stipulation was that a **screen** or other division between the two centres of worship be retained. Only a few screens survive from the Elizabethan period, but Thorpe's plans show that the Injunctions and Prayer Book rubrics had startlingly little influence on the design of the private chapel, as opposed to the parish church.[30] Instead of employing the screen to create a two-centred chapel, it was being used to define the two new forms of chapel that were gaining popularity, the assembly chapel (where screens were, of course, plentiful and versatile) and the narthex chapel.

Three survivors demonstrate that post-Reformation screens had changed in form as well as function. The large openwork screen at Hardwick dividing the dual function space of landing and outer chapel at the upper level from the inner chapel is a severely functional object (fig. 4.12). Whereas early Tudor screens, such as those now in Atherington parish church (fig. 3.19) and at Cotehele, were delicately decorated, that at Hardwick is plain, almost to the extent of being primitive. A screen of similar design is in Sir Michael Willoughby's 1593 chapel of ease, All Saints, near Risley Hall, although in this case two small, carved heads are incorporated into the fabric. In contrast, the Holdenby screen is a highly worked object of great dignity and magnificence, incorporating Doric half-columns with a full entablature (fig. 4.2). This adaptation of correct Classical forms to ecclesiastical fittings must pre-date their use in parish church screens by at least twenty years, and shows how private chapels could set rather than follow an aesthetic agenda.[31] Although a side rather than a west screen, this was very much a showpiece, presumably due to its position on the main processional route through the house. Since in the past it was thought of as a purely secular object similar to the hall screen, the originality of its design can be overlooked. All three screens represent a complete break with the form and decorative language employed in pre-Reformation screens. It is clear that patrons were initiating a new, and Protestant, approach to screen design and function, introducing a new aesthetic and one that was free of decorative imagery and totally independent of the parish church.

Screens do most to set and control the arrangement of a chapel, but other fittings contribute to the overall effect. **Pulpits** can be found in parish churches from the 14th century, and it is surprising that few if any Elizabethan examples survive in private chapels. However, there is no doubt that they existed since some feature in inventories, and a few appear in the Thorpe plans. An early reference is to 'pulpytts of wood' in the Sheffield Castle inventory of 1582, and two other houses connected with Bess of Hardwick, Chatsworth and Hardwick, list pulpits in their 1601 inventories.[32] Sadly, it does not follow that where an inventory makes no mention of a pulpit, none was provided, since they were sometimes considered as fixtures and therefore not listed. However, there is less mention of pulpits than might be expected given the importance of sermons and readings to the Elizabethan liturgy. It is particularly surprising that detailed and well-worked plans by Thorpe such as those for Buckhurst and Wimbledon do not contain pulpits, especially since some of his plans − such as that for Lord Derby's house at Cannon Row, Westminster[33] − do include them. One possible explanation is that lecterns were still preferred − for example the 8th Earl of Northumberland purchased the eagle lectern, which is still in the chapel at Petworth, in 1582.[34] And in houses without chapels (which were of course common) there may well have been pulpits in ordinary rooms.[35]

Desks start to feature in inventories in the Elizabethan period.[36] An early (1565) example is at the Charterhouse in Clerkenwell, London, where the chapel was created from the Carthusian chapter house.[37] However, since the 1600 inventory for Ingatestone lists '2 thick short desks to kneel against', it is clear that the term was used relatively loosely and did not necessarily refer to a fixture from which the chaplain would conduct the service.[38]

Seating for the congregation appears in a number of Elizabethan inventories, and in the lower chapel 'forms' seem to be the most common type. Again, caution is necessary, for the term can also be applied to kneelers.[39] At the Charterhouse, '10 formes after desk fashion, long and stout' could have been for a section of the congregation. On the other hand, it is probable that many of the congregation were accustomed to stand, as they still did in parish churches. Furnishings in the upper chapel also included 'forms', but these tended to be grander and more highly worked.[40]

Pews are sometimes shown in Thorpe's plans. Of fourteen chapels likely to be Elizabethan, six are conventionally arranged, that is, where the pews face east in rows divided by a central aisle. At Lord Burghley's Theobalds, relatively narrow pews were arranged college-style along the north and south walls separated by a wide central aisle.[41] What appears to have been a double screen forms a division east of which are another three box-pews on either side, with the easternmost being significantly larger, perhaps for the chaplain and senior members of the household. An apparent raised or mezzanine pew at the west end was probably occupied by the family − arguably the precursor of the raised pew at Wimbledon (owned by Burghley's son Thomas) and of many other raised west end pews, including 17th-century examples at Althorp in Northamptonshire and Arbury Hall in Warwickshire.[42]

The abandonment of **altars** was required by the Injunctions and Visitation Articles. Post-Reformation stone altars were very rare. Where they did exist, it was in chapels of Roman Catholic families such as at Battle Abbey in East Sussex. Here, after her marriage in 1556, and with Mary on the throne, the Viscountess Montague set up a stone altar complete with steps and rails.[43] The effect on private chapels of the change from stone altars to wooden **communion tables** is clearly reflected in the change of terminology employed, particularly in inventories.[44] Those from the first half of the century, such as for Compton Wynyates I and The Vyne, use the word altar frequently, but after the 1557 inventory of Roman Catholic Kewe the terms 'table' or 'communion table' quickly become standard.[45] Examples include the early Tudor house belonging to the Worsleys at Appuldurcombe House on the Isle of Wight, inventoried in 1566, and the Charterhouse, then owned by the Roman Catholic 4th Duke of Norfolk, whose 1565 inventory listed a table 'standing aulter wyse'.[46]

Decoration: 'Comely whiteness and well-contrived coarctation'

Ecclesiastical Injunctions and Visitation Orders are important in the context of decoration for the insight they give into the thinking of leading churchmen. Protestant patrons would naturally have been aware of them, and generally appear to have followed their lead when building chapels, even though they were rarely actively enforced in existing or proposed private chapels. Moreover, random iconoclasm was rare. More co-ordinated and perhaps specifically anti-Roman Catholic was Elizabeth I's progress to East Anglia in 1578, where the itinerary appears to have deliberately targeted influential Roman Catholics. At Euston Hall in Suffolk, a hidden image of Our Lady was discovered and ceremonially burnt in front of the Queen and the patron, Edward Rookwood, imprisoned.[47] But the effect of iconoclastic and punitive activities of this sort on private chapels does not appear to have been great. It was more the new Protestant attitudes, so clearly reflected in the Injunctions and Visitation Articles, that increasingly affected the content of decorative schemes as powers of patronage passed into the hands of those born after the Reformation, particularly from about 1570 after the Queen's excommunication by the Pope. Perhaps the most noticeable effect was that, in keeping with the Protestant emphasis on preaching and the Word, the east end was no longer the main decorative focus of the chapel.

Proscription of certain types of decoration for walls and glass windows featured for the first time in the 1547 Injunctions that banned 'monuments of feigned miracles, pilgrimages, idolatry and superstition'.[48] But in Article 28 of his 1552 Visitation Articles, Bishop Hooper of Gloucester and Worcester, the former chaplain to Protector Somerset and who was burnt at the stake in 1555, was yet more specific in dealing with painted glass windows. He stipulated that no new or repaired glass window should contain images of saints, and that if they were painted at all, they should depict only branches, flowers or texts from 'Holy Scripture'.[49] It is significant that Hooper did not require existing offending windows to be replaced (due, it is thought, to the expense and shortage of glass), and it is therefore unlikely that any such action would be required in the existing private chapels falling under his jurisdiction. But whereas previously it was only relics and images suspected of veneration which were proscribed, Hooper made it clear that, for new work, the ban now included *any* image, regardless of medium, that could be interpreted as idolatrous. And the branches, flowers and texts that he advocated as idolatry-free alternatives did indeed become popular in both private chapels and parish churches.

It is not possible to pinpoint cases where the Injunctions had a direct influence on decisions affecting the decoration of private chapels. But a comparison between the chapel interiors produced during the early and late Tudor periods is telling, with the pre-Reformation splendour found in the reign of Henry VIII contrasting with a more austere Elizabethan aesthetic. There is little surviving decorative fabric from the Elizabethan period, and it is necessary to depend on documents, particularly on inventories. More travellers' accounts have come down to us from the second half of the 16th century but, although descriptions of country houses increase sharply few, if any, mention private chapels. A well-known account of Theobalds by Baron Waldstein in 1600 paid much attention to the rooms of state and the gardens and yet made no mention of the chapel.[50] In this the baron was not unusual, for no contemporary account of the house mentioned the chapel, perhaps because, devoid of decoration, it was simply not interesting enough. Indeed, with the exception of Hardwick (discussed further below), there are almost no indications of rich decorative schemes in private chapels. Figurative decoration was rarely used, and religious imagery perhaps not at all. This lack of imagery across all decorative media is arresting. New stained glass was rare. One exception was the four-light east window in the detached East Hall chapel at High Legh in Cheshire, where some of the Elizabethan glass, which may have once included images of the patron, Thomas Legh, and his wife, survives now reset in the south window. This depicts the arms of the Legh and Trafford families and a Latin inscription.[51] Although there are medallions of figurative glass in this window from the 14th to the mid–17th centuries, none date from Elizabethan times. Despite possessing a traditionalist outlook, the Legh family seems to have complied with the austere approach

Fig. 4.14: Compton Verney, Warwickshire: detail of a glass panel of 1588 showing Lady Anne Verney and her two children at prayer. It was removed from the chapel on demolition, and is now lost.

advocated by the church authorities. Stained glass was also recorded in the chapel at Compton Verney, Warwickshire, where a panel, dated 1558 and showing Lady Anne Verney and her two children at prayer, contained no religious imagery (fig. 4.14).[52] The rarity of new stained chapel glass is all the more striking since it was fashionable in secular rooms of the period. Francis Bacon, for example, recommended 'stately galleries' with 'fine coloured glass'.[53]

Information about wall decoration is similarly hard to come by. Chapel wall-painting was becoming old-fashioned in the Elizabethan period, and one simple option was to apply whitewash. In a sermon of 1623 Joseph Hall (former chaplain to Henry Prince of Wales, and later Bishop of Exeter and then Norwich) was to praise the 'comely whiteness and well-contrived coarctation'[54] of Thomas Cecil's late 16th-century chapel at Wimbledon.[55] But since the use of whitewash was rarely documented, it is almost impossible to estimate how widespread its use was. The two known examples of Elizabethan painted decoration in Protestant private chapels feature texts.[56] At Bramall, the early Tudor *Ecce Homo* referred to earlier was overpainted with the Ten Commandments (Plate VII). At Little Moreton Hall, texts from Tyndale's Bible, framed within decorative borders in line with Bishop Hooper's instructions, were painted on all three of the east cell walls. These are visible in a James West drawing of 1847 (fig. 4.8). West also shows an east window whose plain glass is certainly consistent with the general climate of austerity, although it is not clear whether it is original. The beams are adorned with a relatively rich pattern based on heraldic elements, showing that care was clearly taken with the decoration, but no biblical (or indeed religious) subjects were used. However, the family was not averse to the depiction of biblical scenes in other rooms. The parlour (where the same beam decoration is found) contains wall paintings of *c*.1570-98 showing scenes from the story of Susannah and the Elders. It is significant that even such a typically Protestant subject was not used in the chapel. And we have seen how at Burghley the survival of 'grotesque' decoration in the chapel suggests that the decorative scheme there was considered of no great import. As with glass, what we know of painted wall decoration follows the spirit of the ecclesiastical Injunctions and Visitation Orders. Whether deriving more from the dictates of fashion or religion, the change in attitudes towards chapel wall decoration was radical and widespread.

Similar standards appear to have governed the choice of subjects for hangings such as tapestries, although few dating from this time can be identified. Plain hangings were replacing those depicting biblical stories. At Chatsworth, no hangings are listed for the lower chapel which was 'in some pt ... waynscotted', but non-figurative hangings were used in the upper chapel. Texts, which had previously been used sparingly and nearly always in conjunction with other decorative forms, were becoming a standard form of tapestry decoration. Heraldry, as always, remained an uncontroversial option. As suggested by Hooper, decorative borders using naturalistic elements were employed. In fact, the sole mention of figurative hangings during the period is at Hardwick, where the lower chapel contained 'too peeces of hanginges imbrodered with pictures Seaven foote and a half deep'.[57] Altar cloths were, for the most part, restrained, with few decorative elements. In the case of Chatsworth at least, the visual emphasis was re-directed to the west end. While the lower chapel not only lacked a distinctive east window, but also contained no items that would have made a decorative impact, the upper chapel, with its colourful hangings and other coverings, could well have formed the richest area, emphasising the importance of family over liturgy.[58]

As with figurative hangings, the only mention of moveable pictures in an Elizabethan chapel also comes from Hardwick. The inventory lists one picture of Our Lady and the Magi, and another of the Annunciation, as well as a crucifix.[59] Depictions of the Virgin Mary were vulnerable to accusations of idolatry: while there is no doubt about her Protestant convictions, one possible explanation is that Bess, in her 80s when Hardwick was being built, belonged to a generation born just before the Reformation which was perhaps less fixed in its ways. Queen Elizabeth also had a crucifix on her altar and, like her queen, Bess tended to be 'a follower of Erasmus, a Christian Believer, but undoctrinal, therefore tolerant'.[60] Although the interiors of newly-built Elizabethan chapels were usually austere, it is likely that in many older chapels pre-Reformation decorative schemes were retained, as was the case at Kirkoswald and in Sandys' Chapel of the Holy Trinity in Basingstoke.

Two contemporary examples of sculptural decoration are known. At Horseheath Hall (Cambridgeshire) before 1591, eighteen heraldic shields decorated the ceiling of the chapel,[61] while the ornate surrounds to the doors of the upper chapel at Copthall could perhaps also qualify as chapel decoration (although strictly they belong to the long gallery's decorative scheme). These are known from Sir Roger Newdigate's drawing of *c*.1748 (fig. 4.15) which shows elaborately decorated doorframes flanking the fireplace.[62] Patrons did not necessarily remove existing sculptural decoration from chapels that came into their possession. For instance, after the Charterhouse was dissolved, subsequent owners did not destroy the vault bosses depicting symbols of the Passion or the corbels with angels in what became the chapel vestibule.

While state rooms in Elizabethan houses reached unprecedented levels of magnificence, the austere requirements of Protestant worship saw to it that the chapel generally no longer ranked alongside them as a room of splendour and expense.[63] What is most noticeable is that great decorative cycles based on biblical stories were no longer introduced in new chapels, and nor was the carefully graded build-up of decorative richness intended to emphasise the east

Fig. 4.15: Copthall, Essex: detail from a drawing by Sir Roger Newdigate (c.1748) showing the elaborately decorated surrounds of the doors leading to the upper chapel from the long gallery.

end. One way of measuring the change from early Tudor times is to compare the value of the contents of the chapel with a room such as the great chamber which would have been a focus for secular display. Whilst in the early Tudor period the chapel contents would often have been the more valuable, this was not so under Elizabeth. For instance, on the death of Sir Roger Woodhouse in 1588, the contents of the chapel at his house, Kimberley in Norfolk, where ten years earlier he had entertained the Queen, were valued at 2s − less than one seventieth of the value of those of the great chamber. As early as 1566, when Sir Richard Worsley's Appuldurcombe was inventoried, the total contents of the chapel were, at 24s 4d, worth less than one of the more valuable beds.[64]

A comparison between the inventories of Lord Sandys' The Vyne, taken in 1541 before the Edwardine Injunctions, and (the Roman Catholic) Sir Thomas Kytson II's Hengrave, not taken until 1603, reinforces the impression of decline.[65] Both chapels were built within about 15 years of each other during the reign of Henry VIII, and they share a number of characteristics, for instance, apsed east ends filled with painted glass cycles of the highest quality. At Hengrave no values are given, but the complete chapel contents consisted of a Bible and service book, a surplice, an old Turkey carpet, a pair of little organs and eleven cushions. In contrast, the Vyne inventory lists tapestry hangings, candlesticks, pictures, crucifixes, canopies, altar frontals, vestments and many other objects. Their total value is £63 2s 3d (a single altar cloth was valued at £8) and, if the plate and chapel accoutrements in the vestry and wardrobe were included, the total would rise considerably. The difference between the contents of two chapels of similar standing speaks eloquently of the changes that followed the Reformation.

5

FROM THE EARLY STUARTS TO THE INTERREGNUM: 'ATTENDED LIKE BERENICE'?

The decisive rejection of Roman Catholicism under Elizabeth was reflected in the whole-hearted promotion of specifically Protestant designs for the private chapel. In the early 17th century, equally far-reaching changes occurred *within* the Protestant Church. Despite urgings that ministers attend to the 'repayring and keeping cleane, and comely adorning of churches', late 16th-century descriptions of neglect and decay abound.[1] An early catalyst for remedial action had been Richard Hooker's *Of the Lawes of Ecclesiasticall Politie* (1594 and 1597) which promoted the improvement of both the appearance of churches and the standards of worship within them. Hooker defended traditional forms of worship, and argued that there should be no objection to the use of ceremonial if it encouraged devotion. This approach was reflected in the Hampton Court Canons of 1604: Canons 85 and 86 required that churches should 'be well and sufficiently repaired ... kept and maintained'. Although the Canons (and the Visitation Articles that followed) were largely directed at parish churches they, like earlier Injunctions and Articles, provide insights into the nature of the dominant strand of religious thinking. They promoted sacramental worship in well-appointed surroundings yet contained no detailed (or potentially contentious) definitions concerning how those attributes were to be recognised or achieved, so opening the way for controversy about how worship was to be conducted, and how places of worship were to be fitted out and decorated.[2] One major area of disagreement was over the conduct of the communion ceremony, with low-church adherents wishing to receive communion sitting, while high-churchmen favoured standing or kneeling. Another battleground was the purpose, form and extent of decorative imagery. Its revival by high-church patrons was an important development, but Puritan chapels comprised an opposing decorative strand, and the tension between the two led to vehement and, during the Civil War and Interregnum, destructive controversy.

The accession of the Stuarts saw a surge in private chapel building. Newly-built houses might incorporate an integral chapel of some distinction, while owners of older houses added linked or detached chapels. Elizabethan designs for Puritan worship, such as the room, assembly and narthex chapels, survived into the 1620s, but many patrons reacted against the predominately low-church attitudes of the Elizabethan period. However, they appear to have made little attempt to create radically new and specifically Protestant high-church spaces. Instead the early experimental phase of Elizabethan Protestantism gave way to architectural features last seen under the early Tudors. Unquestionably, the main architectural development was the revival of the double-cell chapel space in its two-centred form. With numerous adaptations and variations, it became the choice of a wide variety of patrons. In addition, from the earliest years of the 17th century, the chapel was again being given a degree of external differentiation and, in some cases, a formative role in the overall plan. A fundamental cause of these changes was a revival of the practice of consecrating private chapels and the associated tendency to see even unconsecrated chapels as holy spaces.[3]

Jacobean Planning and Architecture: a Rise in Status and the Return of High-church Patrons
(i) The Chapel in the House: Re-emergence of a Sacred Space

The Jacobean period marks the beginning of a new high-church emphasis that predates by some years the movement usually associated with William Laud's influence and the promotion of the 'beauty of holiness'. This change was reflected in the relationship between the chapel and the overall plan of the house. One

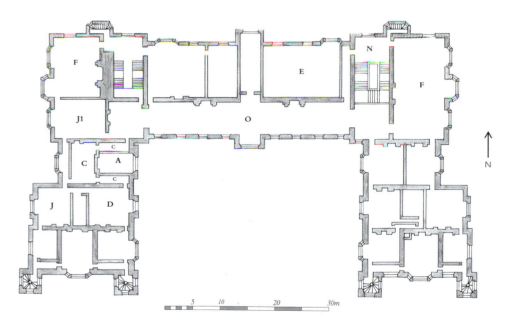

Fig. 5.1: Hatfield House, Hertfordshire: first floor plan, showing the upper part of one of the first cross-range chapels to be built since that at Hengrave. The north and south galleries probably acted as passages from the long gallery and antechamber to the upper chapel at the west end. J = the Queen's bedchamber, and J1 = the Queen's withdrawing chamber.

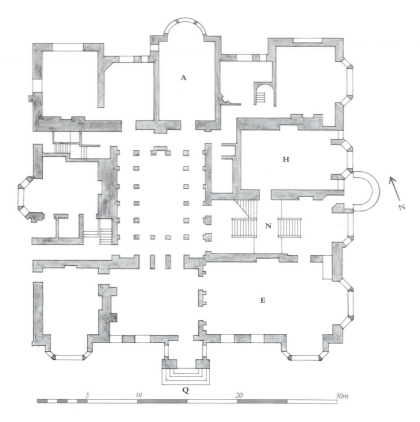

Fig. 5.2: Crewe Hall, Cheshire: ground plan. Though incorrectly oriented, the cross-range chapel played a formative role in the planning process.

direct result of the renewal of the practice of consecrating chapels, with the consequent re-emergence of the chapel as a holy space, was the return of seclusion as an important planning requirement. The Elizabethan practice of placing chapels on a main circulation route declined, and there was a return to a freer, less standardised approach, with an increase in chapels situated away from the hall (this was to become an important element in post-Restoration planning). Often chapels were placed where features such as architectural differentiation that indicated their special function could be provided. Hatfield (fig.

Fig. 5.3: Crewe Hall, Cheshire: detail of the north facade with the chapel apse in the centre.

5.1), Crewe (fig. 5.2) and the unnamed Smythson house already referred to (fig. 4.13) employed the cross-range approach used so successfully in the early 16th century, while a number of other chapels (including those at Audley End in Essex (fig. 5.4), Red House and Chantemarle) lay at the end of a wing. The revival of the cross-range and end of range approaches also facilitated the incorporation of a distinct east-west axis with an emphasis on the liturgical east end, for example by means of an apse (as at Crewe and Chantemarle), and distinctive fenestration (as at Hatfield and Bramshill House in Hampshire). Moreover, contemporary chapels tended to possess windows that accorded well with the internal space.[4]

No particular trends emerge for the provision of access, with some chapels, such as that at Hatfield, possessing a highly complex series of entrances (two or perhaps three at the upper level and three at the lower level), whilst equally grandiose chapels, such as that at Audley End, had only one entrance on each level. On the other hand, there was a notable resurgence of the practice of orienting chapels to the east. Of all the major new chapels of the period, only at Crewe, where the apse faces north, is the chapel clearly incorrectly-oriented.

The revival of the concept of the private chapel as a space apart required it once again to become a formative force in the planning process. Thorpe's unexecuted plan of c.1621, very possibly for the Duke of Buckingham's Burley-on-the-Hill in Rutland (fig. 5.6) which, as Summerson points out, seems to be derived from the Palais du Luxembourg (fig. 4.6), illustrates this well.[5] It is the clearest example of a chapel being afforded a prime position in an English house. Its great axial chapel commands the plan in a way that has no equal, even in early 17th-century English planning. It is bigger than the great hall, and its impressive space is terminated by a large apsed chancel where the altar stands on a raised platform. There can be no doubt that this was the most important space in the house.

Smythson's designs for an unnamed house constitute perhaps the earliest English design of this period for a chapel occupying an important position in a plan, and to some extent dictating the planning process.[6] Here, some 20 years before Thorpe's presumed plan for Burley-on-the-Hill, the chapel is positioned on the main entrance axis, directly across the courtyard from the screens passage, with the central projection of the range forming the (liturgical) east window. The position is not only prestigious but also practical: it is central and easily accessible, yet secluded. At ground-floor level (fig. 4.13a), a generous passageway runs from the great stair and terminates at the large lobby (or ante-chapel) which is screened off from the inner chapel. The passage route is characterised by wide, connecting doorways (about twice the width of the doors leading off it) and terminates at the chapel with no access through to the low end of the house. As a result, the ante-chapel is both approached via an impressive route and yet

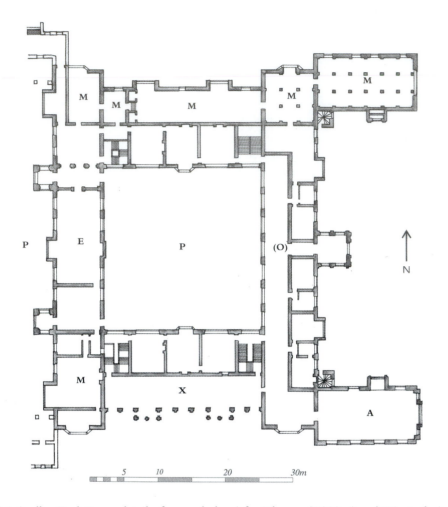

Fig. 5.4: Audley End, Essex: detail of ground plan (after Thorpe (T203–4) and Winstanley). Note the large gathering space immediately to the west of the linked chapel. X = a *loggia*; the long gallery leading to the upper chapel is over the passage marked (O).

undisturbed by passing traffic. A surviving example of this plan type, started in 1615, can be found at Crewe (fig. 5.2). Although the house was much altered and enlarged in the 19th century, the chapel remains positioned on the main entrance axis with its importance emphasised by an apsidal window.[7] Rather than a room to be slotted in where space allowed, the chapel evidently enjoyed a high status, making its positioning a formative influence on the planning process.

At Audley End, the 1st Earl of Suffolk employed a different means of emphasising the importance of his chapel. Instead of being close to the great hall and main stair, the upper chapel stood off the long gallery, at the far end of the main sequence of staterooms which formed a magnificent approach route.

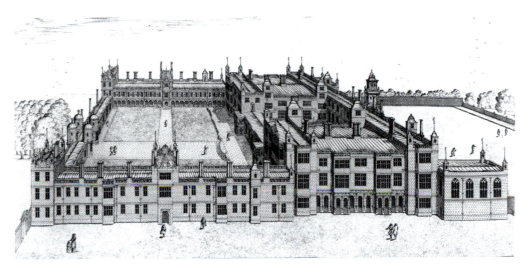

Fig. 5.5: Audley End, Essex: view from the south by Winstanley (1678). The chapel, with its pointed windows, is in the right foreground.

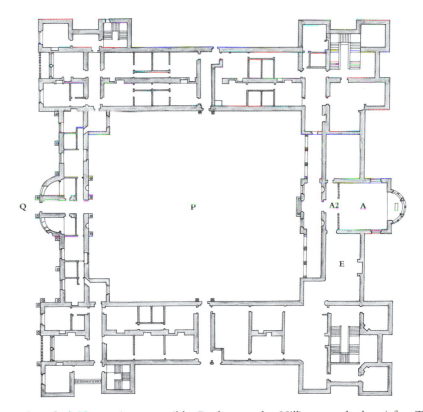

Fig. 5.6: Unidentified House (very possibly Burley-on-the-Hill): ground plan (after Thorpe T105-6). Its great axial chapel commands the plan in a way that was exceptional, even in early 17th-century English planning. It was probably inspired by the Luxembourg Palace in Paris – see fig. 4.6.

Fig. 5.7: Red House, North Yorkshire: south facade of the (originally linked) chapel. Like the east window, the rectangular three-light upper windows were designed to take painted glass.

Equally grandiose was the approach from the ground floor. Henry Winstanley shows an elaborate arrangement of *loggie* and passages which ends in what appears to be a large gathering space before the entrance to the chapel proper (fig. 5.4).[8] This room, with its great bay window, was the culmination of the route to the chapel, and the lack of a fireplace and its open planning make it unlikely that it had any function other than to emphasise the transition between domestic and religious spaces.

Other, smaller, houses also managed to bestow a measure of distinction on the chapel. At Chantemarle, an entire wing (with the exception of the attic level) was given over to it, providing a double-height space as large as the hall in what is a relatively small house (Plate XIII). The chapel in Charlton House in Greenwich, a 'body and four pavilions' (H-plan) house, lay in a wing beyond the great stair and was secluded, correctly-oriented and had a large bay window at the east end.

Although not all Jacobean chapels enjoyed the revival of the features of seclusion and high status, it is clear that from the early years of the 17th century chapel planning was changing in key areas. As we shall see, these changes established trends that were reflected in the exterior architecture, interior decoration and, to a lesser extent, fittings.

(ii) The Exterior Architecture: the Return to Differentiation

For the first time the externally differentiated chapel, whether integrated with the house or detached from it, became a significant feature of Protestant

Fig. 5.8: Red House, North Yorkshire: north facade. While the chapel was sharply distinguished on the south and east sides, from the north (entrance) side of the house it looked more like a shed.

design. Two traditional forms, distinctive fenestration and an apsidal east end, were revived to emphasise its new status. Most clearly documented is the revival of distinctive fenestration.

Many newly-built integrated chapels used medieval or early Tudor window forms, which would of course have been archaic in the 17th century. One of the earliest examples is at Audley End. Winstanley's 1678 view of the house from the south shows a large rectangular chapel projecting from the south-east corner (fig. 5.5). It was balanced by a similarly shaped room at the north-east corner.[9] Although on plan (fig. 5.4) the two spaces appear similar, there are significant differences in the handling of the east end. At first-floor level, the northern room had a central window placed in a flat wall, while the chapel had a projecting central window flanked by two smaller windows which were slightly set back. This indicates that nearly the entire eastern wall of the chapel (but not that of its northern counterpart) was of glass, and that the east window so created was differentiated from the balancing room. Unfortunately, Winstanley's views do not include an east elevation, but the north elevation shows that, while the northern room had large, rectangular, mullioned and transomed windows at first-floor level similar to those used throughout the house, and smaller ones below, the chapel had no lower windows and large, pointed Gothic windows with tracery at first-floor level, giving them a very distinctive character.

At Hatfield, the first recorded cross-range chapel (with the exception of Copthall and Little Moreton Hall) since Hengrave, the east end breaks the symmetry of the original main entrance front by projecting forward from the main facade, a feature not repeated on the balancing east range. It is also easily identifiable by its imposing east window which, spanning two storeys, is the largest on the facade (Plate X). Its aspect is further enhanced by the use of a different fenestration pattern. Instead of variations on the rectangular mullioned and transomed type, the lights are arched. This distinctive form is repeated in the west window of the lower chapel (Plate IX), but that of the upper chapel reverts to the standard domestic form, perhaps because the area which it lit may well have formed an independent passageway linking the queen's withdrawing chamber to her bedchamber.[10]

Other newly-built integrated chapels with differentiated fenestration include Bramshill with its distinctive east window. Visible only from a small courtyard, its purpose was to emphasise the east end internally. Again, arched lights are used, arranged under a four-centred arch. However, the awkward design of this window, with its clumsy brick division in the centre, points either to some later alteration, or to the mason's inexperience. Another example is at Red House, where intriguing evidence of differentiated fenestration is to be found. It came to the Slingsby family in the 16th century, and Sir Henry Slingsby started work on a new house in 1607. However, the chapel, which was to form part of the house, may have been begun as early as 1600, although it is unclear when it was finished. The east end is lit by a large pointed window with panel tracery, while the upper level of the south side has rectangular three-light windows with cusping (fig. 5.7).

Fig. 5.9: Red House, North Yorkshire: looking east through the chapel screen. The eastern cell, where both the communion table and the pulpit are set against the east wall, could have been reserved for the household and chaplain, with the family presiding in the upper chapel and the local congregation occupying the western cell.

Painted glass was intended for all these windows and, although it is difficult to form any clear idea of the fenestration of the original house, it is obvious that from the east and south the chapel would have been sharply distinguished. However, the north side (fig. 5.8), which is now, and may always have been, the most visible on the approach route, has plain, small rectangular windows and a door that leads into a narrow room, about 6ft x 20ft, which is completely separate from the chapel. A similar space above was presumably originally reached from the house. There is no doubt that this is part of the original arrangement.[11] Since this was a purpose-built chapel rather than an adaptation of an existing building, the function of the seemingly awkward spaces is puzzling. There are two possibilities: the upper area might have been, as now, a muniment room, with the space below serving as an extra outhouse or service area; or the design could have been intended to conceal the existence of the ornate, high-church chapel from the casual visitor. If the latter were the case, it would suggest that patrons, at least in some areas, were cautious about the use of stained glass and pre-Reformation style windows. However, no other examples have been found among Protestant chapels of similar attempts at 'disguise', and the purpose of this idiosyncratic arrangement remains unclear.

Another way of giving the chapel distinction was to place an apse in the centre of the facade. The centralised apsidal chapel survives at Crewe (fig. 5.3), while the grandest proposed example can be found in Thorpe's presumed plan for Burley-on-the-Hill (fig. 5.6). An alternative, as at Chantemarle (Plate XIII), was to place a balancing apsidal window to light a domestic space on the other side of the facade – a method that continued (although less clumsily than Sir Thomas Kytson's earlier attempt at Hengrave) the search for a solution to the problem of accommodating a distinct chapel-type space within a symmetrical facade. Here Sir John Strode started work on the E-shaped house in *c*.1612, only nine years after the death of Elizabeth, and his notes make it clear that its form was designed to have religious significance, with the E standing for Emmanuel.[12] But for them, it would have been dismissed as a posthumous tribute to the Queen, or an example of the longevity of the E-shaped plan. This is a salutary reminder that many similar subtleties may have existed in the early 17th century which are now unrecognised. Strode's description of the consecration service (1619) makes it clear that the apse had a liturgical function since the bishop's chair was placed in it.[13] This reflection of the basilical arrangements used by the early Christians may not have been simply a matter of architectural ornamentation, but more an attempt to underline the Protestant claim to connection with the early church.

As well as the creation of integrated chapels, new chapels were linked to earlier (often Elizabethan) houses. In 1621, the 1st Lord Maynard added a chapel to Easton Lodge, a house built by his father. Its appearance is documented by an 18th-century engraving (fig. 5.10).[14] Although the windows of the upper level of the chapel extension were similar to those on the main facade, the lower windows were differentiated, and possessed semi-circular arches and glazing bars. If these were original, they might well have been the first (and perhaps only Jacobean) example of the use of Classical windows to differentiate a private chapel.[15]

Detached chapels, often built to serve earlier, chapel-less houses, form an important group in this period. They gave patrons a better opportunity to exercise

Fig. 5.10: Easton Lodge, Essex: the entrance facade of the Elizabethan house, with the linked Jacobean chapel to the right. Perhaps the only Jacobean example of the use of Classical windows to differentiate a country house chapel.

freedom and imagination in their choice of architectural form and fenestration than did integrated chapels. Here pre-Reformation window types were common, although there was no consensus on their preferred form. At Childerley, the depressed arch east window is composed of seven lights set below panel tracery, while the west window is a smaller four-light version.[16] At Water Eaton, too, depressed arches are used, with the side windows having three cusped, pointed lights while the larger east window has five. At Leweston Manor in Dorset, the east window is pointed, with three pointed lights below simple panel tracery (fig. 5.12), while the side windows have three stepped lights surmounted by a stepped hood-mould (fig. 5.13). The east window at Low Ham in Somerset is pointed with elaborate decorated tracery (Plate XII). The north and south windows are somewhat similar, although the profiles of the chancel windows are considerably steeper than those of the nave aisles. All (except the tower windows which are Perpendicular) have

Fig. 5.11: Easton Lodge, Essex: detail of the upper part of the end of a bench, originally in the chapel but now in Little Easton parish church, illustrating the inevitability of death.

Fig. 5.12: Leweston Manor, Dorset: view of the detached chapel from the south-east showing the distinctive east window.

relatively elaborate Gothic tracery, described by Pevsner as being 'nearest the playful forms of the early 14th century'.[17] The many windows of the chapel built in 1620 by the Puritan Sir Thomas Crewe near his house of Steane Park, Northamptonshire, are bewildering in their variety, and reflect both the unorthodox nature of the chapel and its Puritan purpose.[18] The most impressive window, large and pointed with Decorated tracery, is set over the entrance in the centre of the west facade (Plate XIV). It is flanked by two three-light windows with arched heads set in rectangular frames. On the north and south facades are rectangular windows with three lights with shallow arched heads set under panel tracery, a form also used for the central east window. Finally, the two east windows lighting the outer aisles match their counterparts on the west facade. The range of locations and designs are carefully manipulated to establish a hierarchy which suits the unusual design of the chapel (the traditional east-west axis is noticeably shorter than the north-south width), and adds considerably to its architectural grandeur. And they demonstrate that archaic or differentiated window forms were not confined to the chapels of high-church patrons. Moreover, the absence of an imposing east window underlines the influence that Puritan ideas were bringing to bear on chapel design.

The choice of the forms we would now call Decorated and

Fig. 5.13: Leweston Manor, Dorset: south facade. A single cell, rectangular, detached chapel, with a highly decorated porch or narthex.

Fig. 5.14: Leweston Manor, Dorset: interior of chapel looking east. Perhaps the first surviving post-Reformation example of the conventional pewing arrangement featured in Thorpe's plans. Note the two-decker pulpit in the south-east corner.

Perpendicular was not particularly significant since there was no real understanding of medieval styles, and chapels such as Low Ham and Steane mix them together. And although it is tempting to interpret the new popularity of archaic forms as a high-church return to pre-Reformation ideas, it is unwise so to generalise. The example of Puritan Steane, with its a conspicuously wide range of rich archaic window forms, should provide a warning against such oversimplification. It is probable that, while ornate pre-Reformation tracery may have signalled an ecclesiastical use, it carried none of the Papist implications attached to pre-Reformation decoration, and could be used by any patron, regardless of their place on the religious spectrum.

While Steane may be the most unusual, Low Ham is the most spectacular of the detached chapels. With its west tower, nave with aisles and a clerestory as well as a chancel, it could easily be mistaken for a parish church of some distinction (Plate XII). It also has a degree of external sculptural decoration unrivalled at this date, and includes the staples of medieval parish church design such as battlements, and a cross at the apex of the nave gable. More distinctive are the figures on the four corners of the nave, which appear to be wild men. Their purpose is unknown, although it has been suggested that they might have been intended to ward off evil spirits. Water Eaton also makes use of recognisably ecclesiastical forms, although in a simpler manner, as the roofline draws a clear distinction between nave and chancel. The oldest example, and the only early 17th-century chapel to be built of brick, is at Childerley (from *c.*1600), a rectangular building with a large projecting porch on the north side. Although Leweston, too, is basically a single-cell rectangular building (fig. 5.13), a west entrance porch or narthex is used to house a font. Surprisingly, given the chapel's relatively restrained form, the entrance facade of the porch is the most decorated area to be found at any

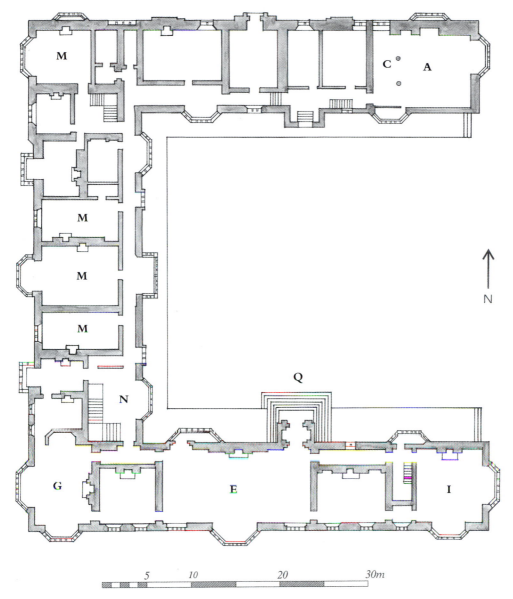

Fig. 5.15: Temple Newsam, West Yorkshire: ground plan. Traditional planning ideas are mixed with more innovative ones. Spanning the basement and ground floors, it is perhaps the earliest surviving example of the provision of a basement entrance to the chapel for servants – a feature that became popular after the Restoration.

of these buildings. The initials IHS are set in a lozenge framed with foliage and placed in a prominent merlin above the entrance; below is an incised frieze, possibly of stylised wreaths alternating with grapes and vine leaves. Finally a strip of nailhead decoration surmounts a coat of arms. Apart from crosses on the gables and a bellcote (all of which may well be later), the main cell of the chapel, including the east end, is extremely plain.

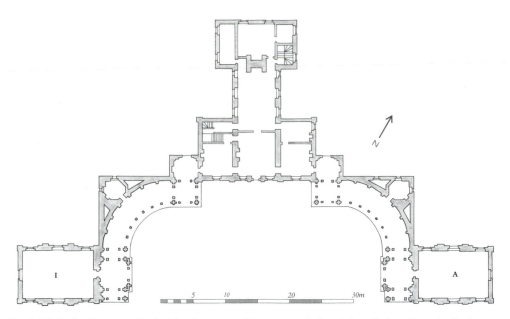

Fig. 5.16: Stoke Bruerne Park, Northamptonshire: ground plan (after Colen Campbell) demonstrating how Palladio's planning principles could be adapted to English requirements. The result was not a total success.

Planning & Architecture 1625–1660: Diversification, Distinction and the Influence of Classical Ideas

The thirty-five years following the death of James I in 1625 offered a wide variety of planning ideas to accommodate different types of worship. The start of the period is associated with Laud's rise (notably as Bishop of London from 1628 and then, from 1633, as Archbishop of Canterbury) and energetic promotion of high-church ideas, but Puritans were also building chapels, and it was their attitudes and liturgy that became dominant from the 1640s. At the same time, architectural fashion was changing, and the arrival of the Classical ideas of Inigo Jones and his followers affected planning as well as architectural style. Temple

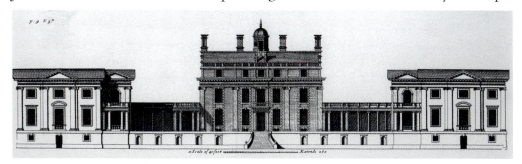

Fig. 5.17: Stoke Bruerne Park, Northamptonshire: the southern elevation (after Colen Campbell) with the supposed chapel on the right. A comparison with fig. 5.18 shows that the line of the roof and entablature were altered at a later date.

Fig. 5.18: Stoke Bruerne Park, Northamptonshire: the east pavilion from the south-west. Perhaps the first example of a wholly Classical private chapel, but the placing of the large windows so low in the elevation casts doubt on whether the pavilion was designed to house a chapel.

Newsam (fig. 5.15) and Stoke Bruerne Park in Northamptonshire (fig. 5.16) are good examples of this diversity. Although close in date, each adopted completely different approaches to planning. As we shall see, Temple Newsam followed an essentially Jacobean plan, while Stoke Bruerne drew its inspiration from Andrea Palladio.

(i) The Chapel in the House: Diverse Influences and Solutions

Two major houses underwent extensive renovation during the period: the early Tudor house of Temple Newsam was largely replaced, while the essentially Elizabethan Castle Ashby House in Warwickshire underwent large-scale renovation. Also significant in terms of overall planning are the three former monastic foundations of Forde Abbey, Woburn Abbey and Wilton, all of which had undergone varying degrees of conversion before additional work was carried out in the 17th century. Finally, four important new houses, Raynham Hall in Norfolk (whose construction in fact started in the Jacobean period), Stoke Bruerne, Tyttenhanger in Hertfordshire, and Belvoir Castle in Leicestershire, enjoyed complete freedom in planning.

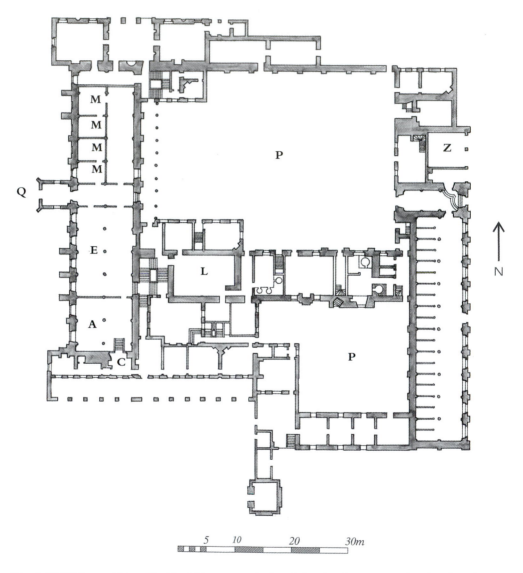

Fig. 5.19: Woburn Abbey, Bedfordshire: ground plan (after Sanderson, 1747). The chapel in this former Cistercian monastery was at the heart of the house. C = the presumed mezzanine level upper chapel; Z = the former Chapter House which was converted into a coach house and washhouse.

Fig. 5.20: Woburn Abbey, Bedfordshire: the west (entrance) facade by John Sanderson 1733. The two Gothic chapel windows are on the right, just north of the south pavilion.

At Temple Newsam (1622–38) and Castle Ashby (*c.*1624–31), the chapel was an important, though not a formative, part of the plan. In each case it was no longer grouped with the hall, great stairs and parlour as had been common in Elizabethan planning. Castle Ashby's chapel harked back to early Tudor times in that it lay across the range and terminated a sequence of staterooms, so providing seclusion from through routes. At Temple Newsam, traditional planning ideas were mixed with more innovative ones. Terminating the side range at the low end of the house, the chapel was again positioned so that it could not become a

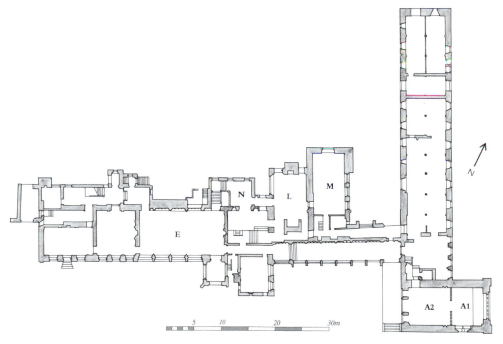

Fig. 5.21: Forde Abbey, Dorset: ground plan. The relatively isolated position of the linked chapel, formerly the Cistercian monastic chapter house, made it easy for local people to gather there without intruding into the main part of the house.

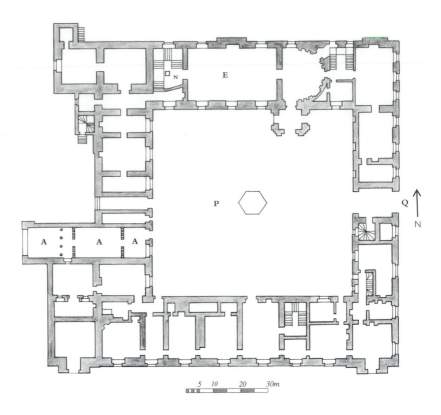

Fig. 5.22: Wilton House, Wiltshire: 1746 ground plan after Rocque (Courtauld Institute, BF 2639/1). It is not clear how the three segments of the chapel (all marked A but apparently chancel, ante-chapel and narthex) would have worked. The sheer size of the liturgical east window would have differentiated it from all other windows.

thoroughfare. However, it spanned the basement and ground floors, and adjoined the kitchens and other service areas. The servants could therefore enter at the lower level, while the family would presumably have used the stairs connecting the long gallery immediately above the chapel to the upper chapel space. The idea of using the basement level for the chapel occurs in some Thorpe plans, but Temple Newsam appears to be the earliest surviving example of an arrangement that was to become popular after the Restoration.[19] It is indeed a good solution to the demand for hierarchical access to the chapel.

Forde (by 1639) and Woburn (c.1630), both originally Cistercian abbeys where only limited work appears to have been carried out after the Reformation, faced very specific planning problems given the set forms employed by the monastic order, and they illustrate what very different solutions could be reached from similarly configured buildings.[20] Both had relatively large chapels but, while at Forde the conventional solution of placing the chapel in the chapter house was chosen, at Woburn the chapter house became a wash-house and coach-house, while the chapel (with two entrances to preserve the hierarchical social structure) and hall were created from the lay brothers' frater (fig. 5.19).[21] This put the chapel at the heart of the house. In contrast the chapel at Forde (fig. 5.21), converted almost certainly by the Puritan Sir Henry Rosewell, and known to have been used for Puritan conventicles, was placed well away from the main apartments, beyond the kitchens and service quarters. In this relatively isolated position it would be easy for local people to gather without entering the main part of the house. The markedly different locations of the two chapels indicate that they were intended to serve different purposes, and illustrate the complex currents which lay beneath the different attitudes to planning. Wilton, on the other hand, a former Benedictine Abbey, had undergone a reasonably thorough conversion in the early Tudor period, and the cross-range late 1630s chapel probably occupied the same position as the early Tudor one (fig. 5.22).[22]

Of the four substantial new houses referred to above, the earliest is Raynham, a double-pile house (*c*.1618-35). The plan in the RIBA library of 1671 (fig. 5.24) shows a large, correctly-oriented chapel occupying a central, slightly projecting position on the east side. Interestingly, given that it adopted a pioneering compact plan, circulation problems and access to the chapel were adroitly handled. Even within a restrictive plan, the chapel is clearly an important and formative element. In contrast, Stoke Bruerne (1629-35) demonstrates how Palladio's planning

Fig. 5.23: Wilton House, Wiltshire: unrealised design by Isaac de Caus for the south elevation of the chapel. He planned to integrate it with the design of the south facade of the house.

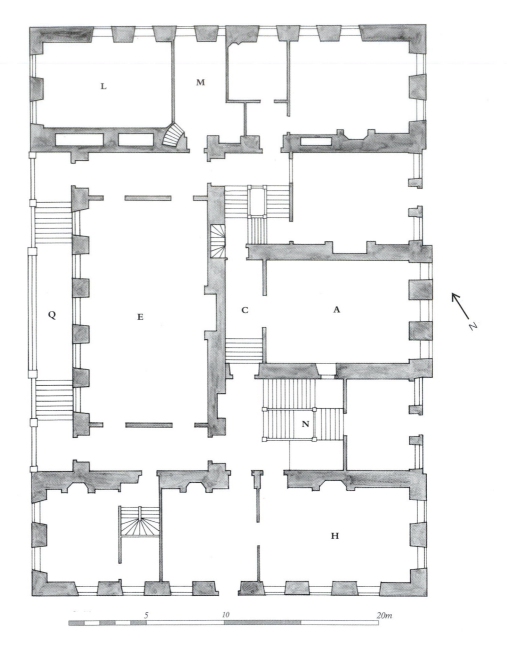

Fig. 5.24: Raynham Hall, Norfolk: ground plan (after a 1671 plan in the RIBA library). Circulation problems and access to the chapel were adroitly handled in this pioneering double-pile house. The entrance to the presumed upper chapel is in the south wall, off the great stair.

principles could be adapted to English requirements (fig. 5.16). Plans and papers relating to the house have been destroyed by fire, and the sole surviving evidence that Stoke Bruerne possessed the first Classical chapel (outside London and for a non-royal patron) is an inscription to that effect by the architect Colen Campbell in *Vitruvius Britannicus*.[23] The chapel and library appear to have occupied balancing pavilions linked to the main house by a covered, quadrant colonnade at raised ground-floor level, and received the treatment accorded to farm buildings in many of Palladio's villas (fig. 5.17).[24] The early 17th-century Anglicisation of these ideas would certainly have achieved an imposing group but it lacked the rigorous practicality of many of Palladio's plans. Although siting the chapel in the east pavilion away from the main block of the house would have avoided the problem of integrating it into a compact plan, it raises questions about flexibility of access, since there was only one entrance and, as far as can be ascertained, no subdivision of the rectangular space and thus no upper chapel. And there are other problems which may cast doubt on the accuracy of Campbell's annotation. The window arrangement suggests that the demands of symmetry and visual aesthetics took precedence over the requirements of the chapel – rather than starting at or above head height, the large windows which light the north and south walls of the pavilions begin at about waist level. While their light might be ideal for a library, their position so low on the elevation was unsuitable for a chapel in that they afforded distracting views of the outside world and the tops of fittings such as pews would have cut across them. On the other hand, the windows might have been lengthened in the 18th century – certainly the fact that the side ground-level windows rise higher in the façade than the top of the entablature of the lower order could indicate that Palladio's plan type was adapted to accommodate the needs of a chapel. Without further information, it is impossible to be certain whether the east pavilion was intended or served as a chapel, but it is not surprising that there are no other contemporary examples of this window arrangement.

The plans of the two remaining major houses, Tyttenhanger (from 1655; fig. 5.25) and John Webb's almost contemporary (but not as built) plan for Belvoir (fig. 5.27), date from the later part of the period and also demonstrate the diversity of options available. They may be close in date but, in terms of chapel planning, they are at opposite ends of the religious and social spectrums. The Belvoir plans demonstrate that, with care and ingenuity, the complex requirements of an important chapel could be incorporated in a large H-plan house. It is a particularly instructive example as this type was much favoured by aristocratic patrons after the Restoration, and many of the planning ideas that Webb employs here were taken up then. The single-storey chapel and its peripheral spaces occupy an entire pavilion, which would otherwise have been used as a set of lodgings. Webb's handling of access and the provision of peripheral spaces demonstrate that it was a room of importance. Providing access for a single-storey chapel that allowed

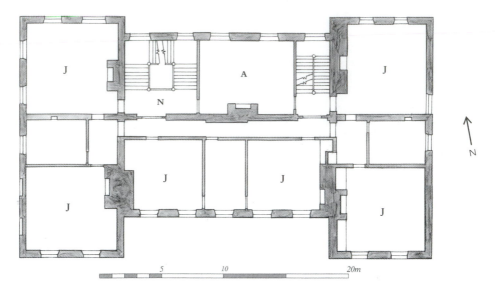

Fig. 5.25: Tyttenhanger, Hertfordshire: second floor plan. The chapel in this relatively unambitious double-pile house is tucked away high on the second floor, but access was easy from both high and low ends of the house.

Fig. 5.26: Tyttenhanger, Hertfordshire: interior of the chapel looking south-west and showing the 17th-century commandment board. The simple Puritan interior harked back to the Elizabethan room chapel.

for hierarchical separation could have been troublesome. Webb resolved it by contriving a flexible system of at least four entrances. Although it cannot be said to be a formative influence on the plan as a whole, this complex and carefully thought-out scheme demonstrates the importance of the chapel within the plan. Its size also proclaimed its significance, for it was about 50ft x 22ft; only the great colonnaded hall and the saloon above, both about 60ft x 30ft, surpassed it.

Tyttenhanger is a far

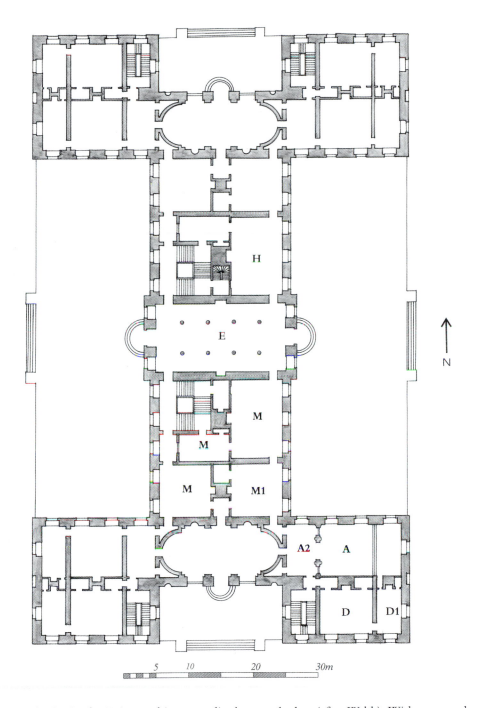

Fig. 5.27: Belvoir Castle, Leicestershire: unrealised ground plan (after Webb). With care and ingenuity, a large chapel could be incorporated in a pavilion of an H plan house – a solution much favoured by aristocratic patrons after the Restoration. D1 = the chapel study; M1 = the steward's dining room.

Fig. 5.28: Staunton Harold Hall, Leicestershire: the detached chapel from the south-east. An exceptionally richly conceived building in the Gothic style that, like Low Ham (Plate XII), resembles a traditional parish church, but reaches new levels of architectural embellishment. Its extravagant opulence helped provoke Cromwell into harrying its creator to his death.

less ambitious, double-pile house.[25] The placing of the chapel on the north front of the second floor, with entrances from two staircases which flank it, was unusual, but the arrangement does provide some of the essentials for a chapel. It is secluded from the main business of the house and, being next to a passageway, is in no danger of becoming a thoroughfare between the two staircases. That it had two entrances, one from the great stair and the other from a smaller staircase connecting directly with the service areas, suggests a hierarchical approach. Indeed the patron, Sir Henry Blount, was said not to care for his servants to go out to church for fear they 'infected one another to goe to the Alehouse and learne debauchery'.[26] This configuration could be accommodated without upsetting the arrangement of the fittings because the chapel appears to have lacked a communion table and therefore had no need of a strong liturgical axis. This small and simple chapel, looking back to the Elizabethan room chapel and tucked away on the second floor, contrasts sharply with the complexity of the large chapel so ingeniously planned by Webb at Belvoir, and again emphasises the sheer range of chapel plan types during this complex period. As will be seen later, this diverse approach is repeated in other aspects of chapel design.

(ii) The Exterior Architecture: Differentiation and the Arrival of Classical Forms

Although Classical forms were used in chapel interiors in the Elizabethan and Jacobean periods, as in the screen at Holdenby and painted Ionic pilasters on the walls at Hatfield, their acceptance as a suitable form of exterior articulation (or ornamentation) took longer to achieve. However, while the reintroduction of distinctive chapel exteriors, whose architectural language tended to look back to pre-Reformation forms, was continued in the early Caroline period, Classical forms were becoming more popular. The range of possibilities was therefore wider than at any other period, making it particularly hard to identify the reasons behind choices made by patrons. The architectural hallmark of this most innovative of periods is its diversity, irrespective of a patron's religious beliefs.

One example is still entirely Jacobean in style. Sir Arthur Ingram's ambitious rebuilding of Temple Newsam looks back to Hatfield, with (it appears) the chapel windows differentiated from those of the rest of the building by arched lights.[27] The present south windows in fact have additions of unknown date to make the lights appear rounded, but a Jan Kip engraving of *c.*1712 shows that the east window (now blocked) had arched lights while the balancing window on the opposite (south) range did not. Apart from the handling of the window(s), there was no attempt to differentiate the chapel from the rest of the house.

Of three detached chapels which employ pre-Reformation forms, two are very simple. At Rug (1637), all elaboration is saved for the interior, and the exterior is a single-cell building with much-restored pointed windows and little elaboration. Bramhope (1649; Plate XI) is a good example of a simple Puritan chapel with unassuming

Fig. 5.29: Staunton Harold Hall, Leicestershire: detail of the west entrance, where prominent Classical forms mingle with the Gothic.

Fig. 5.30: Staunton Harold Hall, Leicestershire: the chapel interior looking east, and showing the best surviving example of decorative clouding in a private chapel.

rectangular windows containing two or three arched lights very similar in type (though not in size) to those at Hatfield. But Staunton Harold (from 1653), which, like Low Ham some thirty years earlier, is easily mistaken for a parish church (fig. 5.28), reaches new levels of architectural embellishment. It has a west tower, chancel and a nave with clerestory and aisles. Its exterior architectural language is largely Gothic: as Pevsner puts it 'completely Gothic, not simply a continuation of the Perp. style but Gothic in a more conscious and general way'.[28] Early English tracery and pointed arches are used in the east windows of the chancel and aisles, and in the north and south windows as well. But the flat-headed clerestory windows have panel tracery, while the large west window over the entrance is pointed but also has panel tracery. There are ornate battlements with openwork quatrefoils surmounted at intervals by pinnacles which, on the tower, are alternated with *fleurs-de-lys*. Gargoyles are resisted in favour of up-to-date lead drainpipes. The intention was clearly not an archaeological reconstruction, for Classical motifs are also included, most prominently at the west end entrance where coupled and garlanded Doric pilasters flank a four-centred entrance arch (fig. 5.29), while a smaller

Fig. 5.31: Staunton Harold Hall, Leicestershire: detail of the (cut down) screen that probably separated the chancel from the nave. It uses Classical forms, albeit of dubious proportions.

110

Fig. 5.32: Higher Melcombe, Dorset: the linked, single-cell chapel from the south-east. It is distinguished from the rest of the house by its pointed windows.

entrance on the south side of the chancel, presumably leading to a crypt, is less flamboyantly and more correctly Classical. This is an extraordinarily richly conceived building. It was no wonder that its sheer, extravagant opulence helped provoke Cromwell into harrying its creator, Sir Robert Shirley, to his death: there was nothing in the realm of private chapel building since the Reformation that came near to rivalling it.

Chapels added to earlier buildings continued this use of archaic forms, with the windows being differentiated from those of the existing house. At Higher Melcombe, Sir Thomas Freke added a chapel to his 16th-century courtyard house before 1633 (fig. 5.32). The chapel, again a simple single cell, was distinguished from the rest of the house with its rectangular mullioned and transomed windows, by the use of pointed windows. The south, or garden, side had two simple windows composed of three lancets under a pointed hood-moulding, while the north sported two-light cusped windows with simple tracery. At Stockton House in Wiltshire, a mid-17th-century addition almost certainly intended as a chapel had windows similar to those at Bramhope. Arched lights were used only in the part of the new facade probably assigned to the chapel, while straight-headed ones are used in the rest of the range.

Other houses using pre-Reformation forms included Littlecote House in Wiltshire, where Sir Alexander Popham – a Royalist but also a Puritan – replaced the medieval chapel in the mid-17th century. His chapel is in the north-west wing which, like the rest of the house, is substantially Elizabethan with some surviving older parts. What is interesting in terms of architectural style is that the chapel fenestration differs on the north and south sides. The latter has plain rectangular two-light windows with mullions and square, cusped lights under simple hood mouldings, while those on the north have two-light windows with cusped heads under similar hood mouldings. It has been suggested that Popham's chapel is a refitting of the earlier medieval chapel but, although it probably does incorporate part of an older chapel, it is unlikely that it occupies exactly the same space. It is, however, possible that medieval windows were reused on the more prominent north, or garden, front whilst the less visible south front received plainer windows. At Woburn, the situation is more complex. An elevation of the entrance facade by John Sanderson of 1733 (fig. 5.20) shows the updating carried out from c.1630 by the 4th Earl of Bedford, a man known for his strict Protestant beliefs.[29] To the right of the entrance porch lie the great hall, and then the chapel lit by two cusped five-light windows. These are sharply differentiated from the other mullioned and transomed windows which also form part of the 4th Earl's updating.[30] Although he went to some lengths to create a classicising, symmetrical facade, it seems that he either retained the old monastic windows or created new differentiated windows of an early Tudor nature to distinguish the chapel. Conversely, the windows of the room chapel at Tyttenhanger conform to the regular fenestration of the house, providing no clue from the exterior of its presence on the second floor.

As in the Jacobean period, different styles of windows continued to be used on the same chapel with no attempt at antiquarianism or consistency. Medieval and Tudor forms were used in a very approximate way, and Classical forms could be thrown in for good measure. The reasons for choosing archaic forms continue to be difficult to clarify. Unlike the early Tudor period, where a number of rooms (particularly the great hall) had differentiated windows, no other rooms appear to have received distinctive treatment. Important rooms may have had bigger windows, but a basic continuity of style was followed, even by garden buildings where possibilities for experimentation were surely higher. It was only the chapel that was not subject to this rule of conformity. There is no direct evidence to throw light on the motivation behind the choice of a particular style, but differentiated windows were presumably used to indicate the ecclesiastical and sanctified character of the chapel.

Windows with tracery would also facilitate the provision of stained glass which, as we shall see, was again becoming popular. However, it is unlikely that all those building chapels with differentiated windows planned to use stained glass, for they included both high-churchmen such as Robert Cecil (Hatfield), and Puritans such as Thomas Crewe (Steane). The Roman Catholic Queen Henrietta

Maria was another patron who, on occasion, chose to provide a Gothic form for a chapel window. In 1638, on the death of Lord Wimbledon, his eponymous house was acquired for her. Among the changes she carried out was the moving of the chapel from the centre of the east range to the south-east corner, where the liturgical east window was altered from a standard Elizabethan mullioned and transomed design to a simple three-light Gothic type (fig. 4.3). Differentiated windows were also installed in the chapels of colleges and hospitals. It is clear that they could be employed by any patron, regardless of his or her religious beliefs.

While Jacobean ideas were permeating through to the provinces, Inigo Jones's disciplined and rigorous new approach to architecture was beginning to appeal to royal and courtier patrons. Although the completion of the Banqueting House in Whitehall in 1622 marked the public arrival of such forms, the catalyst, so far as chapel design was concerned, was the Queen's Chapel at St James's Palace, which Jones was ordered to carry out 'with great state and costliness' in 1623.[31] This was the first instance in England of a Classical chapel being added to an existing early Tudor complex. From the exterior, although conceived on a noble scale, it was a simple, restrained building which employed no architectural forms that would draw attention to its function. Its most noticeable external feature was the great three-light Venetian window at the east end, the first English example of such a window being used in this way. The Queen's Chapel was not, of course, intended as a replacement for the existing Protestant chapel within the palace complex, but as a place of worship for the intended Roman Catholic Spanish bride of Charles, Prince of Wales. In 1625 it became the centre of worship for the Infanta's French replacement, Henrietta Maria, and her entourage. This Roman Catholic chapel was the first religious building in England to use consistently Classical forms and raises the question of the extent to which the Classical style (the style of Rome and the buildings of the Papacy) equated in courtiers' minds with the papist faith. That, as discussed above, Henrietta Maria was also responsible for inserting a Gothic window at the liturgical east end of her Wimbledon chapel appears to rule out any correlation between religious beliefs and architectural style. This supposition is strengthened by the fact that Inigo Jones' 1630s design for the most Classical ecclesiastical building to be built during the Caroline period, St Paul's at Covent Garden, was carried out for the same 4th Earl of Bedford who used pre-Reformation windows for his chapel at Woburn.[32]

Of four large houses owned by prominent courtiers which were either being built or greatly improved in the fifteen years after the building of the Queen's Chapel, one was Temple Newsam where, as already discussed, no Classical forms were used. However, all the others (Castle Ashby, Wilton and possibly Stoke Bruerne) introduced Classical forms into the chapel exterior, although it was not until after the Restoration that they were adopted whole-heartedly.

Fig. 5.33: Castle Ashby House, Warwickshire: east facade. The chapel with its Venetian east window – perhaps the earliest example in a country house chapel – is at the far left.

The 2nd Lord Compton inherited the largely Elizabethan Castle Ashby in 1589 and, as the 1st Earl of Northampton, virtually rebuilt the east range as part of his ambitious programme for updating the house from *c*.1624. In a projecting bay at the southern end was the chapel which was completed by 1630. The facade of the house is not symmetrical, having two large canted bay windows of Elizabethan type at the north end, but its most noticeable feature is the Venetian east window spanning the ground and first floors of the chapel (fig. 5.33).[33] This uses the new architectural language so prominently displayed in an ecclesiastical context in London. It is perhaps the earliest example of a Venetian east window in a country house chapel, and probably directly inspired by Inigo Jones's earlier example at St James's Palace.

Wilton, a 16th-century courtyard house, was also partially remodelled in the Classical style. Here, although the 4th Earl of Pembroke concentrated on rebuilding the south front, he also instructed his architect, Isaac de Caus, to build a new chapel in the west wing, probably on the site of its early Tudor predecessor.[34] A surviving drawing for the south elevation of a Classical chapel by de Caus (fig. 5.23) shows that, in the late 1630s, Pembroke was considering rebuilding his chapel in the same architectural style as the south front.[35] Two other 17th-century drawings survive, one pre-dating the fire of 1648, and the other executed after the 1669 fire.[36] Both show a similar rectangular projection with a hipped roof, and both reflect the position of the chapel as shown in house plans by Colen Campbell (1725) and the surveyor and map-maker John Rocque (1746; fig. 5.22).[37] Rather than differentiating the chapel, de Caus's design shows that he was trying to integrate it with the design of the south facade by following

114

the same basement and *piano nobile* levels, and using similar decorative motifs. The only element in the chapel design not found on the south facade is the decorative frieze. Here the drawing is somewhat free, and it is unclear whether it depicts garlands and masks (as at the Banqueting House in Whitehall) or winged cherubs.

The two 17th-century drawings cannot be relied on as portrayals of the chapel as built because they are indistinct and contradictory, so we are thrown back on the plans. A reconstruction of the mid-18th-century layout based partly on plans in the Wilton archive shows that it projected some 15ft beyond the south-west pavilion, and that the west (liturgical east) end was lit by three windows of equal width on the north, south and liturgical east walls, making it likely that no particular emphasis was placed on it.[38] Rocque and Campbell, on the other hand, while also having the chapel project some 15ft, show no north or south windows, and depict a liturgical east window that took up almost the entire west wall – which would mean that it measured about 13ft across. If this were the case, it would have been about double the width of the central window on the south facade. Since nothing is known about its style (except that neither plan shows a Venetian window), all that can be said is that sheer size would have differentiated it from all the other 17th-century windows.

The way in which Palladio's plan type may have been adapted to accommodate a chapel in the east pavilion at Stoke Bruerne has already been discussed. Since no staircase is shown, the building was probably a single-cell rectangle two storeys high. It is articulated with giant Ionic pilasters which combine with the single-storey order of the colonnade (fig. 5.18). There appear to be no differences between the two pavilions and thus no chapel differentiation. If the east pavilion were truly a chapel, it would be of some importance in the history of chapel design as perhaps the first wholly Classical country house chapel to be built. However, as we have seen, doubts about the access and fenestration raise questions about the function of the east pavilion.

The Rise of Puritan and Low-church Chapels

It is in the early 17th century that the first examples of chapels designed specifically for pulpit-centred, Puritan worship can be found. Perhaps the earliest (1596-1603) is on a sketch plan by John Thorpe of an unidentified house (fig. 5.34).[39] It is unfinished and evidently experimental, but the arrangement of the chapel fittings is clearly indicated: there is no communion table, and a pulpit occupies the centre of the liturgical east end opposite what appears to be the only entrance. On one side there is a conventional row of pews whilst on the other a large box-pew (presumably intended for the patron) is arranged college style. This is a very distinctive arrangement, there being no other example in

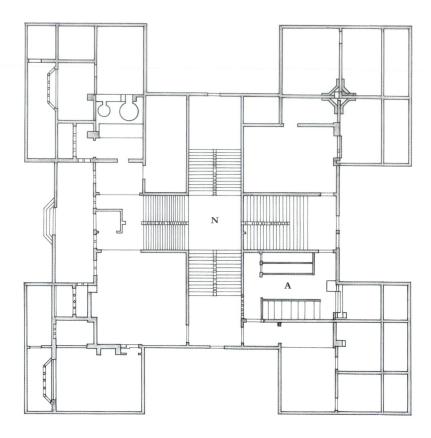

Fig. 5.34: Unidentified Puritan house: incomplete ground plan (after Thorpe T186). With its central pulpit and lacking a communion table, this is the sole Thorpe plan where the emphasis is on the pulpit. Produced 1596-1603, it is perhaps the earliest example of a chapel plan designed specifically for Puritan worship.

Thorpe's collection of a chapel where the emphasis is on the pulpit. It shows how, unaided by architecture, fittings alone can articulate the interior space of a room chapel. The first example of Puritan liturgical priorities demonstrated in a surviving private chapel is at Steane, where the pulpit is at the east end of the central entrance axis. And, for all its differentiated windows, Littlecote offers a particularly uncompromising mid-century example of a chapel interior dominated by its pulpit (fig. 5.35).

Assembly chapels featured in Thorpe's early 17th-century plans for Cannons in Middlesex, and possibly the Blewhouse in Highgate, London.[40] However, with the increasing popularity of consecration, this type declined steeply after about 1620. The narthex type, which co-existed with the assembly chapel in the Elizabethan period, also occurs in the early part of the seventeenth century, and

Fig. 5.35: Littlecote House, Wiltshire: interior of the chapel looking east. Its dominating central pulpit and absence of imagery proclaim its sound Puritan credentials.

Fig. 5.36: Littlecote House, Wiltshire: interior of the chapel looking west. The side galleries contained seating for members of the household, and had a good view of the central pulpit.

three Thorpe designs feature this type of arrangement, those for Aston Hall in Warwickshire, Thornton College in Lincolnshire, and a possible alternative plan for Burley-on-the-Hill.[41] A variant, created by the architecture rather than the fittings, survives at Leweston where, as we have seen, a small west porch, divided by a wall from the main body of the chapel, acts as both a narthex and a baptistery. However, like the assembly chapel, the narthex type became less frequent and less clearly defined as the century progressed. A vestige of the Elizabethan room chapel could also be found in single-cell chapels which occurred predominantly in gentry houses. As the simplest option, these were in some cases little more than ordinary rooms provided with the necessities for worship. A more imposing example was created at Dunham Massey (c.1655), where Sir George Booth amalgamated two existing ground-floor rooms beside the great hall to form a chapel. Few examples of this type survive, but it is possible that they were more popular than this implies, since conversion to a secular space would be simple and leave no sign of the former chapel.

The increased survival rate of known Puritan chapels from the early Caroline period makes it possible to reach some conclusions about their exterior design. Architecturally they follow no recognisable formula. As the Jacobean example of Steane made clear, and as Forde Abbey demonstrates under Charles I, austerity and control were not essential ingredients of all early to mid-17th-century Puritan chapels. Unlike Steane, the chapel at Forde drew its architectural splendour from its past history rather than through the creativity of its Puritan 17th-century patrons. Little is known about the building at this time except that the large and highly ornate east window, which dominates the internal space, was clearly retained from the Abbey chapter house. By 1650, the house was in the hands of Cromwell's attorney general, Sir Edmund Prideaux, who was succeeded on his death in 1659 by his son, also Edmund. The Prideaux family was staunchly Puritan, and made various alterations to the chapel that added to its architectural distinction, including the west end door and the circular window above. These provide an interesting example of the addition of Classical detail to a largely pre-Reformation building (Plate XVII).

During the Interregnum, the climate was of course encouraging to Puritan ventures, and the members of a movement that had previously depended on gatherings in private houses now began to build more openly. The frequent result was purpose-built, detached chapels financed by the patron, although they were often open to fellow worshippers beyond the immediate household. They were frequently near earlier, chapel-less houses, and replaced the inconvenient and often cramped rooms that had served as meeting places. In newly-built houses, room chapels following the Elizabethan format took on a specifically Puritan character, such as that at Tyttenhanger (fig. 5.26), and in other cases, as we have seen at Dunham Massey, rooms were converted to form a chapel.

Although the main interest and defining aspect of Puritan chapels lies in their internal layout and fittings, the handling of the exterior is also of interest. Bramhope chapel has already been mentioned. It was financed and built in 1649 as a private chapel by Robert Dyneley of Bramhope Hall.[42] The simple rectangular exterior is plain with no gratuitous architectural embellishment (Plate XI). There are two exceptions to this regularity: the east window has five lights instead of two or three but is otherwise unadorned, while on the north wall the fenestration pattern is varied to accommodate a small one-light window set at a higher level immediately to the east of the pulpit to provide extra light for the preacher (fig. 5.37). This was an important consideration since sermons could be long: Oliver Heywood records that on 30 January 1665 he preached at Bramhope 'with abundance of inlargement' for four and a half hours.[43]

Like Bramhope, Great Houghton chapel takes the form of a simple, elongated rectangle, a shape presumably chosen to simplify the roof construction. Great Houghton Hall was a chapel-less Elizabethan house. In about 1650 the Puritan Sir Edward Rodes built a chapel close to the house for the use of the household, and probably his tenants and local people as well, since it could hold at least sixty people. Although similar to Bramhope, Great Houghton has greater architectural pretension (fig. 5.38). The parapet is decorated with merlons which on the north and south sides rise to form a small pyramid-like feature over the central window,

Fig. 5.37: Bramhope Hall, West Yorkshire: the chapel interior, looking north-east. To the east of the pulpit, a small one-light window can just be seen. It is set at a higher level to provide extra light for the preacher.

Fig. 5.38: Great Houghton, West Yorkshire: the detached Puritan chapel from the south-east. A simple elongated rectangle, albeit with some architectural embellishment.

while the gables are decorated with half merlons. Two stringcourses mark the bottom of the parapet and the upper window level. The mullioned and transomed windows are relatively large, and the upper lights have pointed heads set within a rectangular frame. As would be expected, the east window has no distinguishing features, although a worn coat of arms is set over the centre. Bramhope and Great Houghton chapels are basically of the same design, with the former, especially, demonstrating the restraint that is often (though not always) found in a Puritan place of worship.

Peripheral Spaces: from Complexity and Variety towards Simplicity and Uniformity

There was a wide variety in the handling of peripheral chapel spaces during the first half of the 17th century. The upper chapel could be found not only in the conventional liturgical west end position, but also along one of the (liturgically north or south) flanking walls. At Blickling Hall in Norfolk (rebuilt 1618-26; fig. 5.39) there is a space which looks like a side gallery but, as the only identifiable peripheral space, was most likely the family upper chapel.[44] There are other examples. At Raynham (fig. 5.24), the main entrance to the chapel was at semi-basement level, but there was another entrance off the main stair to a side gallery at mezzanine level along the south wall which was probably the upper chapel. At

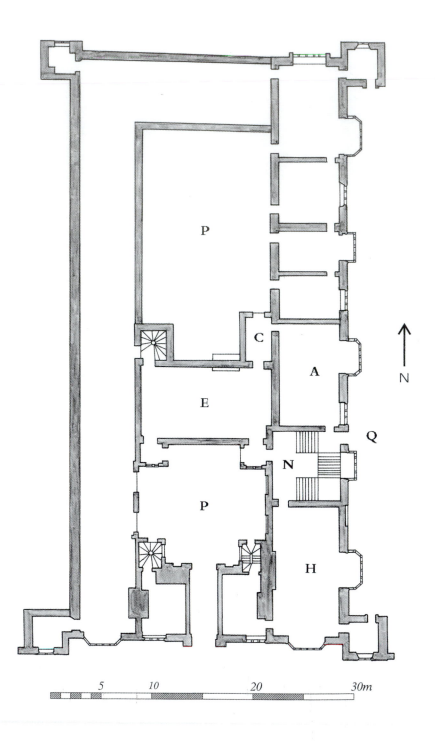

Fig. 5.39: Blickling Hall, Norfolk: ground plan. C = the presumed family upper chapel from which a staircase descended to the main chapel.

Temple Newsam (fig. 5.15), a flue in the south chapel wall at mezzanine level indicates that a side gallery of some size, probably connected by stairs to the long gallery above, acted as the upper chapel.[45] At Woburn, it is not possible to be certain about the orientation of the chapel from the 1747 plan (fig. 5.19), but the positioning of both entrances at the east end suggests that the communion table was at the west end. If so, the space occupying the liturgical north, or side, wall of the chapel would clearly once have been a mezzanine level upper chapel. Although there are still questions about the exact arrangement of these chapels, the fact that so many upper chapel spaces were likely to have been side galleries rather than positioned at the supposedly conventional west end indicates that this was a relatively common practice.

A side gallery was not always used as an upper chapel. The chapels at Hatfield (Plate XIX) and Littlecote (fig. 5.36), were built some forty years apart and come from different ends of the Protestant spectrum: Hatfield is a colourfully decorated high-church chapel, while Littlecote represents an austere, low-church alternative. And their side galleries, which occupy essentially similar peripheral spaces, were put to very different uses. In the latter, the side galleries were probably intended to provide seating for members of the household from where the preaching from the central pulpit could easily be heard. In contrast, the relative narrowness of the Hatfield galleries suggests that their function was to provide access to the west end upper chapel from the long gallery on the north side, and perhaps from an antechamber (see below) on the south side.

Roman Catholic patrons seem to have continued the pre-Reformation practice of hearing Mass in a private closet or oratory. At Naworth, for example, the Roman Catholic convert, Lord William Howard, was extensively renovating the castle from 1618. His substantial, two-storey, household chapel on the main floor had an upper chapel at the liturgical west end which could be entered from the long gallery (fig. 3.11). But an 18th-century description, complemented by one from the early 19th century, notes that Lord William's private apartments in the south-east tower comprised, as well as a library and bed-chamber, an 'oratory, or private chapel, well secured, where Lord William enjoyed his religion in privacy'.[46] Indeed the building accounts for 1624 refer to an oratory (which still survives, as does a 1514 retable), and it is known that Mass was celebrated in the house.[47] A similar arrangement may have existed at Rycote, where the detached chapel appears to have been augmented by a small 'popish' chapel in the house, raising the possibility that, at some stage, the patron had Roman Catholic connections.[48]

There seems to have been one other subsidiary room-type associated with the chapel at this period, although references to it can only be found at Robert Cecil's two major houses, Hatfield, and Salisbury House on The Strand, London

(1602–10). Hatfield inventories list an 'ante chamber adjoining to the upper chapel', on its south side. During royal visits this room functioned as a bedroom, but did not otherwise contain a bed. The record of joiners' work in 1610 suggests that it could have served as an assembly room to be used for prayers and readings. As already noted, early 17th-century household books mention such rooms as an alternative to the chapel. At Salisbury House, inventories list a 'praier house', a room containing only curtains and curtain rods. It seems probable that both houses contained, in addition to a chapel, a room set aside for religious purposes – a subsidiary space which would be particularly suitable for Protestant patrons.[49]

The number of double-height integrated chapels decreased during the period, perhaps due to the rising popularity of spaces designed for low-church worship. One effect of this was to facilitate direct access from the upper chapel to the body of the chapel via a short flight of stairs. The best example is at low-church Woburn (fig. 5.19), but it is also likely to have been the case at high-church Blickling (fig. 5.39), which was consecrated in 1628.[50] A staircase at the latter may well have been installed to enable Sir John Hobart to make a simple descent to the east end of the chapel to celebrate communion, while at Woburn, on the other hand, it was perhaps intended to allow the 4th Earl of Bedford more easily to take an active part in the liturgy from a pulpit or lectern.[51]

Despite the variety of chapel spaces, there was a gradual move away from the complicated and inventive peripheral arrangements of the early Tudor and Elizabethan periods towards a relatively uniform upper chapel at the west end. There was also a decline in specially designated peripheral spaces, perhaps due to the increased introduction of fittings such as pews (see Fittings below) which could be used to order the congregation according to sex and status.

Fittings: Utilitarian Necessities – but Diverse and Inventive

The much improved survival rate for fittings of the first half of the 17th century allows a more detailed consideration of the way in which chapels were ordered, and of the role of key fittings such as screens. There are, however, still caveats: the little documentary information available makes it difficult to obtain an accurate idea of the overall layout of individual chapels, or the extent of later alterations. And, as noted earlier, there is inevitably a bias towards the survival of the more conventional or neutral arrangements.

Fittings played an important role in the revival of the double-cell chapel for, although in some cases the distinction between east and west cells was achieved by architectural means (such as differences in size, the use of a chancel arch, or the pitch of the roof), in numerous other examples the boundary between the two spaces was defined by a screen.[52] At first sight this chapel type appears to be looking back to pre-Reformation ideas, but it is necessary to consider whether patrons were creating a space which followed the post-Reformation liturgical two-centred arrangement seen in parish churches, or whether they were indeed returning to the pre-Reformation practice of separating chapel staff from the household.

Most examples provide a clear answer to this question. For instance, two very different detached chapels, Staunton Harold (fig. 5.30) and the probable chapel of ease at Langley Hall, Shropshire (completed 1601; fig. 5.40), can confidently be assigned to the group following the lead of parish churches. Although the fittings at Langley Hall are simple, and there is no screen, two distinct liturgical areas can be identified. In the slightly raised east cell, seats set against the north, east and south sides, together with a continuous reading shelf, surrounded the modest communion table.[53] Further west, the pulpit stands against the south wall, opposite what is probably the reading pew, complete with a tester. Beyond, are box-pews and then simpler bench pews, all ranged against the north and south walls and separated by a central aisle; what is thought to be a musicians' pew occupies the north-west corner. Although some alterations to the fittings have taken place, the original intention to use the western end of the chapel for daily services and to reserve the eastern section for the celebration of holy communion, remains clear.

The Staunton Harold chapel is much larger and more ambitious.[54] Daily

Fig. 5.40: Langley Hall chapel of ease, Shropshire: the simple interior looking east. The western end was used for daily services and the eastern section was reserved for the celebration of Holy Communion.

services were conducted from the pulpit and reading pew placed west of the chancel arch on the south side. The communion table is raised on three steps at the far end of the east cell, but although the panelling is of the highest quality there are no other fittings in this area, and no specific mention of any appears in the accounts.[55] It seems that the east cell was used solely as the area in which communicants would gather during the celebration of the Eucharist.

The simplicity of Langley Hall contrasts with the richer more sophisticated fittings at Staunton Harold. And while both are two-centred chapels, their layout illustrates very clearly the diversity of practice surrounding the celebration of communion. At Langley Hall communicants would have gathered to sit round the table, while at Staunton Harold they would have stood or knelt to its west. In neither chapel was the table meant to be moved: the surrounding benches at Langley Hall, and its raised position at Staunton Harold, would have made this impractical.

In other chapels, interpretation of the layout can be more problematic. At Red House (fig. 5.9), the most distinctive feature is the way in which all the key fittings are grouped in the eastern cell. Although no specific reading pew or desk can be identified, seats with a continuous reading shelf line the side walls and are returned against the simple screen, while the pulpit is at the north corner of the east wall, with the communion table below the east window. The cell west of the screen contains plain pews, and what was probably the family upper chapel above extends eastwards as far as the screen. Red House is the only example of a two-centred chapel where both the communion table and the pulpit are set against the east wall, implying that in practice, despite the presence of a screen, this was liturgically speaking a single-cell space. The arrangement is closer to the pre-Reformation double-cell model, with the purpose of the screen being to separate the congregation from the eastern cell, and it is certainly ill-adapted to services in which the congregation were to play an active part. A particular problem is to determine for whom the seats in the eastern cell, capable of holding about sixteen to eighteen people, were intended. Since it was unusual for 17th-century gentry to employ more than one chaplain, their use by chapel staff can be ruled out. In 1636, the Slingsby household consisted of six family members, and sixteen male and eight female servants. While it is possible that the family occupied these seats, family pews east of the screen were usually distinct from the fittings used by the chaplain (as at Haddon and Rycote, discussed below).

The diary of Henry Slingsby II, son of the chapel's builder (also Henry), provides valuable information about the way in which the chapel was used. It is clear that preaching was seen as important.[56] This makes the placing of the pulpit so far from the western cell particularly surprising, although there is of course no guarantee that the son's views reflected those of the father. However, given the

Fig. 5.41: Haddon Hall, Derbyshire: interior view of the chapel looking east. Reading shelves project through the balusters of the simple screen. The two-decker pulpit and reading pew are on the left.

relatively large size of the chapel and isolated position of the house, it is possible that it was built to cater for a wider congregation. If so, the eastern cell might indeed have been for the household and chaplain, with the family presiding in the upper chapel and local people filling the western cell.

Rycote (*c.*1610-25) and Haddon (1623-4) represent variations on the liturgical two-centred type. At Haddon, the arrangement was established by refitting what had originally been a small medieval parish church (fig. 5.41). The screen which replaced the rood screen is a simple structure of plain panelling surmounted by simple balusters and a rudimentary cornice. To the west, on the north side, the two-decker pulpit and reading pew are arranged together with a seat facing the pews in the south aisle. A tomb immediately opposite the pulpit is an 18th-century insertion, and probably displaced further pews in the area. The eastern cell contains the communion table, and two large box-pews (presumably for the family since there is no upper chapel) which stand opposite each other immediately east of the screen on the north and south sides. On the west sides of each box-pew (which are formed by the screen), reading shelves facing the congregation project through the balusters. Here the fittings seem well-adapted to the two-centred arrangement, and the fact that the communion table is both raised and railed (and thus impossible to move) shows that communicants were intended to gather, whether standing or kneeling, in the eastern cell. Here is a solution that neatly balances form and function, while also conveying a clear hierarchical message in the emphasis, through their position east of the screen, on the importance of the family. It harks back to the pre-Reformation custom of admitting gentry to the chancel of the parish church and, in the context of the private chapel, perhaps again demonstrates the continuing tension between piety and social status.[57]

Fig. 5.42: Rycote Park, Oxfordshire: looking east through the crested chapel screen. The family pews are immediately to the west of the screen with, on the left, a musicians' gallery above. The pulpit (not visible) is on the right and further to the west. This double-cell layout is well suited to the Word-based Protestant liturgy.

Rycote (fig. 5.42), like Haddon, involved the refitting of a medieval building. Part of the medieval rood screen, augmented with some 17th-century arcading, divides the chapel into two unequal cells. The larger western cell contains the pulpit and a (probably later) reading pew on the south side, set some distance west of the screen. The overall arrangement, incorporating both medieval and 17th-century pews, is well-adapted for the Word-based Protestant liturgy. The placing of two pews for the family and perhaps important guests is somewhat similar to Haddon, but here it is their eastern walls that are incorporated with the screen, since they are placed immediately west of it. Medieval seats returned against the east side of the screen are probably part of the early 17th-century refit. This would suggest that the communion table, previously set at the same level as the seats, was moved into the body of the eastern cell to enable communicants to sit round it there. Certainly the family pews were well-placed to allow their occupants to participate in both types of service with minimum disruption.

The apparently simultaneous existence at Rycote of the small, integral 'popish' chapel and a larger detached chapel set up for Protestant worship suggests that the religious affiliations of a patron cannot be inferred from the layout of the household chapel. Likewise, there was no guarantee that a patron's heirs would remain constant in their affiliations. Four years after the death of the Roman Catholic Lord William Howard in 1640, Naworth was inherited by the Protestant Sir Charles Howard (later the 1st Earl of Carlisle) who used the chapel for Protestant worship, including the celebration of communion.[58] Exactly how the chapel was used before Lord William's death is unclear, but we have already seen that, as at Raglan Castle, households of mixed religion could worship together. Lord William may have planned his chapel as a neutral space where his household could gather for non-denominational worship.

It is possible to piece together something of the layout at Naworth from Hutchinson's 18th-century description, and two 19th-century watercolours (Plates V & VI).[59] Although we cannot know what changes might have been made after Lord William's death, the pictures show a dilapidated early 17th-century interior and, where it is possible to cross-check against the contemporary building accounts, no subsequent changes can be pinpointed. Apart from a box-pew and some venerable benches arranged in conventional manner facing east, the fittings are all east of the screen which, most unusually, does not form a complete division across the chapel. The pulpit stands against the liturgical north wall on the line of the screen which stops just before it, allowing a 180-degree range for the preacher.[60] It is impossible to identify a communion table east of the screen, but this is not conclusive because of the indistinct quality of the paintings and the fact that one is mentioned by Hutchinson. A selection of pews is visible, including what may well be the reading pew, immediately below the pulpit and facing east. There is a large box-pew against the south side of the screen, also facing east, as well as another long box-pew running along the south wall. Finally, another pew is shown in the liturgical north-east corner of the chapel adjoining the east wall. On balance, this would appear to be another example of the two-centred chapel, although the positioning of the pulpit and the relatively large number of box-pews east of the screen might suggest a more flexible use. From the evidence in Lady Halkett's memoirs, the family probably occupied the upper chapel (just visible at the west end in Plate V) for everyday services, and would descend to the chapel proper for the celebration of communion (perhaps using one of the box-pews east of the screen).[61] It is the function of the rest of the seating east of the screen that is problematical. This is not an arrangement, as at Langley Hall and Rycote, where the household could sit on benches surrounding the table for communion. The design and the way the seats are dispersed around the eastern cell suggest that the chapel was not intended primarily for the celebration of communion, and that the seating acted as a tool to distinguish upper servants from their social inferiors.[62] Unfortunately, although the example of Naworth highlights the problems of this turbulent period, it does not provide many clear-cut answers.

That the majority of double-cell chapels followed, at least to some extent, the practice of providing separate spaces for different types of worship seems straightforward, but it implies that they were designed to facilitate the celebration of communion, and this raises the question of consecration and the problem of the extent to which the private chapel usurped the role of the parish church. Put another way, were the chapels which appear to have been designed specifically for communion actually used in this way, or were they intended more as a visual reminder of the liturgy that lay at the heart of the Christian religion? Was the provision of two centres for worship more for show than for use, a kind of visual reference to a liturgy that was the preserve of the parish church? And was it considered acceptable to celebrate communion, or indeed any of the sacraments, in a private chapel whether or not it had been consecrated? References to communion services in private chapels during this period can be found for Chantemarle, Knole (1617, 1619), and Naworth (1649); and of these only the Chantemarle chapel is known to have been consecrated.[63] But records are far from complete, and references to taking communion in private chapels are rare. The answer may be that there is no one general answer to these questions, and that much depended on the attitude of the relevant bishop and the amount of influence wielded by the patron, together with more prosaic practicalities such as the distance of the house from the parish church.

As already stated, rather than using fittings to emphasise the communion table, Puritan chapels often featured the pulpit as the main, and sometimes only, focus.[64] Of the surviving examples, Steane (Plate XV) is the most interesting, although later modifications obscure the original intention. Unlike Thorpe's unidentified Puritan house (fig. 5.34), this purpose-built chapel, wider than it is long, combines fittings and architectural articulation to create a very original Puritan interior. The ecclesiastical standard of high nave with low aisles is used, but with a difference. It is divided longitudinally into three aisles: that to the north is separated from the main body of the chapel by a screen, contains family monuments, and appears to have no liturgical function. The other two are used for worship. The main west entrance is in the middle aisle, with the pulpit at the eastern end, but offset so as to be placed centrally in the space used for worship. The arrangement therefore avoids introducing an imposing west-east vista or the gradual build-up in the richness of fittings so often found in high-church chapels. Although the pulpit is prominent, its presentation and handling is simple and functional. The south aisle now contains an 18th-century altar, making it impossible to reconstruct the original arrangement: a 17th-century communion table cannot be ruled out, although it would not have rivalled the pulpit in importance.

Other examples, such as Littlecote (with its dominating east-end pulpit; fig. 5.35), demonstrate the relative popularity of the pulpit-centred arrangement. However, Bramhope warns against too simplistic an interpretation of Puritan settings (fig. 5.37). Today, the pulpit overlooks the pews from its position about a third of the way down the north wall, while the east end is taken up with a small 19th-century communion table. Although the 17th-century layout is not known, it is unlikely that it would have differed very much since Oliver Heywood's diaries twice record the celebration of communion there (albeit after the Restoration).

The replacement of altars by wooden **communion tables** began under Edward VI and was firmly established in private chapels by the start of the 17th century. The degree of ornamentation varied. Compared with the rudimentary simplicity of the table at Langley Hall, that at Staunton Harold appears positively intricate. There was little reflection of the contemporary controversy which affected cathedrals and parish churches about whether and how the communion table should be positioned at the east end. One point to emerge is the gradual increase in popularity of steps leading up to it and of rails to protect it. At Hatfield, the provision of a raised area at the eastern end of the chapel was clearly an afterthought, carried out with some difficulty in 1611 when the chapel was nearing completion. A number of chapels from the early part of the period did not incorporate rails, regardless, it would seem, of the patron's religious position. Leweston, Red House, Low Ham, and possibly Rycote, probably did not have rails; the absence of any identifiable entry for them in the very detailed accounts suggests that there were none at Hatfield either. It is also notable that in two instances, Rycote and Red House, alterations focusing on the east end and including the provision of rails were carried out after the Restoration, and this, together with the increasingly ornate design of rails, as at Cholmondeley Castle, may point to an increase in their importance as the century progressed. Certainly,

Fig. 5.43: Cholmondeley Castle, Cheshire: looking east through the chapel screen. A rich setting for communion, and created in defiance of the issuing of Parliamentary orders abolishing communion tables, and removing altar rails in parish churches.

the two richest settings for communion to survive from the first half of the century, at Staunton Harold and Cholmondeley Castle, were created some years after a 1643 Parliamentary ordinance abolished communion tables at the east end and ordered the removal of altar rails in parish churches (figs. 5.30, 5.43).[65] Whether these chapels were conceived simply as the protests of individual high-church royalists, or indicated the existence of a more widespread change in attitude, it is difficult to say.[66]

Commandment boards and **reredoses** were used in the early 17th century. Although in 1604 Hampton Court Canon 82 had re-iterated that the Decalogue was to be 'set up on the east end of every church and chapel where the people may best see and read the same', there are surprisingly few signs that private chapels (and particularly those which might be considered to be chapels of ease such as at Langley Hall, Rug and Risley) followed this ruling. The earliest surviving 17th-century commandment board, dated 1610, is at Rycote, and there is another, probably from the mid-century, at Tyttenhanger (fig. 5.26), but they are far from ubiquitous.[67] Since they were not controversial objects, it might be expected that, had they existed in large numbers, the survival rate would have been higher. However, information is limited because they rarely feature in inventories. Even so, a strong impression lingers that the east window (with or without stained glass) was a significantly more popular way of filling the area above the communion table.

Because the **screen** was often the key to the articulation of the interior space, the simple nature of most surviving examples is surprising. Many consist of little more than plain panelling surmounted by simple balusters supporting a rudimentary cornice, sometimes with a central opening. Haddon (1626) provides a typical example (fig. 5.41). In more ornate versions, the central opening is arched and can be emphasised with some form of cresting, such as that at Rycote (fig. 5.42). Of the earlier examples, the richest is at Low Ham, where pre-Reformation forms, mixed with some Classical detail, are revived (fig. 5.44). Here the arched openings are decorated with woodwork reminiscent of Perpendicular tracery, and above, supporting the projecting cornice, are angels bearing texts alternating with winged cherubs' heads. An inscription over their heads is surmounted by a frieze of grapes and vine leaves topped with filigree cresting. Although Classical forms (such as egg and dart) are used, the decorative vocabulary is predominantly medieval. Through its uniqueness, the Low Ham screen highlights the surprisingly characterless designs produced for many other chapels, especially when compared to some of the splendidly ornate Jacobean screens found in medieval parish churches such as at Croscombe in Somerset.[68] Of some interest is the screen at Water Eaton which, on its western face, has a mix of cherubim and animal forms in the spandrels with six green men below, perhaps guarding the entrance to the eastern cell.[69]

The two most impressive screens of the period both date from the 1650s, namely at Staunton Harold and Cholmondeley Castle. At the former (fig. 5.31), what appears to be the original chancel screen, somewhat cut down, is now installed at the west end. Both screens use Classical forms (although of dubious proportions compared with the sumptuous and correctly proportioned Elizabethan screen at Holdenby; fig. 4.2) that rarely featured in screen design

Fig. 5.44: Low Ham, Somerset: the chapel interior looking east. Although Classical forms are used, the decorative vocabulary of the screen is predominantly medieval.

at this date. The upper part of the Staunton Harold screen has ornate pilasters embellished with faceted diamond work between paired arched openings. The screen at Cholmondeley (fig. 5.43) has a less substantial feel and looks back to the inventiveness typical of Jacobean woodwork. Using Corinthian columns and an entablature which includes an ornately pierced frieze, the screen also incorporates elaborate scrollwork in the openings; that of the central arch is decorated with bunches of grapes and vine leaves, clearly a direct reference to the sacrificial function of the eastern half of the chapel.

Pulpits became an almost standard feature in the 17th century.[70] Those at many private chapels, such as Leweston, Haddon, Bramhope and Staunton Harold, were of the two-decker type combining the pulpit with a desk or seat for the chaplain (the three-decker, which added a desk for the parish clerk, remained the preserve of the parish church). In other examples, as at Langley Hall, the pulpit and desk faced each other across a central aisle, while at Red House there is no distinguishable reading pew or desk.

Although the shape of the pulpit was remarkably constant, with the vast majority being octagonal,[71] its position varied considerably. In two cases, pulpits stand against the east wall close to the communion table, one (Leweston) in the south-east corner and the other (Red House) in the north-east corner. But they were normally on a side wall with a preference for the north.[72] The most unusual position for a pulpit was at Salisbury House, where the 1640 inventory records it in the upper chapel. In chapels with Puritan connections, it could supplant the communion table as the focal point at the east end. While evidence for the existence of pulpits under Elizabeth is surprisingly sparse, in the early 17th century it became the most constant, and sometimes the most dominating, feature of the chapel.

The existence of **musicians' pews** emphasises the renewed role of music in the liturgy. Rycote has a musicians' gallery above the family pew (accessed by the medieval stairs to the lost rood screen), and at Langley Hall the larger-than-normal box-pew at the north-west end was perhaps meant for musicians. However, private chapels probably followed the practice of some parish churches in using dismantled rood lofts for singers, and it is unlikely that singers occupied a western gallery in a private chapel before the Restoration.

Leweston (fig. 5.14) is perhaps the first surviving post-Reformation example of the conventional arrangement in which **pews** are placed across the west cell and separated by a central aisle, and which is so often featured in Thorpe's plans. Here all the pews are identical, and thus free from any hierarchical emphasis (other than position). But, as always, diversity is the hallmark of the early 17th century. At Naworth and Rug, rough-hewn benches were provided while at Rycote and Haddon medieval pews are re-used, augmented with 17th-century box-pews. The latter are perhaps best represented at Langley Hall, Bramhope and Steane, although in all cases some re-arrangement has occurred. Hatfield had 'seats benches brackets and desks', at least some of which had 'pew heads'. A 19th-century description of the chapel records 'old high backed seats'.[73] The 1649 Parliamentary Survey recorded a chapel 'well adorned with a pulpitt a reading place and handsome seates or pews' at Wimbledon, while at Trelowarren in Cornwall the accounts include entries for 'pews with partitions', 'seats' and 'desks'.[74] The general impression is that fixed seating became the norm. Although seats are not often mentioned in inventories, builders' accounts almost always specify seating of some type, and the fact that forms, popular in the Elizabethan period, do not often feature perhaps also indicates a move towards fixed seating and the consequent adoption of the term 'pew' to describe them.

Fixed seating raises the issue of the segregation of the sexes, and there is much to be discovered about how seating was used to achieve this. Two private chapels continued the tradition of segregation well into the 20th century. At Staunton Harold until just before the First World War, Lord and Lady Ferrers would lead the entire household from the house to the chapel in segregated crocodiles.[75] The women would sit on the traditional north side under the admonitory gaze of Lady Shirley, whose carved head is featured on the reveal of the north chancel window, while the men sat on the south side supervised by a likeness of Sir Robert. At Hatfield chapel, segregation continues, although here the women sit on the south side.[76]

Segregation may not always have been as simple to arrange as in parish churches.[77] One reason was that men predominated among the retainers of many 17th-century households. This imbalance raises questions about the practicality of segregation by the compass.[78] It is perhaps likely that, at least in some cases, women were accommodated in a specific pew or pews set aside for them rather than filling one side of the chapel. This appears to have been the case at Low Ham a generation or two later, where the pewing occupied by the family is recorded on the death of Ralph, Lord Stawell in 1689 and implies that the women of the household sat behind two far grander pews, presumably containing men, on the north side.[79] It is probable that solutions were varied and, for instance, the fact that all the pews at Leweston have hat-pegs might imply that in some chapels segregation was not an issue.

Whereas the main chapel often contained fixed seating, the upper chapel, when intended for use by the family, almost invariably contained moveable furniture, often richly upholstered to a far higher (and more comfortable) standard. In general, more furniture appears to have been used than in the Elizabethan period. A typical arrangement would be to provide one 'high chair', presumably for the patron, and an assortment of stools and other chairs.

Given the turbulent history of the period, the diverse and inventive ways in which chapel fittings were used is not unexpected. They certainly played a key role in ordering the chapel, but their poor quality is surprising. For the most part, and with the exception of the upper chapel furniture, they were simple and unpretentious, utilitarian necessities rather than objects of display, and often the product of the estate carpenter rather than a skilled craftsman. It is also notable that, Low Ham apart, the two chapels to which this does not apply, those at Staunton Harold and Cholmondeley Castle, date not from the period normally associated with the rise of the 'beauty of holiness', but from the much more austere period of the 1650s.

Decoration: 'Popery may creep in at a glasse window, as well as at a door'

In the 16th century the development of decorative ideas was broadly linear. In the first half of the 17th century the position was more complicated. The revival in importance of the private chapel in the early years of the century was, in the hands of high-church patrons, reflected in a move away from the austerity of the Elizabethan period towards new decorative ideas and the revisiting of old ones. Attitudes towards imagery were complex and variable. In general, designers of richly decorated chapels had two options. One was to use biblical imagery, but this carried the risk of being seen as papist and idolatrous. An alternative, which avoided such difficulties, was to use relatively inoffensive symbolism as the mainstay of the decorative scheme.

Contemporary writings indicate that there were in the main three contrasting views, all vehemently held. There were those who were in favour of 'seemly' beauty and who recognised the didactic possibilities inherent in carefully selected pictorial schemes.[80] But there were also those who remained violently opposed to images of any kind, seeing them as idolatrous and inherently papist. As the Puritan pamphleteer William Prynne put it, 'Popery may creep in at a glasse window, as well as at a door'.[81] This attitude was widespread in low-church circles where there was wholesale condemnation of figurative schemes. Sir William Brereton of Handforth Hall in Cheshire, a patron rather than a theologian, in 1635 condemned the decoration of a parish church in Shrewsbury 'of late gaudily painted' as having 'idle, ridiculous, vain and absurd pictures, representations and stories, the like whereunto I never saw in England'.[82] In 1628, the Puritan divine Peter Smart preached a sermon that was violently critical of the use of ritual at services at Durham Cathedral, and in 1629 he attacked Bishop Richard Neile for wishing to advance 'cathedral pomp and glorious ceremonies' over 'the making of sermons or writing books'.[83] The third position was perhaps the most direct: – decoration was simply irrelevant. To Bishop Joseph Hall, 'one zealous prayer, one orthodox sermon is a more glorious furniture than all the precious rarities of mechanic excellencies or curious imagery'.[84]

Where imagery was not condemned outright, the most contentious debate centred on the question of what constituted 'seemly' decoration? Andrew Willet, a Calvinist and strenuous opponent of Roman Catholicism, demonstrated the difficulties that a man of his beliefs faced when considering the subject. He had no problem with the idea that churches should be well kept and built with 'seemly beauty', but he did not think that great expense should 'be bestowed upon the walls of the Church and idols to garnish and beautify idolatry'. Although he made it clear that 'any images, painted or graven' were 'not safe', this was not clear-cut, for he also stated that images used 'for comeliness and ornament onely, or for historicall use' could be acceptable. In other words, it was not only the choice of images that was important, but also the way in which they were seen to be used.[85]

For high-churchmen, the problem was less acute, although there was the ever-present danger that any fondness for images could be denounced as papist. At the highest level, James I rose magnificently above the confusion. In March 1617, he told the Scottish bishops, who had attempted to dissuade him from including carved figures of the apostles in his chapel at Holyrood Palace in Edinburgh, that it was inconsistent to allow depictions of lions, dragons and devils in their churches but not of the patriarchs and apostles. The king's defence in 1624 of Samuel Harsnett, then Bishop of Norwich, who was charged with setting up religious images in a church, was equally unambiguous. On that occasion he observed 'I am sorrye ... that you call the ornaments of the church idolaturye being nothing but the pictures of the Apostles and such like as I have in myne owne chappell'.[86]

But views were constantly evolving. In the early years of the 17th century, the artist and writer, Henry Peacham, produced a series of publications aimed at promoting the arts of painting and drawing. He dealt in some detail with the question of what painted images were acceptable in church, but did not approach the subject from a theologically entrenched position. Of particular interest is the way in which his views changed. In *The Art of Drawing with the Pen* of 1606 he notes that there were two areas where a painter was not permitted to depict what he liked: first religion and secondly 'filthiness' − that is paintings that induced lust. Of religious subjects he warned against 'reviving from Hell the old heresie of the Anthropomorphites who supposed God to be in the shape of an old man, sitting upon his throne in a white robe with a triple crown on his head'. He also criticised representations of the Trinity, Jesus Christ and the saints.[87] But by 1612, in an edition substantially the same, but renamed *The Gentleman's Exercise or Graphice,* his views have softened. Lust has become the number one danger. Although he still felt that a picture of the Trinity was 'blasphemous utterly unlawful ... an impious thing and not to be tolerated as being expressly forbidden by the word of God', he found pictures of Christ, the apostles and martyrs acceptable. Moreover, he says of one picture of Christ that he would 'scarce change it for the best jewel in the world ... neither of the lawfulnesse thereof I think any wise man will make question'.[88]

The debate about the acceptability of various images continued throughout the period. Before 1641 no authoritative guidelines appear to have emerged, and the legal situation remained unresolved. The extent to which this posed a problem for Protestant patrons is unclear, although it is likely that in the early part of the century critical attention was largely concentrated on public places of worship. However, private chapels certainly featured in the debate. While Peacham supported the Earl of Salisbury's decorative scheme in the chapel at Hatfield, there were those who condemned displays of imagery in private chapels. For the theologically minded, there was the constant danger of patrons falling prey to idolatry and 'superstitioun'. Many mistrusted any rich display in a private chapel as a manifestation of materialistic worldliness and pomp. We have already seen it castigated as 'pomp on earth' in 1614 by Salisbury's former chaplain John Bowle – somewhat surprisingly given his close involvement four years earlier in the design of the painted glass windows at Hatfield. Despite the problematic nature of the use of imagery and the vehement reactions it aroused, it does appear that, until the Parliamentary Ordinances of 1641 to 1644, Protestant private chapels were able to reflect the views and beliefs of their owners relatively unhindered. Biblical imagery was included or proposed in decorative schemes not only of newly-built private chapels, but also in university college chapels, chapels of institutions such as hospitals, and even parish churches. By James I's death in 1625, a relatively wide range of subjects in a number of media was being used, and it is likely that private chapels led the way.

During the third and fourth decades of the century, the Classical forms introduced by Inigo Jones became popular in court circles, but there is little sign that his ideas influenced Protestant chapel decoration, although this may in part be due to the loss of the most important chapels associated with his circle: that at Castle Ashby has lost its original interior (as has the east pavilion at Stoke Brucrne which might have contained a chapel), while that at Wilton has been demolished. As a result, only fragments of information are left — for example, a 1620-3 drawing by Inigo Jones of a wooden coffered ceiling which shows the combination of control with richness that might be expected in a Classical chapel (Plate XXV). If, as has been suggested, it were for the closet of the Duke of Buckingham's chapel at New Hall in Essex, it would comprise the only indication of how a non-royal Jonesian chapel interior could have looked. Jones's estimate for the chapel included fitted paintings, but unfortunately there is no indication of their subject matter.[89]

Glass

The first instances of the 17th-century revival of images can be found in painted glass windows. The earliest example (in this case, of the re-use) of biblical scenes was when the Cutt family transferred medieval glass depicting the 'Passion of Our Saviour flanked by Angels and Doves' from their former seat at Horham Hall to the east window of their new chapel at Childerley. This move had been completed by 1608, and may have occurred as early as 1600.[90] The Passion was a controversial subject, but patrons may well have been prepared to sponsor the depiction of such scenes because leading Reformation figures such as Luther and

Calvin appear to have regarded glass as relatively harmless, its inherent unreality being less likely to encourage idolatry.[91] It was, therefore, the most popular, and indeed the 'safest', medium for biblical scenes. Hence, it seems that it was not only the subject matter but also the medium that affected the degree of controversy attached to a specific image. However, the possibility of misinterpretation was taken seriously: when a window, now in the Victoria and Albert Museum and depicting the Deposition of Christ, was installed in Fitzwilliam Coningsby's chapel at Hampton Court in Herefordshire in 1629, it was felt necessary to include the inscription 'The truth here of is historicall deuine and not superstissious' (Plate XVIII) to emphasise that there was no idolatrous intent.[92] Although more images – particularly of Christ – were created in glass than in any other medium, doubts about their 'safety' evidently persisted.

An alternative strategy, adopted at Hatfield in 1609-10, was to revive the medieval typological approach set out in the *Biblia Pauperum*, in which Old Testament scenes (or ante-types) were held to prefigure events from the life of Christ (types). Apart from Childerley (itself a reworking of an early Tudor scheme), this is the earliest known 17th-century glass cycle, and it is the most important surviving example of Jacobean glass in a private chapel (Plate XXII). The east window contains twelve Old Testament scenes which are (with one exception) linked to New Testament types by means of inscriptions.[93] The use of types and ante-types in decorative schemes has a well-established pre-Reformation history (most famously, at King's College Chapel, Cambridge), and the Hatfield scheme would appear to be an excellent way of bringing contentious subjects such as the Passion and Resurrection to the mind of the worshipper without actually depicting them.

There are no further recorded examples of typological windows in private chapels early in the century, and the choice of subjects shows a surprising unanimity. At Childerley, as we have seen, a Passion was installed. By 1624 Lord Maynard, less cautious than Coningsby at Hampton Court, had set six scenes from the life of Christ in the east window of his richly decorated chapel at Easton Lodge. These are now in Little Easton parish church and include not only the Crucifixion, but also the Resurrection and Ascension.[94] By the third decade of the century, the use of the Crucifixion was relatively widespread. At Red House (by 1622 and probably earlier), the east window had a Crucifixion, flanked by Mary, John and Elizabeth with Peter, Andrew and Paul below. It has also been suggested that the scheme at Temple Newsam chapel of *c*.1636 included glass featuring angels with the instruments of the Passion.[95] And even when major renovations were carried out, medieval glass cycles were often retained. For instance, the east window at Haddon depicting the Crucifixion with John and Mary, together with smaller scenes, including the Annunciation, in the tracery and the saints and apostles in the south windows, was retained in the comprehensive renovation carried out in 1624.

While the Passion was the most popular subject with high-church Protestant patrons, either as the only image, or linked with other scenes from the life of Christ, side windows featured saints and apostles. Many of these images, particularly those of Christ, would have been seen as 'dangerous' by some. The choices reflect pre-Reformation schemes, and mark a return to the emphasis on sacramental worship replaced after the Reformation by a didactic text-based approach. In this, private chapels were not alone, for Episcopal and institutional chapels used similar schemes. At Buckden Palace in Cambridgeshire, Bishop Williams installed a Crucifixion with Mary, John and the Angels. At the chapel of Trinity Hospital, Greenwich, where the foundation stone was laid in 1614, the east window depicts the Passion of Christ flanked by the Agony in the Garden and the Ascension.[96] Wadham College, Oxford, had perhaps the most complete scheme. The north windows of 1614 depicted prophets, whilst the south windows, installed in 1616, showed Christ with apostles and saints. In 1622 the east window, showing ten scenes from the life of Christ together with typological Old Testament scenes in the tracery, completed the cycle. The Calvinist Archbishop Abbot attempted to break the mould in the chapel of the hospital he founded in Guildford by deploying specifically Protestant themes. Here, the (c.1621) windows display very splendid Old Testament scenes depicting the story of Jacob and Esau, almost certainly commissioned as an essay on the covenant between God and Man, and demonstrate that there could be alternatives to the near ubiquitous scenes from the Passion. It is, however, notable that there was little enthusiasm for preferring the specifically Protestant imagery offered by Hatfield and Abbot's Hospital to more contentious scenes from the life of Christ.

Painted Biblical Images

Painted decoration using biblical images returned as cycles on structural elements of the chapel such as walls, panelling and ceilings, and were sometimes combined with moveable pictures designed to hang on walls or act as altarpieces. Documented painted cycles are scarce, although to what extent this is due to a low survival rate rather than inherent unpopularity is not clear. Three examples are known, one being the re-used Tudor work at the Roman Catholic Lord William Howard's Naworth already mentioned.[97] The others are at Hatfield and Temple Newsam.

At Hatfield, two of the most important survivals are the six prophets painted on the reveals of the east window (Plate XX), and the plaster roundels set into the upper galleries which depict Christ and various apostles and saints (Plate XXIII). At least four roundels must have been added to the series when the upper chapel was shortened in the late 18th century, thereby extending the side galleries. Thus it is not certain that the image of Christ (the third of four images set below the west side of the upper chapel) was a part of the original scheme, although a reference in the accounts to Rowland Bucket painting 'Christ and the apostles' makes it likely.[98] The biggest loss at Hatfield is the painting on the ceiling (and probably also on the ante-chapel ceiling beneath the upper chapel). The subjects are not recorded and the main ceiling, whitewashed in 1644, was finally destroyed by fire in the 19th century. The surviving fixed decoration shows a mix of Old Testament and New Testament figures which became (with minor variations) one of the standard features of early 17th-century schemes. If this had been the total extent of the decoration at Hatfield, it would have appeared as a carefully thought-out attempt to revive biblical imagery (in both glass and paint) while avoiding direct reference to the most contentious subjects. However, the scheme also included a series of six paintings of scenes from the life of Christ which are documented as being in the chapel in 1611. What is puzzling about them is that they appear to upset an otherwise carefully considered scheme.[99] The absence of any depictions of events after the Agony in the Garden perhaps reflects a desire to avoid contentious subjects, but it is surprising that only a year or so after the installation of the typological window — apparently designed to refer obliquely to 'difficult' New Testament scenes — vivid and obvious depictions of subjects such as the Annunciation were commissioned specifically for the chapel. Moreover, while some of the scenes from the life of Christ relate to the texts in the east window, others do not. This may be because some elements are now missing, but a more convincing explanation is that it is simply mistaken to assume that schemes would be co-ordinated across different media. No early 17th-century decorative schemes demonstrate sustained cross-media co-ordination. Hatfield is increasingly recognised as being revolutionary in the way that some room schemes co-ordinated the colour of woodwork and textiles but, although the glass and painted wall decoration in the chapel work well together, we should not expect to find a fully co-ordinated cross-media scheme at this date.[100] And some of the contradictions may be due to an apparent change of plan during the creation of the scheme, perhaps caused by a new and more relaxed attitude to the use of certain images. As a supporter of the chapel's scheme, the shift in Peacham's views already noted may well be a reflection of the same influence.

Another partly surviving example of fixed painted decoration combined with canvases is at Temple Newsam, where the owner, Sir Arthur Ingram, wrote to his steward, John Mattison, that he had 'a great desire my chapel may be finely painted'.[101] What now remains, removed from its original context, is a series of battered wooden panels depicting Old Testament figures, but it is possible to reconstruct from the building accounts lost aspects of the scheme. From March 1636, John Carleton spent a year working on the painted decoration. There were eighteen panels depicting Old Testament figures in gilded frames of two different sizes, 124ins x 23ins and 90ins x 20ins. It is probable that they formed the decoration along the side walls of the chapel, and that on the north wall they were hung in two tiers.[102] From an iconographical standpoint, this part of the scheme is coherent. All but one of the panel figures are identifiable, with the final panel almost certainly representing Hosea. The series consists, therefore, of 14 prophets split equally between the two levels. The remaining four figures could act as Old Testament ante-types with Moses prefiguring Christ, and Aaron with his rod acting as an ante-type for the Nativity; Naaman's cleansing in the River Jordan prefigures Christ's Baptism; and Jonah's escape from the whale represents the Resurrection. Two large canvases painted by Carleton at the same time abandon the typological approach, but continue the New Testament emphasis. Of these, the Last Supper (88ins x 112ins) was probably intended as an altarpiece, while the slightly smaller Supper at Emmaus (70ins x 108ins) may have hung opposite it on the west wall.[103] These two subjects would have fitted well into the overall scheme, especially when it is remembered that the east window may have featured the instruments of the Passion. If so, Temple Newsam may represent the first (partially) surviving scheme of decoration that was iconographically integrated across different media, and marking an advance on the confused relationship between them at Hatfield.

Smaller paintings were also used as altarpieces and to hang on walls. At Easton Lodge, there is no way of identifying which pictures, if any, hung in the chapel. However, a 1637 inventory lists a number of religious pictures of which two might well have been altarpieces. One depicted 'Adam and Eve on one side and Christ and his Crosse in the other side', and 'a picture of the same kind' showed Susanna. At Burghley, a list of pictures in the chapel compiled at the end of the 17th century included both Old and New Testament subjects, as well as an altarpiece of 'Lazarus, carried by Angels', although it is impossible to pinpoint the date by which they were in place.[104] But the most popular subject for an altarpiece appears to have been the Last Supper. We have already seen that Carleton's Last Supper may have been used as an altarpiece at Temple Newsam, and a painting of the same subject, reputed to be by Federigo Zuccaro, was recorded at Roehampton House, London, by 1632. College chapels were using similar scenes, although none as early as Hatfield. By 1639 the east wall of Magdalen College chapel was hung with cloths painted by Richard Greenbury depicting the 'birth, passion, resurrection and ascension of our Saviour very largely and exquisitely sett Forth in collours'.[105] At St John's College, Cambridge, large gilt-framed scenes from the life of Christ 'from his conception to his ascension' were displayed in the 1630s.[106] In all these examples Christ's Passion played an important role, a tendency already noted in the choice of subjects for east windows.

Although he does not always specify the medium of the images, Dowsing's journal confirms that painted decoration and pictures were relatively common in newly-built 17th-century chapels in East Anglia, while in older buildings pre-Reformation painted work, both fixed and moveable, was often retained. We have seen him in Suffolk in 1644 ordering the removal of a picture of the Trinity from the medieval chapel at Little Wenham Hall, while at Lord Windsor's chapel at Tendring Hall, he destroyed 'nine superstitious pictures and a crucifix'. At the Waldegrave chapel at Smallbridge Hall, also in Suffolk, 'a picture of God the Father and divers other superstitious images' escaped destruction only when the chapel key could not be found.[107]

Sculpture

Free-standing sculpture was undoubtedly the most contentious medium. A vivid example of the controversy that could ensue occurred when, in 1615-16, James I commissioned major alterations in his chapel at Holyrood, and a contemporary account of the reaction makes it clear that it was the 'graven images' that caused most anger.[108] Few free-standing early 17th-century sculptures are recorded in private chapels but, since the destruction rate in the 1640s must have been high, they may well have been more widespread than is now imagined, and it is clear from Dowsing that crucifixes were still to be found. At the Charterhouse, by then a hospital and school, the refurbishment of the chapel by the Governors under Laud's guidance in the mid-1630s appears to have included the making of alabaster figures of Aaron and Moses which were painted and gilded by Bucket (fig. 5.45). They probably formed part of a more elaborate stone reredos since John Colt also supplied panels with figures of the twelve apostles in an elaborate frame together with seven more decorative panels dated 1637.[109] This is a rare example of sculpture being used to create a specifically Protestant item, in this case a sculptural version of the commandment board. The same cannot be said of the figures on the canopy of one of the family pews (usually known as the king's pew) at Rycote. Two unidentifiable, but reasonably convincingly 17th-century figures survive and, according to the guidebook, a wooden sculpture of the Virgin and Child was positioned on the central pedestal until 1833.[110] If the latter does indeed belong to the early 17th century (the canopy itself is thought to date to c.1625) they are a surprising addition to a Protestant interior.[111]

In general, the only frequently used sculptural forms classifiable as biblical were angels. At Chantemarle in 1618 there were '4 angells in the 4 corners of the Roofe'.[112] Angels were used in a similar way at Low Ham (Plate XVI), Rug (Plate XXIV) and probably Temple Newsam.[113] Here, it seems likely that the ceiling was decorated with at least four wooden angels and possibly eight; and mention is also made of stone angels' heads (some of which came from France), but their function is unclear. The inclusion of angels as part of the roof or ceiling

Fig. 5.45: Charterhouse, London: conjectural reconstruction of the commandment board by Malcolm Dickson. The alabaster figures of Aaron and Moses, painted and gilded by Rowland Bucket, probably formed part of a more elaborate stone reredos.

decoration is yet another example of the revival of decorative ideas used before the Reformation.

Painted Woodwork and Textiles

One of the most elusive aspects of the early 17th-century private chapel is the amount of colour provided by painted woodwork and textiles. At Hatfield, the overall effect of the lower chapel was much enhanced by its *trompe l'oeil* Ionic pilasters which were painted in blue and gilded. Numerous other entries in the Hatfield building accounts also refer to the paintwork (usually blue) and gilding, with perhaps the best surviving example of this type of small-scale, repetitive decoration being the frieze, probably by Bucket, which runs round the chapel at two levels (Plate XXI). Largely executed in blue and gold, its design incorporates winged cherubs' heads, flaming urns (often symbolising piety), and bibles/books – perhaps conveying a simple Protestant message of the importance of the Word.

Textiles not only provided rich textures and colour, but also often introduced biblical images. A number of houses, such as Bramshill, displayed tapestries in the main chapel, but their subjects are not known. The upper chapel at Hatfield was decorated with black hangings, hung in orange baize cases and embroidered with the prophets and patriarchs in coloured satins. A similar hanging, of David, was placed over the fireplace. Inventories often show that upper chapels at this period had particularly rich hangings, whilst in the lower chapels panelling or plainer textiles were used.[114] The rich effect of an upper chapel could be further enhanced by the way in which the furniture was upholstered to match the hangings.[115] This emphasis on the west end is one of the few areas of continuity with the Elizabethan period, but in the early 17th century textiles were used both to emphasise the communion table and the pulpit in the chapel proper, and to balance this concentration of colour at the west end.[116] As late as the 1650s, textiles were still focusing attention on the east end of some chapels. At Staunton Harold, the communion table is still covered by purple velvet with gold and silver trimmings and an embroidered frontal. The pulpit in the nave also retains its original cloth, and the effect would have been enhanced by the covers of the kneeling forms which are no longer *in situ* in the east end.

There are parallels with the pre-Reformation practice of using textiles and canopies to emphasise the east end. But there are also differences. First, it seems that there were neither wooden pulpits nor pulpit cloths in pre-Reformation chapels, where any area of emphasis was connected with sacramental worship (such as a secondary altar or font). Secondly, although post-Elizabethan communion tables certainly had associated textiles (as at Hatfield), there were few if any altar canopies, or cloths decorated with biblical images. A gilded canopy was, however, recorded at Magdalen College, Oxford, while St John's College, Cambridge, possessed a canopy painted with angels, and a frontal showing Christ 'taken from the cross and prepared for His sepulchre'.[117] Whether this is illustrative of a different approach in college chapels is difficult to say, given the small number of examples available.

What should be emphasised about the decorative schemes based on biblical images in high-church private chapels is that, in almost all cases and whatever the medium, the aim was to underline the significance of the Passion. In other words, they were a celebration of sacramental worship, a factor that fits well with early 17th-century developments in other areas of chapel design. The opportunity to develop large-scale, specifically Protestant, iconographic schemes emphasising the importance of the Word does not appear to have been taken up, and instead patrons turned to pre-Reformation ideas to help create rich decorative schemes that celebrated sacramental worship by depicting the family of the Church gathered as onlookers. This approach is particularly clear at Hatfield, where the importance of the communion table is emphasised by the great east window above it, while gathered round are the prophets on the window reveals, the disciples on the exteriors of the galleries, and (perhaps) patriarchs on the ceiling.

Such a scheme represents a comprehensive reversal of the ideas on decoration, with their emphasis on simplicity and austerity, that governed the design of the great majority of Elizabethan chapels.

Symbolism

One option for patrons who wished to avoid contentious biblical imagery and laying themselves open to accusations of idolatry was to use symbols to reflect the function of the chapel. This was an approach often favoured by provincial gentry. At Chantemarle, 'the inside is plastered white and fretted over with the Sun Moone, Starres, Cherubims, Doves & grapes, and pomegranates'.[118] The symbolic references to sacramental worship are clear (and we have seen that communion was celebrated in the chapel) but do not risk provoking controversy. Other chapels provide glimpses of this type of decoration.[119] A number mix symbolic decoration and biblical scenes: at Easton Lodge, the high-quality relief sculpture that decorated the bench ends complemented the life and Passion of Christ depicted in the glass of the east window. The general theme of their decoration appears to be the inevitability of death since symbols such as an hour-glass, a skull and crossed bones, a bell, and a crossed spade and axe (among others) are used (fig. 5.11).[120]

The practice of clouding was a form of symbolic decoration. The best surviving example in a private chapel is at Staunton Harold and, although the aisles and chancel were completed after the Restoration, the overall concept clearly belongs to the first half of the century (fig. 5.30). Clouding is, of course, a neutral subject, although the disturbed state of the clouds at the west end has led some commentators to identify the ceiling there as symbolising the Creation. The importance of the east cell is emphasised by the inclusion of a glory of cherubim singing the *Sanctus*, while over the west side of the chancel arch the controversial letters IHS are a reminder of Sir Robert Shirley's refusal to compromise with the Commonwealth authorities. Clouding appears to have been reasonably common, and examples dating from this period can still be found in parish churches. However, it was not limited to provincial parishes. Perhaps the most sophisticated example was once to be found on the ceiling of St Paul's, Covent Garden, which sported 'little angels and other things'.[121]

The chapel which best demonstrates the way in which symbols rather than biblical images could be used to create a complete and highly decorative scheme is Rug (Plate XXIV), built just a year after the chapel at Temple Newsam was created and which, apart from some 19th-century alterations and restoration, survives in a relatively complete state. The overall impression is of an extremely rich interior, but there are no biblical scenes, and the wall paintings still depend largely on the use of texts.[122] A factor here is the reliance on traditional medieval decorative forms such as those used on rood screens, and a comparison of the upper frieze with the decoration of surviving rood screens in the area shows a generic similarity, if not a direct match. To this is added symbols, some of which (grapes, lamb, pelican) are familiar, together with others whose meaning is now less easy to interpret. While Hatfield and Temple Newsam reflected pre-Reformation schemes through the choice and arrangement of biblical subject matter, at Rug the same idea of continuity is pursued through the use of vernacular symbols which, due to their relatively high survival rate after the Reformation, would have been familiar from local parish churches. Created at virtually the same time, Temple Newsam and Rug represent the two poles of the decorative spectrum. Temple Newsam used biblical characters and scenes to create an apparently co-ordinated scheme which centred round the sacrifice of Christ and the importance of the Eucharist, while the decoration at Rug, richer in terms of sheer volume, balances Christian symbols of salvation with reminders of the horrors that inevitably await the sinner at his death.

Other forms of decoration continued in use. Heraldry featured in the painted frieze at Lytes Cary (1631; Plate XXVI), the roof bosses at Higher Melcombe (by 1633), or the glass in the east window of the detached chapel at Groombridge Place in Kent (by 1635), and was often used on its own or in combination with other images. And texts continued as a standard part of chapel decoration as at Rug, and on commandment boards such as that at Rycote.

A Protestant Iconography?

An important question is whether the revival of interest in decorative schemes in the early 17th century saw the creation of a specifically Protestant iconography before much was swept away in the upheavals of the 1640s and 1650s. The commandment board, first introduced in the reign of Edward VI, provided quintessentially Protestant 'comely ornament', and Elizabethan schemes had comprised a clear and controlled Protestant statement. With the comparative freedom of the early years of the 17th century, does a new Protestant high-church decorative style emerge? Somewhat surprisingly, the answer is 'no': it is difficult to argue that the early 17th-century decorative schemes shared the same distinctive quality. This is due largely to their heavy dependence on pre-Reformation ideas. In general, they tended to borrow from those of the earlier period, albeit with adjustments to make the scheme palatable to the reformed religion, and there was little interest in developing the use of biblical scenes that reflected specifically Protestant ideas or ethics. In part, this must be because those who might have favoured a complete change of imagery in fact preferred no imagery at all – low-church or Puritan chapels like Steane, Bramhope and Littlecote have very little decoration and usually no imagery. The beautiful glass installed by Archbishop Abbot in the chapel of his Guildford hospital, or the sculptural version of the commandment board at the Charterhouse, showed how biblical images could highlight a specifically Protestant theme as opposed to emphasising sacramental worship if private patrons chose to take it up: the fact remains that none did.

6

AFTER THE RESTORATION:
'WE DESIGN'D A HANDSOME CHAPEL'

A patient, high-church strategy of influencing prominent figures at the exiled Stuart court in favour of Anglican ideas quickly paid off once Charles II was restored to the throne in 1660. By 1662, the Church of England and the episcopacy were fully restored, and by 1665 the Clarendon Code was in being to limit and control Puritan activities. It would seem that the scene was set for a return to the splendour of high-church worship celebrated in a rich and seemly setting. Many bishops set about restoring and beautifying their episcopal chapels, and college chapels, too, were renovated and redecorated.

On his appointment as Bishop of Durham in 1660, John Cosin, started work on restoring his palace and chapel at Bishop Auckland which had been roughly treated under the temporary ownership of the Puritan, Sir Arthur Hazelrig. A former friend of Laud and (before the Civil War) the beautifier of the chapel of Peterhouse College, Cambridge, Cosin intended his episcopal chapel to be a *bravura* statement designed to celebrate the re-established ascendancy of the

Fig. 6.1: Bishop Auckland, Durham: south facade of the chapel. It was created out of the old medieval great hall, and intended to set the standards for a revival of high Anglican splendour after the Interregnum.

150

Fig. 6.2: Bishop Auckland, Durham: chapel interior looking east by R. W. Billings (1813-74) after mid-19th-century restoration. Two elderly clerics pausing for thought before Bishop Cosin's tomb are dwarfed by the large proportions of his chapel. The quality of its craftsmanship presented a 'comely' and colourful setting for worship – factors that 19th-century alterations failed to replicate.

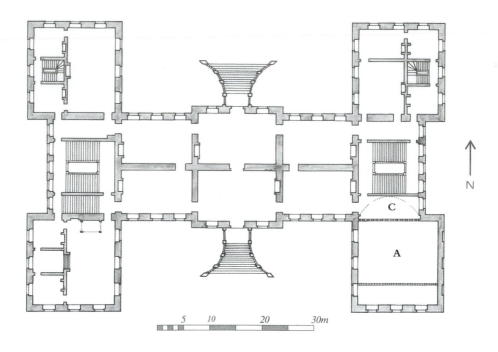

Fig. 6.3: Clarendon House, London: ground plan after Christian Eltester, possibly showing the main and basement levels of the integrated chapel simultaneously. C = the possible family (apsed) gallery, accessible from the ground floor.

Church of England, and to demonstrate the birth of a new Laudian age. Rather than rebuilding the old chapel, he created a much larger one out of the medieval great hall (fig. 6.1). This he did with great dash, but not before consulting other sources, sending his mason a 'patterne, which is taken from the best built plaine chappell in London'.[1] The difference between his chapel and earlier post-Reformation private chapels is striking: only Staunton Harold is in the same class. With its colourful interior, impressive size (84ft x 48ft) and high-quality craftsmanship, it certainly must have presented an impressive setting for worship. At the consecration service in 1665, Cosin's chaplain, George Davenport, made it clear that 'the sight and beauty of the chappell' was intended to persuade high-church Protestants to revive the splendour of the Anglican setting for worship (fig. 6.2), and to 'repair and beautify their own churches and chancells'.[2]

The Chapel in the House: important but not formative

Despite Cosin's urging, there is no evidence of a boom in private chapel building after the Restoration. When a patron did chose to provide a chapel, the

152

favoured position for the typical H-plan house was not at the heart of the house close to the hall, but in a pavilion. Given the denser, more concentrated building plans favoured in this period, it is logical that the most suitable place for the chapel would be in a corner where it would not disturb, or be disturbed by, the main circulation routes. As we have seen, Webb's unrealised plan for Belvoir (fig. 5.27) used this approach and his ideas, probably reflected to some extent in the house he eventually built for the Duke of Rutland, may well have helped set the standards for great houses after the Restoration.[3]

One of the earliest (and grandest) post-Restoration H-plan examples was Clarendon House in Piccadilly, London, begun in 1664 for the 1st Earl of Clarendon. A comparison between Christian Eltester's 1699 plan (fig. 6.3) with Webb's plan for Belvoir is instructive. The general approach is similar, with both houses dedicating a pavilion to the chapel.[4] But at Clarendon the detailed planning is very different. Instead of the careful subdivision of space providing separate areas and entrances to accommodate the hierarchical and practical niceties that characterised the Belvoir plan, sheer size appears to have been the driving force,

Fig. 6.4: Belton House, Lincolnshire: main floor plan. The servants' entrance to the main body of the integrated chapel in this H-plan house is at basement level.

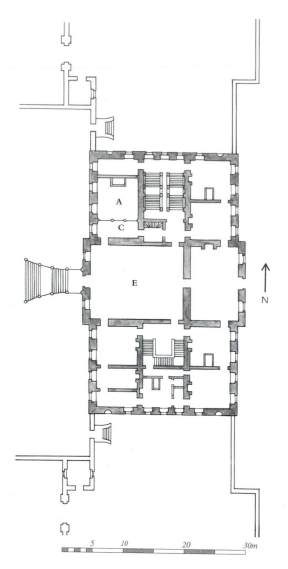

with an entire pavilion given over to the body of the chapel. However, Eltester's plan raises problems of interpretation at the (liturgical) west end. The accounts of Clarendon's architect, Roger Pratt, refer to a 'Passage Betwixt ye Chappell & Dining Roome', but this is not shown on the plan and, with the apsidal west end projecting into the main body of the house as far as the east stair, there was no room for it.[5] Moreover, it appears that the only entrances to the chapel were through this apsed area, but this would have entailed the entire household traipsing through what was almost certainly the family area. It is hard to believe that this would have been acceptable, and it is possible that Eltester's plan shows the main and basement levels of the chapel simultaneously, a method used in the plan for Burlington House (also in Piccadilly).[6] If so, the apsed area could be read as a family gallery and the only part of the chapel that could be accessed from the ground floor. Whatever the exact arrangement, the chapel was certainly large: measuring

Fig. 6.5: Horseheath Hall, Cambridgeshire: ground plan, main block (after Campbell). The chapel in this compact triple-pile house interrupted the circulation. Its liturgical east end consisted of an internal wall, with an awkward space beyond. C marks the chapel gallery on the floor above.

about 38ft x 50ft into the west gallery, it was easily the greatest space in the house. This may have been to accommodate a populous household or was, perhaps, simply an expression of aristocratic pride. Clarendon House was renowned for its splendour and extravagance, and the unusual focus on the west end leads one to suspect that piety was not the main factor.[7]

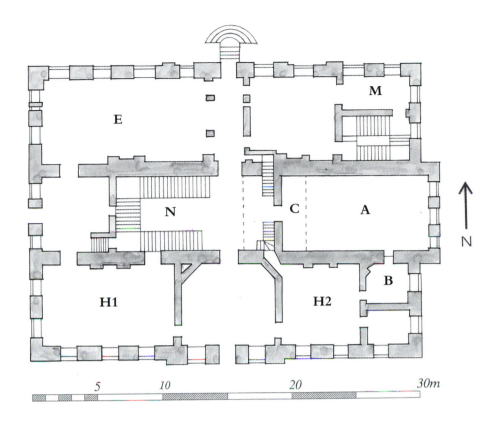

Fig. 6.6: Melton Constable, Norfolk: ground plan (based on the model at Gressinghall, after Alison Maguire). In this standard, triple-pile house, the chapel occupies an imposing, yet flexible, space that clearly affirms its importance within the overall plan. H1 = the great parlour, H2 = the little parlour.

At Burlington (begun *c.*1665), the same format, adapted for a smaller house with only vestigial pavilions, was followed.[8] Here the chapel spanned the basement and main storeys, providing a chapel gallery on the main floor, and access to the body of the chapel for the household at basement level.[9] This arrangement is also found, as we have seen, at Temple Newsam and in some Thorpe plans. Its use in a number of houses built after the Restoration was due to its success in integrating the levels of the chapel with the social groupings that it served. This is clearly demonstrated at Belton in Lincolnshire (1685-8), also an H-plan house (fig. 6.4), where the entrance to the main body of the chapel at basement level survives and demonstrates, by its complete lack of any architectural or decorative pretension, that it was intended for servants rather than family.

One H-plan house appears not to have used a pavilion to house the chapel. At Ragley Hall in Warwickshire (1679-83), two options were discussed.[10] Both

155

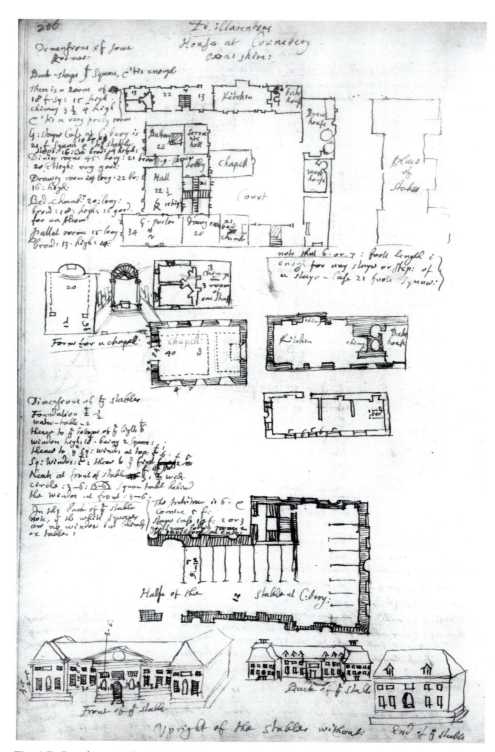

Fig. 6.7: Cornbury Park, Oxfordshire: a page from John Evelyn's notebook of 1664 showing the proposed site of the linked chapel at the heart of the house. His designs for the chapel layout are at left centre.

put the chapel at the centre of the house, next to the hall, while the pavilions were given over to apartments. In one proposal, the arrangement was strictly symmetrical with two staircases either side of the hall, one flanking the chapel and the other the library. The alternative was less symmetrical and had the chapel replacing one of the staircases next to the library. Despite a useful conjunction with the staircase had mezzanine spaces been required, no other contemporary H-plan house seems to have adopted this layout.

Double and triple-pile houses were popular plan types. At Horseheath (built by Pratt, 1663-5), the surviving documentation reveals clearly the difficulties of providing a chapel in a compact, triple-pile house (fig. 6.5). Unusually, the chapel was positioned immediately to one side of the hall on the entrance front, completely interrupting the circulation and leaving an awkwardly small one-bay space in the corner beyond.[11] Given the problems of this plan type, it is not surprising that many similar houses did not have chapels at all. However, both the model and the existing house at Melton Constable in Norfolk (begun in 1664; another triple-pile house) demonstrate that it was possible to provide a relatively magnificent chapel within this compact plan type. The model, which

Fig. 6.8: Cornbury Park, Oxfordshire: interior of the 'Wren' type chapel looking west, showing the west screen and the typically plain family gallery above.

Fig. 6.9: Cornbury Park, Oxfordshire: interior of the chapel looking east. With its single-cell design and the controlled splendour of its decoration and fittings, it set the standard for chapel interiors during the first three decades of the Restoration, and still typifies the ideal country house chapel.

survives and has not been altered, shows a triple-pile design with the single-height chapel and the great stair occupying the central range, together with a small room linking the great hall with the great parlour to keep the circulation route open.[12] The advantages of this arrangement are clear from the plan (fig. 6.6). It allows for a chapel which is second only to the great hall in size and easily

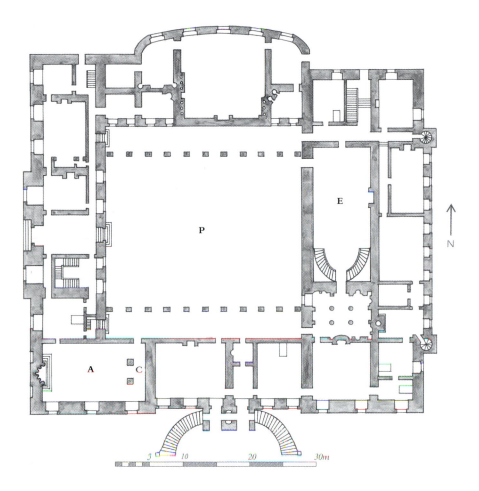

Fig. 6.10: Chatsworth, Derbyshire: ground plan before the 6th Duke's 19th-century reconstruction. The chapel combines practicality with impressive size. There was originally an Elizabethan tower on the southern angle of the west front.

accessible, and yet removed from main circulation routes; the mezzanine level chapel gallery can be reached from both the hall and the little parlour; and there is a connection between the chapel and the closet east of the little parlour, as well as direct access from Sir Jacob Astley's closet directly above the chapel gallery. The result is an imposing yet flexible space that clearly affirms the importance of the chapel within the overall plan. As built, some modifications were made and later alterations to the chapel spaces have slightly obscured the original intention, but it remains an imposing and well-manipulated space.

Some older houses had new chapels incorporated or added. They included Ham House in Surrey (1673–5) and Arbury (c.1678), but one of the earliest was Cornbury Park in Oxfordshire (1666–7). An irregular, Tudor house updated in

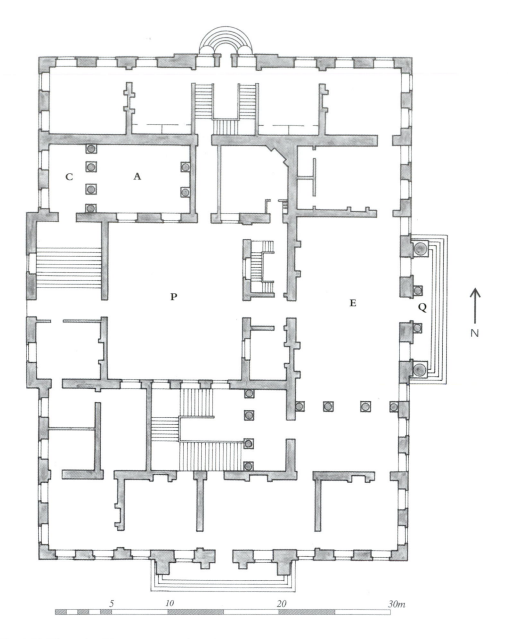

Fig. 6.11: Thoresby House, Nottinghamshire: ground plan (after Campbell). A not particularly skilful plan, and one that was not influential, but perhaps the first to utilise baroque principles in planning the approach to the upper chapel.

the early 17th century, it had no chapel when it was granted to the future Lord Clarendon in 1661. In October 1664, two years before work was finished at Clarendon House and attention switched to Cornbury, Clarendon visited the site with his son, Lord Cornbury, and John Evelyn who recorded in his diary that 'We design'd a handsom Chapell that was yet wanting'.[13] His record shows considerable understanding of the practical needs of a chapel. Centred on the main entrance axis, it was to be at the heart of the house, close to the hall, the stairs and the servants' hall and yet separated from the bustle of daily life by a spacious lobby (fig. 6.7). Access was easy from both high and low ends of the house, and the provision of a chapel gallery with a separate entrance ensured that social hierarchies were maintained. The ideas set down by Evelyn were not followed exactly, and it is not possible to be certain about the arrangements as built, but the chapel was constructed on the site he outlined. That this discussion occurred at such an early stage suggests that some importance was attached to the design of the chapel and its position in the overall plan.

Two important courtyard plan houses, Chatsworth (1687-91) and Thoresby House in Nottinghamshire (1683-7), were undergoing major renovation during this period. Both show how a large and imposing chapel could be provided within an old-fashioned plan type. In spite of the piecemeal development of late 17th-century Chatsworth, the chapel there combines practicality with impressive size (fig. 6.10). Spanning two floors, there were four entrances: one at the (liturgical) east end, two at the west end, and the fourth giving the family access to the chapel gallery. Fenestration too is matched with the needs of the chapel. The lack of an east window is explained by the presence of an Elizabethan tower on the southern angle of the west front, which was not removed until some years later, but more significant is that the basement windows were not carried across the western end of the south facade with three blind windows being incorporated instead. In the context of the chapel, proper windows would obviously have been inappropriate, and priority was given to its needs in preference to the pursuit of exact symmetry.

Thoresby followed an idiosyncratic and not particularly skilful plan which was presumably conditioned by the existence of an earlier house (fig. 6.11).[14] Although not influential, it is important as a demonstration of one way in which overall planning could enhance the importance of the chapel. Here, perhaps for the first time, truly baroque principles were applied to the planning of the approach to the chapel gallery. The access route lay across the courtyard on the main axis of the house. A vestibule, accessible from both the exterior and the courtyard, gave on to a flight of ten stairs, each about 20ft wide (the same width as the chapel itself), which led only to a mezzanine level chapel gallery, presumably for the family. The arrangement has all the hallmarks of a processional route, and it confers a new importance on the chapel approach. It is difficult to see how it fulfilled any religious purpose. Although it is the only contemporary example of this planning type, it reflects, as we shall see, the somewhat worldly developments found in other areas of chapel design in the last two decades of the century.

Not only was there no marked revival in chapel building after the Restoration, but there was also a certain ambivalence towards chapel planning in that no sustained attempt was made to create chapels of high status that would exert a formative influence on the overall plan. While some patrons, particularly aristocratic ones, tended to see the positioning of the chapel as an important element of the overall design, most did not accord it a controlling influence. Thoresby apart, in terms of their planning and status nothing could begin to rival chapels such as that thought to have been proposed by Thorpe in 1621 for Burley-on-the-Hill (fig. 5.6).

The Exterior Architecture: Purposefully Understated

Externally, Bishop Cosin's chapel challenged clergy and laity to take advantage of the new, high-church ascendancy to build chapels celebrating a return to the 'beauty of holiness' (fig. 6.1). He added a clerestory level, and elaborately refaced the most prominent facade, the south, in ashlar with his bishop's fret, a diamond, appearing emphatically on every other stone above the stringcourse.[15] His work contained a mixture of reworked medieval elements, such as the pointed windows of the lower level, and a 17th-century *mélange* of Gothic and Classical forms, as in the large round-headed clerestory windows. And there was a rich scattering of battlements, pinnacles (each surmounted by a cross) and finials, as well as a coat of arms set into a 'pediment' over the east window.

But this highly individual design had no close followers among private patrons. It was in fact rare for integral country house chapels to have any exterior characteristics at all due, at least in part, to the architectural fashion for strict symmetry and a simple rectangular shape. The liturgical east end of the chapel was usually given no importance in terms of its windows. At Horseheath, it was an internal wall, and at Belton the two lower windows are blind, while the upper two, partially blocked by the reredos, play a negligible part in the overall effect. Even at Chatsworth where, as we shall see, the grandiose decoration of the interior reflects its high status, the chapel remains (apart from the blind basement windows) anonymous from the outside. However, the example of Melton Constable shows that it was

Fig. 6.12: Berwick House, Shropshire: north facade of the chapel. A modest rectangular building with simple mullion and transom windows.

Fig. 6.13: Woodhey Hall, Cheshire: the formerly linked chapel from the south-east. The sophisticated simplicity of this rectangular brick box indicates the Puritan sympathies of its patron.

possible to emphasise the position of the chapel in a relatively standard triple-pile house while largely following the prevailing architectural fashion (Plate XXVIII). The three central bays of the lower two storeys of the east facade project forward, and the three-arched chapel windows interrupt the standard fenestration pattern. These are set close together, and the slightly larger central opening has a winged cherub as a keystone, while those of the smaller windows have plain corbels. But Melton Constable was the house of a relatively unimportant provincial patron. Throughout the second half of the century, major houses, such as Chatsworth and Belton, as well as the most prominent of London ones, Clarendon House, and its slightly later near neighbour, Burlington House, do not appear to have used any form of exterior differentiation.[16]

As usual, it is in detached chapels and those only loosely linked to existing houses that there is a greater interest in architectural forms. Here the Classical style became the accepted architectural language, supplanting the earlier preference for pre-

Fig. 6.14: Woodhey Hall, Cheshire: interior of the chapel looking west. The plain gallery contained fireplaces across the corners

Fig. 6.15: Locko Park, Derbyshire: the linked chapel from the south-east. "Another rectangular box". Part of the adjoining 18th-century house can be seen on the right.

Reformation forms. One of the earliest examples was at Cornbury. Clarendon was no stranger to architectural magnificence, but his chapel, linked to the house, is a simple rectangular building of ashlar with semi-circular windows on the north and south elevations. The east end is very plain, decorated only with three blind windows, and lacking the apse suggested by Evelyn. It gives no hint of the richness and quality within.

At Berwick House in Shropshire (1672; fig. 6.12), after discounting the tower, the south entrance porch and the east end with its transepts, all of which are later additions, the chapel remains a modest rectangular building with plain mullioned and transomed windows, closer to early 17th-century forms than those of the 1670s. A more sophisticated simplicity is achieved at Woodhey Hall in Cheshire (1697-9), a rectangular brick box enlivened only by quoins (fig. 6.13). Here the low-church affiliation of the patron, Lady Wilbraham, is indicated by the regularity of the large but straightforward round-headed windows which continue in an uninterrupted rhythm round three sides of the building. The only break is at the west end where small circular windows (to light the chapel gallery) are set above entrance doors. Like the north and south facades, the east end has two regular windows, rather than the more traditional single, centralised window used in conjunction with a communion table. At the west end a Classical *loggia*, thought to have belonged to the demolished Elizabethan house, is reused to give access to the chapel gallery.

Even at Locko Park in Derbyshire (1669-73), where the linked chapel (added to a vanished earlier house) has one of the most magnificent ceilings to survive

Fig. 6.16: Bretby Hall, Derbyshire: detail of Knyff and Kip view of *c*.1708 from *Britannia Illustrata*. The linked chapel occupied the projecting right-hand wing. It is the only confirmed example of an apsidal private chapel at this time, and was architecturally the grandest late 17th-century chapel.

from this date (Plate XXVII), the external character is reticent (fig. 6.15). It is another rectangular box with a slightly pitched roof surrounded by a parapet with an inscription. The parapet has ball finials, except at the centre of the east end where there is a cross, and at the west end where there is a simple arch within which a bell is suspended. The chapel is lit by two large round-headed windows with small, undecorated keystones on the south facade, and by a similar but smaller central window in the east facade surmounted by a simple architrave centred on the keystone. The most elaborate architectural feature is the west front, where the Doric entablature above a simple round-headed door is surmounted by a large segmental pediment containing a coat of arms. There is no emphasis on the east end and no figurative sculpture.

Relatively few private chapels were built in the last fifteen years of the century, but two examples from the 1690s illustrate that the architectural language of the chapel could become grander and more assertive. The linked chapel at Bretby Hall in Derbyshire, (demolished towards the end of the 18th century), is well illustrated in a Leonard Knyff view of *c*.1708 (fig. 6.16), and many of the details shown are documented in 18th-century descriptions.[17] The U-shaped house was

Fig. 6.17: Culverthorpe Hall, Lincolnshire: the chapel portico. This sadly dilapidated, detached building in the woods appears to have been the first Classical temple-style private chapel to be built outside London.

completed in 1639 and updated later in the century by the French architect Louis le Vau. The chapel, attributed to William Talman, was added to the east side of the house in 1696 and, although this was some time after Le Vau's death, it is reminiscent of his style. Described shortly after its destruction as by a 'Grecian' architect and 'very light and handsome', it was three, or possibly four, bays long, and terminated in an apsidal east end.[18] This form, with its historical resonances, might be expected to appeal to high-church patrons, but it is the only confirmed example of an apsidal private chapel at this time. According to the

Fig. 6.18: Gwydir Castle, Caernarvonshire: the detached chapel from the north-east. Gothic in style, but with the reticence of a Classical chapel.

diarist and traveller Celia Fiennes, there was a plain, oval east window of clouded glass over the altar.[19] Knyff shows the chapel (somewhat surprisingly) as being the same height as the main range and, if correct, it must indeed have been a magnificent building. The architectural articulation consisted of coupled, possibly giant, columns on a high basement, surmounted by a balustrade and finials which reflected the rhythm of the order – architecturally, it was the grandest chapel of the period.

One other Classical chapel worthy of note is the sadly dilapidated, detached building standing in the woods at Culverthorpe Hall in Lincolnshire (fig. 6.17).[20] Although the chapel does not appear to have been fitted out until 1702, it is first mentioned in correspondence as early as 1685, when it is implied that it would act as a chapel of ease to which others, in addition to the patron Sir John Newton, would make a financial contribution. It is clear from further references that by 1690 work on it was well advanced. It is highly likely that the portico was conceived and built along with the body of the chapel. This is important because Culverthorpe appears to have been the first Classical temple-style private chapel to be built outside London, and as such is a landmark of some importance in the history of chapel design. The form proposed by Inigo Jones for St Paul's, Covent Garden in the 1630s (itself consecrated as a chapel of ease), and seemingly so suitable for detached chapels, appears to have taken nearly fifty years to catch on in the provinces.

Except for Culverthorpe and Bretby, there does not seem to have been much interest in creating grandiose Classical chapel exteriors. Although patrons included men of such distinction as Lord Clarendon and the 4th Earl of Devonshire, there is little evidence that the exterior appearance of the private chapel was seen as a

Fig. 6.19: Compton Wynyates II, Warwickshire: the (relatively restrained) south facade of the detached chapel. Despite the angled corner buttresses, there is a rudimentary attempt to give the building a semblance of Classical articulation (note the 'Classical' pilasters and semi-circular doorway). Overall, a deliberately archaic form could have been chosen to commemorate the earlier chapel largely destroyed in the Civil War.

Fig. 6.20: Compton Wynyates II, Warwickshire: the simple interior looking east from the pulpit.

suitable area for display, and the possibilities inherent in the Classical language were for the most part not exploited.

There were of course exceptions to the use of a purely Classical style. The detached chapel at Gwydir Castle in North Wales (1673-4) used medieval forms exclusively. Gwydir was the only wholly new

Fig. 6.21: Burford Priory, Oxfordshire: the linked chapel from the liturgical south-west. Its external sculptural decoration is rivalled only by that of Staunton Harold. The combination of motifs from the Classical and pre-Reformation traditions is carried out with assurance and a refined eccentricity. The balustraded walkway to the upper chapel is on the left.

chapel using the Gothic style, but displayed the same external reticence seen in most Classical chapels (fig. 6.18). Rather than copying Cosin's carved frets and large clerestory windows and pinnacles, this is a simple, rectangular building with a cross at the east apex and a bellcote at the west end. The windows are mullioned with square or shallow-arched heads, while the larger east window is pointed and has panel tracery. There are no other external decorative elements, and the chapel is very similar to many of the earlier 17th-century 'medieval' style examples.

Three chapels that mix both Classical and pre-Reformation features are less reticent in their architectural character. Compton Wynyates II (1665–6), and Burford

Fig. 6.22: Burford Priory, Oxfordshire: chapel interior, looking to the liturgical west, showing the 'two box' gallery. It is difficult to understand why this awkward form was adopted, unless it was to facilitate segregation of the sexes, or the result of later changes.

Priory in Oxfordshire (1660-2), are close in date but demonstrate very clearly the wide range of choices available to the patron, while the later Tabley (1674-8) has a somewhat provincial feel. Compton Wynyates II (fig. 6.19) is a rectangular building occupying the site of the pre-Reformation chapel which had been destroyed – with the possible exception of the west tower – during the Civil War. The windows of the north and south facades are rectangular with four cusped lights, while the two east windows (each centred on an aisle) have shallow arches and simple tracery. Despite the angled corner buttresses, there is a rudimentary attempt to give the building a semblance of Classical articulation. Thin pilaster strips with diamond-shaped decorations in place of corbels meet a simple stringcourse, creating an approximation of an entablature. The door is similarly idiosyncratic, rusticated and with a semi-circular arch but also with a hood moulding that ends in diamond-shaped stops. Below them are strange, flat, scrollwork decorations.

In spite of the oddity of the detail, Compton Wynyates II is relatively restrained, a quality which cannot be said of Burford, the most idiosyncratic of private chapel exteriors (fig. 6.21). Built of stone for Sir William Lenthall, the rectangular building is attached to the house by a covered passage which also provides an open, balustraded first-floor walkway to the chapel gallery. A high parapet,

Fig. 6.23: Burford Priory, Oxfordshire: detail of a burning bush over the entrance, possibly symbolising the Nativity or the Virgin Mary. This, and the gesturing angels on either side, are most visible to those leaving the chapel.

Fig. 6.24: Tabley Hall, Cheshire: the detached chapel from the north-west (the tower is a later addition). An inventive mix of Classical and Gothic, but with a provincial feel and showing only a rudimentary grasp of the finer points of architectural articulation. The sole sculptural decoration is above the entrance: an inscription surmounted by a winged cherub set below a pediment.

boasting pinnacles and two highly decorative pediments oddly separated from windows below the entablature, conceals part of the steeply pitched roof. The shaped gables are also surmounted by (larger) pinnacles but, while the liturgical east end, window apart, is plain, the liturgical west end has two doors. At first-floor level, the pedimented entrance has a flamboyant royal coat of arms balanced on the apex of the pediment, and over the lower entrance are the Lenthall arms in a cartouche of cornucopias, surmounted by birds. The whole building is sparsely articulated, with composite pilasters placed at wide intervals supporting an entablature which in some places doubles as a window architrave. But it is the windows that give the chapel its extraordinary quality. The liturgical east window, set in a square frame, has three main lights with radiating lights within a semi–circle above. On the sides, towards the liturgical west end, there are large pointed windows with thick curvilinear tracery set in rectangular frames, while nearer the liturgical east end, square frames surround rose windows. The latter have no figurative decoration, but the spandrels of the two pointed windows are decorated with, on the liturgical north, a scaly dragon facing a serpent with a forked tongue and to the liturgical south, a winged creature, possibly a harpy, facing an archer with his bow drawn. Although there is no direct connection between these features and the more primitive decoration on the walls and benches at Rug, the general similarity of the subject matter is striking, and it is possible that both were based on

Fig. 6.25: Tabley Hall, Cheshire: detail of the family pew occupying the north wall of the west end. A gallery above was used by singers.

medieval sources. Burford is rivalled only by Staunton Harold in the amount of exterior sculptural decoration. Although decorative forms were used by the latter in a very different and often more conventional way, the two buildings share something of the same *élan*. This is perhaps incongruous in the case of Burford, whose patron summed up his career (as a lukewarm Roundhead and unconvincing convert to the Royalist cause) in the words '*vermis sum*' ('I am a worm') on his tombstone.

The detached chapel at Tabley (fig. 6.24) is nearly twenty years later than Burford. The exterior gives the impression of a more rudimentary grasp of the finer points of architectural articulation. Similar to Compton Wynyates II in form, with a (later) tower set at the west end of a rectangular building, Tabley shares with Burford the use of shaped gables, though here the somewhat clumsy curves lack the refined eccentricity of the latter. While most of the windows are mullioned and transomed with straight hood-mouldings, the large east window has a flattened arch profile into which the arched lights of the highest level are awkwardly fitted. Where they become regular, they differ little from those at Hatfield some sixty years earlier. Apart from the window, the east end is completely undecorated, and it is only above the north entrance that there is any sculptural decoration – an inscription surmounted by a large winged cherub set below a pediment.

All three chapels combine Classical and pre-Reformation motifs. While perhaps more inventive than their purely Classical counterparts, only at Burford is the handling of the detail carried out with assurance, and this is more likely to be connected with the style of a local school of craftsmen (who may well also have worked on the chapel at Brasenose College, Oxford, and a number of secular buildings) than with any particular specification by the patron. As always, it is tempting to try to relate the use of a particular style to a specific religious affiliation, but there is again little evidence that this would prove fruitful. The most that can be said is that a deliberately archaic form could have been chosen for Compton Wynyates II to commemorate the earlier destroyed chapel.

What emerges very strongly across the stylistic variations is the lack of architectural emphasis on the east end, not just in the chapels of a low-church patron such as Lady Wilbraham at Woodhey. The number of chapels with no centralised east window is surprisingly large. That there were so many blank, or nearly blank, east walls is particularly arresting in a period when high-church experimentation with architectural forms might have been expected. Although architectural fashion may play some part, it does not (as Melton Constable demonstrates) provide a complete explanation. Another factor could have been a difficulty in obtaining stained and painted glass (discussed further below). Tabley and Gwydir had 'traditional' large east windows, and we know that at Gwydir painted glass was intended but could not be obtained. Perhaps the clouded glass observed at Bretby by Fiennes was a response to this problem. But in general, it would seem that while patrons, irrespective of their religious beliefs, increasingly favoured Classical styles, chapel exteriors, with only a very few exceptions, remained surprisingly understated. In terms of external architecture, Bishop Cosin's call for beautification went unanswered.

Peripheral Spaces: Predominance of the West End Gallery

The variety of peripheral rooms and spaces connected with the chapel in earlier times declined markedly, and uniformity was undoubtedly a major post-Restoration characteristic. Although it was not quite as all-pervasive as surviving examples imply, by the 1660s a certain regularity and relative lack of inventiveness had set in. Some chapels, such as at Locko and Compton Wynyates II, have no special arrangements for the family at all, though the latter may not be typical given the continued existence of the chapel in the house. And some galleries, especially those in detached chapels where there could be no direct entry from

Fig. 6.26: Petworth House, West Sussex: detail of the altar rail. Ornate rails such as these were designed to enhance the status of the altar.

the house, were not designed for use by the family. At Tabley, where the gallery was used by singers, the family occupied two distinctive pews at the west end of the lower level (fig. 6.25). This arrangement also occurred in some single-storey chapels, as at Arbury and Ham where, the installation of a gallery or mezzanine level being impractical, the patrons sat at the west end. On the other hand, following the late 17th-century reconstruction at Rycote, the family forsook their pews in the western cell and moved into the eastern cell.[21]

A few chapels were equipped with family closets to facilitate segregation of the sexes, such as those at Bretby, Durdans in Surrey, and Melton Constable.[22] But the great majority of integrated or linked household chapels had an upper gallery for family members at the west end, usually accessible from the first floor – for example at Cornbury, Belton, Chatsworth, Petworth and (though now detached) Woodhey, and no side or other peripheral spaces. In general, the upper galleries were relatively plain as at Cornbury (fig. 6.8) and Woodhey (fig. 6.14), with the latter possessing a central entrance and fireplaces across the western corners. An unusual feature at Woodhey is the benches along the west walls, behind which are cane screens separating off more space. Whether these discreet rear galleries were for servants, or for women who wished to remain anonymous, is not known. The gallery at Burford consists of two boxes flanking a much narrower entrance area (fig. 6.22). The result is that very little space is available, and it is difficult to understand why this awkward form was adopted, raising the possibility that it was to allow a degree of segregation, or the result of later changes. The arrangement at Burford requires the patron to enter the body of the chapel by returning to the house along the open-air first-floor walkway, and then making his way back via the ground-floor passage. No other linked chapel provides quite such a tortuous route, but the planning of both Belton and Chatsworth suggest that direct access from the family gallery to the main body was considered unnecessary.

Fig. 6.27: Petworth House, West Sussex: the chapel interior is dominated by the 'Proud Duke's' gallery at the west end. Complete with curtains held by tasselled chords, it resembles nothing so much as a box at the opera.

Fittings: 'a mere spacious, oblong room, fitted up for the purpose of devotion'

The fittings of Bishop Cosin's chapel worked with the decorative scheme to form a clearly designated chancel, and the result is second to none in its ornate complexity. However, perhaps due in part to the sheer size of his chapel (fig. 6.2), here too his example appears to have had little influence on the patrons of private chapels, and a formula based on dignified, solid and restrained fittings, loosely similar to those in college chapels, began to emerge.

The diversity of the first half of the century did not disappear immediately. The simplicity of the fittings at Compton Wynyates II (fig. 6.20) contrasts with the controlled splendour at Cornbury (fig. 6.9), but both shared the single-cell arrangement which was to dominate chapel design until the end of the century. The rejection both of the two-centred arrangement so popular before the Restoration, and of an integrated narthex area, effectively signalled the end of a major role for the **screen**. Chancel screens became redundant in post-Restoration chapels, and only Cornbury and Tabley have west screens – the latter being the last to feature in a private chapel in the 17th century.

Pulpits continued to be more or less essential equipment. Exceptions were Ham and Chatsworth, but Chatsworth had no fittings at all, while at Ham it appears that two lecterns were used instead. Elsewhere, the location of the pulpit

Fig. 6.28: Rycote Park, Oxfordshire: the richly architectural 1682 reredos obscures much of the chapel east window. Its high level of craftsmanship is typical of the period.

continued to reflect the liturgical priorities of the patron. Those with Puritan leanings tended to favour the central east end position as at Woodhey, where there was no communion table – perhaps because the formidable Lady Wilbraham and her household used the local parish church on Sundays. At Compton Wynyates II, the communion table is placed at the centre of the east end, but the pulpit in the centre of the south wall exerts an equally dominating presence, commanding the box-pews in front of it. At Cornbury and Tabley, the pulpit, though clearly an important part of the fittings, takes second place to the communion table. The positioning of the pulpit appears to be relatively flexible. At Tabley, Compton Wynyates II and Petworth, the south side is preferred while at Cornbury it is on the north. A Chaplain's **desk** or reading pew continued to be used and was usually associated with the pulpit: either opposite it (Cornbury and probably Arbury) or next to it (Compton Wynyates II and Tabley). In general they were less obtrusive than pulpits, but some (as at Arbury) may have had sounding boards.

Communion tables and the area associated with them became more dignified. Particularly noticeable is the increased popularity of communion rails which, in the early 17th century, had been comparatively rare. The post-1660 alterations at Red House focused on this aspect, while at Rycote considerable alterations took place in the 1680s at the east end, only some fifty years after the

176

Fig. 6.29: Pembroke College, Cambridge: the interior looking east. Its 'Wrenian' formula of plain, rectangular box with refined and seemly decoration set the standard for country house chapel design. The chapel was extended and the chancel arch added in 1880.

Fig. 6.30: Pembroke College, Cambridge: the interior looking west. The decoration avoided biblical imagery, and the ceiling would not have appeared out of place in a saloon. The gallery, designed to hold an organ, was added when the shell of the building was complete, and there has been debate about whether or not it formed part of Wren's original plan.

refit of the medieval chapel. Here the provision of steps, rails, and a large reredos was clearly designed to enhance the status of the communion table, and to ensure that it could not be moved into the centre of the eastern cell. In some cases, as at Petworth, the rails are extremely ornate (fig. 6.26), serving perhaps to divert at least some attention away from the 'Proud Duke's' west end gallery (fig. 6.27).

The stained glass favoured in the early 17th century as the focal point of the east end tended to be replaced by high-quality fittings. **Reredoses,** in particular, appear to have taken over from the east window as the main focus above the communion table, and simple commandment boards often (but not always) gave way to magnificent displays of sumptuous craftsmanship. The crested panelling across the windowless east wall at Cornbury (fig. 6.9) provides a good example of this new use of highly-crafted and dignified fittings early in the post-Restoration period. Twenty years later, the reredos at Belton (Plate XXIX) dominated the east end, and at Petworth, although the earlier east window with its heraldic glass was retained, the panelling behind the altar represents the decorative culmination of the painted and gilded woodwork which covers the north and south sides of the chapel. At Rycote, the earlier and much smaller reredos would have fitted into the space above the communion table and below the east window, but its 1682 replacement obscures about a third of the latter (fig. 6.28). The use of fittings to increase the richness of the east end reached its apogee with the great marble and alabaster reredos installed against the (windowless) liturgical east wall at Chatsworth (1687-91; Plate XXXI).

The arrangement of **seating** was relatively uncomplicated. In family galleries, it was still usual to rely on upholstered seating rather than benches or pews (as at Chatsworth and Belton, and probably Petworth and Burford). Downstairs, in most surviving examples it was arranged college-style. This is a very distinct change. Before the Restoration the only examples of private chapels with college-style seating appear to have been at Knole, and at Red House where Slingsby remarks in his diary that such seats were used.[23] It is difficult to identify why there was such a definitive change. It may be that this type of arrangement was seen as a way of concentrating attention on the east end, with the communion table terminating an uncluttered vista, but it is also possible that it facilitated the provision of certain types of singing. Alternatively, it could simply be that college-style seating became fashionable, due to the lead given by the many college chapels built in the early 17th century. Sir Peter Leycester, for example, modelled Tabley on his old Oxford college chapel, Brasenose.[24]

Another possibility is that the arrangement was related to the wish to segregate the sexes, which is well documented during this period. The traveller, collector and cleric Sir George Wheler advocated 'strict separation' in the parish church, but suggested that in a domestic context it was sufficient 'that men be ranged on the one side of the chapel, or room, and the women on the other'.[25] In an aisled chapel such as Low Ham, college-style seating was obviously impossible and the arrangements could be somewhat haphazard, but elsewhere, as at Arbury where seating was college-style, it could perhaps provide for a simpler and tidier division of the sexes.[26] At Tabley, the conventional system of allocating the south side to women was followed at least in respect of what were called the 'tenants' benches', although there is nothing to indicate how the seating for other members of the congregation was arranged. In some chapels, the patron's immediate family and friends were accommodated by sex in separate closets.[27] However, it is difficult to see how segregation of family members could have been achieved in west end gallery type chapels such as those at Cornbury, Belton and Chatsworth.

Two chapels have very few fittings. At Burford, because of the parlous state of the chapel before its restoration early in the 20th century, it would be unwise to attach too much importance to the omission of pulpit, reading pew, and seating. Chatsworth is altogether more puzzling (Plate XXXI). There was a pulpit in the chapel at Elizabethan Chatsworth but, for about a hundred years from its Baroque recreation in the 1690s, it had no pulpit and, as is still the case, no fitted seating.

Compared with the practical style of the first half of the century, the hallmark of most fittings after the Restoration is their high quality, and restrained and dignified yet opulent design. Often they were the work of master craftsmen rather than of estate workers. However, the abandonment of the chancel screen and almost universal adoption of the single-cell chapel space contrasts sharply with the earlier diversity and ingenuity. The similarity of many chapels is notable, particularly the way in which they used fittings to articulate the interior space. Perhaps this is not surprising. A small but influential group of people were involved in the design of two seminal chapels early in the period. As we have seen, Clarendon was discussing the form of his proposed chapel at Cornbury with Evelyn in 1664. At about the same time (1663-5), at the request of his uncle Matthew Wren, Bishop of Ely, Christopher Wren was building a chapel at Pembroke College, Cambridge, in the form of a plain rectangular box (fig. 6.29). All this is well known, but what is less often remarked upon in this context is that at this time Clarendon's secretary was none other than Bishop Wren's son (also Matthew). Since the design of Cornbury and Pembroke had been discussed by some of the most influential minds of the time, the subsequent popularity of the 'Pembroke option', with its near-formulaic approach to the handling of fittings, should not come as a surprise.[28] It is not fanciful to see these two chapels (and perhaps also that at Clarendon House) as standing at the head of a long line of 'mere spacious, oblong' rooms 'fitted up for the purpose of devotion', often with a gallery for the family at the west end.[29]

Decoration in the 1660s and 1670s: 'seemly beauty'

An air of opulence is created in Bishop Cosin's chapel by the combination of varied media, the use of colour in the ceiling and east end and, in particular, the rich and complex woodwork. Coloured glass was also used, but only a small amount (depicting Cosin's fret in blue on a white ground) survives in the west end. The clearly designated chancel was emphasised by the ceiling decoration. In the nave (Plate XXX), the ceiling panels alternated Cosin's fret with his coat of arms and bishop's mitres, but at the east end, the rhythm of the design altered, as did the colour scheme, a factor that later restorations have not taken into account. The climax was the area around the communion table which was destroyed during 19th-century alterations. A *trompe l'oeil* Classically-articulated chancel area was formed in the easternmost bay. Over the altar, the text '*Laudate Deum in decore sancto*' was inscribed in gold on the blue frieze, and on either side '*Sancta sanctis*' and '*Sursum corda*'. This colourful chapel did not continue the emphasis on biblical scenes found in many early 17th-century chapels. Only one biblical image is recorded: a tapestry showing the meeting of Solomon and the Queen of Sheba (often an Old Testament ante-type for the Adoration of the Magi), which hung below the east window and above the communion table. Whether this avoidance of images was intentional, or to some extent due to difficulties in finding painters skilled in the depiction of biblical scenes, is difficult to say.

Fig. 6.31: Magdalen College, Oxford: 1698 engraving of the east end of the chapel by M. Burghers. Isaac Fuller's Resurrection above the altar canopy and Richard Greenbury's hanging in grisaille of the Last Supper (barely distinguishable beneath) combined with fittings and architectural features to create perhaps one of the first Baroque displays in a religious context in England.

The decorative scheme of another early statement of the renewed power of high-church Anglicans, the Pembroke option, provided an alternative to Cosin. The decoration at Pembroke College avoided biblical imagery entirely, and the motifs had much in common with domestic interiors of the period. The rich plaster decoration of the ceiling features the standard fruit, foliage, garlands and architectural enrichments (fig. 6.30). Just as the Bishop Auckland ceiling concentrated on heraldry and the insignia of office (suitable decoration for the great hall that the chapel once was), so that at Pembroke would not have appeared out of place in a saloon. Although the two chapels appear very different, they are united in the use of well-crafted decoration that was controlled, ordered and, above all, seemly. Both created by high-church bishops, they demonstrated two possibilities open to post-Restoration Laudian patrons.

There was, however, a third possible approach which was adopted at three Oxford colleges – Magdalen, All Souls, and Wadham. At Magdalen, the chapel had suffered damage during the Civil War, probably including the destruction of much, if not all, of Greenbury's east end. However, in 1664 Evelyn noted a Last Supper 'on blue cloth in *chiara oscuro*' by Greenbury at the east end. This could indicate that part of his original work survived the interregnum – it would have been easy to remove and store – or that he produced a new hanging to go below the altar canopy. By the same date, Isaac Fuller had painted a Resurrection in the area above the canopy.[30] This is an important example of an early attempt to revive large scale wall painting and recreate the spirit of the pre-Civil War east end with its colourful use of images. The two paintings, captured by Michael Burghers in his engraving of 1698 (fig. 6.31), were designed to relate to the position of the altar and its canopy. The ensemble created what must have been one of the first Baroque displays in a religious context, uniting paintings, fittings and architectural features into a convincing whole.

At All Souls, a similar scheme was also begun soon after the Restoration. Again Fuller was involved, producing a painting of the Resurrection and Last Judgement which was in place by 1664 – when Evelyn described it as the 'largest piece of fresco painting … in England'.[31] The scheme included painting the boarded ceiling (of which fragments survive, but the subject is no longer identifiable). Evelyn found the finished product 'too full of nakeds for a chappell'.[32] At Wadham, Fuller completed the early 17th-century decorative scheme with a near-monochrome depiction on cloth of the Last Supper flanked by Abraham and Melchizedek (ante-types for the Last Supper) on one side and the Israelites Gathering Manna (an ante-type for the Eucharist) on the other.[33]

These schemes represent the first examples of a Baroque, counter-Reformation style of ecclesiastical decoration in the service of the Protestant Church in England, and in a sense they build upon the early 17th-century attachment to biblical images by applying up-to-date techniques learnt from the Continent, and by ignoring the earlier, more equivocal, attitude to images. Moreover, it would seem that schemes which were integrated across different media, especially stained glass and wall painting, were now being created and that – particularly important when completing unfinished or damaged schemes – those at both Magdalen and Wadham show a degree of diachronic coherence.

One private patron to take up the Baroque approach pioneered by the Oxford colleges was Sir Richard Wynn, whose scheme at Gwydir contains a significant amount of painted glass and wall decoration. He employed a painter to decorate his boarded ceiling, and the primitive quality of the work carried out in glue tempera, with the gaps between the boards taped over with cotton strips, is plain to see. Though the rendering is naïve, the iconographical scheme is relatively sophisticated and, in terms of imagery, surprisingly daring. The three main bays of the roof depict the three persons of the Trinity: Christ and the Holy Ghost are represented by the standard symbols of IHS and a dove, but God the Father is portrayed as a seated figure in the centre of the ceiling (Plate XXXIV). This first known depiction of God in a private chapel since the Reformation, in effect revived 'from Hell the old heresie of the Anthropomorphites' spurned so vehemently earlier in the century by Henry Peacham.[34] At the west end, two angels over the gallery proclaim with trumpets the Day of Judgement. Texts underline and reinforce the message.[35] This careful and considered programme was not done justice in its execution by the craftsman, and is easy to dismiss as primitive. It acts as a warning not to underestimate the intellectual qualities of figurative post-Restoration schemes. There appears to have been a genuine attempt to combine the two strands of early 17th-century decorative schemes – the symbolic and the biblical – and to provide a new form of Baroque ecclesiastical ceiling decoration.

Most other patrons followed the Pembroke option. Of the surviving interiors from this period, Cornbury chapel is the most rewarding to study. It is not the earliest post-Restoration chapel – Burford, Horseheath and Melton Constable, as well as the high profile London examples at Clarendon House and Burlington House, all predate it – but it is the earliest to have survived relatively untouched. The decoration is simple and avoids biblical images and most religious symbolism. The ceiling is, like that at Pembroke College, typical of a domestic room of the period (fig. 6.9), with a laurel garland at the top of the coving and a central oval, devoid of images, bordered with flowers and foliage in the contemporary fashion. Other decorative elements are also drawn from the conventional vocabulary of the period: there is nothing here that would not be familiar to a plasterer used to working on secular commissions, and the inclusion of bunches of grapes provides the sole potentially religious reference. The east end is emphasised only by the richer woodwork in the form of a reredos covering the entire wall. Again, the motifs are conventional, even secular, in their inspiration. The dominant element is the large coat of arms, decorated with swags of fruit and flowers and flanked by flaming urns, which surmounts the reredos over the communion table. The panelling below is articulated with coupled Corinthian pilasters flanking the communion table. The crossed palm leaves and winged cherubs' heads which decorate the frieze are, with the flaming urns, the only symbols capable of a religious interpretation. However, all three are standard motifs often found in secular settings and, with the bulk of the decoration depending on motifs such as swags of fruit and flowers and lions' masks, it is difficult to attach much importance to them as part of a specifically religious programme. It is now impossible to say whether the rectangular panel immediately above the communion table was designed to incorporate a figurative altarpiece or rich textile infill.

Fig. 6.32: Halston Hall, Shropshire: the east end of the chapel possessed one of the few commandment boards of the period to incorporate images.

Cornbury establishes the so-called 'Wrenian chapel' (or Pembroke) type that was to predominate during the first three decades of the Restoration, and which even today remains the popular ideal of the typical country house chapel. The rich and colourful mixed media, used with such enthusiasm in the early part of the 17th century, was supplanted by restrained decoration, always decorous and usually of a very high standard. The general approach employed at Cornbury was followed at, for example, Arbury, Tabley and Belton (Plate XXIX) which still bear witness to its appeal. All are richly decorated spaces making liberal use of the vogue for naturalistic decoration in plaster or woodwork, but demonstrating a controlled use of imagery, with few if any specifically religious motifs. Again, the predominant characteristic is a controlled 'seemliness'. There is no evidence before the late 1670s of painted canvases being set into the ceilings, and in general the effect of both wall and ceiling decoration is of rich but controlled work suitable for any important room.

There are, however, exceptions. Some contemporary chapels, such as that at Ham, had completely plain ceilings. And at Locko, the richly decorated coffered wooden ceiling (Plate XXVII), with its blue ground and lavish gilding, provides perhaps the only surviving example of the use of colour for ceiling decoration in a private country house chapel of the period. At Melton Constable (another early example), the barrel vault is divided into sections decorated with plaster coats of arms and winged figures. At Burford, although it is said that the early 20th-century restoration re-created as closely as possible (albeit in different materials) the elliptical stone barrel-vault, a 1736 description of the chapel 'with its fretwork roof of scripture history' shows that the restrained and Classical vault copied by the restorers could not have been original.[36] The link between these exceptions is that they would all have given the chapel a character that contrasted with the domestic rooms, emphasising the unique purpose of the space in a way that the somewhat domestic decorative style of the 'Wren chapel' did not.

The controlled seemliness of the Pembroke option was followed in the choices made for subjects displayed in the east end. Most notably, biblical images were rarely used as altarpieces or set in reredoses during the first decades after the Restoration. A number of chapels did not use imagery at all. Ham sported a hanging of crimson velvet and damask. At Belton a crimson silk velvet panel was put in place in 1771, but there is no record of it replacing a biblical image. Similarly, at Petworth the present painting of cherubim was set into the reredos in the 18th century, and there is no mention in the accounts of an earlier image. Commandment boards of various designs continued in use to the end of the century.[37] At Rycote, the richly architectural (1682) reredos with four panels displaying the usual texts provides a good example of the 'seemly beauty' and control combined with a high level of craftsmanship that was typical of the period (fig. 6.28). A simple and somewhat homespun board of c.1610 was replaced by one of exemplary craftsmanship which is larger, very detailed architecturally, and more carefully related to other elements of the space. Its high standard of craftsmanship makes the earlier version seem rough and provincial. One of the few post-Restoration commandment boards to incorporate images was at Halston Hall in Shropshire, where the traditional figures of Moses and Aaron are featured with a glory of cherubim (fig. 6.32).

Sculptural decoration (except for conventional plaster motifs) was not popular. Apart from the trumpeting angels surmounting the reredos (now removed) at Berwick, the one major exception is the chapel at Burford. We have seen that the present restrained character of the interior was at least partly the product of later alterations, and it is possible that, like the exterior, the interior also contained some very unusual sculptural decoration. W.H. Godfrey (writing in the early 20th century) records the two free-standing columns twined with vines and thistles flanking the altar which are still in the chapel, while at the west end he noted the two carved stone angels which still flank the west door and which look upwards to a stylised representation of the burning bush which surmounts it (fig. 6.23).[38] In the *Biblia Pauperum*, the Burning Bush is the Old Testament ante-type for the Nativity, but it could symbolise the Virgin Mary, and other meanings have also been ascribed to it. However, a text beneath the left-hand angel reading '*exue calceos tuos nam terra est sancta*' ('put off thy shoes from off thy feet, for the place whereon thou standeth is holy ground') is wholly appropriate to a chapel entrance as well as being associated in Exodus with the burning bush, while a text beneath the right-hand angel, reading '*salvabimur quasi per ignem*' ('we shall be saved; yet so as by fire') relates more directly to the theme of burning.[39] But it is strange to place the richest sculptural decoration at the west end, and the group is awkwardly constructed round and over the west door so that it is all but invisible except when leaving the chapel (rendering the angel's instruction to 'put off thy shoes' redundant), and cannot be seen at all from the gallery above. Burford was clearly not a conventional chapel, and the decorative arrangements should be viewed with extreme caution. There are no other examples of similar sculptural decoration, and the arrangement is awkward enough (especially in the lack of any cohesive relationship between the angels and the burning bush) to suggest that parts have been brought together at a later date, and may have had no original connection with the chapel. However, their exuberant quality, especially that of the angels, has resonances with the exterior reliefs, so their presence in the original interior cannot be ruled out.

The restrained approach of the Pembroke option, with its lack of colourful imagery, contrasts strongly with the exuberance that characterised the earlier years of the century, and marks an important change in the decoration of high-church chapels. That so many patrons chose to follow it must in part be due to the early influence exerted by Wren and Clarendon, but it may also have stemmed from an absence of materials. Painted glass was difficult to obtain, and even as late as 1697 Fiennes commented when describing the coloured glass at Salisbury House that it was 'an art which is now lost amongst us'.[40] On the other hand, despite the clumsy evocations at Gwydir, there does not appear to have been a similarly acute shortage of artists to paint decorative schemes.

186

Certainly, two painters with experience on the Continent were available: Fuller, who studied under François Perrier, and Robert Streater, who was said to have been in Italy during the Commonwealth.[41] Both had sons who followed in their trade. Moreover, foreign craftsmen were trying to take advantage of the new opportunities in England.[42] A contrary factor may have been a perception that fresco painting lacked durability. Evelyn remarked not long after Fuller's painting at All Souls was completed 'yet I fear it will not hold long', and this may reflect a general (and well-founded) suspicion of the medium.[43] But it is difficult to see why painting on canvas would have posed technical problems. While it appears that images were deliberately avoided, it is possible that other more innovative and potentially controversial schemes were initiated but have simply disappeared, victims of their own technical incompetence or of subsequent generations' wish to replace or efface them – something that could be achieved in a matter of hours at very little cost. Whatever the case, other than at Gwydir, there appear to be no recorded examples of painted decorative schemes in private country house chapels before the 1680s. The main components of most surviving schemes are plaster and wood: more durable than paint and, especially in the case of plaster, less easy to alter. In addition, the conventional motifs applied in most chapels were uncontroversial and thus less likely to offend succeeding generations. Moreover, plasterers and woodworkers displayed great artistic skills during the period, and the design of chapels often reflected this.

Decoration before and after the Glorious Revolution of 1688: 'All the Pride of Pray'r'?

While in the first two decades after the Restoration, legislation was aimed at restricting the power of the Puritans, from the late 1670s increasing unease centred on the fact that the heir to the throne, the Duke of York, was openly Roman Catholic. The purported discovery of the Popish Plot in 1678 seriously alarmed Protestants. By July 1683, according to Evelyn, 'the whole Nation was now in greate Consternation, upon the late Plot and Conspiracy; ... the Papists in the meane while very jocund, and indeede they have reason'. Two years later James II was King, and in the same year an heir was born. Evelyn described 'the Romanists swarming at Court with greater confidence than had ever been seen in England since the Reformation so as everybody grew Jealous as to what this would tend.'[44]

It might be thought that this surge of Roman Catholic confidence would have created a climate in which images in Protestant buildings were avoided lest they give rise to accusations of popish practices, but in 1684 a case in Lincolnshire helped clarify the official line. The parishioners of Moulton wanted to put up a painting of the apostles in the east end of their parish church, but their application

ELEVATION

LOWER PLAN | UPPER PLAN

was turned down by the Bishop Barlow of Lincoln as 'superstitious' and tending 'to idolatry'. They appealed to the Court of Arches on the grounds that 'under such pretended fears of superstition and idolatry most of the churches, chapels, colleges and other pious and religious places in England may be in danger of being pulled down and demolished'. Their appeal was upheld.[45]

Although interiors similar to that at Cornbury continued to be created during the 1680s, for example at Belton and Culverthorpe, a new attitude to decoration was becoming fashionable, and giving rise to high-quality, Baroque decorative schemes. This was made possible by the arrival of foreign painters and craftsmen such as Antonio Verrio, Louis Laguerre, Caius Cibber, René Cousin and Grinling Gibbons. As a result, the possibilities for chapel decoration began to expand. Moreover, not only was painted decoration now a realistic (technically speaking) option, but the wider range of media available could be co-ordinated by architects such as Talman and Hugh May, who were able to exploit the new cross-media possibilities in a way that was far removed from provincial efforts such as those at Gwydir.

The new standard had been set by the redecoration of the King's Chapel at Windsor for Charles II in 1680–2, where many of the immigrant artists had first worked together, and where the overall effect was obtained through the use of illusionistic painting by Verrio combined with richly carved woodwork (Plate XXXV).[46] To what extent the iconographic scheme of the chapel was intended to express the King's piety is questionable, especially since the chapel and the adjoining St George's Hall were designed as part of the same, highly political scheme – the size and grandeur of the King's throne in the latter would have left little doubt about where the main focus of the two rooms lay.[47] Even so, as a demonstration of the possibilities of illusionistic painting, the chapel interior at Windsor had no rival, and it is unlikely that any of Verrio's work in country house chapels pre-dated it.[48]

James II lost little time in altering some of the royal chapel decoration, but most important was his creation of the new and specifically Roman Catholic chapel at Whitehall Palace.[49] It appears that the decorative scheme centred on the Virgin Mary, emphasising its Roman Catholic nature. The painted decoration included an Assumption on the ceiling, 'according to their tradition' as Evelyn put it, and an altarpiece of the Annunciation, as well as unspecified subjects on the ceilings of Queen Mary's oratory and closet. Perhaps the most eye-catching

Opposite: Fig. 6.33: Whitehall Palace, London: a partial reconstruction of the reredos for James II's chapel, a multi-media ensemble that would have been more at home in Rome than in London (reproduced from H. Colvin (editor), *The History of the King's Works*, 5 (London 1976), p. 292).

decorative feature was the reredos, designed by Wren, with statuary by Gibbons and Arnold Quellin. While Verrio's (liturgical) east end at Windsor was entirely illusionistic, at Whitehall, white marble was combined with free-standing purple rance columns to create a multi-media ensemble more at home in Rome than in London (fig. 6.33).[50] The painted altarpiece was surrounded by silvered sculptural reliefs by Cousin and flanked by statues of Peter and Paul (Plate XXXIII) and two female figures, probably Faith and Hope. Two adoring angels, possibly positioned at the highest points, completed a display that Evelyn noted was of 'exquisite art and greate cost'.[51]

Painted and highly decorated chapels were to be found in a number of Protestant private houses. Illusionistic paintings by Verrio were commissioned at Woodcote Park in Surrey (a ceiling depicting the Resurrection) and at Snape, where a coved ceiling depicting the 'Wonder and War in Heaven' survives, albeit in a parlous state. At Chatsworth chapel (begun 1687), Laguerre painted the walls and ceiling, while Verrio provided an altarpiece for the highly sculpted marble reredos. In 1695, Verrio was paid £130 'for painting the chapel' at Thoresby after a fire.[52] This sum emphasises the relative splendours of Thoresby and Windsor, for at the latter Verrio was, some ten years earlier, paid £1,000 for his work on 'Henry VIII's chapel'.[53] It is likely that many more such schemes, not just in great houses, have disappeared without trace. Certainly, the fashion for such imagery continued well into the 18th century, and was popular enough to attract Pope's scornful reference to the sprawling 'saints of Verrio or Laguerre' quoted in Chapter 1. On the other hand, major programmes of redecoration in some great houses ignored the chapel, for example at Burghley. When Fiennes visited the house in 1697 after Verrio and Laguerre had finished their work there, she praised their craftsmanship but also noted that 'the chaple is old and not to abide, the painting is good but the place is not suteable to any part else'.[54] This was presumably the same chapel scheme whose grotesques were noted later by Walpole.[55]

Another aspect of chapel decoration that changed in the last decades of the 17th century was the handling of the reredos. Well into the 1680s the most favoured type was a wooden structure of architectural nature such as those at Rycote or Belton. But the great altarpiece for James II at Whitehall, which was ready by Christmas 1686, set new standards. From the late 1680s, richer materials such as marble and alabaster were also being used by Protestant patrons, with less conventional and more flamboyant arrangements being pioneered. At Bretby, 'the altarpiece of Italian marble was remarkably fine' and its magnificence would have been further enhanced by having been set in an apsed east end.[56] Fiennes remarked in 1698 that the arrangement, including the plain glass oval window over the altar already mentioned, 'look'd pretty as being particular and uncommon'. At Thoresby, it is likely that payments to Cibber in 1695 and to Cibber and John van Nost the elder in 1696 were related to work for an ornate east end arrangement.[57] Now all that can be seen is the magnificent scale of the freestanding columns flanking the altar. But one splendid reredos created by Cibber, Verrio and others does survive and illustrates the level of splendour that could be achieved in a Protestant family chapel. This is at Chatsworth and will be discussed in greater detail below.

Given the Roman Catholic ascendancy of the three years of James's reign, and the subsequent firm re-instatement of Protestant values after 1688, it might seem difficult to explain or be easy to misinterpret this unprecedented rise in the scale and amount of decoration lavished on some Protestant chapels. It was in this period, perhaps more than any other, that the tension between fashionable grandeur and the expression of piety was at its most acute. Contemporary writers noted the secular, even worldly, nature of chapels created 'Purely out of Form and to set off the Grandeur of the Family'.[58] It is undoubtedly true that many of them were created more to enhance the patron's standing than to encourage the spiritual well-being of the household. A measure of these secular priorities is the relative degree of grandeur allotted respectively to the altar and to the family gallery. At Belton, for instance, it is only in the gallery that cedarwood is used; the rest of the chapel is panelled in deal, and the decorative carving in the gallery is of far higher quality even than that of the reredos. Similarly, at Petworth, the first truly mixed-media private chapel of the late 17th century to survive, the painted angels trumpet equally at the east and west ends, while the windows demonstrate the illustrious ancestry of a great family rather than Christ's sacrifice. The 'Proud Duke's' west end gallery, set up like an opera box, complete with curtains held by tasselled chords illusionistically carved and then painted and gilded, dominates the chapel (fig. 6.27).

The chapels at Belton and Petworth are among the most prominent of this date in the country, and there is a tendency to dismiss all the Baroque chapels of the late 17th century as pure demonstrations of wealth and status. But this would be to misunderstand the way in which many Protestant patrons saw their role as promoters of their religion, not only by word and personal example, but also through the decoration of their chapels. One example in particular, that of Chatsworth (Plate XXXI), demonstrates the deliberate use of chapel decoration to promote Protestant ideas.

Certainly, contemporaries admired the worldly grandeur of Chatsworth. It was, as White Kennett (later Bishop of Peterborough) put it, 'a Monument of Beauty and Magnificence that perhaps is not exceeded by any Palace in Europe'; while Joseph Grove wrote ' ... Chatsworth, which for the grandeur and elegance of the structure ... and great variety of well-chosen decorations ... (is) not unworthy of the greatest prince in Europe'.[59] It is, therefore, not surprising that the chapel, with its grandiose display of painted decoration set against alabaster and marble fittings, the rival of many in Rome, was widely seen simply as a statement of aristocratic pride. But the political role and personal beliefs of the 4th Earl (later 1st Duke) of Devonshire, as well as a detailed scrutiny of the decorative scheme of the chapel, suggest otherwise.

During the rise in Roman Catholic influence of the late 1670s and early 1680s, the 4th Earl was one of the leaders of the anti-Romanist party. He argued strongly for the exclusion of the Duke of York from the succession, and his speeches calling for stricter enforcement of laws against popery, and for a new bill designed to limit its growth, were printed in a popular pamphlet. Soon after James became king in February 1685, the Earl withdrew from London and spent his enforced retirement planning the rebuilding of Elizabethan Chatsworth. Contemporary descriptions of his private life confirm that he was a man deeply committed to the Protestant faith: he was 'a steady and magnanimous Opposer of Popery' who had 'a reverence for the scriptures and read them with a diligent eye and defended whatever he thought the fundamental doctrines.' Moreover, 'he saw Popery and Arbitrary Power coming in like a mighty stream. He dar'd swim against it ... with steady resolution never to depart from the Interests of England and the Protestant religion'.[60] No contemporary household regulations survive to throw light on the role of his chapel, but it is reasonable to suppose that the paternalistic attitude to the spiritual life of all members of the household, which features in so many other regulations, existed at Chatsworth.[61] This is supported by the description of the earl's widow's devotional habits by her chaplain, Williamson, after her death in 1710. Although (as ever with this genre) a certain degree of hagiography should be allowed for – the 4th Earl was a racing man with a reputation for profligacy – Williamson's description of the family's attitude to the chapel and their religious responsibilities does not seem extravagant. The Duchess aimed, he said, to promote piety among the household by means of example and environment, and was well aware that her family's duty was to exert 'the face of their Authority and Example for the interests of Virtue and Religion'. The chapel was decorated to 'excite Devotion' amongst the household, and to 'convey a Train of Holy (and Protestant) Ideas to the mind'.[62]

The dominant theme of the decoration in the chapel is the importance of faith, and the key to its message lies in the configuration of the east end. Verrio's altarpiece shows the moment when Christ takes Thomas's finger and, placing it in his wound, says 'be not faithless but believing'.[63] This is flanked by two great marble statues by Cibber: on the liturgical north Faith looks directly up at Thomas, and to the south Divine Justice gazes across the space of the chapel. Next to the statues, Laguerre has painted, to the same scale, illusionistic sculpted

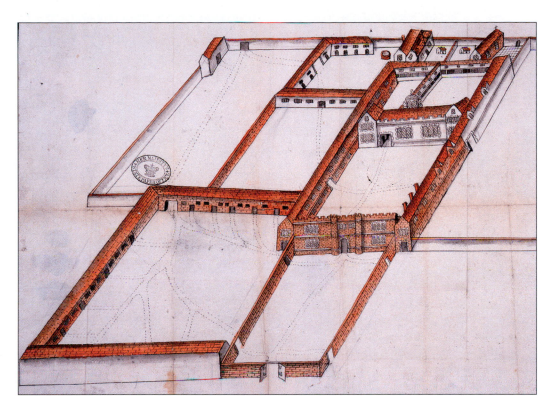

Plate I: Shurland, Kent: a survey map of 1572. The chapel (top right) is distinguished by crosses on the gable ends. The tall west window rises above the two-storey inner courtyard.

Plate II: Gipping Hall, Suffolk: the south facade of the detached chapel, showing evidence of the expense and craftsmanship lavished on a building of some splendour.

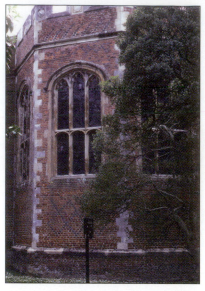

Plate III: The Vyne, Hampshire: the chapel apse as it is today. An apse could impart an individual character to the outside of the chapel, as well as enhancing the interior by supporting a magnificent display of coloured glass.

Plate IV: The Vyne, Hampshire: detail of the east facade showing the chapel apse – from a 1640s Sandys family portrait. If this were the original entrance range, the apse would have contributed to the magnificence of the house as seen by approaching visitors.

Plate V: Naworth Castle, Cumbria: watercolour by George Howard (1843-1911) of the dilapidated 17th-century chapel interior looking towards the liturgical west. Part of the early Tudor compartmented ceiling, originally at Kirkoswald, can be clearly seen, and the family west-end upper chapel is just visible.

Plate VI: Naworth Castle, Cumbria: watercolour by Samuel Rayner (1821–1874) of the chapel interior looking towards the liturgical east. Apparently a two-centred chapel, it was not obviously designed for the celebration of communion, and may have been used for ecumenical worship.

Plate VII: Bramall Hall, Lancashire: detail of the medieval *Ecce Homo* on the west wall of the chapel. This fragment could have formed part of a much larger scheme. It was later over-painted with the Ten Commandments.

Plate VIII: Chatsworth, Derbyshire: needlework view of *c*.1590–1600, sometimes attributed to Bess of Hardwick. It shows the entrance (west) front. The window of the liturgical east end of the double-height chapel was most likely to the left of the right-hand tower, and had no external distinguishing features, but the two staterooms on the second floor (the one at top right lit the end of the Long Gallery) were highlighted by large pedimented windows.

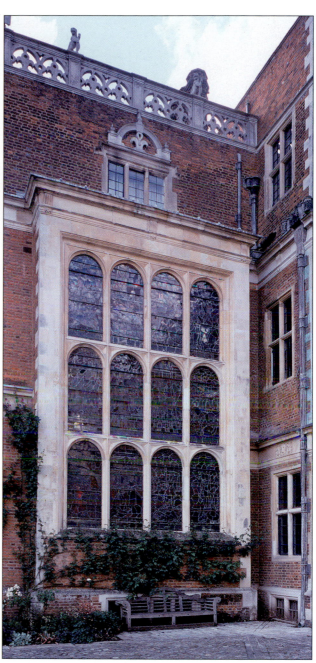

Plate IX: Hatfield House, Hertfordshire: the west windows of the chapel. The lower window is distinctive, but the upper window reverts to the standard domestic form.

Plate X: Hatfield House, Hertfordshire: the imposing east window of the chapel, with its distinctive arched forms, projects slightly forward from the main facade of the west range.

Plate XI: Bramhope Hall, West Yorkshire: view from the south-west. A simple, detached Puritan chapel.

Plate XII: Low Ham, Somerset: the detached chapel from the south-east. In contrast to Bramhope, a spectacular building, with much external sculptural decoration and 'playful Gothic' windows, that could easily be mistaken for a parish church.

Plate XIII: Chantemarle House, Dorset: main facade. The E-shape of the plan symbolised Emmanuel. The double-height chapel, with its apsed east end, was on the right.

Plate XIV: Steane Park, Northamptonshire: the west front of the purpose-built, detached, Puritan chapel is wider than it is long. The windows display a variety of eye-catchingly rich archaic forms, and reflect the unorthodox nature of the chapel.

Plate XV: Steane Park, Northamptonshire: the interior looking east. With the pulpit at the east end, it is the first surviving example of Puritan liturgical priorities demonstrated in a private chapel, and combines fittings and architectural articulation to create a very original Puritan interior.

Plate XVI: Low Ham, Somerset: detail of angel beneath the roof of the chancel. The inclusion of angels as part of the roof or ceiling decoration was one facet of the revival of pre-Reformation decorative ideas under the early Stuarts.

Plate XVII: Forde Abbey, Dorset: the west facade of the chapel. The entrance door and the circular window above are Classical details that were added, probably in the 1650s, to this largely pre-Reformation building.

Plate XVIII: Hampton Court, Herefordshire: painted glass window, by Abraham Van Linge, originally in the chapel and now at the V&A. The inscription reassures the viewer that the depiction of the Deposition carried no idolatrous intent.

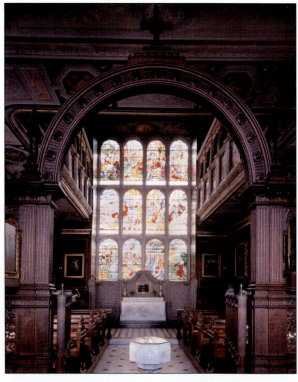

Plate XIX: Hatfield House, Hertfordshire: the interior of the colourfully decorated high-church chapel looking east.

Plate XX: Hatfield House, Hertfordshire: detail of prophets painted on the reveals of the chapel east window, south side. The reign of James I saw the return of biblical images painted on structural elements of chapels.

Plate XXI: Hatfield House, Hertfordshire: detail of the chapel frieze, probably by Rowland Bucket. The books and flaming urns (at the bottom) conveyed a simple Protestant message.

Plate XXII: Hatfield House, Hertfordshire: the chapel east window. Containing a typological scheme depicting twelve Old Testament scenes, it is the most important surviving example of Jacobean glass in a private chapel.

Plate XXIII: Hatfield House, Hertfordshire: the chapel interior looking west. The plaster roundels on the west gallery depict Christ (second on the left) with apostles and saints. The west window probably originally contained painted glass.

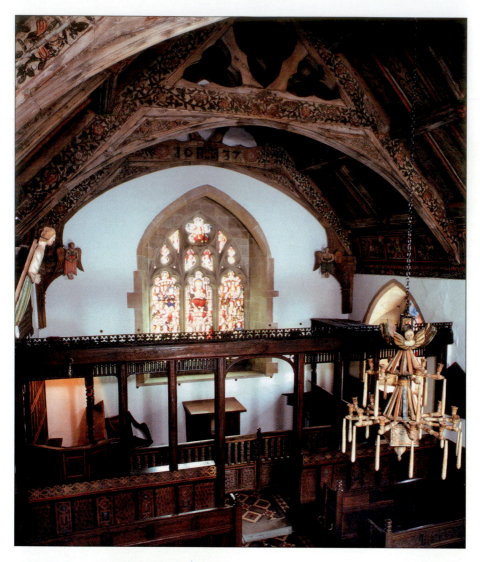

Plate XXIV: Rug Chapel, Caernarvonshire: the interior looking east. The plain exterior of this single-cell, detached building belies its richly decorated interior. The bulk of the roof decoration, including the cut-out angels, is original, though the altar, screen and stained glass are more recent.

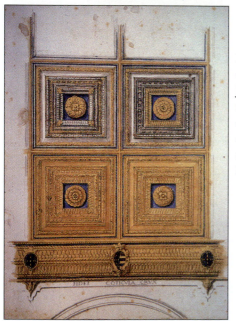

Plate XXV: Newhall, Essex: ceiling design by Inigo Jones. Possibly meant for the ceiling of the chapel closet, it shows how part of a non-royal Jonesian chapel interior might have looked.

Plate XXVI: Lytes Cary, Somerset: detail of the painted heraldic decorative frieze on the chapel wall. Heraldry could be used as an alternative to decoration based on biblical themes.

Plate XXVIII: Melton Constable, Norfolk: the east facade showing the arched chapel windows that interrupt the standard fenestration pattern.

Plate XXVII: Locko Park, Derbyshire: with Bishop Auckland (Plate XXX), one of two surviving examples of colourful post-Restoration chapel ceiling decoration.

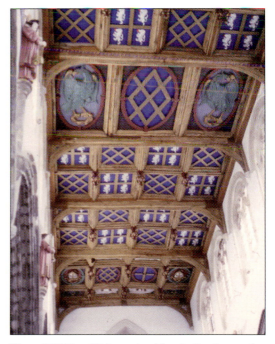

Plate XXIX: Belton House, Lincolnshire: chapel reredos. A restrained and decorous wooden structure of an architectural nature, there is no record that it originally displayed a biblical image. The crimson silk velvet panel was installed in 1771.

Plate XXX: Bishop Auckland, Durham: the chapel ceiling looking east. The decoration, which suffered from unsympathetic 19th-century restoration, is secular in character, concentrating as it does on heraldry and the insignia of office.

Plate XXXI: Chatsworth, Derbyshire: interior view of the chapel looking to the liturgical east, showing the reredos with Verrio's altarpiece flanked by Cibber's statues of Faith and Divine Justice, and Laguerre's paintings of True Religion and Hope. The 4th Earl of Devonshire planned this grouping as a repudiation of the Roman Catholic message of James II's chapel at Whitehall. Part of Laguerre's paintings for the ceiling and south wall can also be seen.

Plate XXXII: Chatsworth, Derbyshire: Laguerre's chapel ceiling looking to the liturgical east. It depicts Christ in Glory, and was intended as a riposte to Verrio's Assumption on the ceiling of the Whitehall chapel.

Left Plate XXXIII: Whitehall Palace, London: statue of St Paul by Grinling Gibbons. Formerly a proud part of the altarpiece in James II's chapel, it now addresses a stunted lamp-post in the College Garden of Westminster School.

Right Plate XXXIV: Gwydir Castle, Caernarvonshire: detail of the central panel of the chapel ceiling. This first known depiction of God the Father in a private chapel since the Reformation would have caused consternation earlier in the century.

Plate XXXV: Windsor Castle, Berkshire: an early 19th-century painting of the interior of Charles II's chapel, looking towards the altar, by Charles Wild (1781-1835). The effect was achieved by a combination of illusionistic painting and richly carved woodwork. The scenes by Verrio of Christ healing the sick that ran along the liturgical south wall may have provoked the 4th Earl of Bedford to commission Laguerre to depict the same subject on the equivalent wall of his chapel at Chatsworth.

figures representing (on the south) True Religion (who holds an unusually large book, perhaps emphasising the importance of Protestant bible-based doctrines), and to the north Hope, who may represent both the hope that faith can bring and also, given the turbulent times, that Protestant doctrines would triumph. Linked to this central core are three grisaille panels which show scenes from the life of Christ illustrating the importance of faith and demonstrating that it can be found amongst the humble and outcasts. Completing the decoration in the coving of the ceiling are the four evangelists, one in each corner, demonstrating the importance of the Gospels.[64]

The decoration of the walls and ceiling combine with the reredos and these scenes to create a space of great richness. The liturgical north (or window) wall is relatively simple with two fictive niches set between giant illusionistic columns. The chapel is watched over from the niches by Charity, who completes the three theological virtues, and Divine Grace, through whose strength True Religion can flourish. Both are shown as gifts from God, symbolised by the flames on their heads, and in this they are linked to the prominently flaming urns set high on the reredos. Great illusionistic schemes by Laguerre fill the ceiling and the liturgical south wall. On the latter, a scene of Christ healing the sick reminds the congregation that, for the faithful, he intervenes in daily life, and that his mercy is available to all who believe, both rich and poor. This is emphasised by the boy at the west end who, looking towards the occupants of the chapel gallery, points to Christ further down the wall. Given the position of this scene in a family chapel, it can also be interpreted as representing the patron's duty of care to all who belong to his household, while in a wider context it is a metaphor for spiritual healing wrought through faith. Laguerre's depiction of Christ in Glory fills the ceiling with, unusually, the figure of Christ placed at the liturgical west end close to the family gallery (Plate XXXII).

The 4th Earl's choice of subjects may best be interpreted as references to the two recent royal chapels. Verrio had painted scenes of Christ healing the sick along the equivalent wall in Charles II's chapel at Windsor. The ceiling there contained a depiction of the Resurrection with Christ rising of his own volition, but a Christ in Glory as at Chatsworth has him born aloft by angels and cherubim. This could well have been a reference to Verrio's Assumption painted on the ceiling of James II's Whitehall chapel just as the 4th Earl was beginning to plan his own chapel. The Whitehall ceiling no longer survives so no detailed comparison is possible, but the standard form for an Assumption is to show the Virgin borne aloft by choirs of angels and cherubim. Could the ceiling at Chatsworth, therefore, comprise a Protestant riposte to James's chapel? Certainly the dating of the two chapels fits well with this interpretation. Gibbons and Quellin were asked in March 1686 to make a model of the altarpiece for the

Whitehall chapel, and the contract stipulated that it should be completed by September 25th. The first service held was the Christmas midnight Mass in that year. At Chatsworth the fitting out of the chapel began less than a year later, and was largely complete by September 1691.

While only brief descriptions of the painted scheme at Whitehall survive, enough is known about the reredos to allow a more detailed comparison of the similarities and significant differences from that at Chatsworth to be made (fig. 6.33 and Plate XXXI). Both are of two storeys with superimposed orders; both use carefully graded marble (white marble with veined pilasters and purple rance columns at Whitehall; white and veined marble with black alabaster columns at Chatsworth); and both support life-size, three-dimensional, sculpted images. Both also use apsidal forms. At Whitehall, the wings of the reredos curved forward, leaving a large central recess, while at Chatsworth, there is a more conventional central apse. No other reredoses even remotely approach the same level of grandeur at this date. Both were confections that would have been at home in the Baroque Counter-Reformation churches of Rome, but which in England were isolated in the extreme.

The links between the two structures appear to extend beyond the general similarities of form. At Whitehall, in 1686, the altarpiece of the Nativity was flanked by Peter and Paul, and probably (although the figures are now very worn) Faith and Hope, a fairly conventional ensemble. At Chatsworth, the east end, together with the two illusionistic statues on the north wall, form an unusual group of figures which works well as a direct repudiation of the Roman Catholic message of Whitehall, emphasising instead Protestant values and faith. The source for the Chatsworth figures was Cesare Ripa's manual of Classical and Baroque symbolism, *Iconologia*, which was in standard use for Roman Catholic decoration.[65] However, each Chatsworth figure has been carefully altered to emphasise the Protestant nature of the iconography. For example, the figure of Divine Faith has the crown and distinctive long, centrally parted hair shown in the manual, but lacks the dove and the use of gold specified by Ripa. In the same way the Charity depicts two children in place of Ripa's three.

What all this amounts to is that Chatsworth chapel was conceived by the 4th Earl of Devonshire as an affirmation of his Protestant faith during a time of great religious turbulence, and as a stimulus to devotion through the promotion of beleaguered Protestant beliefs. The decorative programme comprised a carefully considered exposition of the Protestant doctrine of Faith through Divine Grace, as well as a direct and very splendid rebuttal of the Roman Catholic scheme at Whitehall. It should be understood as a means of 'Promoting solid Piety' and Protestant beliefs rather than as a demonstration of worldly pride. Pope's condemnation is not applicable here. Indeed, it is with Chatsworth that the dependence on reworking pre-Reformation ideas is removed, and the evolution of a specifically Protestant decorative scheme comes of age. Making full use of the technically sophisticated craftsmen now available, the chapel provides the Protestant answer to the Roman Catholic use of Baroque decoration by means of a fully-integrated mixed-media scheme. It was as if the events of this decade forced the Protestants to reconsider their often ambivalent attitude to decoration, and to 'come out', using decoration to underline and advertise their religion, and offering a counter Counter-Reformation alternative. Some 150 years after the Reformation, Protestant decoration in private country house chapels had found an independent voice.

Notes

Introduction

1. My thanks to Nicholas Cooper for this information.

2. D. Gurney, 'Extracts from the Household and Privy Purse Accounts of the Lestranges of Hunstanton', *Archaeologia*, 25 (1834), p. 413.

3. Although the rich decoration of the eastern cell in some chapels showed that a sense of hierarchy of worship could still exist.

4. For supporting material, see Annabel Ricketts, 'The Evolution of the Protestant Country House Chapel *c*.1500–*c*.1700' (unpublished Ph.D thesis, University of London, 2003), p. 88.

5. *Of Household Stuff: the 1601 Inventories of Bess of Hardwick* (S.M. Levey and P.K. Thornton, editors), (London, 2001).

6. Hatfield House, Cecil MSS, Box A/I; Box A/5 fol. 6r. [Editor's note: my thanks to Sue Bracken for clarifying these references].

7. Only one post-Restoration example of a fireplace incorporated into a chapel gallery survives – at Woodhey in Cheshire.

8. West Yorkshire Archive Service, Leeds: WYL 150 TN EA3, 3/10, 13/18 (i) & WYL (Pawson MSS) 178/1, 2, 14.

9. The use of the word 'oratory' to denote a personal chapel in a country house seems to have originated in the 1620s – such spaces are invariably referred to as closets in 16th-century country houses. In the 17th century, it may have carried an implication of Roman Catholicism, with patrons perhaps celebrating Roman Catholic Mass in private, with a Protestant-type service being held in the main household chapel – as was the case at Naworth Castle in Cumbria and possibly Rycote in Oxfordshire. But the term could also be used to denote a standard private chapel or a pulpit – see J. Florio, *A Worlde of Wordes or Most Copious, and Exact Dictionarie in Italian and English* (London, 1598) and *Queen Anne's New World of Words or Dictionarie of the Italian and English Tongues* (London, 1611); Ricketts, [note 4], pp. 90-2.

10. *The Household Papers of Henry Percy, 9th Earl of Northumberland (1564-1632)* (G.R. Batho, editor), (London, 1962), p. xx.

11. T. Bayly, *Certamen Religiosum: A Conference between Charles I and Henry, Marquess of Worcester concerning religion* (London, 1649).

12. For the sake of brevity, the word 'fittings' is used to embrace 'fixtures'. It includes altars and communion tables (but not their coverings) and their immediate adjuncts, such as rails and reredoses (although insets such as paintings are considered as decoration). It also covers structures which enable the business of the chapel to be conducted such as screens, pulpits, stalls, reading desks, lecterns and fonts, as well as seating for the congregation, the patron and his family, and panelling. Often the fittings are of wood, but stone, marble and metalwork also feature.

13. The term 'decoration' refers to the decoration of the chapel 'shell' and fittings, and includes paint, textiles, fabrics and metalwork.

14. Where it is necessary to draw the distinction, the house chapel will continue to be referred to as Compton Wynyates I, and the detached chapel as Compton Wynyates II.

15. Especially since Dugdale writes that the fabric of the house 'was totally reduced to rubbish' (W. Dugdale, *The Antiquities of Warwickshire* (London, 1730), p. 550).

16. *The Journal of William Dowsing* (T. Cooper, editor), (Woodbridge, 2001), pp. 238, 248, 270, 320.

Chapter 1

1. J. G. Nichols, 'Memoir of Henry Fitzroy, Duke of Richmond and Somerset', *Camden Miscellany*,

3 (1855), p. xxi. Thomas, Lord Darcy's residence was Temple Hurst, now Temple Newsam, while that of Richard Nevill, 2nd Lord Latimer, was Snape Castle.

2. J. Bowle, *A Sermon Preached at Flitton in the Co of Bedford at the Funeral of the Rt Hon Earle of Kent* (London, 1614).

3. A. Pope, 'Epistle IV. To Richard Boyle, Earl of Burlington', in *The Poems of Alexander Pope* (J. Butt, editor), (London, 1965), p. 593.

4. Dorset Record Office, D/BVL/M4 fol. 22v. My thanks to Nicholas Cooper for alerting me to these papers.

5. *English Orders for Consecrating Churches in the Seventeenth Century* (J. Wickham Legg, editor), (London, 1911), p. 131.

6. Letters from the Duke of Lauderdale to Sir William Bruce, quoted in J.G. Dunbar 'The Building Activities of the Duke and Duchess of Lauderdale, 1670-82', *Archaeological Journal*, 132 (1975), pp. 215-17.

7. J.T. Cliffe, *The Puritan Gentry; The Great Puritan Families of Early Stuart England* (London, Boston, Melbourne and Henley, 1984), p. 168.

8. M. Aston, *England's Iconoclasts* (Oxford, 1988), p. 220.

9. *Inventories of Worcestershire Landed Gentry 1537-1786* (M. Wanklyn, editor), (Worcester, 1998), p. 40.

10. E.W. Crossley, 'Two Seventeenth Century Inventories', *Yorkshire Archaeological Journal*, 34 (1939), pp. 182-98.

11. C. Giles, *Rural Houses of West Yorkshire, 1400-1830* (London, 1986), p. 197.

12. S.R. Westfall, *Patrons and Performance: Early Tudor Household Revels* (Oxford, 1990), pp. 23-4.

13. The terms 'high-church' and 'low-church', although perhaps anachronistic, are used for convenience since they have commonly understood, but not too specific, religious and social connotations.

14. *Diary of Lady Margaret Hoby* (J. Moody, editor), (Stroud, 1998), pp. xxxvii–viii, 134, 136 etc.

15. John Knox described how Somerset would not 'dainyie himself to ga frome his gallerie to his hall for heiring of a sermon'. J. Knox, *Works*, Bannatyne Edition, 3 (Edinburgh, 1854), p. 176, quoted in N. Pevsner, 'Old Somerset House', *Architectural Review*, 16 (1954), p. 163.

16. R. Brathwaite, *Some Rules and Orders for the Government of the House of an Earle (c.1605)*, (London, 1821), pp. 12, 26.

17. J. Nichols, *History and Antiquities of the County of Leicester*, 3 (London, 1804), p. 594.

18. The Montacute inventory of 1638 was taken on the death of Sir Robert Phelips, the builder's son (Somerset Record Office, DD/PH 224/98).

19. See Ricketts, [Intro., note 4], pp. 34-5, and A. Maguire, 'Country House Planning in England from 1600-1700' (unpublished Ph.D thesis, University of London, 1989).

20. 'Household Regulations of John, Earl of Bridgewater (1622-84)' transcribed in H.J. Todd, *History of the College of Bonhommes at Ashridge* (1823), pp. 47-55.

21. S. Fairclough, *The Saints Worthinesse and the Worlds Worthlessnesse* (London, 1653), p. 17.

22. J. Williamson, *A Modest Essay upon the Character of her late Grace the Duchess-Dowager of Devonshire* (London, 1710), p. 4.

23. W. Darrell, *A Gentleman Instructed in the Conduct of a Virtuous and Happy Life. Written for the Instruction of a Young Nobleman* (2nd ed., London, 1704), pp. 157-8.

Chapter 2

1. Injunction 28 reads: 'Also, That they shall take away, utterly extinct and destroy all shrines, all tables, candlesticks, trindles or rolls of wax, pictures, paintings, and all other monuments of feigned miracles, pilgrimages, idolatry, and superstition: so that there remain no memory of the

same in walls, glass-windows, or elsewhere within their churches or houses. And they shall exhort all their parishioners to do the like within their several houses.' W.H. Frere and W.M. Kennedy, *Visitation Articles and Injunctions of the Period of the Reformation*, 2 (London, 1910), p. 126.

2. Frere and Kennedy, [note 1], pp 177-8, 189.

3. H. Gee and W. Hardy, *Documents Illustrative of English Church History* (London, 1896), p. 361.

4. See G. Addleshaw and F. Etchells, *The Architectural Setting of Anglican Worship* (London, 1948), pp. 30-4; Frere and Kennedy, 3, [note 1], pp. 108-9.

5. Dowsing, [Intro., note 16], p. 12.

6. These are clearly set out as Appendix 5 of Dowsing, [Intro., note 16], p. 338.

7. *Dowsing*, [Intro., note 16], p. 238.

8. *Dowsing,* [Intro., note 16], pp. 358-60.

9. Hatfield House, Cecil MSS, Bills 216; Box A/9.

10. Gee and Hardy, [note 3], pp. 623-32.

11. O. Heywood, *Oliver Heywood, His Autobiography, Diaries, Anecdotes and Event Books* (J. Horsfall Turner, editor), 1 (Brighouse, 1882), e.g. pp. 192, 196, 226, 251-2, 254-5, 269, 293 etc.

12. D. Crankshaw, 'The Elizabethan Faculty Office and the Aristocratic Patronage of Chaplains', in *Patronage and Recruitment in the Tudor and Early Stuart Church* (C. Cross, editor), (York, 1996), pp. 24-7, 61-2; R.C. Palmer, *Selling the Church: the English Parish in Law, Commerce, and Religion, 1350-1550* (Chapel Hill and London, 2002), pp. 161-2.

13. Thomas Wood to the Earl of Warwick, 20th August 1576 in *Letters of Thomas Wood, Puritan, 1566-1577* (P. Collinson, editor), *Bulletin of the Institute of Historical Research*, Special Supplement No. 5 (1960), p. 16.

14. British Library, Add. MSS 42,275 f. 66, quoted in W. Gibson, *The Social History of the Domestic Chaplain 1530-1840* (Leicester, 1997), p. 15.

15. Gibson, [note 14], p. 2.

16. W. Laud, *Works*, 5 (facsimile edition, Hildesheim and New York, 1977), pp. 307-8; *Visitation Articles and Injunctions of the early Stuart Church*, 2 (K. Fincham, editor), (Woodbridge and Rochester, 1998), p. 38.

17. Bishops who included the substance of the Instructions in their Visitation Articles included Richard Neile and Thomas Morton at Durham, Richard Montagu at Chichester, Robert Wright at Coventry and Lichfield, Matthew Wren at Hereford and Norwich, and William Juxon at London (*Visitation Articles*, [note 16], 1, pp. 88, 116; 2, pp. 27, 69, 141-2, 160, 230).

18. [Editor's note: of 57 Puritan families listed by Cliffe as possessing chaplains in early Stuart England, Annabel Ricketts securely identified only eleven as possessing private chapels (Cliffe, [Chap. 1, note 7], pp. 237-240); similarly, of 73 Puritan families listed by Cliffe as possessing chaplains 1650-1700, she identified only fifteen with private chapels (J.T. Cliffe, *The Puritan Gentry Besieged, 1650-1700* (London and New York, 1993), pp. 206-28).]

19. My thanks to Maurice Howard for allowing me to see his transcript of The Vyne inventory of 1541. [Editor's note: now reproduced at pp. 142-55 in M. Howard and E. Wilson, *The Vyne: a Tudor House Revealed* (The National Trust, 2003).]

20. And Chaloner Chute states that it was not consecrated – see C.W. Chute, *A History of The Vyne in Hampshire* (Winchester, 1888), p. 15.

21. Although the chapel in the Hospital of the Holy Trinity in Croydon was consecrated in 1599 by the order of its founder, Dr Whitgift, Archbishop of Canterbury (Legg, [Chap. 1, note 5], p. xviii).

22. *The Works of James Pilkington* (J. Scholefield, editor), (Cambridge, 1842), p. 129. My thanks to Margaret Aston for this reference.

23. Legg, [Chap. 1, note 5], pp. 199-200.

24. Cliffe, [Chap. 1, note 7], pp. 167–8.

25. T.W. Davids, *Annals of Evangelical Nonconformity in the County of Essex* (London, 1863), p. 172. My thanks to Margaret Aston for this reference.

26. G.M. Griffiths, 'A Report on the Deanery of Penllyn and Edeirnion, by the Rev. John Wynn 1730', *Merioneth Historical and Record Society, Extra Publications, ser. 1, no. 3* (1955), pp. 38–44.

27. *The Life and Opinions of Robert Roberts as told by Himself* (J.H. Davies, editor), (Cardiff, 1923), p. 421.

28. H. Slingsby, *The Diary of Sir Henry Slingsby of Scriven, Bart.*(D. Parsons, editor), (London, 1836), p. 19.

29. [Editor's note: my thanks to Margaret Aston for this insight.]

30. A.T. Hart, *The Man in the Pew 1558-1660* (London, 1966), p. 170.

31. *Diary of Lady Anne Clifford* (D. Clifford, editor), (Stroud, 1992), pp. 57, 74, 159, 180, 193, 251.

32. A number of licences for marriages in private chapels survive, for instance at Snape Castle.

33. J. Hutchins, *History and Antiquities of the County of Dorset,* 4 (London, 1870), p. 367.

34. According to B. Wood ('The Chapel at Red House, Moor Monkton, Yorkshire', *Country Life*, 27 Oct. 1944, p. 730), the chapel was consecrated in 1618. However Sir Henry Slingsby II makes it clear in his *Diary*, [note 28], p. 19, that the chapel was not consecrated in 1638. It is likely that it was consecrated by Bishop Morton, whose arms are in the east window, before 1641.

35. Slingsby, [note 28], pp. 3, 18.

36. Legg, [Chap. 1, note 5], pp. 323–4.

37. See Leycester's documents which used to be held at Tabley Hall. The uncatalogued collection has now been transferred to the John Rylands Library at Manchester.

Chapter 3

1. *The Regulations and Establishment of the Household of Henry Algernon Percy, the Fifth Earl of Northumberland, at his Castles of Wresill and Lekinfield in Yorkshire* (T. Percy, editor), (London, 1827) pp. 367–76; otherwise known as *The Northumberland Household Book.*

2. Although integrated chapels had of course existed in some medieval houses, particularly in fortified buildings.

3. Percy, [note 1], pp. 331–8; 367–76.

4. Because so few plans of upper storeys survive, there is very little complete evidence about access. In many cases, an upper chapel would be reached from the same level, but there are also examples of staircases in, or adjacent to, a chapel that may have served the upper chapel.

5. West Sussex Record Office, Petworth archives 3538–47 (cited by kind permission of Lord Egremont, the owner of those documents). Although Wressle is a medieval building, the plans show the considerable updating that occurred in the early 16th century, and could well be the most detailed record of an early Tudor chapel interior to survive.

6. R. Coope, 'The Long Gallery: its Origins, Development, Use and Decoration', *Architectural History,* 29 (1986), pp. 43–72.

7. The only surviving early Tudor description of this type which mentions the chapel: A. Boorde, *A Compendyous Regyment or Dyetary of Health* (F.J. Furnivall, editor), (London, 1870), pp. 233–5.

8. M. Airs, *The Tudor and Jacobean Country House: a Building History* (Stroud, 1995), p. 55.

9. The east end window in the chapel at Cotehele has a pointed arch, but this is explained by its medieval origins.

10. After the Dissolution of the monasteries, monastic windows were re-used in new buildings and, by association, may have been thought suitable for chapel windows. It is difficult to find documented examples, but it is likely that the chapel window at Samlesbury Hall in Lancashire was brought from the nearby Whalley Abbey by Sir Thomas Southworth who was a Commissioner

(see M. Howard, *The Early Tudor Country House: Architecture and Politics 1490-1550* (London, 1987), p. 142). However, the re-use of monastic windows in newly built chapels as opposed to domestic rooms was not a frequent enough occurrence to count as a common feature.

11. M. Howard, *The Vyne* (National Trust, 1998), p. 45.

12. For further information about Shelton, see A. Emery, *Greater Medieval Houses of England and Wales,* 2 (Cambridge, 1996), pp. 149-51.

13. M. Girouard, 'The Development of Longleat House between 1546 and 1572', *Archaeological Journal,* 116 (1961), pp. 200-22.

14. The word pew is here used in its late medieval sense, that is, as a 'place (often enclosed) usually raised on a footpace, seated for and appropriated to certain of the worshippers, eg for a great personage, a family etc.'. *Shorter Oxford English Dictionary,* 2 (Oxford, 1967), p. 1484. Very few examples of a lord's pew survive, but the late medieval one at Berkeley Castle in Gloucestershire (although not *in situ*) gives an idea of what the Wressle pew might have been like (pictured in Ricketts, [Intro., note 4], Plate 12).

15. S. Thurley, *The Royal Palaces of Tudor England* (New Haven and London, 1993), p. 196.

16. M. Aston, 'Segregation in Church' in *Women in the Church* (W.J. Sheils and D. Wood, editors), (Oxford, 1990), pp. 269-81.

17. [Editor's note: for a full exposition of the recent investigations and discoveries at The Vyne, see Howard and Wilson, [Chap. 2, note 19]. Pp. 85-91 and 110-11 refer to the chapel and its peripheral spaces.]

18. Transcribed in W.B. Compton, *History of the Comptons of Compton Wynyates* (London, 1930), pp. 308-11.

19. Larke's Survey of Ingatestone, Essex Record Office D/CP M186; for the 1600 inventory, see Essex Record Office D/CP F215.

20. Percy, [note 1], p. 332, and West Sussex Record Office, Petworth archives, [note 5]; the plan of the principle floor at Wressle (fig. 3.14a) shows two small rooms immediately off 'my lord's chamber', one of which is probably the closet referred to.

21. Extracts from the Castle Hedingham documents, the whereabouts of which are now unknown, have been published in *Archaeologia,* 66 (1915), pp. 275-348.

22. 'Inventory of the Goods of Dame Agnes Hungerford' (J.G. Nichols and J.E. Jackson, editors), *Archaeologia,* 38 (1860), pp. 353-72; Howard and Wilson, [Chap. 2, note 19].

23. A lectern is included in the 1565 Charterhouse inventory (Bodleian MS North b.12 f. 31v-2; my thanks to Stephen Porter for his help with this inventory); and the inventory of Henry VIII (*c.*1550) lists a ' foldinge lecture couered all ouer with greane vellet and fringed with grene Sylke' which had formerly belonged to the duke of Norfolk – *The Inventory of King Henry VIII* (D. Starkey, editor), (London, 1998), pp. 174-5.

24. A. Hayward, 'Thornbury Castle', *Transactions of the Bristol and Gloucester Archaeological Society,* 95 (1977), p. 54; G.R. Batho, 'The Percies at Petworth 1574-1632', *Sussex Archaeological Collections,* 95 (1957), p. 10.

25. For further discussion of the fittings at Wressle, see Ricketts, [Intro., note 4], pp. 138-9.

26. Batho, *Petworth,* [note 24], pp. 6-7.

27. See Howard and Wilson, [Chap. 2, note 19], p. 110.

28. The construction of the stalls is solid up to first-floor level, and the only breaks in their solidity are the small cusped openings in the upper half of the central doors.

29. Percy, [note 1], pp. 40-1, 44, 48, 368-74; J. Gage 'The Household Book of Edward Stafford, Duke of Buckingham', *Archaeologia,* 25 (1834), pp. 318-27; reference to Sir Robert Jermyn's 'godly chapel of syngyng men' at Rushbrooke in H. Machyn, 'Diary of Henry Machyn, Citizen and Merchant-Taylor of London from AD 1550 to AD 1563' (J. Nichols, editor), (London, 1848), p. 27.

30. The 1541 inventory does show that there was a schoolmaster's room at The Vyne, but this need not suggest that his charges were employed as singing boys.

31. E.g. why, in work of this quality, is the junction with the door in the south wall so awkward? Why does the form of some individual stalls vary in an apparently random way? And why does the distribution of the figurative poppy heads appear not to relate to the general form of the stalls? It may be that undocumented changes (such as to the panelling below the east windows) were made during the 17th and early 18th centuries, or perhaps the changes made in the later 18th century have not been fully understood.

32. B. Winchester, *Tudor Family Portrait* (London, 1955), p. 112.

33. Although no great reliance can be placed on individual decorative details, the basic structure of the ceiling appears to be original.

34. Kenninghall's altarpiece was a 'fair table of the Birth, Passion and Resurrection of Christ wrought upon wainscot. Imagery all gilt' (National Archives, LR 2/115).

35. A Wilton 1561 inventory lists a 'table plated with sylver and gylte for the Altare with the picture of Christ and his Apostells' (Victoria and Albert Museum Library, NAL KRP.D.30).

36. Compton Wynyates (1522): see Compton, [note 18]; The Vyne (1541/2): see Howard and Wilson, [Chap. 2, note 19].

37. Extracts from both documents have been published in 'The Last Testament and Inventory of John de Vere, Thirteenth Earl of Oxford', *Archaeologia* (W.H. St J. Hope, editor), 66 (1915), pp. 275-348. The whereabouts of the originals are not known.

38. National Archives, LR 2/115.

39. Only at Wilton were the altar cloths and wall hangings of similarly high quality.

40. Information from the inventories for Kenninghall (1547): National Archives, LR 2/115); and Chesworth (1549): H. Ellis, 'Inventories of Goods etc in the Manor of Chesworth, Sedgewick and Other Parks', *Sussex Archaeological Collections*, 13 (1861), pp. 118-26. See also Ricketts, [Intro., note 4], p. 188 for more detail.

41. H. Peacham, *The Complete Gentleman*, (London, 1622), p. 109; *The History of the King's Works* (H. Colvin, editor), 4 (London, 1982), pp. 315, 341.

42. At The Vyne there was a canopy of 'crimson satin and yellowe damaske' (5s) – see Howard and Wilson, [Chap. 2, note 19]; for Heytesbury, the 1523 inventory lists 'a canabe of russet velvet fringed with red and green silk with all the silk things belonging to the sepulchre' (J.G. Nichols and J. E. Jackson, [Note 22]).

43. Although it is likely that the glass in The Vyne chapel came originally from Lord Sandys' Chapel of the Holy Ghost at Basingstoke – see H. Wayment 'The Stained Glass in the Chapel of the Vyne and the Chapel of the Holy Ghost, Basingstoke', *Archaeologia,* 107 (1982), pp. 141-52.

44. See Ricketts, [Intro., note 4], p. 189 for examples at Compton Wynyates I, The Vyne, Collyweston in Lincolnshire, Wilton and Kenninghall.

45. Inventory quoted in *Royal Institution of Cornwall Journal*, 2 (1867), pp. 226-37. It is possible that the flowers could have had a symbolic meaning, but there are no clearly documented examples of this practice in the early Tudor period.

46. See also Ricketts, [Intro., note 4], p. 191, which argues that, for example, the scheme at Kenninghall, although centred on the Passion, was not coordinated across different media.

47. Pl. V shows that the size and arrangement of the panels along the upper part of the south wall are similar to the panels on the ceiling. W. Hutchinson, *The History of Cumberland,* 1 (Carlisle, 1794), p. 135, and D. and S. Lysons, *Magna Britannia,* 4 (London, 1816), pp. cciv and 32-3. [Editor's note: though Hutchinson and Lysons describe the ceiling scheme as extending to the east wall, the pictures there as shown in Plate VI seem to be of a different type. See further comments in note 48 below.]

48. See Hutchinson, p. 136 and Lysons, p. cciv, [both note 47]. [Editor's note: Annabel Ricketts, [Intro., note 4] states (pp. 190–1) that the Tree of Jesse was on the liturgical east wall of the chapel, and is visible in the 19th-century view at pl.VI. On the other hand, Hutchinson and Lysons agree that it was on the ceiling, a description followed by Croft-Murray (E. Croft-Murray, *Decorative Painting in England, 1537–1837*, 1 (London, 1962), p. 16), and I cannot myself distinguish it on the east wall in pl.VI. It may be that the depiction of Jesse was not a wall painting already *in situ* at Naworth, but formed part of the scheme transferred from Kirkoswald in 1622. Indeed it is difficult to see how there could otherwise have been space for it on the ceiling because, as pls.V and VI show, it was (in the mid-19th century at any rate) tightly packed with portraits. However, since Hutchinson and Lysons describe the ceiling scheme as extending to the east wall, Annabel Ricketts may well be correct in that Jesse himself was represented on this wall, with his progeny, in the form of the portraits of kings and patriarchs, spreading across the ceiling.]

49. F. Baigent and J. Millard, *A History of the Town and Manor of Basingstoke* (London, 1889), p. 111.

Chapter 4

1. The Thorpe collection is in the Soane Museum, and the Smythson collection is in the Royal Institute of British Architects, both in London.

2. Note Francis Bacon's description of the planning of a great house in his essay *On Building*: 'on...the household side, I wish it divided at first into a hall and a chapel, ... and those not to go all the length, but to have at the further end a winter and a summer parlour' (F. Bacon, *The Works of Francis Bacon* (J. Spedding, L. Ellis and D. Heath editors), 6 (London, 1858), pp. 482–3).

3. This was most likely due both to the demands of symmetry, and because more flexible internal arrangements made an external entrance unnecessary.

4. This observation is based on a study of those of Thorpe's pre-Jacobean plans where a chapel can be identified, including those belonging to Summerson's Primary Series (i.e. produced *c*.1596–1603; see J. Summerson, *The Book of Architecture of John Thorpe* (Glasgow, 1966), p. 22). The plans are: T19/20, T63/64, T65/66, T113/14, T149, T163/64, T183/84, T193/94, T211/12, T221, T239/40 (and alternatives) and T245. [Editor's note: 'T' numbers refer to references coined by Summerson. They are not included in the text, but may be found in footnotes, captions to illustrations and the Gazetteer.]

5. J. Husselby, 'Architecture at Burghley House: The Patronage of William Cecil 1553-1598' (unpublished Ph.D thesis, University of Warwick, 1996), pp. 99, 270–2.

6. H. Walpole, *Horace Walpole's Journal of Visits to Country Seats etc.* (P. Toynbee, editor), (Glasgow, 1928), pp. 58–9.

7. John Norden describes an oratory in the corner of the great chamber at Cecil House, perhaps in this case referring to a pulpit: see J. Norden, 'Speculum Britanniae', 1593 (British Library, Harleian MS 570 I, f. 39r). In the recently discovered late 16th-century plan of Cecil House, no room is clearly identifiable as a chapel. Although this is not conclusive proof that it did not possess one, it must strengthen the possibility since chapels, with their specific access needs and lack of fireplace, are often easily identified on plan. William Cecil may have held household prayers in the great chamber, with the congregation being addressed from the pulpit/oratory by his chaplain. See J. Husselby and P. Henderson, 'Location, Location, Location! Cecil House in the Strand', *Architectural History,* 45 (2002), pp. 159–93. My thanks to Paula Henderson for illuminating discussions about the plan.

8. One of the few consistent characteristics of the private chapel during the period 1500-1700 is that it is extremely rare for a fireplace to be provided other than in the upper chapel. Only one exception, at Bere Court in Berkshire, has been found.

9. It is unlikely that the celebration of communion was intended in a simple narthex chapel.

10. The site of the Elizabethan chapel is not securely documented, but it is likely that it occupied the same position as its 17th-century successor at the west end of the south range, a supposition that the order of the rooms in the 1601 inventory appears to confirm - see *Of Household Stuff*, [Intro., note 5].

11. It should, however, be noted that the Copthall plan is of 18th-century date, and could therefore incorporate later changes.

12. Much can be learned of the 'little' and 'great' chapels from a 1574 report on the house and a 1576 survey. The 'great' chapel originally extended a further 8ft west. See Batho, *Petworth*, [Chap. 3, note 24], pp. 4-8.

13. [Editor's note: see A. Ricketts, 'Designing for Protestant Worship: the Private Chapels of the Cecil Family' (with C. Gapper and C. Knight) in *Defining the Holy: Sacred Space in Medieval and Early Modern Europe* (A. Spicer and S. Hamilton, editors), (Aldershot, 2005), pp. 117, 124-5.]

14. T183-4.

15. The screen now in the parish church at Holdenby was set up there in the 18th century. For a discussion of this screen see M. Girouard, *Town and Country* (London, 1992), pp. 208-9.

16. The passage was about 12ft 6ins wide at its narrowest point and some 40ft long.

17. N. Nichols, *Memoirs of the Life and Times of Sir Christopher Hatton* (London, 1847), p. 224. The fact that Lord Burghley particularly praised the arrangement suggests that it was not considered impractical.

18. RIBA, Smythson, I/24.

19. See Ricketts, [Intro., note 4], pp. 78-9 for a detailed discussion of the Wimbledon chapel.

20. Little is known of the extent to which outdoor staff and tenants might use a household chapel. However, Cope refers to a door into the chapel at Bramshill from the courtyard 'by which, as I have been informed by ancient people who remembered it in use, not only the domestics, but even the dependants and tenants, had access to the chapel' (W.H. Cope, *Bramshill, Its History and Architecture* (London, 1883), pp. 34-5).

21. See 'Country Seats', [note 4], p. 29.

22. A design for the Great House, Chelsea at Hatfield House, Cecil MSS, CPM II/x, shows a similar arrangement.

23. Some confirmation of this is provided by the 1601 inventory which lists 'in the half pace at the stare head ... fyve formes' (*Of Household Stuff*, [Intro., note 5], p. 51). But it should be noted that forms are also listed on the landing outside Bess's withdrawing chamber.

24. See Ricketts, [Intro., note 4], p. 80 which explains in more detail why the alterations were due to a late (but nonetheless contemporary) change of plan.

25. Of twenty-three Thorpe plans in which a chapel is securely identifiable, thirteen depict assembly chapels. Of these, four can definitely be associated with Elizabethan houses and five are Jacobean.

26. Although some examples are still to be found among Thorpe's early 17th-century plans, for example T62 depicting the Blewhouse in Highgate, London.

27. Hatfield House, Cecil MSS, CPM II 6-7, 9-10, 15-16. My thanks to Nicholas Cooper for sharing his thoughts on these plans.

28. A stacked chapel is one in which the upper chapel has the same dimensions as the lower chapel.

29. RIBA, Smythson II/2(2).

30. The two possible exceptions are, as usual, Copthall and Little Moreton Hall.

31. Though it is fair to say that few new parish churches were built during this period.

32. S.L. Ticker, 'Descent of the Manor of Sheffield', *Journal of the British Archaeological Association*,

30 (1874), pp. 251-60; *Of Household Stuff,* [Intro., note 5].

33. T109.

34. Batho, [Intro., note 10], p. 117.

35. See, for example, Norden's description of Cecil House in the Strand (Norden, [note 7]). It will also be recalled, [Intro., note 9], that Florio's *Dictionary* recorded that the word 'oratory' could also be used to mean 'pulpit', the probable explanation being that a pulpit was provided in the room in which the household gathered for prayers.

36. Although the mention of one in *The Northumberland Household Book* (Percy, [Chap. 3, note 1], pp. 370, 374) underlines the fact that they were not a Protestant introduction.

37. Charterhouse 1565 inventory − Bodleian MS, [Chap. 3, note 23].

38. Essex RO, D/DP F215.

39. See Ricketts, [Intro., note 4], p. 149 for further discussion about forms versus kneelers.

40. For instance, at Hardwick and Chatsworth − see Ricketts, [Intro., note 4], p. 149 − where there were also single chairs, presumably for the patrons, together with stools.

41. T245.

42. For Althorp see Colen Campbell's plan which clearly shows a chapel with a west end platform raised by three steps (C. Campbell, *Vitruvius Britannicus*, 2 (London, 1717), pl. 95-7).

43. R. Smith, *The Life of the Most Honourable and Vertuous Lady, the Lady Magdalen, Viscountess Montague* (St Omer, 1627), p. 43.

44. For example, a 1554 survey shows that Sir William Petre had, in the chapel of his house in Aldersgate, London, an 'alabaster table... a gift from Compagni' (Essex RO, D/DP T286). However, the 1600 inventory of his country house, Ingatestone, lists a wooden table in the chapel (Essex RO, D/DP F215). This was a short plain table on a frame, and likely to have been the communion table.

45. The term 'altar' does, however, survive in descriptions of objects connected with the communion table such as 'altar rails'.

46. Information from the relevant inventories. Compton Wynyates: see Compton, [Chap. 3, note 18]; The Vyne (1541/2): see Howard and Wilson, [Chap. 2, note 19]; Kewe (1556/7): see *Royal Institution of Cornwall Journal*, 2 (1867), pp. 226-37; Appuldurcombe (1566): see J.L. Whitehead, 'An Inventory of the Goods and Chattels of Sir Richard Worsley, of Appuldurcombe, A.D. 1566', *Papers and Proceedings of the Hampshire Field Club*, 5.3 (1906), pp. 277-95; Charterhouse (1565): see Bodleian MS, [Chap. 3, note 23].

47. E. Lodge, *Illustrations of British History*, 2 (London, 1791), p. 187; Aston, [Chap. 1, note 8], p. 318; Z. Dovey, *An Elizabethan Progress* (Stroud, 1999), pp. 53-4.

48. Frere and Kennedy, [Chap. 2, note 1].

49. Frere and Kennedy, [Chap. 2, note 1], p. 289.

50. Baron Zdenkonius Brtnicencis Waldstein, *The Diary of Baron Waldstein: A Traveller in Elizabethan England* (G.W. Groos, editor/translator), (London, 1981).

51. R. Richards, 'The Chapels of The Blessed Virgin Mary and St John at High Legh, Cheshire', *Transactions of the Historic Society of Lancashire and Cheshire*, 101 (1949), pp. 116-17.

52. H.T. Kirby. 'Compton Verney Glass', *Country Life,* 115 (15 April 1954). The current whereabouts of the panel is not known.

53. Bacon, [note 2], p. 483.

54. Quoted in J.F. Merritt, 'Puritans, Laudians, and the Phenomenon of Church-Building in Jacobean London', *Historical Journal,* 41, 4 (1998), p. 956. The Oxford English Dictionary records one meaning of coarctation in 1605 as 'confinement or restriction as to limits'.

55. It is clear that he was referring to the Earl's assembly chapel in his house at Wimbledon, begun in 1588, since the Exeter chapel in Wimbledon parish church was not started until 1626. [Editor's

note: my thanks to Caroline Knight for this clarification.]

56. It is interesting that the walls of the presumed Roman Catholic chapel at Kirkby Hall, Furness, Cumbria, are decorated with heraldic devices, texts of prayers, and the Ten Commandments. They may well date from this period.

57. *Of Household Stuff*, [Intro., note 5], pp. 25, 28.

58. For instance, the upper chapel contained: 'a forme Covered with blewe cloth and grene silk frenge, a Chare of tawnie and yellowe velvet ... a turkie Carpet, a silk Curtin as well as of three cusions of different materials'. *Of Household Stuff*, [Intro., note 5], p. 25.

59. *Of Household Stuff*, [Intro., note 5], pp. 51-2.

60. Aston, [Chap. 1, note 8], pp 313-14; A. Wells-Cole, *Art and Decoration in Elizabethan and Jacobean England* (New Haven and London, 1997), p. 295.

61. Forty heraldic shields were listed at Horseheath in 1591; besides those in the chapel there were also ten in the hall and twelve in the parlour (C. Parsons, 'Horseheath Hall and its Owners', *Proceedings of the Cambridge Antiquarian Society*, 41 (1948), pp. 1-51).

62. Essex Record Office, D/DW E26, 27. See also Coope, [Chap. 3, note 6]. It is possible that each of the two doors opened on to a closet in much the same way as the arrangement proposed for Great House, Chelsea (fig. 4.10).

63. Harrison's description of 1587 mentions great houses 'so magnificent and stately as the basest house of a baron doth often match in our day with some honours of princes in old time'. W. Harrison, *The Description of England* (G. Edelen, editor), (Ithaca, 1968), p. 199.

64. Information from inventories for Kimberley (1588 – see: L.G. Bolingbroke, 'Two Elizabethan Inventories', *Norfolk Archaeology*, 15 (1904), pp. 93-107) and Appuldurcombe (1566 – see note 46). See also Howard, [Chap. 3, note 10], pp. 37, 114.

65. Vyne Inventory (1541): see Howard and Wilson, [Chap. 2, note 19]; Hengrave inventory (1603): see Cambridge University Library, Hengrave, 81. The latter inventory was taken when surviving members of the Kytson family were suffering heavy penalties for recusancy.

Chapter 5

1. See Homily III in the *Second Tome of Homilies* (1562/3); also 'The Anglican Canons 1529-1947' (G. Bray, editor), *Church of England Record Society*, 6 (1998), pp. 726, 743.

2. Bray, [note 1], pp. 378-81; K. Fincham and P. Lake, 'Ecclesiastical Policy of James I', *Journal of British Studies*, 24.2 (1985), pp. 169-207.

3. Houses whose chapels were consecrated in the Jacobean period included Bramshill House in Hampshire, Chantemarle House in Dorset, Charlton House in Greenwich, Childerley, Clay Hall in Essex, Hatfield, Langley Park in Kent, Easton Lodge, and Oxhey in Hertfordshire (e.g. Legg, [Chap. 1, note 5], pp. 318-20).

4. Although it should be noted that of Thorpe plans for eleven houses shown as containing a chapel and likely to be of Jacobean date, three – T39-40 for Loseley Park (Surrey), T62 for the Blewhouse (Highgate, London), and T171-2, probably for Little Charlton (East Sutton, Kent) – show fenestration patterns that fitted awkwardly with the internal divisions of the chapel.

5. T105-6; Summerson, [Chap. 4, note 4], p. 74.

6. This set (II/2) is usually dated to *c*.1600 on the grounds that it is similar to Smythson's unrealised design (I/19) of about 1599 for Slingsby Castle North Yorkshire, and because the same type of paper is used.

7. This window appears to have been rebuilt, but other chapels (such as that at Chantemarle) made use of apsidal east ends at this time and it is quite likely that the feature is original.

8. Thorpe's plan (T203-4) accords with this, though it differs from Winstanley's in many other respects.

9. P. Drury, 'No other Palace in the Kingdom will Compare with it: the Evolution of Audley End 1605-1745', *Architectural History*, 23 (1980), pp. 1-39. Although Winstanley's view was executed after the house had passed into royal ownership, it is unlikely that the chapel was significantly altered since the royal accounts show that only minor remedial work was carried out; Colvin, [Chap. 3, note 41], 5, pp. 131-3.

10. For a detailed discussion see C. Gapper, J. Newman and A. Ricketts, 'Hatfield: a House for a Lord Treasurer' in *Patronage, Culture and Power, The Early Cecils 1558-1612* (P. Croft, editor), (London, 2002), pp. 67-95.

11. The east window is centred on the chapel's internal space so that, when viewed from the outside, it is offset to the south.

12. Dorset Record Office, [Chap. 1, note 4].

13. Dorset Record Office, [Chap. 1, note 4], ff.

14. P. Morant, *The History and Antiquities of the County of Essex*, 2 (London, 1768), p. 430.

15. Though Raynham Hall in Norfolk (started in 1618) may be another example. According to an elevation of the east front of 1671 in the RIBA Library, the majority of windows had mullions and transoms, but the three chapel windows are shown without detailing, possibly indicating a different treatment from the rest of the house.

16. The east window at Childerley may well have been altered, since documents refer to a six-light window, while the present window has seven lights.

17. N. Pevsner, *The Buildings of England, Northamptonshire* (Harmondsworth, 1990), pp. 413-14.

18. 'A great promoter of the Reformation', Crewe was a leading Puritan (Cliffe, [Chap. 1, note 7], p. 108).

19. Although a variant on a basement approach was also used at Raynham, and is shown in the 1671 plan (fig. 5.24).

20. For Woburn, see D. Duggan, 'The Architectural Patronage of the 4th Earl of Bedford, 1587-1641' (unpublished Ph.D thesis, University of London, 2002), pp. 25-68.

21. My thanks to Dianne Duggan for discussing this with me before the publication of her article 'Woburn Abbey: the First Episode of a Great Country House' in *Architectural History*, 46 (2003), pp. 57-80.

22. See Ricketts, [Intro., note 4], p. 58 for more on the position of the chapel at Wilton.

23. The identification of the two pavilions as, respectively, a library (west pavilion) and a chapel (east pavilion) rests solely on inscriptions to that effect in C. Campbell, *Vitruvius Britannicus*, 3 (London, 1725), pl. 9.

24. Palladio's aim in plans of this type was to combine practicality (the farm buildings being carefully positioned to be easily accessible and yet not intrusive) with grandeur by using the physical presence of the outbuildings to create an imposing group.

25. A recently discovered plan in the Hertfordshire Record Office (D/EC/P2) shows that, in the late 18th-century, the form and fittings of the chapel were substantially as they are now. But there were 19th-century alterations at Tyttenhanger and, although the existence of a 17th-century chapel is documented, more changes could have been made than are usually recognised.

26. Blount also bid his servants attend public executions on the grounds that it would do them more good than 'all the oratory in the Sermons' (J. Aubrey, *Aubrey's Brief Lives* (O.L. Dick, editor), (London, 1958), p. 27).

27. Although a view of Temple Newsam in 1699 by Knyff and Kip does not show a differentiated east window, this may be explained by the small scale – see L. Knyff, and J. Kip, *Britannia Illustrata* (J. Harris, and G. Jackson-Stops, editors), (Bungay, 1984), pl. 42. And the drawing *The prospect of Temple Newsam from (....) first outer court c.1712* in the Leeds City Art Gallery's collection (38.1/79) clearly shows that the upper register of the east window had arched lights.

28. N. Pevsner, *The Buildings of England: Leicestershire and Rutland* (Harmondsworth, 1970), p. 238.

29. Woburn Archive (uncatalogued). My thanks to Dianne Duggan for bringing this chapel to my attention, and for the very useful discussions about the house.

30. See Ricketts, [Intro., note 4], p. 116 for arguments supporting the contention that the chapel at Woburn was created by the 4th Earl of Bedford rather than the 2nd Earl.

31. State Papers 14/144, no. 11.

32. According to Hugh Walpole (*Anecdotes of Painting in England,* 1 (Strawberry Hill, 1765), p. 175n.), Bedford instructed Jones to make it 'not … much better than a barn'.

33. The date of this window, which is considerably larger than the Venetian window on the main entrance front, has been questioned. However, as Heward and Taylor have pointed out, the *voussoirs* appear to be contemporary with those of the *loggia* (J. Heward and R. Taylor, *Country Houses of Northamptonshire* (Swindon, 1996), p. 132).

34. In 1635, he told de Caus to 'take downe … that side of Wilton house which is towards the Garden & such other parts as shall bee necessary & rebuild it anew with additions according to ye Plott' (quoted in A.A. Tait, 'Isaac de Caus and the South Front of Wilton House', *Burlington Magazine*, 106 (1964), p. 74).

35. J. Harris and A.A. Tait, *Catalogue of Drawings by Inigo Jones, John Webb and Isaac de Caus at Worcester College, Oxford* (Oxford, 1979), p. 49 (no. 111) and pl. 92.

36. British Library, Add MS 33767B, f. 24. These are discussed in J. Bold with J. Reeves, *Wilton House and English Palladianism* (London, 1988), pp. 40-3.

37. For Campbell's plan see Campbell, [note 23], p. 18; for Rocque's plan see Courtauld Institute BF2639/1.

38. The reconstruction appears in Bold, [note 36], p. 64.

39. T186. Included in J. Summerson's 'Primary Series' dated 1596-1603, [Chap. 4, note 4].

40. T43-4, T62.

41. Respectively T201 and T205, T67 and T81-2.

42. Bramhope was ostensibly built as a chapel of ease but, being owned by Robert Dyneley, it was in effect a private chapel. The appointment of a minister was controlled by Dyneley and five Trustees rather than by Dyneley alone.

43. Heywood, [Chap. 2, note 11], p. 194.

44. However, the orientation of the chapel cannot be verified. If it were correctly-oriented, with (unusually) the east end terminating the short axis, it would then be incorrect to see the space as a side gallery.

45. My thanks to Anthony Wells-Cole for this information. Since the long axis of the chapel runs east-west and terminates in a large (and originally differentiated) east window, the orientation of this chapel is not in question.

46. See Hutchinson, p. 137 and Lysons, pp. cciv-v [both Chap. 3, note 47].

47. See the incomplete, partially transcribed 17th-century building and household accounts in *Household Books of the Lord William Howard of Naworth* (G. Ornsby, editor), (Durham, 1878), pp. xlii-lxxi, 132-3, 194; State Papers Dom. Eliz. clxiv. 48.

48. S. Markham, *John Loveday of Caversham, 1711-1789* (Salisbury, 1984), pp. 216-17. This chapel could have been left over from the tenure of a previous patron, Lord Williams (died 1559), or was perhaps installed and/or used by subsequent owners ranging from the Norreys family to the high-church, Jacobite Bertie family.

49. Hatfield [Intro., note 6]; Hatfield, Cecil MSS, Box C/8.

50. D. Duggan, [note 21], pp. 57-80; C. Stanley-Milson and J. Newman, 'Blickling Hall: The Building of a Jacobean Mansion', *Architectural History,* 29 (1986), pp.1-42.

51. Both family pews at Haddon, created about ten years earlier than Woburn, had reading shelves fitted to their west sides, presumably so that the assembled household could be addressed by the patron.

52. Because of their strong pre-Reformation connotations, the terms 'chancel' and 'nave' have largely been avoided in the ensuing discussion. Instead the more neutral terms east and west cells have been used.

53. Although Horton Davies, writing about the chapel in 1975, describes benches surrounding the communion table on the north and east sides only (H. Davies, *Worship and Theology in England*, 2 (Princeton, 1975), pp. 26-7).

54. Again, various alterations have been made, but the survival of the building accounts helps in understanding the original arrangement. J. Simmons and H. Colvin, 'Staunton Harold Church', *Architectural Journal*, 112 (1955), pp. 173-4.

55. The National Trust guidebook (1990) notes that 'instead of the present altar rails there were originally moveable kneeling forms, covered in dark purple houseling cloths' (p. 10). I have not been able to trace the source for this statement.

56. Since Henry Slingsby II writes 'it would be of great ease to us yt live here at Redhouse to have a sermon in ye Chapple being so far from our Parish Church'. Slingsby, [Chap. 2, note 28], pp. 7-8, 19-21.

57. Aston, 'Segregation in Church', [Chap. 3, note 16], pp. 209, 246.

58. *The Memoirs of Lady Anne Halkett and Lady Ann Fanshawe* (J Loftus, editor), (Oxford, 1979), p. 41.

59. Hutchinson, [Chap. 3, note 47], pp. 135-6.

60. This arrangement is emphasised by the pulpit cloth which runs the whole way round the exposed part of the pulpit (with the exception of the door), thus confirming that it was possible to address both the east and west cells of the chapel with equal ease.

61. See *Halkett*, [note 58], pp. 41-2: 'the gallery was the usual passage to the chapell'.

62. Certainly this was the interpretation favoured in the 18th century, since Hutchinson writes (Hutchinson, [Chap. 3, note 47], p. 135) that 'a long elevated stall faces the pulpit, which perhaps was the place of the chief domestics'.

63. In 1619 (see Legg, [Chap. 1, note 5], p. 319).

64. This type of chapel is often known as a 'Cromwellian chapel'. However its documented existence from the 1620s together with the strong possibility that other chapels of this type existed earlier makes this a misleading description.

65. See Dowsing, [Intro., note 16], Appendix 5, pp. 337-50.

66. A close reading of the accounts (Simmons and Colvin, [note 54]), reveals that the provision of altar rails cannot be ruled out as part of the original design at Staunton Harold.

67. At Staunton Harold, payment for 'erecting the Kings arms and tenn commandments' was made in 1662 (Simmons and Colvin, [note 54], p. 175).

68. There is some doubt as to the date of the Low Ham screen. Although the decoration suggests the 1620s, it is possible that biblical quotations refer to the Civil War, and were therefore a later addition.

69. There is a tradition of green men and forms related to them being used in this way. At Chastleton a house of very similar date, and also in Oxfordshire, they are used to guard the windows of the long gallery. My thanks to Claire Gapper for this information.

70. For a list of chapels with pulpits, see Ricketts, [Intro., note 4], p. 166.

71. Exceptions include Rycote and Langley Hall, where the pulpits are square.

72. For example at Naworth, Chantemarle, Haddon, Knole and Bramhope (as well as in Laud's chapel at Lambeth Palace in London). However, at Langley Hall, Rycote and Staunton Harold

the pulpits are on the south side.

73. W. Butterfield, *Alterations in and about Hatfield House since 1868* (privately printed, 1908).

74. 'The Parliamentary Survey of Richmond, Wimbledon & Nonsuch in the County of Surrey, AD 1649' (W. Hart, editor), *Sussex Archaeological Collections,* 5 (1871), pp. 104–11; Cornwall Record Office, V/EC/4/2, 8-98.

75. G. Jackson Stops and J. Pipkin, *The English Country House, a Grand Tour* (London, 1985), p. 212.

76. Although it is likely that the tradition has not continued unbroken. My thanks to Robin Harcourt-Williams for this information.

77. See Aston, 'Segregation in Church', [Chap. 3, note 16], for a detailed discussion of this subject.

78. For example, in 1612 the household at Hatfield consisted of 61 people of whom 56 were male and only 5 were female; this remained fairly constant for in 1637 there were 62 males and 11 females. The proportions were similar at Naworth, although the household was smaller (Hatfield House, Accs 160/3, 33/1 and Box 1/4; for Naworth, see Household Books, [note 47]).

79. G.D. Stawell, *A Quantock Family* (Taunton, 1910), p. 473.

80. Cf John Donne: 'if the true use of Pictures be preached unto them, there is no danger of abuse; and so, as remembrances of that which hath been taught in the Pulpit, they may be retained'. J. Donne, *Sermons,* 7 (E. Simpson and G. Potter, editors), (Berkeley, 1954), p. 432.

81. W. Prynne, *Canterburies Doome, or The First Part of a Compleat History of the Commitment, Charge, Tryall, Condemnation and Execution of William Laud, Late Archbishop of Canterbury* (London, 1646), p. 466.

82. W. Brereton, *Travels in Holland, The United Provinces, England, Scotland and Ireland* (E. Hawkins, editor), (Manchester, 1844), p. 187. My thanks to Margaret Aston for this reference.

83. See Dictionary of National Biography and *The Acts of the High Commission Court within the Diocese of Durham* (W.H.D. Longstaffe, editor), (Durham, 1858), pp. 201-2. Smart was subsequently imprisoned for some twelve years on refusing to pay the fine levied as a punishment for the views expressed in his sermon.

84. J. Hall, *Works* (P. Wynter, editor), 5 (Oxford, 1863), p. 191.

85. A. Willet, *Synopsis Papismi* (London, 1613), pp. 465, 484-6.

86. British Library, Harleian MSS 159 f. 136; J. Spottiswoode, *History of the Church of Scotland*, 3 (Edinburgh, 1851), pp. 238-9.

87. H. Peacham, *The Art of Drawing with the Pen* (London, 1606), p. 8.

88. H. Peacham, *The Gentleman's Exercise or Graphice* (London, 1612), pp. 7, 11-12.

89. J. Harris and G. Higgott, *Inigo Jones: Complete Architectural Drawings* (London, 1989), pp. 178-9.

90. Laud, [Chap. 2, note 16], pp. 364-5. Laud notes that in 1639 Cutt claimed that the chapel had been consecrated by Bishop Heton between 1600 and 1609.

91. Aston, [Chap. 1, note 8], p. 156.

92. Victoria and Albert Museum, C.62-1927, ID 632.

93. For comment and a full list of the subjects and the inscriptions, see Croft (editor), [note 10], pp. 88-9 and 92. The west window probably also originally contained painted glass.

94. Morant, [note 14], 2, p. 433; M. Archer, 'Seventeenth Century Painted Glass at Little Easton', *Essex Journal,* 12.1 (1977), pp. 3-10.

95. In July 1622 Richard Butler was paid for '9: of the 12 Apostles for a window in the Chappell at Redhowse of 3: lights' which was for the south window. Slingsby, [Chap. 2, note 28], p.31; M. Archer, 'Richard Butler, Glass-painter', *Burlington Magazine*, 132 (1990), pp. 310-11; J. Pocklington, *Altare Christianum or the Dead Vicar's Plea* (London 1637), p. 87; A. Wells-Cole 'The Dining Room

at Temple Newsam', *Leeds Arts Calendar,* No. 110 (1992), pp. 23-4.

96. These scenes have all been cut at the top, and may not be in their original setting.

97. This scheme was, of course, retained for Protestant worship after Howard's death in 1640.

98. It is tempting to identify the image of Christ as the picture Henry Peacham would not have exchanged 'for the best jewel in the world' – see p. 138 and Peacham, *Graphice,* [note 88].

99. See Ricketts, [Intro., note 4], p. 211 for further discussion of the seemingly incongruous nature of the six paintings at Hatfield.

100. See Croft, [note 10], p. 80 for a description of possibly intentional co-ordination of colour schemes in the king's bedchamber at Hatfield.

101. Quoted in C. Gilbert, 'Light on Sir Arthur Ingram's Reconstruction of Temple Newsam 1622-38', *Leeds Arts Calendar,* 51 (1963), p. 11.

102. It is unlikely that the panels were split evenly between the north and south walls – see Ricketts, [Intro., note 4], pp. 213-4.

103. Two pictures listed in the chapel in the 1666 inventory (West Yorkshire Archive Service, Leeds: WYL 150 TN EA 3/10) are almost certainly those by Carleton mentioned here.

104. Information from inventories for Easton Lodge: F.W. Steer, *Easton Lodge Inventory, 1637* (Great Dunmow, 1952); and Burghley: F. Peck, *Desiderata Curiosa* 1.6 (London, 1732-5), p. 44.

105. *The Travels of Peter Mundy in Europe and Asia 1608-67* (R.C. Temple, editor), (London, 1924), p. 26.

106. British Library, Harleian MS 7017 f. 74, quoted in N. Tyacke, *Anti-Calvinists: The Rise of English Arminianism c.1590-1640* (Oxford, 1987), p. 194.

107. Dowsing, [Intro., note 16], pp. 238, 248.

108. British Library, Lansdowne MS 973 'A Letter sent out of Scotland'.

109. S. Porter and A. White, 'John Colt and the Charterhouse Chapel', *Architectural History,* 44 (2001), pp. 228-36.

110. J. Salmon, *Rycote Chapel,* (guidebook, reprinted 1996): unfortunately no reference is given and the source of this information cannot now be found.

111. But, as already noted, in 1624 the family may have had Roman Catholic connections.

112. Dorset Record Office, [Chap. 1, note 4].

113. The chapel at Temple Newsam did not have an open timber ceiling since the long gallery was immediately above it, but the accounts appear to indicate that it was decorated with angels – see Temple Newsam accounts (West Yorkshire Archive Service, Leeds: WYL 150 TN EA3, 3/10, 13/18 (i) & WYL (Pawson MSS) 178/1, 2, 14). NB it is easy to confuse the Temple Newsam accounts with those for chapels which Ingram was building at the same time at Bootham and in his town house, both in York.

114. See Ricketts, [Intro., note 4], p. 217 for Salisbury House and Easton Lodge.

115. See Ricketts, [Intro., note 4], p. 217 for Hatfield and Easton Lodge.

116. See Ricketts, [Intro., note 4], pp. 217-8 for Hatfield, Easton Lodge and Red House.

117. Magdalen College archive, C3/38/2/1; Tyacke, [note 106], p. 194.

118. Dorset Record Office, [Chap. 1, note 4], ff.

119. For instance the spandrels of the roof timbers at Halston, the decoration of the pulpit originally at Gorhambury (which is likely to be early 17th century) and the mix of cherubim and what appear to be green men on the west side of the screen at Water Eaton.

120. These are now in Thaxted parish church. The ends survive in good condition, although the benches themselves have been altered, and it is no longer possible to reconstruct their original disposition.

121. L. Huygens, *The English Journal 1651–1652* (A.G.H. Bachrach and R.G. Collmer, editors and translators), (Leiden, 1982), p. 55.

122. For a detailed description of the decorative scheme at Rug, see Ricketts, [Intro., note 4], pp. 220-1.

Chapter 6

1. J. Raine, *A Brief Historical Account of the Episcopal Castle, or Palace, of Auckland* (Durham, 1852), p. 85 (the identity of the 'plaine chappell' is not known). See also Emery, [Chap. 3, note 12], 1, p. 52.

2. J. Cosin, *The Correspondence of John Cosin, Lord Bishop of Durham*, 2 (Durham, 1872), p. xxii.

3. It would have been useful to include an analysis of the chapel at Belvoir, but unfortunately I was not granted access to the archives.

4. See F-E. Keller, 'Christian Eltester's Drawings of Roger Pratt's Clarendon House and Robert Hooke's Montagu House', *Burlington Magazine*, 128 (1986), pp. 732-7); R. Pratt, *The Architecture of Sir Roger Pratt*, (R.T. Gunther, editor), (Oxford, 1928), p. 148.

5. Pratt, [note 4], p. 162.

6. C. Campbell, *Vitruvius Britannicus*, 1 (London, 1715), pl. 31.

7. In the handling of the upper chapel, it is tempting to see the Clarendon House gallery as a forerunner of the magnificently baroque gallery at Petworth built by the 6th Duke of Somerset ('the Proud Duke').

8. See 'Parish of St James Westminster, Pt 2, North of Piccadilly', *Survey of London*, 32 (London, 1963), pp. 393 ff.; Campbell, [note 6], pl. 32.

9. However this layout may not have been successful, since the plans in *Vitruvius Britannicus* suggest that the basement area had been removed by the early 18th century. It is not clear whether the chapel was then extended upwards.

10. P. Leach, 'Ragley Hall Reconsidered', *Archaeological Journal,* 136 (1979), pp. 265-8.

11. Pratt was clearly aware of the weakness of his design, since he felt the need to suggest possible uses for this little room: 'a Vestry ... or a small stair... or if you should ... thinke your chappell too little, by taking away ye partition ye might thus easily inlarge it'. Pratt, [note 4], p. 90.

12. The model is at the Norfolk Museum of Rural Life at Gressenhall in Norfolk.

13. *The Diary of John Evelyn*, (E.S. de Beer, editor), 3 (London, 1955), pp. 381-2.

14. Campbell, [note 6], pp. 90-1.

15. To an extent this is a revival of a pre-Reformation custom: for instance the heraldic badges displayed on the facade of the gatehouse of Butley Priory in Suffolk, *c.*1320, record the support of influential local families.

16. Campbell, [note 6], pl. 32.

17. L. Knyff, and J. Kip, [Chap. 5, note 27] pl. 26.

18. 'Tour thro' the Midland Counties', *The Topographer*, 2.3 (1790), pp. 161-2.

19. Over the altar is 'a large ovall of glass of the sort of Private glass used in windows to obscure the sight from without, but hinders not the light within side'. C. Fiennes, *The Journeys of Celia Fiennes* (C. Morris, editor), (London, 1947), p. 171.

20. For a detailed discussion of this chapel see J. Lord, 'A Chapel and some Garden Walls: Culverthorpe in the 1690s', *Architectural History*, 40 (1997), pp. 99-109.

21. 'The chancel in which sit the Chief of the family is paved with marble; in the body which is something lower, sit the Servants'. Markham, [Chap. 5, note 48], pp. 216-17.

22. For Bretby and Durdans, see Fiennes, [note 19], pp. 171, 342; for Melton Constable, see R. North, *Of Building, Roger North's Writings on Architecture* (H. Colvin and J. Newman, editors), (Oxford, 1981), p. 75.

23. Slingsby, [Chap. 2, note 28], p. 3.

24. Information from transcribed documents at Tabley Hall [Chap. 2, note 37].

25. G. Wheler, *The Protestant Monastery: or Christian Oeconomicks. Containing Directions for the Religious Conduct of a Family* (London, 1698), p. 100. In his earlier *An Account of the Churches, or Places of Assembly, of the Primitive Christians* (London, 1689), pp. 119-20, Wheler comments that 'the general mixture of all ages and sexes, as in most of London and Westminster churches, is very indecent; not to say … scandalous'. Both passages are quoted in Aston, 'Segregation in Church', [Chap. 3, note 16], p. 290.

26. It is not clear whether men sat on one side and women on the other at Arbury, or whether men and women sat behind one another on both sides – see Ricketts, [Intro., note 4], pp. 174-5.

27. As at Bretby, Durdans and Melton Constable, [note 22], and possibly Arbury (Warwickshire Record Office, Newdigate papers CR136: B2446, B2451).

28. And, of course, Christopher Wren was to exert great influence on the 'language' of Protestant interiors as a consequence of his involvement in the rebuilding of the London city churches.

29. The quotation is from a description of the fictional Sotherton Court in J. Austen, *Mansfield Park* (New York, 1964), p. 69.

30. Evelyn, [note 13], p. 386.

31. Evelyn, [note 13], pp. 385-6.

32. Evelyn, [note 13,] pp. 381-2.

33. An invaluable work on Isaac Fuller's career at Oxford is M.J.H. Liversidge, 'Prelude to the Baroque: Isaac Fuller at Oxford', *Oxoniensia*, 57 (1993), pp. 311-29.

34. See Peacham, [Chap. 5, note 87].

35. See Ricketts, [Intro., note 4], pp. 228-9, for a fuller description of the decorative scheme at Gwydir.

36. Markham, [Chap. 5, note 48, p. 221].

37. For example a 1690s design survives for a typical Wrenian reredos which may have been intended for Culverthorpe (Lincolnshire Archive Office, MON 7/12/101; illustrated in Lord, [note 20], p. 107).

38. W. H. Godfrey, *Burford Priory* (n.d.).

39. Respectively Exodus 3.4 and 1 Corinthians, 3.15. [Editor's note: my thanks to Nicholas Cooper for drawing my attention to the origin and possible significance of these texts.]

40. Fiennes, [note 19], p. 125. However, in 1662 the Master Glazier, Thomas Bagley, made glass which included a Crucifixion and two coats of arms for the Roman Catholic Queen's Chapel at St James's Palace (*History of the King's Works* (H. Colvin, editor), 5 (London, 1976), p. 245).

41. *Grove Dictionary of Art.*

42. For instance, in the *London Gazette* of July 29th 1669, Philibert Beydaels advertised his services in 'the Art or Mistery of Painting and Guilding of Leather in Forrest-works, Flowers and Figures, proper for the adorning of Chappels, Dining Rooms Chambers, Galleries and Closets, with Beauty and Lustre, which will endure many ages ...'. Croft-Murray, [Chap. 3, note 48], 2 (Feltham, 1970), p. 47.

43. Evelyn, [note 13], 2, p. 70.

44. Evelyn, [note 13], 4, pp. 330-1, 418.

45. Cited in R.J. Phillimore, *The Principal Ecclesiastical Judgements Delivered in the Courts of the Arches 1867-1875* (London, 1876), pp. 380-2.

46. *History of the King's Works*, [note 40], pp. 326-7.

47. For an analysis of the meaning and implications of the decoration of these two rooms see K. Gibson, 'The Decoration of St George's Hall, Windsor, for Charles II', *Apollo*, 147 (May 1998), pp. 30-40.

48. Although it is possible that Verrio's work at Euston for Lord Arlington, the Lord Chamberlain

and co-ordinator of the Windsor project, may have included the chapel.

49. *History of the King's Works*, [note 40], pp. 290-3.

50. Queen Anne gave the Whitehall reredos, altered to suit its new, Protestant, setting, to Westminster Abbey in 1706. In the 19th century, shorn of four statues which now stand in the grounds of Westminster School, much of it was removed to the church of St Andrew's at Burnham-on-Sea where fragments can still be seen.

51. Evelyn, [note 13], pp. 26, 30.

52. British Library, Egerton MSS 3562.

53. *History of the King's Works*, [note 40], p. 328.

54. Fiennes, [note 19], p. 70.

55. See Walpole, *Country Seats*, [Ch. 4, note 6].

56. *The Topographer* [note 18].

57. Fiennes, [note 19], p. 171; Egerton MSS [note 52].

58. Williamson, [Chap. 1, note 22], p. 4.

59. W. Kennett, *A Sermon Preach'd at the Funeral of the … Duke of Devonshire* (London, 1708); J. Grove, *Lives of all the Earls and Dukes of Devonshire* (London, 1764).

60. Kennett, [note 59], p. 48.

61. E.g. in Todd, [Chap. 1, note 20].

62. Williamson, [Chap. 1, note 22], p. 4.

63. John 20.27.

64. For a fuller description of this iconography see Ricketts, [Intro., note 4], p. 243, and A. Ricketts, "'All the Pride of Prayer": the Purpose of the Private Chapel at Chatsworth' in *Baroque and Palladian: the Early 18th- Century Great House* (M. Airs, editor), (Oxford, 1996).

65. C. Ripa, *Iconologia* (facs. edn., New York and London, 1976). This Italian guide to symbolism, first published in Rome in 1593, was very influential in the 17th century and also existed in French and Dutch translations (it was translated into English and German later).

GAZETTEER

Editor's note: this Gazetteer covers private chapels which Annabel Ricketts considered when preparing her Ph.D thesis because they were built or altered during the period 1485-1700, or otherwise came to her notice. It does not cover all private chapels in existence during the period, and has been compiled largely from notes and other material on which she was working when she died in 2003. The emphasis is on English country house Protestant chapels, but some chapels in Wales and in English towns (notably London) of particular historical, architectural or decorative interest are included, as are some pre-Reformation (and therefore Roman Catholic) chapels which she used as yardsticks against which to measure post-Reformation changes. Certain chapels of ease which had particular associations with a private patron are also included. Chapel features discussed in the main text are largely omitted (where there is a 'see also' referral to the main text, the associated page numbers can be found in the Index).

Some of the sources and literature that contributed to Dr Ricketts' thinking are cited but it has not been possible to produce an exhaustive list, and her conclusions often derived from her own on-site observations and analysis. A few works published after her death have also been cited.

The Gazetteer is not a 'gazetteer of gazetteers' – references to recent guide-books, general histories and other useful and comprehensive compendiums and gazetteers, such as Pevsner's *Buildings of England* series and various excellent county country house surveys and histories, are excluded except where particularly justified by the context. Other useful and wide-ranging books that are likewise mentioned more sparingly than they deserve include: M. Airs, *The Tudor & Jacobean Country House: a Building History* (Stroud, 1995); A. Emery, *Greater Medieval Houses of England and Wales, 1300-1500*, 1-3 (Cambridge, 1996-2006); O. Hill and J. Cornforth, *English Country Houses: Caroline 1625 – 1685* (London, 1966); and M. Howard, *The Early Tudor Country House* (London, 1987).

Some of the episcopal, college, hospital and post-Marian Roman Catholic chapels that were considered by Dr Ricketts are listed separately at the end.

Abbreviations:

a.	active (of a person)
A	*Archaeologia*
AC	*Archaeologia Cantiana*
Addleshaw	G.W.O. Addleshaw and F. Etchells, *The Architectural Setting of Anglican Worship* (London, 1948)
AH	*Architectural History* (Journal of the Society of the Architectural Historians of Great Britain)
Airs	M. Airs, *The Tudor & Jacobean Country House: a Building History* (Stroud, 1995)
AJ	*Archaeological Journal*
AR	*Architectural Review*
BL	British Library
CL	*Country Life*
Cherry	B. Cherry and N. Pevsner, *The Buildings of England: Devon* (London, 1989)
Cliffe	J.T. Cliffe, *The Puritan Gentry Besieged 1650-1700* (London and New York, 1993)
Cliffe, *World*	J.T. Cliffe, *The World of the Country House in Seventeenth-Century England* (New Haven and London, 1999)
Clifford	*Diary of Lady Anne Clifford* (D. Clifford, editor), (Stroud, 1992)
Coope	R. Coope, 'The Long Gallery', *AH*, 29 (1986)
Croft	*Patronage, Culture and Power, The Early Cecils 1558-1612* (P. Croft, editor), (London, 2002)
Crossley	E.W. Crossley, 'Two Seventeenth Century Inventories', *YAJ*, 34 (1939)
Devon	*Reports and Transactions of the Devonshire Association*
Dowsing	*The Journal of William Dowsing* (T. Cooper, editor), (Woodbridge, 2001)
Emery	A. Emery, *Greater Medieval Houses of England and Wales, 1300-1500*, 1-3 (Cambridge, 1996-2006)
Evelyn	*The Diary of John Evelyn* (E.S. de Beer, editor), 1-6, (London, 1955)
Fiennes	C. Fiennes, *The Journeys of Celia Fiennes* (C. Morris, editor), (London, 1947)
Giles	C. Giles, *Rural Houses of West Yorkshire, 1400-1830* (London, 1986)
Heward	J. Heward and R. Taylor, *The Country Houses of Northamptonshire* (Swindon, 1996)
Howard	M. Howard, *The Early Tudor Country House* (London, 1987)
Hussey	A. Hussey, 'Chapels in Kent', *AC*, 29 (1911)

JBSMGP	*Journal of the British Society of Master Glass Painters*
Knyff	L. Knyff and J. Kip, *Britannia Illustrata* (J. Harris and G. Jackson–Stops, editors), (Bungay, 1984)
LAC	*Leeds Arts Calendar*
Legg	*English Orders for Consecrating Churches in the Seventeenth Century* (J. Wickham Legg, editor), (London, 1911)
Leland	J. Leland, *The Itinerary of John Leland in or about the Years 1535-1543* (L.T. Smith, editor), (London, 1906-10)
Markham	S. Markham, *John Loveday of Caversham, 1711-1789* (Salisbury, 1984)
MHRS	*Journal of the Merioneth Historical and Record Society*
NA	National Archives
Ormerod	G. Ormerod, *History of the County Palatine and City of Cheshire* (T. Helsby, editor), 1-3 (London, 1882)
Oswald	A. Oswald, *Country Houses of Dorset* (London, 1935)
RIBA	Royal Institute of British Architects
RO	Record(s) Office
SAC	*Sussex Archaeological Collections*
Ricketts, *Cecil*	A. Ricketts, 'Designing for Protestant Worship: the Private Chapels of the Cecil Family' (with C. Gapper and C. Knight) in *Defining the Holy: Sacred Space in Medieval and Early Modern Europe* (A. Spicer and S. Hamilton, editors), (Aldershot, 2005), pp. 115-36
Robinson	J.M. Robinson, *A Guide to the Country Houses of the North-West* (London, 1991)
Smith	J.T. Smith, *Hertfordshire Houses, Selective Inventory* (London, 1993)
Stell	C.F. Stell, *Nonconformist Chapels and Meeting-Houses in the North of England* (London, 1994)
T	Plan number in J. Summerson, *The Book of Architecture of John Thorpe* (Glasgow, 1966)
Tyack	G. Tyack, *Warwickshire Country Houses* (Chichester, 1994)
VB	C. Campbell, *Vitruvius Britannicus*, 1-3 (London, 1717-25)
VCH	*The Victoria History of the Counties of England* (for the county concerned)
Westfall	S.R. Westfall, *Patrons and Performance: Early Tudor Household Revels* (Oxford, 1990)
Walpole	*Horace Walpole's Journals of Visits to Country Seats, etc.* (P.J. Toynbee, editor), (Glasgow, 1928)
Wanklyn	*Inventories of Worcestershire Landed Gentry 1537-1786* (M. Wanklyn, editor), (Worcester, 1998)
YAJ	*Journal of the Yorkshire Archaeological Society*

ACLAND BARTON, DEVON (house, altered, survives; chapel shell survives)
Patrons: Acland family.
Date: 1591 alterations.
The chapel in the 15th-century stone manor house, for long the home of the Acland family and remodelled in 1591, was at right angles to the house, and possessed a wagon roof with carved bosses. It is not clear whether there was direct access from the house, and it may have originally been detached.
Sources/literature: *CL*, 22 Sep. 1950.

ACTON BURNELL CASTLE, SHROPSHIRE
See **LANGLEY HALL, SHROPSHIRE**

ADLINGTON HALL, CHESHIRE (house, much altered, survives; chapel does not)
Patron: Thomas Legh (d. 1519).
Date: 1498 event.
Legh obtained a licence in 1498 for the holding of divine service in the late 14th-century chapel in his moated, timber-framed house. The licence included permission for his chaplain to celebrate mass there.
Sources/literature: Ormerod, 3, pp. 658, 663.

AGECROFT HALL, LANCASHIRE (house, much restored and transported to Richmond, Virginia, USA, in 1926, survives; chapel does not)
Patrons: Robert Langley (d. 1527); William Dauntsey (d. 1695).
Dates: 1525 event; 1694 event.
The correctly-oriented chapel was at the E end of the S range in Langley's timber-framed, courtyard house – which was probably begun in the 1490s by his father John (d. 1496). The chapel had two entrances, one via a door in the NW corner from the courtyard, and the other from the adjacent vestry to the W. In his will of 1525, Langley left the chapel trappings to his grandson and heir, Robert.
The Dauntseys inherited before 1571 on marrying a Langley heiress. A deed and inventory of 1694 mention the chapel, chapel chamber and 'the farther' chapel chamber.
Sources/literature: 'A Collection of Lancashire and Cheshire Wills' (W.F. Irvine, editor), *Record Society for the Publication of Original Documents Relating to Lancashire & Cheshire*, 30 (1896), pp. 62-3; J.P. Earwaker, 'Charters and Deeds at Agecroft Hall', *Transactions of the Lancashire & Cheshire Antiquarian Society*, 4 (1886) pp. 213-14; *VCH*, 4 (1990), pp. 399-403; Westfall, pp. 23-4.

ALBRIGHT HUSSEY, BATTLEFIELD, SHROPSHIRE (house survives; chapel does not)
Patrons: Hussey family.
Dates: 16th century rebuild/addition.
The timber-framed (early Tudor) and brick (Elizabethan) house had long been in the Hussey family. In the 16th century, there was a chapel near the great hall.
Sources/literature: N. Pevsner, *The Buildings of England: Shropshire* (Harmondsworth, 1958), pp. 55-6.

ALDERSGATE (SIR WILLIAM PETRE'S HOUSE), LONDON (demolished)
Patron: Sir William Petre (*c*.1500–72).
Date: 1554 event.
As well as at Ingatestone (*q.v.*), Petre also possessed a chapel in his London house in Aldersgate. In 1554 it contained an alabaster table that presumably served as the altar. The use of stone instead of wood for the altar table was contrary to Protestant practice, and may reflect a conscious return to Roman Catholic usage after the restoration of papal supremacy with the accession of Mary Tudor in 1554.
Sources/literature: Essex RO, D/DP T286.
See also: main text.

ALTHORP, NORTHAMPTONSHIRE (house, remodelled, survives; chapel does not)
Patron: Robert Spencer (1641–1702), 2nd Earl of Sunderland.
Dates: 1665–8 alterations.
Architect: Anthony Ellis (1620–71) and others.
Sunderland inherited the red brick, early Tudor and Elizabethan house in 1643. He remodelled it in 1665–8 to resemble a U-shaped Italianate *palazzo*. The (more or less) correctly-oriented, integral chapel was on the first floor of the E range. A raised W-end platform, presumably to accommodate the family, was reached from the great stair. Another entrance at the NE end was accessed from a staircase leading up from the kitchen.
Sources/literature: Knyff, pl. 27; *VB*, 2 (London, 1717), pl. 95–7.
See also: main text.

APETHORPE HALL, NORTHAMPTONSHIRE (house, much altered survives; chapel does not)
Patron: Francis Fane (1580–1628), 1st Earl of Westmorland.
Dates: *c*.1622–5 additions.
Westmorland acquired the early Tudor house, which had been enlarged in the 16th century by Sir Walter Mildmay (*c*.1520–89), on marrying the latter's granddaughter, Elizabeth. In 1622, at the prompting of James I, he started work on the state apartments in the S range. The range contained a low, ground-floor chapel.
Sources/literature: Heward, pp. 58–66.

APPULDURCOMBE HOUSE, ISLE OF WIGHT (replaced)
Patron: Sir Richard Worsley (d. 1565).
Date: *c*.1566 event.
The Worsleys had acquired the house on the marriage of Worsley's father, James (d. 1538), to the heiress Anne Leigh. Richard Worsley inherited a Tudor house of *c*.1527 comprising three ranges embracing a flagged court, and two wings. A 1566 inventory shows that the contents of the linked chapel were worth less than one-sixth of the contents of his bedroom.
Sources/literature: Howard, pp. 114, 207; J.L. Whitehead, 'An Inventory of the Goods and Chattels of Sir Richard Worsley, of Appuldurcombe, A.D. 1566', *Papers and Proceedings of the Hampshire Field Club*, 5.3 (1906), pp. 277–95; R. Worsley, *History of the Isle of Wight* (London, 1791), p. 180.
See also: main text.

ARBURY HALL, WARWICKSHIRE (house, much altered, survives; chapel, somewhat altered, survives)

Patrons: Sir John Newdigate (1571-1610); Sir Richard Newdigate, Bt (1602-78); Sir Richard Newdigate, Bt (1644-1710).

Dates: 1600 event; c.1678 alterations; 1683 event; 1694 event.

John Newdigate inherited the Elizabethan courtyard house, built on the site of a former Augustinian monastery, from his father, also John, in 1592. An inventory of 1600 lists a chapel chamber with a bed, but contains no reference to a chapel.

Richard Newdigate began alterations in c.1674, probably under the management of his son, also Richard, to whom he had handed over the house. In c.1678, he created a single-storey, rectangular, correctly-oriented, integral chapel in a side (NE) range with one internal entrance from a passage. There was no differentiation in floor or decoration to distinguish the E end. The patron sat in a partly partitioned off pew placed on a dais at the W end. The chaplain's desk or reading pew, complete with sounding board, was halfway down the N side, probably opposite the pulpit. Seating was college-style, and separate seating was provided for men and women, who were also segregated and possibly separated by a partition. The plaster ceiling decoration by Edward Martin follows the 'seemly' Cornbury (*q.v.*) example of naturalistic decoration comprising coats of arms, foliage, fruit and scallop shells. The design of the commandment boards flanking the E window does not appear to match that of their surrounds.

In 1683, troops arriving to search the house for evidence of complicity in the Rye House Plot waited to search the chapel until the service had been concluded.

Some or all of the woodwork, including strings of fruit and winged cherubim, may have been installed in 1694, probably by Grinling Gibbons.

Sources/literature: Warwickshire RO, Newdigate papers, CR136 B551, B571, B2446, B2451; *Miscellaneous Designs and drawings by Sir Christopher Wren and Others* (A.T. Bolton and H.D. Hendry, editors), (Oxford, 1935), pp. 21-2, pls. L, LII; R. Newdigate, *Cavalier and Puritan in the Days of the Stuarts* (A.E. Newdigate, editor), (London, 1901), pp. 215-16; *CL*, 13 Sep. 1913, 8 Oct. 1953, 7, 14 Jan. 1999.

See also: main text.

ARMATHWAITE CASTLE, CUMBRIA (house survives with additions; chapel, restored, survives)

Patron: Richard Skelton (d. c.1668).

Dates: 1660s restoration.

Skelton restored a 15th-century chapel of ease near his 15th-century pele tower in the 1660s, creating a single-cell detached chapel. He endowed it in his will of 1668 with £100.

Sources/literature: N. Pevsner, *The Buildings of England: Cumberland and Westmoreland* (Harmondsworth, 1967), p. 61; Robinson, p. 86.

ARNOLDS (later ARNOS GROVE), SOUTHGATE, LONDON (house replaced; chapel demolished)

Patron: Sir John Weld (d. 1623).

Date: 1615 event.

Weld erected a detached, brick chapel of ease near his house for his family and local inhabitants. He also made financial provision for a minister or curate. The chapel

measured 42ft x 20ft and was consecrated in 1615.
Sources/literature: Legg, pp. 29-32; *VCH*, 5 (1976), pp. 181-7.

ASHBY DE LA ZOUCHE CASTLE, LEICESTERSHIRE (house and chapel survive as ruins)
Patron: Henry Hastings (1586-1643), 5th Earl of Huntingdon.
Date: 1609 event.
The formidable castle had been acquired and further strengthened by the Hastings family in the latter half of the 15th century. The large, correctly-oriented, loosely linked chapel was added at this time. The castle was slighted in 1648. Huntingdon's religious affiliations were strongly influenced by his Puritan great uncle, Henry Hastings (3rd Earl; 1536-95). His 1609 household book makes it clear that prayers and sermonss were conducted in the chapel.
Sources/literature: C. Cross, *The Puritan Earl: The Life of Henry Hastings Third Earl of Huntingdon, 1536 – 1595* (London 1966), pp. 54, 60; J. Nichols, *History and Antiquities of the County of Leicester,* 3 (London, 1804), p. 594; *VCH*, 2 (1954), p. 109.
See also: main text and fig. 3.16.

ASHRIDGE HOUSE, HERTFORDSHIRE (house replaced; chapel does not survive)
Patrons: Thomas Egerton (*c.*1540-1617), Viscount Brackley; John Egerton (1622-84), 2nd Earl of Bridgewater; John Egerton (1646-1701), 3rd Earl of Bridgewater.
Dates: 1604-8 rebuild; 1643 event; 1662 event; 1699 event.
On buying the site of a dissolved conventual church and cloisters that had belonged to the Bonhommes and then became a temporary home to Princess Elizabeth, Brackley adapted, repaired and beautified the remains in 1604-8. His accounts include payment for black velvet textiles for the chapel.
The chapel was presumably severely damaged when the house was looted in 1643, during which ceilings were 'beaten down' (it may well have been subsequently repaired by the 2nd Earl during an extensive upgrade of the house).
Household regulations of 1662 enjoined all servants immediately to heed summons to attend the chapel or other appointed place for prayer or sermons. In the winter, the Wardrobe Keeper was to light the chapel lights for evening prayers, and to light the family's way to and from the chapel.
A new (detached or linked) chapel, entered from the cloisters, seems to have been built in 1699, when a sermon was preached to celebrate its opening.
Sources/literature: H.J. Todd, *History of the College of Bonhommes at Ashridge* (London, 1823).

ASTON HALL, CHESHIRE (demolished)
Patron: Sir Thomas Aston (d. 1645).
Dates: 1637 event; 1645 event.
The chapel was consecrated by John Bridgeman, Bishop of Chester, in 1637. Aston was buried there in 1645.
Sources/literature: P. Leycester, *Historical Antiquities*, 2.4 (London, 1673), p. 214.

ASTON HALL, WARWICKSHIRE (house and second chapel survive)
Patrons: Sir Thomas Holte, Bt (1571-1654); Sir Charles Holte, Bt (d.1722).

Dates: 1618–35 new build; from 1679 alterations.

Architect: probably John Thorpe (*c*.1565–*c*.1655).

Thomas Holte inherited the site in 1592 and built a spectacular, red brick, U-shaped house. Thorpe's plans (supported to some extent by archaeological evidence) indicate that an integral, incorrectly-oriented, narthex-type chapel lay behind the great stair on the W (garden) front. On plan, it had college-style seating arranged along the liturgical N and S walls. That it does not feature in the 1654 inventory suggests that it was destroyed when the house was sacked by Parliamentary forces in 1643, or that it was never built.

Charles Holte converted the great parlour in the S wing into a chapel after inheriting the house in 1679, lowering the floor and removing the fireplace and a canted bay at the S end.

Sources/literature: T201, 205; O. Fairclough, 'John Thorpe and Aston Hall', *AH*, 32 (1989), pp. 30–51; *CL*, 20 Aug. 1953.

See also: main text.

ASTWELL CASTLE, NORTHAMPTONSHIRE (house, much altered, survives; chapel does not)

Patrons: Thomas Lovett (d. 1586); Sir George Shirley (1559–1622).

Dates: late 16th and early 17th-century alterations; 1622 event.

Lovett and Shirley considerably enlarged the medieval, moated, courtyard house on the site. The integral chapel that emerged from their alterations was in the S range, adjoining the E end of the great parlour. The hall, in the W range, lay between the service rooms to the N and the great parlour in the S range.

Shirley outwardly conformed to Protestant beliefs and used the Book of Common Prayer in his chapel, but died (and perhaps surreptitiously lived) as a Roman Catholic. On his death in 1622, the chapel contents were very basic.

Sources/literature: Leicestershire RO, 26DS3/2602; J. Bridges, *The History and Antiquities of Northamptonshire* (P. Whalley, editor), 1 (Oxford, 1791), p. 214; C.A. Markham, 'Astwell Castle in Northamptonshire', *Associated Architectural Societies' Reports and Papers*, 37 (1925), pp. 308–15; E.P. Shirley, *Stemmata Shirleiana* (London, 1841), pp. 71–4; J. Wake, 'History in Stone: the Story of Astwell Manor House', *Northamptonshire Past and Present*, 2.6 (1959), pp. 324–9.

ATHELHAMPTON HALL, DORSET (house survives; chapel demolished)

Patrons: Sir William Martyn (d. 1504); Robert Martyn (d. 1550).

Dates: *c*.1490s new build; by 1550 addition.

William Martyn built the battlemented stone house with towers probably during the 1490s. It was added to by succeeding generations through the 16th century. His grandson, Robert, built the gatehouse before 1550. Beyond the gatehouse was a large walled forecourt on the S side of which stood a chapel. It is not clear precisely when the chapel was built.

Sources/literature: Oswald, p. 18.

AUDLEY END, ESSEX (house, much altered and reduced, survives; chapel demolished)

Patrons: Thomas Howard (1561–1626), 1st Earl of Suffolk; Charles II (1630–85).

Dates: *c*.1605–14 new build; 1671 event.

Architect: possibly John Thorpe (*c*.1565–*c*.1655).

The magnificent, double-courtyard, early 17th-century, 'prodigy' house was built on the site of Thomas Audley's large, c.1540s house which he had fashioned from the dissolved Walden Abbey. The creation of the linked, correctly-oriented, double-height, double-cell chapel is one of the earliest examples of the post-Elizabethan re-introduction of a splendid and distinctive space for religious worship. It occupied a projection at the SE corner of the main house off the main circulation routes, and well away from the great hall. It was balanced by a similar projection in the NE corner comprising a cellar below and council chamber above. The chapel had a screen at the W end which supported an upper chapel. There appears to have been a porch in the centre of the N wall, perhaps with a staircase in the thickness of the wall. It seems originally to have had only two internal entrances, one at each level, but both were approached by a magnificent series of rooms and walkways. The fenestration was highly distinctive. It is not known how the interior was decorated, and there may have been changes later in the century.

Charles II bought the house after the Restoration, taking possession in 1669. A 1671 inventory of chapel hangings lists eight pictures depicting the Passion and nine showing the Acts of the Apostles. Horace Walpole, writing in 1762, noted that the chapel was very sumptuous with marble pillars.

Sources/literature: T203-4; Audley End, 'scrapbook': 1752 survey; Essex RO, Library, E/WALD (IE5A): Winstanley plans and views of c.1678; NA, 1671 inventory of hangings, LC 5/14, pp. 43-4; H. Colvin (editor) *The History of the King's Works*, 5 (London, 1976), pp.131-3; P.J. Drury, 'No other palace in the kingdom will compare with it: The Evolution of Audley End 1605-1745', *AH,* 23 (1980), pp.1- 39; R. Griffin, *The History of Audley End and Saffron Walden* (London, 1836); Walpole, p. 33.

See also: main text and figs. 5.4, 5.5.

AYSHFORD, BURLESCOMBE, DEVON (house and chapel, restored, survive)
Patrons: Ayshford family.
Dates: 17th-century event.
The detached medieval chapel, built for the private use of the Ayshford family, stands near the house. It contains 17th-century family tombs.
Sources/literature: Cherry, p. 146.

BACHYMBYD FAWR, LLANYNYS, DENBIGHSHIRE (replaced)
Patron: Sir Robert Salesbury (d. 1601).
Date: 1601 event.
An inventory on Salesbury's death indicates that the chapel 'loft' was filled with bedding, suggesting that the chapel itself was not used as such.
Sources/literature: W.J. Smith, 'Three Salesbury Mansions', *Bulletin of the Board of Celtic Studies*, 15.4 (May 1954), pp. 293-9.

BARDEN TOWER, NORTH YORKSHIRE (house a ruin; chapel survives)
Patron: Lady Anne Clifford (1590-1676), Countess of Pembroke.
Dates: 1650 or 1658 new build.
Lady Anne Clifford repaired the large, early Tudor tower house in 1650 and 1658. She also built its single-cell, linked chapel – probably at the same time.
Sources/literature: Clifford, pp. 113, 140.

BASINGSTOKE (CHAPEL OF THE HOLY GHOST), HAMPSHIRE

(a ruin)

Patrons: William Sandys (*c*.1470–1540), 1st Lord Sandys; George Morley (1598–1684), Bishop of Winchester.

Dates: early Tudor restoration; post–1670 restoration.

Sandys has been credited with building the detached, correctly-oriented chapel to the N of Basingstoke, but it is more likely that he restored a 13th-century chapel already on the site, and added a side chapel dedicated to the Holy Trinity. The ceiling of the former featured early Tudor figurative wall paintings of biblical history and portraits. Sandys had coloured glass for the windows, comprising episodes from the lives of Christ and the Virgin Mary, shipped from Antwerp in the 1520s. Some of this may now be found in the chapel at The Vyne (*q.v.*), as well as in the parish churches of Mottisfont, Hampshire; Woolbeding, West Sussex; and St Michael, Basingstoke.

The chapel seems to have suffered during the Civil War, and Loveday notes that it was restored after 1670 by Bishop Morley.

Sources/literature: F. Baigent and J. Millard, *A History of the Town and Manor of Basingstoke* (London, 1889), pp. 110–61; S. Loggon, *History of the Brotherhood or Guild of the Holy Ghost* (Reading, 1742); Markham, p. 380; H. Wayment, 'The Stained Glass of the Chapel of the Vyne and the Chapel of the Holy Ghost, Basingstoke', *A*, 107 (1982), pp. 141–52.

See also: main text.

BEAUFORT HOUSE, CHELSEA, LONDON – see GREAT HOUSE

BEAUPRÉ HALL, OUTWELL, NORFOLK (demolished)

Patron: probably Nicholas Beaupré (d. 1540–50).

Date: *c*.1530 rebuild.

The *c*.1500 house was transformed *c*.1530 into a standard courtyard type. The chapel was either freestanding or at the end of a range to the W. It ran W–E and was therefore probably correctly-oriented.

Sources/literature: *CL*, 1 Dec. 1923.

BELSAY CASTLE, NORTHUMBERLAND (a ruin)

Patron: Sir William Middleton (*c*.1636–90).

Date: 1673 events.

Middleton had his Jacobean manor house with its 14th-century tower licensed as a Presbyterian meeting-house in 1673. His chaplain was said to have 'preached constantly in the chapel'.

Sources/literature: Cliffe, p. 221.

BELTON HOUSE, LINCOLNSHIRE (house and chapel survive)

Patron: Sir John Brownlow, Bt (1659–97).

Dates: 1685–8 new build.

Architect: possibly William Winde (d. 1722).

Brownlow inherited the original house on the site in 1679, and replaced it with an accomplished H-plan house. The integral, double-height, single-cell chapel, oriented to the N, occupied the NE pavilion off the main circulation route. It probably had no exterior architectural differentiation. Inside, like other chapels of the period, the predominant characteristic is a controlled 'seemliness' that makes liberal use of the vogue for naturalistic decoration in plaster and woodwork, with few if any specifically religious motifs. The ceiling is by Edward Goudge. The chapel contained a communion table, pulpit and reading desk, and the area round the communion table is raised.

Sources/literature: O. Hill and J. Cornforth, *English Country Houses: Caroline 1625-1685* (London, 1966), pp. 193-202.

See also: main text and fig. 6.4; Plate XXIX.

BELVOIR CASTLE, LEICESTERSHIRE (house remodelled)

Patrons: John Manners (1604-79), 8th Earl of Rutland; John Manners (1638-1711), 1st Duke of Rutland.

Dates: 1654-8 event; 1662-8 rebuild; 1685 event.

Architects: John Webb (1611-72); John Webb and perhaps Samuel Marsh (*fl.* 1650s-70s). Webb's 1650s designs for an H-plan house to replace the medieval and mid-16th-century castle, slighted in 1649, were not taken up, but they afford a useful insight into planning during the period. The correctly-oriented, single-storey chapel and its peripheral spaces were to have occupied a whole pavilion. There were to have been three entrances to the ante-chapel: in the NW corner from the steward's dining-room and the service area of the ground floor; in the centre from the exterior via the central *loggia* of the side range; and just W of the screen on the S side, presumably for the family, through a lobby formed in the thickness of the wall to a staircase leading up to the long gallery above. This lobby also gave access to another space set in the thickness of the S wall, which could have been used as a small gallery or pew. Finally, there was to be direct access to the E end of the chapel from the chapel study.

The house was rebuilt after the Restoration as a solid square block. It may well have incorporated elements of Webb's earlier plans as well as designs by Samuel Marsh. It certainly had a chapel which, in 1735, Loveday found to be 'crowded'.

The archives at Belvoir may contain 1685 references to the chapel decoration.

Sources/literature: Markham, p. 200. Access to the Belvoir archives was denied. However, information from more fortunate researchers suggests that, among others, the following papers may contain references to the post-Restoration chapel: Misc MS 67; Maps 95, 127, 129-32; Acct 461.

See also: main text and fig. 5.27.

BERE COURT, BERKSHIRE (house, updated, survives; chapel demolished)

Patron: John Breedon (*c.*1622-85).

Date: 1671 event.

The post-Reformation brick house, built on land that had formerly belonged to Reading Abbey, was partially rebuilt after the Restoration. Breedon bought it from Sir John Davis in 1671. A detached, single-cell (consecrated) chapel stood nearby. In 1735 Loveday noted a Crucifixion in the E window, and the painted initials HF (presumably for Hugh Faringdon, the last abbot of Reading, hanged after the Dissolution) and arms of Reading Abbey at the W end. Unusually for this period, the chapel contained a fireplace.

Sources/literature: Markham, p. 245; J. Wilcox, *Pangbourne, an Illustrated History* (Pangbourne, 1992), pp. 4-5.

See also: main text.

BERKELEY CASTLE, GLOUCESTERSHIRE (house, remodelled, survives, as does the room formerly occupied by the chapel).
Patrons: Henry VII (1457–1509).
Dates: early Tudor event.
The integral chapel within the medieval castle, that had been remodelled in the 14th century, contained the wooden 'King's pew', now removed to the long drawing room, at the W end. It sports the arms of Henry VII and was presumably installed during his reign when the castle was temporarily in royal ownership. A projecting box resting on Renaissance pillars, it is one of very few surviving examples of what a lord's pew, such as that at Wressle Castle (*q.v.*), might have been like.
Sources/literature: N. Kingsley, *The Country Houses of Gloucestershire*, 1 (Cheltenham, 1989), pp. 57-61.
See also: main text.

BERWICK HOUSE, SHROPSHIRE (house replaced; chapel, altered and restored, survives)
Patrons: Sir Samuel Jones (a. 1672).
Date: 1672 new build.
Nothing is known of Jones' house. He built a rectangular, correctly-oriented, modest, stone chapel in the grounds. There is a W gallery.
Sources/literature: D.H.S. Cranage, *The Churches of Shropshire*, 2 (Wellington, 1912), pp. 847-8.
See also: main text and fig. 6.12.

BEVERSTON CASTLE, GLOUCESTERSHIRE (house a ruin; chapel shell survives)
Patrons: Berkeley family.
Date: 16th-century alterations.
The original 13th-century castle was extensively remodelled in the 14th century. The integral, correctly-oriented, 14th-century chapel was on the first floor of the SW tower, and entered via a stair from the great hall. The W window was replaced in the 16th century.
Sources/literature: none given.

BICKERSTAFFE HALL, LANCASHIRE (replaced)
Patron: Lady Mary Stanley (a. 1672 and 1674).
Dates: 1672 event; 1674 event.
Lady Stanley had Bickerstaffe Hall licensed for Presbyterian worship in 1672. Nonconformist ministers preached in the chapel, which had a family gallery.
In 1674, soldiers burst into the chapel and arrested and imprisoned the chaplain, Nathaniel Heywood (younger brother of the more celebrated Oliver), just as he was about to deliver his sermon and despite Lady Stanley's heated objections.
Sources/literature: Cliffe, pp. 117-18, 224.

BINDERTON HOUSE, WEST SUSSEX (house, remodelled, survives; chapel a ruin)
Patrons: Thomas Smyth I (d. 1658); Thomas Smyth II (d. 1684).
Dates: before 1658 event; *c.*1677 new build.

Thomas Smyth I inherited the medieval manor house, that had belonged to the nuns of Tarrant Abbey until the Dissolution, in 1624. In the 1650s, he pulled down the parish church because it stood in the way of a new house he was planning.

Thomas Smyth II built a new house on the site in 1677, and probably also built the replacement church, in the form of a rectangular, 28ft x 18ft, single-cell chapel, at the same time. He was buried in the chapel, which was never consecrated and swiftly degenerated to become a barn.

Sources/literature: *VCH*, 4 (1953), pp. 89-91.

BLACKMORE MANOR, SOMERSET (house and chapel survive)
Patrons: Sir Thomas Tremaill (d. 1508) and John Tremaill (d. 1534).
Dates: early Tudor new build.

Thomas (father) and John (son) bought the site in 1476 and built a stone house comprising a central, rectangular block facing E, with a diagonally opposed wing at either end. The square, correctly-oriented, linked chapel occupies the NE wing. It was bisected by the screen to create a chancel and ante-chapel, each being roughly the same size. A passage linking the hall and parlour terminates in a chamber which has a doorway and squint giving onto the ante-chapel. There is a separate external entrance at the W end of the S wall of the ante-chapel. The large, distinctive E window has three lights.

Sources/literature: N. Cooper, *Houses of the Gentry 1480-1680* (New Haven and London, 1999), pp. 70-4.

BLENCOW HALL, CUMBRIA (house survives; chapel does not)
Patrons: Blencowe family.
Dates: 16th-century new build.

The house, comprising a hall range between two towers, was built in stages. The centre was built by Henry Blencowe in 1590. In the walled courtyard at the back of the house is a window with Y-tracery that belonged to the former chapel.

Sources/literature: N. Pevsner, *The Buildings of England: Cumberland and Westmorland* (Harmondsworth, 1967), p. 134; Robinson, p. 89.
.

BLEWHOUSE (HIGHGATE; also known as DORCHESTER HOUSE), LONDON (demolished)
Patron: John Warner (d. *c.*1619).
Dates: pre 1617 new build.

The house was built in the form of a rectangular block, presumably by John Warner. It possessed what was probably an assembly chapel since an openwork screen separated it from the complex great stair which could have served as a peripheral chapel space. It was lit only by a bay window set off-centre in what appears to be the north wall.

Sources/literature: T62.

BLICKLING HALL, NORFOLK (house, much reduced, survives; chapel does not)
Patrons: Sir Henry Hobart, Bt (*c.*1560-1625); Sir John Hobart, Bt (1593-1647).
Dates: 1618-26 rebuild; 1627 and 1629 events.
Architect: Robert Lemyinge (d. 1628).

Formerly the home of Anne Boleyn, Henry Hobart transformed the existing moated medieval manor house, rebuilding the S and E ranges and substantially altering the N and W ranges, to create a substantial red-brick, double-courtyard house. The integral, single-storey chapel was on the ground floor in the centre of the E range, above the wine cellar and below the long gallery. It occupied a rectangular space with the long axis running N–S along the range, and its orientation is unclear. The great hall, which separated the two courtyards, lay to the W and was linked at the dais end to the chapel by a closet that was probably at mezzanine level. It had a view into the NW of the chapel through a screen, and presumably constituted the family upper chapel. Depending on the chapel's orientation, this comprised a side or W end space for worship. There may also have been a closet at the S end of the chapel. The chapel could be entered from the S via the great stair or by means of a bridge across the moat, and probably also from the presumed upper chapel via a stair. The chapel was lit by two windows in the E wall, one with a bay. There is no evidence of distinctive fenestration.

In 1627 an organ, and chairs and stools covered with green cloth, were installed.

The chapel was consecrated in 1629.

Sources/literature: Norfolk RO, Lothian papers MC3/52; Legg, p. 321; C. Stanley and J. Newman, 'Blickling Hall, the Building of a Jacobean Mansion', *AH*, 29 (1986), pp. 1–42.

See also: main text and fig. 5.39.

BOLSOVER CASTLE, DERBYSHIRE (castle and associated buildings, altered, survive; no sign of projected chapel)

Patron: William Cavendish (1593–1676), 1st Duke of Newcastle.

Date: *c.*1630 possible new build.

Architect: John Smythson (d. 1634).

Formerly a large medieval castle, Bess of Hardwick's third son, Sir Charles Cavendish, leased Bolsover from 1608, and began to transform the keep into the 'Little Castle' to designs by Robert Smythson. Cavendish's son William, who inherited in 1617, completed his father's work, and employed Smythson's son, John, to undertake further building work there. This included the W ('terrace') range. Smythson's plan of *c.*1630 shows a double-cell chapel at the S end of the range. There is no evidence that the chapel was ever built.

Sources/literature: RIBA, Smythson III/1/4.

BOUGHTON HOUSE, NORTHAMPTONSHIRE (house, much altered, survives; chapel does not)

Patrons: Edward Montagu (1562–1644), 1st Lord Montagu; Ralph Montagu (*c.*1638–1709), 1st Duke of Montagu.

Dates: 1612–20 alterations; from 1683 rebuild.

Edward Montagu updated the medieval and 16th-century house in 1612–20. His work included remodelling the S wing which housed the chapel.

The 4th baron (later 1st Duke) inherited the house in 1683 and rebuilt it. It is not clear what happened to the chapel.

Sources/literature: Heward, pp. 94–109.

BOUGHTON PLACE, KENT (house survives, greatly rebuilt; chapel does not)

Patron: Sir Edward Wotton (d.1551).

Dates: early Tudor new build.

One range survives of the ragstone house built between 1519 and 1529. It was extended *c.*1553. The finding of a piscina in what is now the drawing-room suggests that there

was once a chapel there.
Sources/literature: A. Oswald, *Country Houses of Kent* (London, 1933), pp. 17, 33; *CL,* 22 Apr. 1922.

BOWRINGSLEIGH, DEVON (house, restored and enlarged, survives; chapel, much altered, survives)
Patrons: Bowring (till 1543) and/or Gilbert (till 1695) families.
Dates: uncertain survival.
It is difficult to assess the date of the chapel – which survives within a 19th-century tower attached to the medieval, 16th and 17th-century house.
Sources/literature: *CL,* 6 Mar.1915.

BRADGATE HOUSE, LEICESTERSHIRE (house a ruin; chapel, much altered, survives)
Patron: Thomas Grey (1451-1501), 1st Marquis of Dorset.
Dates: 1490-1500 new build.
Dorset built a brick, U-shaped house, soon to become the childhood home of Lady Jane Grey, with the hall in the N range, kitchens to the W, and the chapel at the S end of the E wing (where Bess of Hardwick married Sir William Cavendish in 1547). It has a large, rectangular, six-light, mullioned and transomed east window, originally occupied two storeys, with a sealed crypt below, and contained an upper chapel with (unusually) external access via a staircase, as well as internal access from an apartment on the first floor. The main entrance is from the W end.
Sources/literature: Knyff, pl. 12; M. Forsyth, *The History of Bradgate* (Leicester, 1974).

BRADLEY MANOR, DEVON (house and chapel survive)
Patrons: Yarde family.
Dates: 1547-53 presumed event.
The early 15th-century, correctly-oriented, double-height chapel is linked to the NE corner of the largely 15th-century house. There is a squint, formerly the parlour window, in the W wall. A small alabaster angel from the 15th-century reredos was found concealed in the socket previously used to support the rood beam, which was presumably destroyed under Edward VI during 1547-53.
Sources/literature: Cherry, pp. 587-91.

BRAMALL HALL, CHESHIRE (house and chapel, both altered, survive)
Patrons: Sir William Davenport (1446-1528); William Davenport I (1472-1541); William Davenport II (1521-76).
Dates: early 16th-century alterations; 1541 events; probably post-1558 event.
Sir William Davenport inherited the medieval, timber-framed, T-shaped house in 1478. He reconstructed the S cross wing (containing the chapel and parlour). The integral, correctly-oriented chapel, which was probably at one stage detached from the house, is a low, single-storied space with a nine-light E window containing three small early 16th-century figures from the Crucifixion. There are traces of an *Ecce Homo* on the central beam of the W wall.
The earliest mention of the chapel is in William Davenport I's Will of 1541. According to the inventory taken after his death, the chapel contained three old yellow cushions and two andirons, while the chapel chamber above contained bedding.

The *Ecce Homo* was replaced by texts by William Davenport II after the accession of Elizabeth in 1558 or, less likely, before the death of Edward VI in 1553.

Sources/literature: Cheshire RO, EDA 2/1 pp, 153b, 200; E.B. Dean, *Bramall Hall, the Story of an Elizabethan Manor House* (Stockport, 1977); Howard, pp. 114; G. Ormerod, 3, p. 89; E. Twycross, *The Mansions of England and Wales,* 2 (London, 1847-50), p. 89; *CL,* 13 Jun. 1903.

See also: main text and Plate VII.

BRAMHOPE HALL, WEST YORKSHIRE (house demolished; chapel, restored, survives)

Patron: Robert Dyneley (1609-89).

Dates: 1649 new build; 1665 event.

In 1649, the Puritan Robert Dyneley financed and built the simple, correctly-oriented, detached chapel in the grounds of the 16th-century Dyneley family house on land that had belonged to the dissolved Kirkstall Abbey. Ostensibly a chapel of ease, it was in reality a private chapel for use by the immediate household and local people. Inside, the walls are rendered, and the roof has undecorated king-post trusses. The appointment of a minister was controlled by Dyneley and five local squires who were trustees.

After the Restoration, the chapel became a chapel of ease to Otley parish church, but Puritan worship continued. In 1665, Dyneley was charged by the authorities with holding a conventicle.

Sources/literature: O. Heywood, *His Diaries, Anecdote and Event Books* (J. Horsfall Turner, editor), 1 (Brighouse, 1881), p. 194 etc.; Stell, pp. 239-41; *CL,* 20 Jun. 1963.

See also: main text and fig. 5.37; Plate XI.

BRAMSHILL HOUSE, HAMPSHIRE (house, much altered, survives; chapel, except for E window, does not)

Patrons: Edward Zouche (*c.*1556-1625), 11th Lord Zouche; Sir Edward Zouche (d. 1634).

Dates: 1605-21 rebuild; 1634 event.

Lord Zouche bought the massive, medieval, courtyard house in 1605, and largely replaced it with a courtyard 'prodigy' house, whose NW and SE ranges extended to form a further, three-sided, courtyard. The two-storey, integral, double-cell chapel was oriented to the NE, and situated at the SW end of a narrow courtyard between two staircases and behind the great hall. Sir Henry Wotton, who thought that the architectural design of a house could usefully emulate aspects of the human body, was a friend of Zouche, and it is possible (just) to read the plan as a human figure with the chapel in its central position representing the heart. There was a distinctive liturgical E window of awkward design. Inside, the family pew may have been between the upper and lower levels, and the upper chapel may have had a fireplace. It is difficult to determine where the entrances were. One source suggests that there were two to the lower chapel: from an inner hall at the foot of the great stair, and from the courtyard for staff, dependents and tenants. There was also a way into the upper chapel from the adjacent chapel drawing room, which was itself next to the chapel chamber. The chapel was consecrated in 1621.

A 1634 inventory indicates that the upper chapel was in use as a storeroom, while the chapel chamber was furnished as a bedroom. The total value of the chapel contents was £35, compared with £230 for those of the privy chamber and £200 for the long gallery.

Sources/literature: NA, 1634 inventory, C108/187; W.H. Cope, *Bramshill, Its History and Architecture* (London, 1883), pp. 34-5; H.M. Hills, 'Bramshill House' (unpublished MA thesis, University of London, 1984); H. Wotton, *The Elements of Architecture*, facs. edn. (C.F. Hard, editor), (Charlottesville, 1968); *CL*, 2, 9, 16, 23 Jun. 1923, 10, 17 Oct. 1985 See also: main text.

BREDE PLACE, EAST SUSSEX (house, somewhat altered, survives; chapel largely gutted by fire)
Patron: Sir Goddard Oxenbridge (d. 1531).
Dates: 16th-century alterations.
Oxenbridge's father, Robert, created a 15th-century sandstone house, then known as Ford Place, to which his successors contributed brick additions. The integral, correctly-oriented chapel is at the S end of the hall range. It has an external main entrance in the NW wall, and contained an upper chapel and screen. A small room to the S may have been a vestry and a room above, accessible by means of a ladder, may have been the priest's room. The altar is lit from the S by a long, three-light window with vertical tracery. The E end of the chapel was truncated by a 16th-century staircase, possibly inserted by (the allegedly cannibalistic) Sir Goddard, and causing rearrangement of earlier fabric.
Sources/literature: *VCH*, 9 (1973), pp. 165-7; *CL*, 3 Nov. 1906.

BRETBY HALL, DERBYSHIRE (house replaced; chapel demolished)
Patron: Philip Stanhope (1633-1714), 2nd Earl of Chesterfield.
Date: 1696 new build.
Architect: possibly William Talman (1650-1719).
The late16th/early 17th-century, U-shaped, S-facing house was updated by the 1st Earl before 1639, and again before 1670 by the architect Louis Le Vau for the 2nd Earl. The main range was nine bays long, with a sumptuous Classical centrepiece. The linked, correctly-oriented chapel was added in 1696, in a style reminiscent of Le Vau but possibly by Talman, to the E of the main range. It was situated off main circulation routes at the end of a passage leading to offices, and illustrates how the architectural language of the late 17th-century chapel could become grander and more assertive, with the architectural rhythms being emphasised by the large urns which stood on the parapet above the orders. Inside, the altarpiece of Italian marble struck Loveday later as having 'a grave solemn Monument look.' The ceiling was plastered with fretwork of fruit and foliage, panelling was probably of cedar, and the floor of black and white Italian marble. There were separate closets for the male and female members of the patron's family and friends, while an organ occupied a gallery at the W end.
Sources/literature: Fiennes, p.171; 'Tour thro' the Midland Counties', *The Topographer*, 2.3 (1790), pp. 161-2; Knyff, pl. 26; Markham, pp. 191-2.
See also: main text and fig. 6.16.

BROUGHAM CASTLE, CUMBRIA (a ruin)
Patron: Lady Anne Clifford (1590-1676), Countess of Pembroke.
Dates: 1661 and 1662 events.
Lady Anne Clifford restored the medieval castle 1651-2. She received communion in the (unconsecrated) late 14th-century chapel there in 1661 and 1662.
Sources/literature: Clifford, p. 159.
See also: main text.

BROUGHAM (ST WILFRID'S CHAPEL), CUMBRIA (chapel survives, heavily restored)
Patron: Lady Anne Clifford (1590-1676), Countess of Pembroke.
Date: 1658 rebuild.
Lady Anne Clifford rebuilt a medieval chapel on the site, probably as a chapel of ease, in the form of a simple, single-cell rectangle.
Sources/literature: Addleshaw, p. 195; Clifford, p. 142.

BROUGHTON CASTLE, OXFORDSHIRE (house and chapel, both restored and redecorated, survive)
Patrons: Sir William Fiennes (d. 1573); William Fiennes (1582-1662), 1st Viscount Saye and Sele ('Old Subtlety').
Dates: 16th and 17th-century events.
The moated, 13th and 14th-century manor house was crenellated in the 15th century and updated in the second half of the 16th century. The 14th-century, correctly oriented chapel is in the east wing. The state-bedroom, probably built by William Fiennes early on in during the 16th-century updating, was provided with a squint into the chapel.
The chapel is thought to have been plastered and the lower walls wainscoted in the 17th century, perhaps by Saye and Sele.
Sources/literature: H. G. Slade, 'Broughton Castle, Oxfordshire', *AJ*, 135 (1978), pp. 138-94.

BUCKHURST HOUSE, EAST SUSSEX (largely demolished; chapel does not survive)
Patrons: Sir John Sackville (*c*.1484-1556); Thomas Sackville (1536-1608), 1st Earl of Dorset.
Dates: 1556 event; *c*.1599 event.
Only the stone gatehouse remains of the (probably) half-timbered, *c*.1510-25 house with an enclosing wall. On John Sackville's death in 1556, his will decreed that his widow should have 'free passage' through the gallery to the chapel closet.
Thorpe's unrealised plan was probably drawn up for Thomas Sackville, perhaps in 1599 when he was appointed Lord Treasurer. The correctly-oriented, integral, narthex-type chapel is shown set in the angle where the N and E ranges meet. It is entered from the S. The fenestration follows the dictates of external symmetry at the expense of a strong liturgical E-W axis.
Sources/literature: T19-20; J.B. Burke, *A Visitation of Seats and Arms* (London, 1853), p. 162; Coope, pp. 60-1; W.D. Scull, 'Old Buckhurst', *SAC*, 54 (1911), p. 69; *CL*, 11, 18 May 1912, 18, 25 Oct. 1919.
See also: main text and fig. 4.5.

BULLHOUSE HALL, PENISTONE, WEST YORKSHIRE (house and chapel survive)
Patron: Elkanah Rich (a. 1692).
Date: 1692 new build.
Rich inherited the 1655 house, which his father had had licensed for Presbyterian meetings, in 1683. In 1692 he built a simple, detached, rectangular, stone chapel nearby.
Sources/literature: C.F. Stell, 'Bullhouse Chapel, Penistone', *AJ*, 137 (1980), p. 461.

BULWICK HALL, NORTHAMPTONSHIRE (house, reduced, survives; chapel does not)
Patron: James Tryon (*c.*1655–85).
Dates: 1676 rebuild.
Tryon inherited a 16th-century house and, on coming of age in 1676, rebuilt it in the form of a large courtyard house. At this point it contained a chapel although its location is unknown.
Sources/literature: Northamptonshire RO, T(B) 567.

BURFORD PRIORY, OXFORDSHIRE (house, greatly remodelled, survives; chapel, restored, survives)
Patron: William Lenthall (1591–1662).
Dates: 1660–2 new build.
Architect: perhaps John Jackson (*c.*1602–63).
The late 16th-century, E-shaped house, built by Sir Laurence Tanfield on the site of an Augustinian priory, was remodelled and enlarged in the 17th century, probably by Lenthall, who had bought it from Lucius Cary, 2nd Viscount Falkland, in the 1630s. He began to build the loosely linked, rectangular, SSW-oriented, single-cell, stone chapel in 1660, and had it consecrated in 1662. It has a very idiosyncratic exterior, comprising a mix of pre-Reformation and Classical forms, and is unique for its time in the amount of sculptural decoration used. Probably built by local craftsmen, the assurance of its execution suggests that the work was supervised by John Jackson. Inside, it probably also contained more unusual sculptural decoration in contrast to the somewhat domestic decorative style of the conventional 'Wren' chapel. The shallow, barrel-vaulted, stone ceiling, its ribs decorated with guilloche, contained biblical scenes in plastered fretwork. Stone commandment boards, each surmounted by an angel and supported by a winged cherub, flank the liturgical E window. The floor in this area has a differentiated pattern. The two boxes of the gallery are supported by spirally fluted columns with Corinthian capitals incorporating birds' heads that also feature above Lenthall's arms outside. There are few original fittings, but it is possible that benches ran around the walls.
Sources/literature: W.H. Godfrey, *Burford Priory* (n.d.), pp. 80–7; Markham, p. 221; *CL*, 3 Mar. 1911, 3, 10 Jun. 1939. [Editor's note: thanks to Nicholas Cooper for sharing his draft *VCH* contribution on Burford with me.]
See also: main text and figs. 6.21, 6.22, 6.23.

BURGHLEY HOUSE, LINCOLNSHIRE (house survives; chapel replaced)
Patrons: William Cecil (1520–98), Lord Burghley; John Cecil (1648–1700), 5th Earl of Exeter.
Dates: 1556–64 rebuild; 1573–87 alterations; 1690s event.
William Cecil started building a stone, single courtyard house on the site of a pre-existing house that he had inherited in 1552. His integral chapel appears to have been situated at the E end of the S wing on the first floor. If this is correct, it was close to the great Chamber and over the great parlour which abutted the high end of the great hall.
Cecil's chapel did not survive major alterations started in 1573 (by which time his son Thomas was in residence) which completed the transformation of Burghley into one of the foremost Elizabethan 'prodigy' houses. A new chapel was created as an afterthought out of a suite of private apartments.

A large-scale redecoration programme in the 1690s, employing Verrio and Laguerre among others, omitted the chapel. Pictures in the chapel at this time depicted biblical themes.

Sources/literature: T57-8; Burghley House, Exeter MS 51/18; Fiennes, p. 70; J.A. Gotch, 'The Renaissance in Northamptonshire', *Journal of the Proceedings of RIBA*, n.s., 6 (1890), p. 157; J. Husselby, *Architecture at Burghley House; The Patronage of William Cecil 1553-1598* (unpublished Ph.D thesis, University of Warwick, 1996), pp. 99, 270-2; J. Husselby, 'The Politics of Pleasure: William Cecil and Burghley House' in Croft, pp. 21-45; F. Peck, *Desiderata Curiosa*, 1.6 (London, 1732), p. 40; Ricketts, *Cecil*; Walpole, pp. 58-9; *CL*, 3, 10, 17, 31 Dec. 1953.

See also: main text.

BURLEY-ON-THE-HILL, RUTLAND (replaced)

Patrons: George Villiers (1592-1628), 1st Duke of Buckingham; Daniel Finch (1647-1730), 2nd Earl of Nottingham.

Dates: *c*.1620 new build; from 1696 new build.

Buckingham bought the site in *c*.1620. Three Thorpe plans have been associated, not entirely securely, with the house he built there. They provide interesting alternatives for a chapel of differing status, ranging from an extremely dominant chapel to a small, relatively self-effacing one. T105-6 is the most securely linked to Buckingham's house, and shows a very large chapel in the hall range on the main axis opposite the entrance. It has an apsidal E window and a kind of narthex leading to the ante-chapel which is divided from the main chapel by a screen. Access is from both the high and low ends of the house, as well as from the courtyard. Such treatment is without precedent at this date in England. Another version (T81-2) has the chapel in a corner pavilion of the hall range and immediately behind the high end. It lacks the dominating force of the first example, but is still an imposing chapel, well positioned for both seclusion and easy access. In the third alternative (T101-2), the chapel is much smaller in relation to the hall, and relegated to part of the corner pavilion of the entrance range, where access is from the courtyard *loggia* via a staircase hall, or from the state apartments.

Nottingham demolished Buckingham's house and started a new house in 1696. His work may have included altering the chapel which, in 1735, Loveday found 'plain and neat'.

Sources/literature: T81-2, T101-2 and T105-6; Markham, p. 201.

See also: main text and fig. 5.6.

BURLINGTON HOUSE (WESTMINSTER), LONDON (house remodelled; chapel does not survive)

Patron: Richard Boyle (1612-97), 1st Earl of Burlington.

Dates: new build completed 1665-8.

Architect: Hugh May (1621-84).

Burlington bought, and finished building, a comparatively small, rectangular house with vestigial pavilions. The double-height chapel, oriented to the S, occupied the E range and was consecrated.

Sources/literature: *VB*, 1 (London, 1715), pl. 31; 'The Parish of St James, Westminster. Part 2, North of Piccadilly', *Survey of London*, 32 (1963), pp. 391ff.

See also: main text.

BURTON AGNES HALL, EAST YORKSHIRE (house, little altered, survives; chapel does not)
Patrons: Sir Henry Griffith (1558-1620); Sir Matthew Boynton (1591-1647).
Dates: *c*.1598-1610 new build; 1630s event.
Architect: Robert Smythson (*c*.1535-1614).
Griffith inherited the site and built a square, red brick, Elizabethan house, with an ornate and imposing entrance facade. Smythson's ground plan, which was not strictly adhered to, shows a correctly-oriented, integral chapel in the centre of the E block, opposite the great stair. It was entered from the parlour at the NE corner. There is some evidence of an upper chapel.
The Puritan Boynton acquired the house in 1620, having married the childless Griffith's sister, Frances. In the 1630s he employed, as a chaplain, the nonconformist Henry Jessey who had refused to follow high-church liturgies.
Sources/literature: RIBA, Smythson I/2.

BUTTERCRAMBE HALL, NORTH YORKSHIRE (replaced)
Patron: Sir Richard Darley (d. *c*.1654).
Dates: 1630s event.
In the 1630s, Darley allowed his Puritan chaplain to officiate, unlicensed, at the local parish church since, not being a conforming Anglican, he was not permitted by Laudian regulations to serve in the house chapel.
Sources/literature: W. Gibson, *A Social History of the Domestic Chaplain* (London, 1997), p. 30.

CALVELEY HALL, MILTON GREEN, CHESHIRE (house, altered, survives; chapel does not)
Patron: Lady Mary Calveley (d. 1705), née Hoghton.
Date: 1690 installation.
Mary Calveley, widow of Sir Hugh (d. 1648), erected a domestic chapel in the late 17th century house in 1690.
Sources/literature: Ormerod, 2, pp. 724, 769.

CALVERLEY HALL, WEST YORKSHIRE (house, enlarged, and chapel shell survive)
Patrons: Calverley family.
Dates: 1485-95 addition.
In the early Tudor period, the main components of the stone and timber-framed house of *c*.1400 were a hall, solar and linked stone chapel. The latter, oriented to the SE and added in 1485-95, occupied a projection at the SW end. There are a liturgical two-light Perpendicular E window, and an upper chapel or closet that opened off the solar and was divided from the body of the chapel by a traceried screen.
Sources/literature: Giles, pp. 18-20, 194-5.

CANNON ROW (LORD DERBY'S HOUSE, WESTMINSTER), LONDON (demolished)
Patron: William Stanley (*c*.1561-1642), 6th Earl of Derby.
Dates: post-1594 rebuild.
Derby inherited the site in 1594, and started rebuilding shortly thereafter. Thorpe's

plan shows a square courtyard house incorporating an assembly chapel separated by an openwork screen from a passage leading to an external entrance, and opposite a landing of the great stair. Unusually for this period, the plan shows a pulpit.
Sources/literature: T109.

CANNONS, MIDDLESEX (demolished)
Patron: Sir Thomas Lake (*c.*1567-1630).
Dates: post-1604 rebuild.
Lake acquired Cannons in 1604. Thorpe's plans of the U-plan house show a (probably) correctly-oriented, assembly chapel in the form of a small room off the high end of the hall, close to the great stair, and with its liturgical W wall separated from a passage by an openwork screen.
Sources/literature: T43-4, T224.

CANONS ASHBY HOUSE, NORTHAMPTONSHIRE (house, altered, and church/chapel survive)
Patrons: Sir Erasmus Dryden, Bt (1553-1632); Sir John Dryden, Bt (d. *c.*1658).
Dates: 1611 event; *c.*1640s event.
Erasmus Dryden inherited the 16th-century courtyard house, largely built by his father, in 1584. He seems to have acquired from his neighbours and relations, the Copes of Canons Ashby Priory (*q.v.*), the right to present to the church/chapel, formed from the nave and tower of the old priory church. It was deemed to be a peculiar and therefore outside the jurisdiction of the local bishop. In 1611, James I ordered the removal from the ministry there of the Puritan John Dod, known as 'Decalogue Dod', who was living under Dryden's protection.
Erasmus' son John, uncle of the (Roman Catholic) poet and dramatist John Dryden, was later reported as having converted most of the church into a barn and store-house.
Sources/literature: J.T. Cliffe, *The Puritan Gentry: Great Puritan Families of Early Stuart England* (London etc., 1984), pp. 180-1.

CANONS ASHBY PRIORY, NORTHAMPTONSHIRE (house demolished; chapel/church survives)
Patron: Sir John Cope (d. *c.*1558).
Dates: 1538-58 conversion.
Cope bought the suppressed Augustinian priory in 1538, and converted part of it into a house. He retained the nave and tower of the priory church to form a family chapel and serve as the church for the parish – whose population had been greatly reduced by enclosures.
Sources/literature: Heward, p. 114.

CASSIOBURY PARK, HERTFORDSHIRE (demolished)
Patron: Arthur Capel, 1st Earl of Essex (1631-83).
Date: 1680 event.
Architect: Hugh May (1621-84).
Capel inherited the Elizabethan H-plan house, built by the Morrison family on land that had belonged to St Albans Abbey, following his father's execution by order of Parliament in 1649. After the Restoration, he commissioned Hugh May to modernise it. Evelyn recorded that he attended prayers in Essex's chapel on 1 April 1680.
Sources/literature: Evelyn, 4, p. 201; Smith, pp. 202-2.

CASTLE ASHBY HOUSE, NORTHAMPTONSHIRE (house, somewhat altered, survives, as does chapel, redecorated in the 19th century)

Patrons: Henry Compton (1538-89), 1st Lord Compton; William Compton (c.1568-1630), 1st Earl of Northampton; Spencer Compton (1601-42), 2nd Earl of Northampton; James Compton (1622-81), 3rd Earl of Northampton.

Dates: from c.1574 new build; c.1624-31 partial rebuild; 1660-c.1679: refit.

By the time Henry Compton acquired the site in 1574, the original house, bought by his grandfather Sir William Compton (c.1482-1628) in 1512, had become a ruin. He built a two-storey, single-pile, courtyard house alongside it, with a three-storey pavilion at each corner. There may have been a chapel in the SE pavilion.

William Compton rebuilt the E range, incorporating an ashlar front. His correctly-oriented, cross-range, double-height, integral chapel with its large Venetian E window occupies a projecting bay in the SE corner, terminating a sequence of staterooms. The interior and upper chapel were completed in 1630-1. The house was sacked by Parliamentary troops during the Civil War, and the E range, including the chapel, gutted by fire.

The chapel was repaired 1660-c.1679.

Sources/literature: Castle Ashby, FD 1001-53, FD 1261-76, FD 1319; Soane Museum, Adam Survey, (29, 20-2; 54i, 56); *VB*, 3, (London, 1725), pl. 8; Warwickshire RO, CR 556/274; *CL*, 30 Jan. 1986.

See also: main text and fig. 5.33.

CASTLE HEDINGHAM, ESSEX (keep survives; chapel does not)

Patron: John de Vere (d. 1513), 13th Earl of Oxford.

Dates: 1509 and1513 events.

The pre-Reformation chapel was immediately to the S of the 12th-century keep which had been subjected to considerable late 15th-century additions. It is well documented in Oxford's will of 1509 and the inventory taken on his death in 1513. It contained particularly splendid decoration and metalwork. The records show that Oxford also possessed a highly decorated chapel in his private closet.

Sources/literature: 'The Last Testament and Inventory of John de Vere, Thirteenth Earl of Oxford' (W.H. St J. Hope, editor), *A*, 66 (1915), pp. 275-348; L.A. Majendie, 'On a Plan of Hedingham Castle, as described by recent excavations, and compared with a survey made in 1592', *Transactions of the Essex Archaeological Society*, 4 (1869), pp. 240-3.

See also: main text.

CECIL HOUSE (THE STRAND), LONDON (later Burghley House and then Exeter House) (demolished)

Patrons: William Cecil (1520-98), Lord Burghley; John Cecil (1628-78), 4th Earl of Exeter.

Dates: 1560-2 rebuild; 1657 event.

The original house on the site of the rectory of St Clement Danes was begun by Sir Thomas Palmer (d. 1553) under Edward VI, and acquired by Cecil in 1560. He built a brick and timber, double-courtyard house which he made his London headquarters. The location of any chapel has not been identified, and services may well have been held in the great chamber which contained a pulpit.

By 1657 a chapel had been created in the house, for in that year the diarist John Evelyn celebrated Christmas Day there, noting that it was 'one of the principal places of worship

for Anglicans until the Restoration'.
Sources/literature: Burghley, MS 358; Evelyn, 3, p. 95; J. Norden, *Speculum Britanniae* (London, 1593) (*BL*, Harleian MS 570, I, f. 39v); J. Husselby and P. Henderson, 'Location, Location, Location! Cecil House in the Strand', *AH*, 45 (2002), pp. 159-93; Ricketts, *Cecil*.
See also: main text.

CHANTEMARLE HOUSE, DORSET (much of house survives; chapel does not)
Patron: Sir John Strode (*c*.1561-1642).
Dates: 1612-19 rebuild.
Architects: Sir John Strode, with Gabriel Moore (*fl.* early 17th century).
Strode bought the medieval house from the Cheverell family in 1606. He pulled most of it down (including a small, dark, low chapel with a four-light E window) and created an E-facing, standard Jacobean, E-plan, stone house, incorporating religious inscriptions on the entrance front. Strode's integral, correctly-oriented, double-height, double-cell chapel occupied most of the N wing. Unusually for the period, the windows were not differentiated. The fittings included a pulpit along the N wall, together with the minister's pew, another pew, and two lower pews behind. Against the S wall stood two higher and two lower pews, and there were also seats round the walls. The plastered walls were painted white and the plastered ceiling (probably by Robert Eaton) displayed symbolic (but uncontroversial) references to sacramental worship. The chapel was consecrated in 1619.
Sources/literature: Dorset RO, D/BVL/M4, f. 22v ff.; Oswald, pp. 41-3; Hutchins, 4, pp. 4-7; J. Hutchins, *Vitruvius Dorsettienses* (London, 1816), pl. 5; Legg, pp. 43-6; *CL*, 30 Jun., 7 Jul. 1950.
See also: main text and Plate XIII.

CHAPELFORD HOUSE, NORWICH, NORFOLK (disappeared)
Patron: Lady Frances Hobart (d. 1664), née Egerton.
Date: *c*.1661 event.
The Calvinist Lady Frances converted some lower rooms of her house into a chapel which could accommodate some 200 people. Suspicious that she might be allowing illegal services to be conducted there, the authorities searched the premises in *c*.1661, but found nothing incriminating and later apologised for the disturbance. Earlier, she had 'won' her husband, Sir John Hobart of Blickling (*q.v.*) 'from what had been the vanity of his youth' so that he would seriously 'reprove others (especially his servants) and admonish his friends of those errors which had formerly been too much his own pleasure and delight'.
Sources/literature: Cliffe, pp. 18, 111.

CHARLTON HOUSE (GREENWICH), LONDON (house survives; chapel does not)
Patron: Sir Adam Newton (d. 1630).
Dates: *c*.1607-16 new build.
Newton bought the site, once the property of Bermondsey Priory, in 1607. There he built an H-plan house, of which the correctly-oriented, double-cell chapel occupied the NE wing. It was situated beyond the great stair and some distance from the great hall. It was consecrated in 1616. There was a large bay window at the E end. Unusually for this

period, the fenestration was undifferentiated.
Sources/literature: D.L. Lysons, *The Environs of London*, 4 (London, 1796), pp. 326-7.

CHARTERHOUSE (CLERKENWELL), LONDON

Patrons: Edward North (d. 1564), 1st Lord North; Thomas Howard (1536-72), 4th Duke of Norfolk; Thomas Howard (1561-1626), 1st Earl of Suffolk; Thomas Sutton (1532-1611); Charterhouse Governing Body (from 1611).

Dates: post-1545 alterations; 1565 event; 1608 event; from 1611: alterations as a hospital and school.

North bought the dissolved Carthusian monastery in 1545 and transformed it into a standard courtyard house. He, and the Roman Catholic Norfolk who bought the house from North's son in 1565 and was imprisoned there 1570-1, created and refashioned the chapel out of the early 14th-century monastic chapter house.

At the time of a 1565 inventory, the chapel had a lectern, desk, communion table, seating, cloths and curtains etc.

An inventory taken in 1608, by which time Norfolk's second son Suffolk was in possession (having been granted the house by the Crown in 1601), does not mention a chapel.

Thomas Sutton bought the house from Suffolk in 1611, and founded a hospital and school on the site. A N aisle was added to the chapel in 1612-14, and Sutton was buried in it in 1614. Further alterations in the mid-1630s under the guidance of Archbishop Laud (who was chairman of the governing body) included the making by John Colt of a commandment board, probably intended as part of a stone reredos. This featured figures of Aaron and Moses standing on pedestals and flanking white marble text panels. Below was a cherub's head and above was another cherub's head surrounded by heavenly clouds. The upper cornice supported two incense bowls which flanked a central urn, and (position uncertain) clouds surrounding the name of Jehovah. Colt later supplied a panel carved with figures of the apostles in a frame decorated with *putti* and seven decorated panels. This was perhaps designed to go above the commandment board. The chancel was raised at this time and altar rails installed. Further alterations took place after the Restoration, presumably to make good depredations during the Commonwealth – whose authorities regarded the Charterhouse as a 'nest of unclean birds'.

Sources/literature: Bodleian MS, 1565 inventory, North, b.12 ff. 31v-32; London Metropolitan Archives ACC/1876/AR/03/017a, 018a, 028c (consulted by kind permission of the Governors of Sutton's Hospital in Charterhouse); S. Porter, 'John Colt and the Charterhouse Chapel', *AH*, 44 (2001), pp. 228-36.

See also: main text and fig. 5.45.

CHATSWORTH, DERBYSHIRE (house, altered, and 17th-century chapel survive)

Patrons: Sir William Cavendish (1505-57) and Lady Cavendish, née Hardwick (Bess of Hardwick; 1518-1608); William Cavendish (1640-1707), 4th Earl and 1st Duke of Devonshire.

Dates: *c.*1551-77 new build; 1687-91 alterations.

Architects: any of Thomas Archer (*c.*1668-1743); Sir Thomas Fitch (1637-88); William Talman (1650-1719); or perhaps Devonshire himself.

Bess of Hardwick persuaded Cavendish to buy the site in 1549, and replaced the existing house with a single-pile courtyard house. The position of the original chapel is not securely documented, but it probably occupied the same site as the present chapel (but perhaps with different dimensions) in the W end of the S range. It comprised an upper and lower chapel, the former containing rich fittings and blue and white hangings.

Soon after the accession of James II in 1685, Devonshire withdrew from London and began to plan the rebuilding of Elizabethan Chatsworth. From 1687 he created a large, double-height, rectangular, integrated chapel, oriented to the W and with a simple family gallery at the liturgical W end. Three basement windows were incorporated into the lower part of the liturgical N wall (blind to prevent the intrusion of distracting views from the outside), but the exterior was not otherwise distinguished. With its grandiose display of painted decoration set against alabaster and marble fittings, the interior, which Walpole was to describe in 1760 as 'magnificent', was primarily intended to promote Protestant ideas, and to rebut the high-church and Roman Catholic messages conveyed in the two recent royal chapels of, respectively, Windsor (1684) and Whitehall (1686). With Chatsworth, the evolution of a specifically Protestant decorative scheme for a private chapel came of age.

Sources/literature: *Of Household Stuff: The 1601 Inventories of Bess of Hardwick* (S.M. Levey and P. Thornton, editors), (London, 2001), pp. 25, 28; Knyff, pl. 17; C. Ripa, *Iconologia* (facs. edn., New York and London, 1976); G. Vertue, 'Notebook A.1', *WS*, 30 (1955), pp. 24, 72-3; W. Kennett, *A Sermon Preach'd at the Funeral of the 1st Duke of Devonshire* (London, 1708); J. Grove, *Lives of all the Earls and Dukes of Devonshire* (London, 1764), p. 48; Walpole, p. 28.

See also: main text and fig. 6.10; Plates VIII, XXXI, XXXII.

CHELMSCOTE MANOR, BUCKINGHAMSHIRE (house, much altered, survives; remains of chapel survive)

Patrons: Corbet family.

Dates: late 16th/early 17th-century alterations.

The 14th-century chapel was incorporated into the house in the late 16th/early 17th centuries.

Sources/literature: *VCH*, 3 (1925), pp. 414-20.

CHELSEA (SIR JOHN DANVERS' HOUSE), LONDON (demolished)

Patron: Sir John Danvers (d. 1655).

Dates: from 1623 new build.

Danvers bought the site in 1622-3, and started to build shortly thereafter. John Aubrey found the house 'elegant and ingeniose' with two high turrets, but not sufficiently Classical. He noted that there was a 'neate little Chapell or Oratorie, finely painted' next to the drawing room. Thorpe's plan is of a square house containing a square chapel with one, undifferentiated, four-light window at what was probably the liturgical E end. The main entrance is from the hall at the W end. There is another entrance in the centre of the S wall from a corridor N of the parlour and linking the great stair and a turret staircase. A third entrance, at the W end of the N wall, leads from a self-contained room to the N.

Sources/literature: T21-2; J. Aubrey, 'Natural History of Wiltshire', Bodleian Library, Aubrey MSS, 2ff. 56, 58v.

CHESWORTH, WEST SUSSEX (house survives as a farm house; chapel demolished)

Patron: Thomas Howard (1473-1554), 3rd Duke of Norfolk.

Date: 1549 event.

According to the inventory taken on Norfolk's attainder in 1549, the Tudor, brick house with medieval hall contained a chapel, chapel chamber and chapel closet, all very richly decorated.

Sources/literature: H. Ellis, 'Inventories of Goods etc in the Manor of Chesworth, Sedgewick and Other Parks', *SAC*, 13 (1861), pp. 118-26.

See also: main text.

CHILDERLEY HALL, CAMBRIDGESHIRE (house, much altered, and chapel, part derelict, survive)
Patrons: Sir John Cutt (d. 1615); Sir John Cutt (d. 1646).
Dates: from 1600 new build; by 1609 event; 1639 event.
The detached, correctly-oriented, rectangular, brick chapel stands about 35 yards from the site of the early Tudor, brick house built by Sir John Cutte (d. 1520), and was erected by his descendant, Sir John Cutt. It is the only early 17th-century chapel known to be built of brick, and used pre-Reformation window types. The six-light E window contained a medieval painted glass Passion which was moved from the former Cutt seat at Horham Hall in Essex (*q.v.*), marking the beginnings of the 17th-century revival of the use of biblical scenes in private chapels. Inside, there was an upper chapel at the W end.
The chapel was consecrated between 1600 and 1609 by Bishop Heton of Ely.
In 1639, Laud informed Charles I that the Bishop of Ely (Matthew Wren) had contested Cutt's right to worship in his private chapel instead of a parish church. The bishop had claimed that Cutt's presumed dereliction was compounded by his having built outhouses on the ruins of the former parish church, and employed a chaplain without entitlement while claiming that he was the curate of the defunct parish.
Sources/literature: Relhan drawings (Cambridge Antiquarian Society Library); W. Laud, *Works*, 5 (facs. edn., Hildesheim and New York, 1977), pp. 365-6; The Royal Commission on the Historical Monuments of England, *An Inventory of the Historical Monuments in the County of Cambridge*, 1 (London, 1968), pp. 44-6; Legg, p. 318.
See also: main text.

CHILTON LODGE, WILTSHIRE (replaced)
Patron: Bulstrode Whitelocke (1605-75).
Date: 1672 event.
After the Declaration of Indulgence of 1672, Whitelocke applied for and received a licence for a chaplain to preach in his house and 'to allowe a roome there for preaching'. In the 1630s he had lived at the chapelled Fawley Court in Buckinghamshire (*q.v.*) which he had inherited from his father.
Sources/literature: Cliffe, p. 116.

CHIPCHASE CASTLE, NORTHUMBERLAND (house, altered, survives; chapel replaced)
Patrons: Heron family.
Dates: by end of 17th-century event.
A detached chapel is believed to have stood near the *c.*14th-century pele tower and small Tudor manor house that was largely replaced in *c.*1621. It is likely that the chapel had fallen into disuse by the end of the 17th century.
Sources/literature: *CL*, 21 Jun. 1956.

CHOLMONDELEY CASTLE, CHESHIRE (house replaced; chapel rebuilt, but E cell and much 17th-century woodwork survive)
Patrons: Richard Cholmondeley (*c*.1475-1518); Sir Hugh Cholmondeley (d. 1597); Robert Cholmondeley (*c*.1584-1659), 1st Earl of Leinster.
Dates: by 1518 event; Elizabethan rebuild; 1651-5 refit.
There was probably a detached, correctly-oriented chapel on the site from *c*.1200 near the moated, half-timbered house. Richard Cholmondeley may have reinforced the chapel roof before his death in 1518, at which stage it was probably of half-timbered construction, and he left money for prayers to be said there.
The house was rebuilt under Elizabeth as a timber-framed courtyard house to which the chapel may have been linked.
House and chapel were damaged during the Civil War, and repaired by Robert Cholmondeley. He refitted the chapel in 1651-5, creating an ornate two-centred chapel in defiance of Parliamentary ordinances forbidding altar-centred worship and conspicuous display. A reading desk and pulpit are to the immediate W of the screen. The commandment boards above them were originally probably over the communion table.
Sources/literature: Cholmey, H., *The Memoirs of Sir Hugh Cholmey* (Malton, 1870); F.I. Dunn, *The Ancient Chapel of the Lords of Cholmondeley* (Taporley, 1991); *CL*, 19 Jul. 1973.
See also: main text and fig. 5.43.

CHURSTON COURT, CHURSTON FERRERS, DEVON (house and chapel, both much restored, survive)
Patrons: Yarde family.
Dates: 1480-90 event.
The church near the house was once the private chapel of Churston Court, but the family handed it over for parochial use in 1480-90.
Sources/literature: M. Adams, 'Some Notes on the Church and Parish of Churston Ferrers', *Devon*, 36 (1904), p. 508.

CLARENDON HOUSE (WESTMINSTER), LONDON (demolished)
Patron: Edward Hyde (1609-74), 1st Earl of Clarendon.
Dates: 1664-6 new build.
Architect: Sir Roger Pratt (1620-85).
One of the earliest, grandest and most influential of post-Restoration great Classical houses, it was of the H-plan type, double-pile, and with four pavilions. Its chapel probably occupied the SE pavilion, was oriented to the S and not externally distinguished. It may well have occupied the basement and ground-floor levels, with a family gallery accessible from the latter. It was consecrated in 1667.
Sources/literature: F-E. Keller, 'Christian Eltester's drawings of Roger Pratt's Clarendon House and Robert Hooke's Montagu House', *Burlington Magazine*, 128 (1986), pp. 732-7; R. Pratt, *The Architecture of Sir Roger Pratt* (R.T. Gunther, editor), (Oxford, 1928), p. 162; Legg, p. 324.
See also: main text and fig. 6.3.

CLAY HALL, ILFORD, ESSEX (house and chapel demolished)
Patron: Sir Christopher Hatton (d. 1619).

Dates: 1616 and 1619-22 events.

Hatton leased the house, probably from the Colney family, in *c*.1608-19. He built a small, red-brick, detached chapel there which was consecrated in 1616. After his death, its contents were listed in an inventory taken during 1619-22, and included a table, carpet, cushions, curtain and rods, gilt leather forms and 'other lumber'. The total value was £12.11s.4d.

Sources/literature: Essex RO, T/P/93/2, f. 222; Northamptonshire RO, FH 617 & 2666; Legg, p. 319; D.L. Lysons, *The Environs of London*, 4 (London, 1796), pp. 82-3; *VCH*, 5 (1966), pp. 195-6.

CLOPTON HOUSE, WARWICKSHIRE (house, altered, survives; as does chapel)

Patron: John Clopton (a. 1660s).

Dates: 1660s rebuild.

Clopton rebuilt and added to the moated, 16th-century house that he had inherited from his father. The chapel under the roof, painted with religious texts, seems to date from this period.

Sources/literature: Tyack, pp. 50-2.

COBHAM HALL, KENT (house, altered, survives, as does chapel with Gothicised interior)

Patrons: William Brooke (1527-97), 10th Lord Cobham; Henry Brooke (1564-1619), 11th Lord Cobham.

Dates: *c*.1580-1603 alterations.

William Brooke created a red-brick, U-shaped house by adding N and S wings to an earlier central block in 1584 and 1594 respectively. Work stopped in 1603 on Henry Brooke's imprisonment for treason. The central block had disappeared by 1641, and was replaced after the Restoration. The chapel is in the N wing with a long gallery above. An impressive Classical porch serves as the entrance to the chapel.

Sources/literature: NA, State Papers: Correspondence of R. Williams to 11th Lord Cobham; 'Cobham Hall: Inventory of Furniture and Pictures in 1672' (W.A. Scott Robertson, editor), *AC*, 17 (1887), pp. 392-408.

COLLETON BARTON, DEVON (house, altered, survives; chapel shell survives)

Patron: Humphrey Bury (a. 1612).

Date: late 16th/early 17th-century remodelling.

Bury substantially rebuilt the medieval house in 1612. The detached gatehouse block contained the 15th-century chapel, remodelled in the late 16th/early 17th centuries – perhaps by Bury. However, the main constructional details appear to be medieval.

Sources/literature: W.G. Hoskins, *Devon* (London, 1954), p. 368; *CL*, 28 Aug. 1915.

COLLYWESTON, NORTHAMPTONSHIRE (demolished)

Patrons: Margaret Beaufort (1443-1509), Countess of Richmond; Henry Fitzroy (1519-36), Duke of Richmond.

Dates: early 16th-century event; 1526 event.

The stone house was probably built by Margaret Beaufort, mother of Henry VII. Her household in the early 16th century included choirboys who had separate accommodation in the house (the same arrangement pertained at Fotheringay Castle (*q.v.*).

The crown acquired the house on the attainder of Edward Stafford, 3rd Duke of Buckingham in 1521. It was subsequently settled on Henry VIII's illegitimate son, Henry

Fitzroy, probably becoming his main residence. In 1526 the duke's household included the Archdeacon of Richmond, the dean of his chapel, four chaplains, and their eight servants. The chapel hangings contained seven scenes from the Passion.

Sources/literature: Leland, pt. 1, p. 22; St John's College, Cambridge MS 102.9; J. Nichols, *Progresses and Public Processions of Queen Elizabeth*, 1 (London, 1823), p. 204; J.G. Nichols, 'Memoir of Henry Fitzroy, Duke of Richmond and Somerset', *Camden Miscellany*, 3 (1855), pp. xx-xxvi; J.G. Nichols (editor), 'Inventory of the Goods of Henry Fitzroy, Duke of Richmond', *Camden Miscellany*, 3 (1855), pp. 1-21.

COMBE ABBEY, WARWICKSHIRE (house, much altered, survives; chapel does not)

Patrons: John Harington (d. 1613), Lord Harington; William Craven (1606-97), 1st Earl of Craven.

Dates: after 1581 conversion; possible alterations 1684-9.

Architect: William Winde (d. 1722).

Harington acquired a three-sided courtyard house, formed from a dissolved Cistercian monastery, on the death of his father-in-law Sir William Wigston in 1581, and converted it into a substantial country house. The integral, correctly-oriented chapel was at the E end of the hall (N) range with a large seven-light window, and may have posessed stairs to an upper level.

Craven inherited the house from his mother who had bought it in 1622 from Harington's heir. Winde's alterations, overseen by Craven's nephew and presumed heir Sir William Craven (d. 1695), included remodelling the N range. A contemporary plan shows the chapel to the E of the hall, and separated from it by the great stair. There was an entrance at the N end of the W wall from the stair, and another from the cloisters at the W end of the S wall. A third entrance lay at the E end of the N wall and gave access from an ante-chamber, bed chamber and other accommodation.

Sources/literature: Bodleian MS, Gough drawings a.2, ff. 70v-1; D. King, *The Cathedrall and Conventuall Churches of England and Wales Orthographically Delineated* (London, 1656); Knyff, pl. 47; 'Winde-Craven Correspondence' (H. M. Colvin, editor), *WS*, 1 (1984).

COMPTON CASTLE, DEVON (house and chapel, restored, survive)

Patrons: John Gilbert (d. 1539) or Otho Gilbert (1417-94).

Dates: *c*.1520s or 1450-80 alterations.

[Editor's note: Annabel Ricketts, following Everett and Cherry, noted that John Gilbert extended the original manor house and erected showy fortifications from *c*.1520, making the mid 15th-century, north-oriented, double-height chapel an integral part of the house. However, Emery, publishing three years after Dr Ricketts', death, persuasively attributes the above alterations to John's father Otho, and puts them at 1450-80.]

Sources/literature: Cherry, pp. 285-6; Emery, 3, pp. 519-22; A.W. Everett, 'Compton Castle', *Devon*, 71 (1939), p. 345; A.W. Everett, 'The Rebuilding of Compton Castle', *Devon*, 88 (1956), pp. 75-85; *National Trust Guide Book* (1985), pp. 4 (A.W. Everett: 'Plan of Compton Castle'), 10-11.

COMPTON VERNEY, WARWICKSHIRE (house rebuilt; chapel replaced)

Patrons: Verney family.

Date: 1558 event.

The detached, correctly-oriented, medieval chapel, originally a parish church before the nearby village became depopulated, stood to the E of the mid-15th-century courtyard house. It contained a (lost) glass panel of 1558 depicting members of the Verney family, as well as 16th-century armorial glass.

Sources/literature: *CL*, 15 Apr.1954.

See also: main text and fig. 4.14.

COMPTON WYNYATES, WARWICKSHIRE (house survives)

A large, red-brick, early Tudor, courtyard house, Compton Wynyates was unusual in that it possessed both a fair-sized household chapel (Compton Wynyates I) and a detached chapel (Compton Wynyates II) a few hundred yards away.

Compton Wynyates I (chapel shell survives)

Patron: Sir William Compton (*c*.1482-1528).

Dates: early 16th-century rebuild.

Compton inherited the site in 1493, and is thought to have largely replaced the existing medieval manor house with the house that survives today. The double-height, integral, SE-oriented chapel is in the E range and distinguishable externally by a projecting liturgical E end and large window. A screen separated the chancel from the nave. Tapestry hangings were of 'verdure trailed with roses'.

Compton Wynyates II (chapel survives)

Patron: James Compton (1622-81), 3rd Earl of Northampton.

Dates: 1665-6 rebuild.

The detached chapel is a rectangular, correctly-oriented, single-cell building occupying the site of the pre-Reformation chapel which had been largely destroyed during the Civil War. The exterior contains a mix of early Tudor and (rudimentary) Classical styles. Inside, there are two aisles, each with a separate E window above. The ceiling of one aisle was painted with the sun and clouds to represent day, and the other with the moon and stars to represent night.

Sources/literature: W.B. Compton, *History of the Comptons of Compton Wynyates* (London, 1930); W. Dugdale, *The Antiquities of Warwickshire* (London, 1730), p. 550; *CL*, 30 Oct., 6 Nov. 1915.

See also: main text and figs. 3.8, 3.9, 3.10, 6.19, 6.20.

COPTHALL, ESSEX (demolished)

Patron: Sir Thomas Heneage (d. 1595).

Dates: post-1564 alterations.

Heneage was granted the manor, formerly the property of the dissolved Abbey of Waltham, in 1564, and created a single courtyard house with the hall on the main entrance axis. The integral, cross-range chapel appears to have been in one of the side ranges, perhaps oriented to the W. The ante-chapel possessed an impressive bay window. Unusual for the period was the chapel's size: it was about the same width as the hall and, counting the ante-chapel, not much shorter. Its appearance and layout are known mainly from a plan and drawing of *c*.1747, undertaken shortly before the house was demolished, and its somewhat Jacobean feel may be due to unrecorded early 17th-century alterations. The inner chapel containing box-pews arranged college-style was separated from the outer chapel by a screen, with an ante-chapel beyond. Access to the latter was from a passageway to the liturgical N, and via an external entrance opposite the kitchen on the liturgical S. There was no upper chapel, but it seems that two small closets, each capable of holding perhaps two people, overlooked the chapel. The decoration of the closet doorways and the general arrangement of the gallery in relation to the closets are thought to owe much to French influence.

Sources/literature: BL, King's Maps, 124, nos. 28-9; Essex RO, D/DW E26/1 & 2, E27/14; Coope, p. 61.

See also: main text and fig. 4.15.

CORNBURY PARK, OXFORDSHIRE (house, exterior relatively unspoiled, survives; chapel, its eastern half more or less as originally conceived, survives)

Patron: Edward Hyde (1609-74), 1st Earl of Clarendon.

Dates: 1666-7 new build (NB: until recently, it was thought that Clarendon's son erected the chapel in 1677, along with completing building work interrupted following his father's disgrace and exile in 1667).

Architect: Hugh May (1621-84).

Charles II granted the Tudor house, which had been updated in the early 17th century, to Clarendon in 1661. May's work includes a linked, single-cell, double-height, N-oriented chapel. It was accessible via a narthex or ante-chapel, originally much larger than the present arrangement, from the high and low ends of the house. Externally, it is a simple rectangle of ashlar with a steep hipped roof linked to the main house at its liturgical W end. Although it has three external walls, no attempt is made to give them a specific architectural character. Inside, the decoration is largely secular, with a controlled emphasis on the area around the communion table. The plasterwork is of high quality and, apart from the area above the gallery, appears to be original. The ceiling is typical of a domestic room of the period. The woodwork is remarkably complete. The basic scheme is of rectangular panels with simple mouldings divided by pilasters. At the liturgical W end, the family gallery is accessed from the first floor, though there might have been a 17th-century stair as much has altered in the area of the ante-chapel. The gallery's woodwork is of high quality but relatively plain. It is supported below by a three-bay W screen with openwork scrolls and foliage built round large Corinthian columns – apart from that at Tabley (*q.v.*), this was the last W screen to be installed in a private country house chapel in the 17th century. The entablature above is decorated with masks and swags. The pulpit is on the liturgical N side and clearly of less importance than the communion table. The chaplain's desk or reading pew stands opposite it. The floor was of uniform bluish stone with a border round the edge laid diamond-wise, except for the raised E end where dark and white stone alternated. Cornbury typifies the popular conception of the country house chapel.

Sources/literature: BL, Add. MS 78341, f. 101v; Evelyn, 3, pp. 381-2; NA, C 104/109; J. Newman, 'Hugh May, Clarendon and Cornbury', in *English Architecture Public and Private* (J. Bold and E. Chaney editors), (London, 1993), pp. 81-7; V. Watney, *Cornbury and the Forest of Wychwood* (London, 1910); *CL*, 22 Sep. 1950.

See also: main text and figs. 6.7, 6.8, 6.9.

COTEHELE, CORNWALL (house and chapel survive)

Patrons: Sir Richard Edgcumbe (d. 1489); Sir Piers Edgcumbe (1472-1539).

Dates: early Tudor alterations.

Richard Edgcumbe inherited the modest, medieval, stone house in *c.*1460. He probably retained its 13th-century walls when creating the double-height, correctly-oriented chapel which replaced an earlier chapel. He or his son Piers inserted a horizontal window just below eye level in the W wall of the chapel, perhaps to allow retainers a view of the altar at the E end. Piers extended the house, principally by the addition of a N (hall) range that linked the chapel to the family rooms. Inside, the chapel has a plastered barrel vault with wooden ribs incorporating roof bosses depicting the Tudor rose. Its floor contains some of the original green and white glazed tiles. The altar cloth – purple and decorated with appliqué figures of the twelve apostles and the arms of Piers and his wife Joan Durnford – is pre-1520. The family may have occupied seats in the chancel. A squint linked Sir Piers' solar at first floor level.

Sources/literature: R. Marks and P. Williamson (editors), *Gothic Art for England 1400-1547* (London, 2003), p. 339.

See also: main text and fig. 3.1.

COTHERIDGE COURT, WORCESTERSHIRE (house, altered, survives)

Patrons: Margery Ketelby (d. 1548); John Ketelby (d. *c*.1573).

Date: 1548 event; 1573 event.

Margery Ketelby inherited the early Tudor house from her husband John when he predeceased her in 1541. The inventory taken on her death lists a chapel chamber containing bedding, but no chapel is mentioned.

An inventory taken on the death of John and Mary Ketelby's son, John, also lists bedding in a chapel chamber, but again no chapel is mentioned.

Sources/literature: Wanklyn, pp. 13-14, 48.

COWDRAY HOUSE, WEST SUSSEX (house, including chapel shell, survives as a ruin)

Patrons: Sir David Owen (d. 1535); William Fitzwilliam (1490-1542), Earl of Southampton; Sir Anthony Browne (*c*.1500-48).

Dates: early Tudor new build.

Owen inherited the site in 1492, and built the E range that contains the integral, rectangular, double-height, correctly-oriented chapel, set at right angles to the hall. The main chapel entrance was from the N, just off the dais end of the hall. There may also have been an entrance on the S side which would have communicated directly with the servants' quarters. At first-floor level, the upper chapel at the W end appears to have been reached from the great chamber above the hall. There is a three-sided apse at the E end. No decoration survives from the Tudor period. The final shape of the house was set by Southampton (who had bought it from Owen) and his half-brother Browne. Together they created a fine, courtyard house of brick and stone.

Sources/literature: 'A Book of Orders and Rules of Anthony Viscount Montagu in 1595' (S.D. Scott, editor), S*AC*, 7 (1854), pp. 172-212; W.H. St J. Hope, *Cowdray and Easebourne Priory* (London, 1919); C. Roundell, *Cowdray, the History of a Great English House* (London, 1884).

See also: main text and figs. 3.3, 3.4, 3.5.

CREWE HALL, CHESHIRE (house, much enlarged, and chapel survive)

Patron: Sir Ranulph Crewe (1558-1646).

Dates: *c*.1615-39 new build.

Crewe bought the site and built a new house in the shape of a square block. His centralised, cross-range, integral, double-cell chapel was evidently an essential and formative part of the plan. Oriented to the N, it is positioned on the main entrance axis and approached via an impressive route but undisturbed by passing traffic. Its fenestration is differentiated, and its importance is emphasised by a (probably original) apsidal window. It was consecrated in 1635.

Sources/literature: Legg, pp. 199–203.

See also: main text and figs. 5.2, 5.3.

CULVERTHORPE HALL, LINCOLNSHIRE (house, remodelled, survives; chapel portico survives as a 'garden feature')

Patron: Sir John Newton, Bt (1626-99).

Dates: 1690s new build.

Architect: perhaps William Stanton (1639-1705).

Newton acquired the site by *c.*1672, and erected a house on it in *c.*1679. The building of the detached chapel, first considered in 1685, was well advanced by 1690, although it was not fully fitted out until 1702. It stood about 200 yards E of the site of the 1670s house, was severely Classical in appearance, correctly-oriented, and of single-cell design. The surviving portico has Ionic columns – St Paul's Covent Garden (*q.v.*) apart, it appears to be the first example of a private chapel with a Classical portico in England. The ceiling was of coloured plasterwork and the floor of marble.

Sources/literature: Lincolnshire Archive Office, MON 7/12/101; J. Lord, 'A Chapel and Some Garden Walls: Culverthorpe in the 1690s', *AH*, 40 (1997), pp. 99–109.

See also: main text and fig. 6.17.

DARLASTON MANOR, STAFFORDSHIRE (no trace survives)

Patron: Sir Thomas Offley (*c.*1505-82).

Date: 1582 event.

It is clear from Offley's will of 1582 that Darlaston contained a chapel.

Sources/literature: NA, PROB2 423.

DEIGHTON, NORTH YORKSHIRE (no trace survives)

Patron: Sir William Ingleby (d. 1617).

Date: 1617 event.

An inventory taken on Ingleby's death indicates that the household chapel was used as a lumber room.

Sources/literature: Crossley, pp. 198–203.

DENHAM PLACE, BUCKINGHAMSHIRE (house, somewhat altered, survives; chapel, greatly altered, survives)

Patron: Sir Roger Hill (d. 1729).

Dates: 1688-1701 new build.

Architect: probably William Stanton (1639-1705).

Hill bought the property in 1673, and started building an H-plan house. The integral chapel, oriented to the N, is in the NE wing. There is a family gallery at the liturgical W end, of which the ceiling is dated 1692. The present, highly ornate fittings, including a screen separating the inner and outer chapels, are a mix of Tudor and late 17th-century, and were installed during 19th-century renovations.

Sources/literature: *CL*, 18 Apr.1925.

DORCHESTER HOUSE, LONDON: see **BLEWHOUSE**

DRAYTON HOUSE, NORTHAMPTONSHIRE (house and chapel, altered, survive)
Patron: Henry Mordaunt (1623-97), 2nd Earl of Peterborough.
Dates: from *c*.1676 rebuild; 1688 event.
Architect: Isaac Rowe (*fl*. 1660s-80s).
Peterborough inherited the rectangular, courtyard house in 1643. Late 13th-century in origin, it had subsequently been updated and extended, notably in the 1580s. It possessed a chapel in early Tudor times but its location is not known. He transformed the house in the 1670s, creating a new entrance in the SE wall. Here, in 1676, Rowe designed ranges on either side of the gate, including a SW-oriented, single-cell, integral chapel running NE-SW along the range. It has three bays and had casement windows with mullions and curved transoms reflecting the curve of the window head. Access was probably via a door to the ante-chapel. The family may well have used the chapel chamber above the latter as a gallery. The ceiling – divided by narrow ribs into 60 panels decorated with coats of arms – is thought to date from Rowe's time, as is the wooden reredos at the (windowless) liturgical E end. Peterborough declared himself a Roman Catholic in 1687, but there are no indications that his chapel was fitted out for Roman Catholic worship.
The chapel was pillaged in 1688, but repaired and redecorated some 30 years later. It is likely that the present gallery was installed at that stage.
Sources/literature: R. Halstead, *Succinct Genealogies* (London, 1685), p. 402; *CL*, 13, 20, 27 May, 3 Jun. 1965.

DUDDESTON HALL, BIRMINGHAM (disappeared)
Patron: Thomas Holte (1495-1546).
Date: 1546 event.
A 1546 inventory taken on Holte's death (he was the grandfather of the builder of Aston Hall, Warwickshire, *q.v.*), indicated that the house contained twelve chambers, including a hall, great chamber, gallery, chapel and kitchen.
Sources/literature: A. Davidson, *History of the Holtes of Aston* (Birmingham, 1854), pp. 15-16.

DUKINFIELD HALL, CHESHIRE (house demolished; chapel, much altered, survives)
Patrons: Dukinfield family; Robert Dukinfield (1619-89); Sir Robert Dukinfield (1642-1729).
Dates: Jacobean new build; 1640-1 event; 1653 event; *c*.1695 event.
The linked Jacobean chapel, oriented to the N, was added to an earlier house, perhaps on the site of a medieval oratory. Built of stone and of nave-and-chancel design, it is lit on the liturgical N and S sides by six three-light, round-arched windows. The liturgical E window is similar, although the window heads are cusped. The chancel has a door with a segmental head to the S, and there are two round-headed doors to the N and S of the nave. The interior has a simple hammer-beam roof and semi-circular chancel arch. There was also a wooden chancel screen.
In 1640-1, Robert Dukinfield's radical chaplain, Samuel Eaton, led an 'independent' congregation in worship in the chapel.

From 1653 the chapel was used as a gathering place for nonconformists.

In c.1695, Sir Robert had the chapel licensed for nonconformist worship.

Sources/literature: Cliffe, pp. 193-5, 211-12; G.J. Oliver "Samuel Eaton 1597-1665 – First Congregational Chapel in England", *History Alive - Tameside*, 2 (2001), p. 48; Stell, pp. 7–8.

See also: main text.

DUNHAM MASSEY, CHESHIRE (house and chapel, remodelled, survive)

Patron: George Booth (1622-84), 1st Lord Delamere.

Date: *c.*1655 conversion.

The early Tudor, courtyard house on the site was largely rebuilt in the early 17th century to form a brick, E-shaped house with Flemish gables. In *c.*1655, Booth converted two ground-floor rooms in the N range off the great stair to form a simple, rectangular, integral chapel, oriented to the W. It was refitted in *c.*1710, and the extent to which the 17th-century scheme was altered is uncertain. There was a central communion table at the liturgical E end, flanked by the servants' entrance and a reading pew. There was a further entrance from the hall. Benches and pews are arranged college-style. The family pew was raised, with no access to the main body of the chapel. Knyff's view of 1697 shows a small building with Flemish gables to the SE of the house, which might have been a detached chapel, and which had disappeared some 50 years later.

Sources/literature: Knyff, pl. 37; J. Swarbrick, 'Dunham Massey Hall', *Transactions of the Lancashire and Cheshire Antiquarian Society,* 42 (1925), pp. 53-78.

See also: main text.

DUNSTER CASTLE, SOMERSET (house, much altered survives; chapel does not)

Patron: George Luttrell (d. 1629).

Date: 1626 event.

Architect: probably William Arnold (*fl.* late 16th/early 17th centuries).

The Luttrell family started reconstructing their medieval castle in *c.*1576, and in 1617 George Luttrell instructed Arnold to transform it into an E or H-plan house. The chapel received a licence in 1626.

Sources/literature: Somerset RO, Luttrell Papers, Box 39/12.

DURDANS, SURREY (demolished)

Patron: George Berkeley (1628-98), 1st Earl of Berkeley.

Dates: 1673-89 rebuild.

Berkeley rebuilt the late 16th-century house, which had been expanded in 1639, possibly using materials from the demolished Nonsuch Palace. Fiennes described the 'pretty' chapel as being entered from the little parlour. There was a 'balcony closet' for the patron and his wife, and a separate closet for women accessible from the dining room.

Sources/literature: Fiennes, p. 342; J. Harris, *The Artist and the Country House* (London, 1979), pp. 61-2.

EASTINGTON HALL, WORCESTERSHIRE (house survives; chapel does not)

Patron: Giles Bridges (*c.*1515-59).

Date: 1559 event.

Bridges inherited the early 16th-century, timber-framed, U-shaped house from his mother, Alice Bridges, née Eastington, in 1539. An inventory taken on Bridges' death lists a chapel containing candlesticks, bells, a mass book etc. The inventory also lists a chapel chamber containing bedding.
Sources/literature: Wanklyn, p. 29.

EASTON LODGE, ESSEX (demolished)
Patron: William Maynard (1586-1640), 1st Lord Maynard.
Dates: by 1621 new build.
Maynard added a richly decorated, linked, correctly-oriented chapel, consecrated in 1621, to his Elizabethan house. The main chapel was richly carpeted in gold, silver, orange, black and purple. Textiles were used to emphasise the communion table and the pulpit, the former being decorated with a cushion of gold and silver, and the latter with one of embroidered purple velvet. The colour of the E end was balanced by the rich effect of the upper chapel which possessed gilded leather hangings. Its furniture was upholstered to match, and covered with two long cushions of green and gold satin.
Sources/literature: Essex RO, I/Mp129/1/1; NA, Prob 11/85, ff. 185, 190, 194; F.W. Steer, *Easton Lodge Inventory, 1637* (Chelmsford, 1952); M. Archer, '17th Century Painted Glass at Little Easton', *Essex Journal,* 12:1 (1977), pp. 3-10; P. Morant, *History and Antiquities of the County of Essex,* 2 (London 1768), pp. 430, 433.
See also: main text and figs. 5.10, 5.11.

EASTON MAUDIT HALL, NORTHAMPTONSHIRE (demolished)
Patron: Sir Henry Yelverton (1633-70).
Date: 1671 event.
The inventory taken after Yelverton's death lists a main chapel and an 'upper' chapel in the house. The latter contained a fireplace, chairs, hangings, etc., and was evidently intended for use by the family.
Sources/literature: NA 4/7,269 quoted in Cliffe, *World*, pp. 34-5.

EASTON NESTON, NORTHAMPTONSHIRE (replaced)
Patrons: Richard Empson/William Compton. (a. early 16th century).
Date: 1511 alterations.
The medieval house, updated in 1511, contained rooms for singers and a chaplain, but there was no other evidence of a chapel. The rooms did not appear in a 1540 inventory, by which time it had become the property of the Fermor family.
Sources/literature: NA, C 142/26/21.

EATON HALL, CHESHIRE (replaced)
Patron: Sir Thomas Grosvenor, Bt (1656-1700).
Date: 1669 event.
Grosvenor inherited the gabled, moated manor house from his grandfather in 1664 and was to replace it on a new site from 1675. According to Sir Peter Leycester of Tabley Hall (*q.v.*), Eaton Hall possessed a chapel in 1669.
Sources/literature: P. Leycester, Historical Antiquities (London, 1674), pp. 193-7, quoted in Cliffe, *World*, pp. 33-4.

EDINGTON PRIORY, WILTSHIRE (house survives; chapel does not)
Patron: Anne, Lady Beauchamp (d. 1665).

Date: 1665 event.

Anne Beauchamp rented the 16th-century house, built on the site of the living quarters of the canons of the Bonhommes, from the Paulett family. The inventory taken on her death valued the contents of her chapel – which included two round tables, nine chairs, twelve pictures, some cushions and a carpet – at 40s.

Sources/literature: 'Anne, Lady Beauchamp's Inventory at Edington, Wiltshire 1665', *Wiltshire Archaeological & Natural History Magazine*, 58 (1963), pp. 383-9.

ELSYNG (ENFIELD), LONDON (demolished)
Patron: Sir Thomas Lovell (d. 1524).

Date: 1524 event.

Lovell acquired the large courtyard house in 1492 and further extended it. A 1524 inventory attached to his will mentions a chapel near the porter's lodge and a parlour. The house, restyled Elsyng Palace, was later acquired by Henry VIII.

Sources/literature: NA, Prob 2/199.

ELTON HALL, CAMBRIDGESHIRE (house replaced; chapel undercroft and some chapel fabric survive)
Patrons: Sir Richard Sapcote (d. 1477) or Sir John Sapcote (a. late 15th century).

Date: late 15th-century new build.

Richard Sapcote and/or his son, John, built the gatehouse range which included a chapel and chapel undercroft. The hall range is thought to have lain to the north.

Sources/literature: N. Pevsner, *The Buildings of England: Bedfordshire and the County of Huntingdon and Peterborough* (Harmondsworth, 1974), pp. 238-40.

EUSTON HALL, SUFFOLK (house, remodelled, survives; chapel does not)
Patron: Henry Bennet (1618-85), 1st Earl of Arlington.

Dates: 1666-70 alterations.

Arlington bought the house in 1666, formerly the property of the Roman Catholic Rookwood family, and transformed it into an H-plan house with corner pavilions in the French style. Verrio was employed there, and may have created a painted scheme for the chapel.

Sources/literature: Fiennes, pp. 150-1; M. Aston, *England's Iconoclasts* (Oxford, 1988), p. 318; E. Lodge, *Illustrations of British History*, 2 (London, 1791), p.187; *CL*, 10, 17, 24 Jan. 1957.

See also: main text.

FAWLEY COURT, BUCKINGHAMSHIRE (replaced)
Patron: Sir James Whitelocke (1570-1632).

Dates: 1621-32 event.

Whitelocke's chapel was consecrated by John Williams, Bishop of Lincoln, between 1621 and 1632.

Sources/literature: F. Heal and C. Holmes, *The Gentry in England and Wales, 1500-1700* (Basingstoke, 1994), p. 369.

FINESHADE ABBEY, NORTHAMPTONSHIRE (replaced)
Patron: Robert Kirkham (d. 1653).

Dates: 1647-53 new build.

The former Augustinian Priory, converted into a modest house with mullioned windows, is said to have contained a chapel, perhaps created by Kirkham after he inherited the house in 1647.

Sources/literature: J. Bridges, *The History and Antiquities of Northamptonshire* (P. Whalley, editor), 2 (London, 1791), p. 307; Heward, p. 222.

FIRLE PLACE, EAST SUSSEX (house remodelled; chapel does not survive)
Patron: Sir John Gage (1479-1556).
Dates: 1540s event.

Gage was said to have built his double-courtyard house using stone from a nearby dissolved monastery. His chapel was 57ft long and 10ft wide at its broadest point. The area round the altar was to be paved with tiles of the highest quality ordered from Antwerp in the 1540s. Further W, they were to be less costly, while the W end was to be paved with plain green and yellow stone.

Sources/literature: B. Winchester, *Tudor Family Portrait* (London, 1955), p.112.
See also: main text.

FORDE ABBEY, DORSET (house and chapel survive)
Patrons: Sir Henry Rosewell (d. 1656); Sir Edmund Prideaux, Bt (1601-59); Edmund Prideaux (c.1634-1702).
Dates: by 1639 conversion; after 1649 addition.

The correctly-oriented, loosely linked chapel was created out of the chapter house of the former Cistercian abbey, most probably by the Puritan Rosewell.

In 1649 or 1650, Rosewell sold the house to Cromwell's Attorney General, Sir Edmund Prideaux (second son of Sir Edmund Prideaux of Netherton Hall, *q.v.*). The Prideaux family added Classical detailing. The pulpit is to the SE of the carved screen, and the seating was college style.

Sources/literature: Cliffe, pp. 113, 162, 222; J.T. Cliffe, *The Puritan Gentry: Great Puritan Families of Early Stuart England* (London etc., 1984), pp. 167-8; Oswald, pp. 54-8; *CL*, 14, 21, 28 Mar., 4 Apr. 1963.
See also: main text and fig. 5.21; Plate XVII.

FOTHERINGAY CASTLE, NORTHAMPTONSHIRE (a ruin)
Patron: Margaret Beaufort (1443-1509), Countess of Richmond.
Dates: early 16th-century event.

The medieval castle, rebuilt in the 15th century, contained two chapels in the 14th, and was later to be the site of the execution of Mary Queen of Scots. Margaret Beaufort, mother of Henry VII, owned it in the early 16th century when her household included choirboys who had their own accommodation (the same arrangement pertained at Collyweston, (*q.v.*).

Sources/literature: St John's College, Cambridge MS 91.7.

GIPPING HALL, SUFFOLK (house demolished; chapel survives)
Patrons: Sir James Tyrell (d. 1502); Tyrell family.
Dates: c.1474-1502 new build and addition; late 16th/early 17th-century addition.

Tyrell had made his money under the patronage of Richard III, and probably built the detached, correctly-oriented chapel, which stands about 200 yards from the site of his 15th-century house, shortly before Henry VII came to the throne in 1485. He subsequently added an annex to the N of the chancel. Of a simple 'nave and chancel' design, it replaced an earlier chapel, perhaps built on the same site. The walls are of knapped flint arranged in chequer patterns. Inside, there are doors in the N and S walls midway down the nave, with two-light windows above.

A small tower was added in the later 16th or early 17th century.

Sources/literature: Emery, 2, pp. 108-9; W. H. Sewell, *Sir James Tyrell's Chapel at Gipping, Suffolk* (Needham Market, reprint of 1871 edn.); R. Tricker, *The Chapel of Saint Nicholas Gipping, Suffolk, Brief Guide* (1998).

See also: main text and Plate II.

GLASSENBURY, KENT (house, updated, survives; chapel does not)

Patron: Sir Thomas Roberts (1658-1706).

Date: 1672 event.

In 1672, Roberts' mother, Lady Bridget Roberts (d. 1706), sought a licence for nonconformist worship in the domestic chapel adjoining the moated, early Tudor house. Services were attended by local people as well as the Roberts household. Roberts himself 'catechised' his servants and children every Sunday following the afternoon sermon.

Sources/literature: Cliffe, pp. 116, 140-1, 196, 223.

GORHAMBURY, HERTFORDSHIRE (house replaced; chapel does not survive)

Patrons: Sir Nicholas Bacon (1509-79); Lady Ann Bacon (1528-1610), née Cook; Francis Bacon (1561-1626), Viscount St Albans; Edward Radcliffe (d. 1643), 6th Earl of Sussex; Sir Harbottle Grimston, Bt (1603-85).

Dates: 1560s new build; early 17th-century event; 1630s event; 1668-75 alterations.

Nicholas Bacon bought the medieval manor house, until the Dissolution the property of the Abbey of St Albans, in *c*.1561, and replaced it with a new courtyard house to which he later added a two-storey cloister and gallery. The integral chapel, orientation unclear, was probably a continuation of the hall range, close to the upper end of the great hall and to the great stair, but off the main processional route. There was one ground-floor (internal) entrance, and there may have been an upper chapel at the liturgical W end.

The decoration of the (probably early 17th-century) pulpit, presumably installed by Nicholas Bacon's widow Ann or son Francis, and now in St Michael's church, St Albans, avoids contentious biblical imagery by using symbolic references to sacramental worship.

In the late 1630s, large amounts of wafers were bought at various times of the year, presumably for communion. This would have been for the Earl and Countess of Sussex who were renting the house at the time.

Grimston bought the house in 1652. He repaired the chapel windows, and planned to extend the W wall by 20 feet. This work does not appear to have been carried out, though a new window was planned in 1673. In the same year, wainscoting was installed, perhaps incorporating four Corinthian columns. In 1675, the main body of the chapel was to be floored with white Purbeck stone and black marble and the altar area with black and white marble, all laid 'cornerwise'. Steps to the altar were also to be built. Walpole visited the house in *c*.1753 and pronounced the chapel 'pretty'.

Sources/literature: Gorhambury House Book 1637-9; N. King, *The Grimstons of Gorhambury* (Chichester, 1983), pp. 19, 38-40; Walpole, p. 21.

See also: main text.

GREAT FULFORD, DEVON (house survives; chapel does not)

Patron: Sir John Fulford (d. 1546).

Dates: mid-Tudor alterations.

Fulford transformed the 12th-century house into an essentially Tudor, courtyard house. The placing of the integral chapel in the E range, S of the gatehouse, effectively isolated it from the main circulation route. The former chapel now has late 17th-century panelling, but probably originally contained the wooden panels of Cain, Abel, Isaac and Esau, dated 1534, which are now in the hall.

Sources/literature: *CL*, 1 Aug. 1914.

GREAT HOUGHTON, WEST YORKSHIRE (house demolished; chapel survives)

Patrons: Sir Edward Rodes (1600-66); Godfrey Rodes (1631-81); William Rodes (1639-96).

Dates: *c*.1650 new build; 1669 event; 1689 event.

In *c*.1650 the Puritan Sir Edward Rodes erected a large, detached, rectangular, correctly-oriented chapel to the W of the chapel-less, Elizabethan H-plan house built by his ancestor, Francis Rodes. Overall, it combines simplicity with some architectural pretension. The N and S walls now have two windows each, a third having been blocked up. The undifferentiated E window is slightly off-centre to the S. Above it, and centred on the gable, are the arms of the Rodes and Milne families. There was an entrance towards the W end of the S wall. Inside, the plaster ceiling has been removed to expose king-post roof trusses. A contemporary octagonal pulpit with tester and box-pews with acorn finials survive, though the former has evidently been moved from its original position.

In 1669, conventicles were reported in the chapel.

In 1689, William Rodes had the chapel licensed for nonconformist worship.

Sources/literature: Cliffe, pp. 113, 193, 195, 223-4; Stell, pp. 254-5.

See also: main text and fig. 5.38.

GREAT HOUSE (CHELSEA; also known as BEAUFORT HOUSE), LONDON (demolished)

Patrons: Sir Thomas More (1478-1535); William Cecil (1520-98), Lord Burghley or Robert Cecil (1563-1612), 1st Earl of Salisbury.

Dates: early Tudor build; 1595-9 rebuild.

More built the L-shaped, brick house. His integral chapel was oriented to the N and entered from the liturgical W via a small hallway leading from the great stair. There was a stacked upper chapel with an opening of about 4ft x 6ft immediately over the communion table. It was entered from a landing off the great stair.

Cecil inherited the house in 1595 and gave it to his son Robert in 1597. They rebuilt it (after considering various options for the chapel) in the form of a modified U before selling it to Henry Clinton, 2nd Earl of Lincoln (*c*.1540-1616) in 1599. Thorpe's post-1595 plan shows an integral assembly chapel. Assuming it was correctly oriented, it was positioned at the E end of the main block, E of the great stair and N of the parlour.

Sources/literature: T63-4; Hatfield House, Cecil MSS, CPM II 6-7, 9-10, 15-16; T63-4; Knyff, pl. 13; A.W. Clapham and W.H. Godfrey, *Some Famous Buildings and Their Story* (London, 1913), pp. 79-103; R. Davies, *Chelsea Old Church* (London, 1904), pp. 106-18; Ricketts, *Cecil*.

See also: main text and figs. 4.9, 4.10.

GREAT HUMBY, LINCOLNSHIRE (house demolished; chapel, rebuilt, survives)
Patron: Sir William Brownlow (1595-1666).
Date: by 1666 rebuild.
Brownlow, a younger son, inherited the house from his father, Richard. By 1666 he had rebuilt the medieval chapel, possibly a chapel of ease, in the form of a simple single cell with a bell-gable at the W end.
Sources/literature: N. Pevsner and J. Harris (revised by N. Antram), *The Buildings of England: Lincolnshire* (London, 1989), p. 402.

GREAT LEVER HALL, LANCASHIRE (demolished)
Patrons: Bridgeman family.
Date: 1634 event.
The Bridgeman family bought the house in 1620 and rebuilt it in 1631 in the form of a timber-framed and brick quadrangle. The linked chapel, built of brick, was added in 1634.
Sources/literature: Robinson, p. 187.

GRIMSTHORPE CASTLE, LINCOLNSHIRE (house and chapel, both altered and restored, survive)
Patron: Robert Bertie (1631-1701), 3rd Earl of Lindsey.
Date: *c.*1685 alterations.
Architect: possibly William Winde (d. 1722).
Lindsey rebuilt the N front of the double-courtyard, post-1540s house, originally a quadrangular medieval castle, in *c.*1685. It is not clear whether the present double-height, N-oriented chapel, that seems to date from the Hawksmoor and Vanbrugh 18th-century reconstructions, replaced or modified an earlier chapel installed or refashioned by Lindsey.
Sources/literature: Knyff, pl. 20-3; *CL*, 19 Apr. 1924.

GROOMBRIDGE PLACE, KENT (house replaced; chapel, restored, survives)
Patron: John Packer (d. 1649).
Dates: by 1625 new build.
Packer bought the medieval, moated house from the Sackvilles in 1618. It may have already contained a small private chapel, but he built a detached, single-cell chapel in the Gothic style nearby, possibly to serve as a chapel of ease, to celebrate the failure of the future Charles I's Spanish match. The original font and pulpit with sounding board survive, as does a panel of heraldic glass in the E window.
Sources/literature: Evelyn, 2, p. 43; E. Hasted, History of Kent, 1 (Canterbury, 1797), p. 432.

GURNEY STREET MANOR, SOMERSET (house, somewhat altered, and chapel survive)
Patrons: Agnes Michell (d. 1503), née Peryman; Thomas Michell (d. 1539).
Dates: early Tudor addition.
Agnes Michell was left the N-facing house with a small inner courtyard and a forecourt flanked by two wings by her uncle, William Dodesham (d. 1480 or 1482). In the late 15th or early 16th century, she or her grandson, Thomas, installed an integral, correctly-

oriented chapel or oratory to the E of the parlour. It is entered from a staircase lobby to the N, across which lies the hall. There was also probably an external entrance from the courtyard. It is capable of holding only four to five people. As well as a view into the chapel from the chamber above via a trap door, there may also have been a squint from the parlour in the W wall.

Sources/literature: N. Cooper, *Houses of the Gentry 1480-1680* (New Haven and London, 1999), pp. 70-4; oral information from N. Cooper; Emery, 3, pp. 574-7; *VCH*, 6 (1992), pp. 82-3.

See also: main text.

GUY'S CLIFFE, WARWICKSHIRE (house replaced; chapel, remodelled, survives)

Patron: Sir Andrew Flammock (a. 1547).

Date: 1547 event.

On the Dissolution of the chantries in 1547, Flammock was granted the site. It contained a two-storeyed, stone house with gabled projections and a steeply-pitched roof built to house the priest who served the adjacent medieval chantry chapel that was partly built into the rock.

Sources/literature: *VCH*, 8 (1969), pp. 442, 534-5.

GWYDIR CASTLE, GWYNEDD (house, much reduced, survives; chapel survives virtually intact)

Patron: Sir Richard Wynn, Bt (d. 1674).

Dates: 1673-4 new build.

Wynn inherited an early Tudor house that had been enlarged and transformed into a large, double-courtyard, Elizabethan house by the incorporation of material from a neighbouring demolished Cistercian abbey. He built a simple, correctly-oriented, rectangular, single-cell chapel above the castle, near the 17th-century summer house of Gwydir Uchaf. The traditional E window was designed to take a crucifix in painted glass. The entrance is in the NW corner of the N wall. Inside, the ceiling decoration is technically primitive but iconographically sophisticated. As well as painted biblical figures and texts, other devices are employed. For example, two of the three sections are patterned with stars, but the bay dedicated to the Holy Spirit features tongues of fire representing Pentecost. The primitive cut-out angels which mark the terminations of the trusses carry inscriptions that are appropriate to the scene depicted − in the case of the Holy Ghost *'Veni Spiritus Sanc'* and *'et reple corda fidelium'*. In the bay devoted to Christ angels point with one hand to earth and with the other to heaven, while those in the panel devoted to God are kneeling and worshipping, and those flanking the Holy Spirit stretch out their arms in a gesture of dispensation. The remainder of the interior is relatively standard for the time. The communion table is raised by one step and surrounded by a rail. The floor slabs towards the E end are set in a diagonal pattern. The pulpit is in the middle of the S wall, with a reading desk to the W. Seating is college style with panelling above. There is a gallery at the W end that was intended to accommodate singers.

Sources/literature: The Royal Commission on the Historical Monuments of Wales, *An Inventory of the Ancient Monuments of Caernarvonshire*, 1 (London, 1956), pp. 182-5; *CL*, 27 Jun. 1908.

See also: main text and fig. 6.18; Plate XXXIV.

HACKNESS HALL, NORTH YORKSHIRE (house replaced)
Patron: Lady Margaret Hoby, née Dakins (1571-1633).
Dates: 1589-1605 events; 1608 event.
The impressive, stone, Elizabethan, U-shaped house was built from the remains of monastic buildings on the site. In 1589, it was bought for the Puritan Lady Margaret and her first husband, Walter Devereux (d. 1591; brother of Elizabeth I's favourite, 2nd Earl of Essex). The family did not use the chapel in the house for household prayers.
A survey of 1608 lists a chapel in the house.
Sources/literature: *Diary of Lady Margaret Hoby* (J. Moody, editor), (Stroud, 1998), pp. xxxvii–viii, *passim*; North Yorkshire RO, MIC/1608.
See also: main text.

HADDON HALL, DERBYSHIRE (house and chapel survive)
Patrons: Sir George Vernon (d. 1567) and Sir William Coffin (*c*.1492-1538); Sir George Manners (d. 1623).
Dates: early 16th-century alterations; 1623-4 renovation.
The integration of an accretion of medieval buildings to form a double-courtyard house was probably overseen by Vernon's stepfather and guardian, Coffin. It incorporated, in the SW corner, the correctly-oriented, double-cell chapel which was originally the detached parish church. It has an external entrance in the N wall. A striking feature of the chapel is its medieval wall paintings.
Manners inherited the house from his father who had (allegedly) eloped with a Vernon heiress. His refit established a liturgical two-cell arrangement, in which the accommodation of the family east of the screen looked back to the pre-Reformation custom of admitting gentry to the chancel of the parish church. By 1760, Walpole found the chapel 'almost in ruins'.
Sources/literature: W.A. Carington, 'Selections from the Stewards' Accounts Preserved at Haddon Hall for the Years 1549 and 1564', *Journal of the Derbyshire Archaeological and Natural History Society*, 16 (1894), pp. 61-83; Walpole, p. 29.
See also: main text and fig. 5.41.

HAILES ABBEY, GLOUCESTERSHIRE (a ruin)
Patron: William Tracy (d. 1712), 4th Viscount Tracy.
Date: *c*.1694 event.
The Tracy family bought the remains of the former Cistercian monastery – the abbot's lodgings – in the early 17th century. In *c*.1694, Celia Fiennes described it as 'a good old house', and noted that it had 'a pretty chappel with a gallery for people of quality to sitt in' which was entered via the 'lofty large' hall.
Sources/literature: Fiennes, p. 54.

HALL PLACE, BEXLEY, KENT (house survives, greatly extended; chapel does not)
Patrons: Sir John Champeneis (d. 1556); Sir Justinian Champeneis (d. 1596).
Dates: from 1537 new build; from 1556 alterations.
John Champeneis acquired the site in 1537 from the Shelley family, and probably built most, if not all, of the house which then comprised a hall range with cross wings of flint and ex-monastic stone. He probably also installed the correctly-oriented chapel in the W wing. It was a small (20ft x 10ft), single-storey room N of the parlour, and lit by a

pointed E window of three trefoiled lights that is clearly differentiated from the other windows of the facade, and beneath which the altar presumably stood. There is a small window at the W end. The room would not have been large enough to accommodate the entire household unless there was a peripheral space for worship to the N with an exterior door opposite the kitchen in the opposing E range. Alternatively, it could have been a private oratory that the family would have entered from the parlour, but it was unusual for an oratory to possess a distinctive E window.

The house was enlarged from 1556 by Champeneis' son, Justinian. He installed a recess in the chapel N wall that may have been an aumbry or credence for storing sacramental vessels. If so, it would be an interesting example of the revival of Roman Catholic customs under Mary Tudor.

Sources/literature: J. Shaw and M. Scott, *Hall Place, a Short History* (Bexley, 1984); P. Tester, 'Hall Place, Bexley'. *AC*, 71 (1957), pp. 153-61; *CL*, 21 Jan. 1922.

See also: main text.

HALNAKER HOUSE, WEST SUSSEX (house, including chapel walls, survives as a ruin)

Patron: Thomas West (*c*.1472-1544), 9th Lord de la Warr.

Dates: early Tudor alterations.

De la Warr acquired the fortified, medieval, stone house on marrying the heiress, Elizabeth Bonville, before 1494. He remodelled and extended it, largely in brick, to incorporate the hitherto detached, correctly-oriented chapel. In 1540 he was obliged to exchange the house with Henry VIII for other properties.

Sources/literature: J.L. André, 'Art in Sussex', *SAC*, 43 (1900), pp. 201-13; G.H. Cook, *Letters to Cromwell and Others on the Suppression of the Monasteries* (London, 1965), p. 90; T.W. Horsfield, *The History, Antiquities and Topography of the County of Sussex*, 2 (Lewes, 1835), p. 58.

See also: main text.

HALSTON HALL, SHROPSHIRE (house replaced; chapel, with additions, survives)

Patrons: probably Edward Mytton (1553-83); Mytton family (post-1660).

Dates: *c*.1570s-80s new build; post-1660 alteration.

Built on the site of a dissolved Hospitallers' preceptory, the detached, timber-framed, correctly-oriented chapel, with an upper chapel at the W end, stands to the N of what may have been the site of the original house, and about a mile from Whittington parish church. Mytton inherited the house in 1568, and the chapel may date from the 1570s-80s. The decoration of the spandrels of the roof timbers avoids contentious biblical imagery by using symbolic references to sacramental worship.

The post-Restoration commandment board is one of the very few of that date to have incorporated painted images.

Sources/literature: Addleshaw, p. 192.

See also main text and fig. 6.32.

HAM HOUSE, LONDON (house and chapel survive, both virtually unchanged)

Patrons: Elizabeth Maitland (*c*.1626-1698), née Murray, Duchess of Lauderdale, and John Maitland (1616-82), 1st Duke of Lauderdale.

Dates: 1673-5 alterations.

Elizabeth Murray inherited the single-pile, three-storey, H-plan, Jacobean house updated in the late 1630s, on her father's death in *c*.1654. In 1673-5, she and Lauderdale, her second husband, undertook a major programme of remodelling and redecoration. Their work included the transformation of the parlour in the NE wing off the hall and great stair into an integral, single-storey, N-oriented chapel. Externally, it has no distinctive features. Inside, the chancel area is paved in black and white marble. The original altar cloth of crimson velvet and gold survives. The altar rails have a central opening. Panelling throughout the chapel is plain, and there were crimson velvet and damask hangings with gold fringes. Seating is college style with two box-pews for the duke and duchess at the liturgical W end.

Sources/literature: J.G. Dunbar, 'The Building Activities of the Duke and Duchess of Lauderdale, 1670-82', *AJ*, 132 (1975), pp. 202-30.

See also: main text.

HAMPTON COURT, HEREFORDSHIRE (house, remodelled, survives, as does chapel)

Patron: Fitzwilliam Coningsby (a. 1625 and 1629).

Date: 1629 event.

Coningsby inherited the medieval and Tudor courtyard house from his father in 1625. He installed a painted glass window, by Abraham Van Linge dated 1629, in the correctly-oriented, linked chapel which projects from the NE corner.

Sources/literature: Victoria and Albert Museum, C.62-1927, ID 632.

See also: main text and Plate XVIII.

HANDFORTH HALL, CHESHIRE (house, reduced, survives; chapel does not)

Patrons: William Brereton (d. 1610), or Sir William Brereton, Bt (1604-61)

Dates: early 17th-century alterations.

The half-timbered house was built *c*.1562 by Sir Urian Brereton, who had married the heiress Margaret, née Handforth. It is not now possible to say whether it followed a rectangular, E-shaped or courtyard plan. The screens passage contains an early 17th-century, elliptical, four-centred arch to the former chapel, perhaps installed by Urian Brereton's grandson William, or by the latter's son, also William, who made a number of alterations to the house (and was a successful commander of Parliamentary forces during the Civil War).

Sources/literature: P. De Figueiredo, and J. Treuherz, *Cheshire Country Houses* (Chichester, 1988), pp. 107-110; Ormerod, 3, pp. 644-5.

HARDWICK HALL, DERBYSHIRE (house survives, as does part of first floor chapel arrangement)

Patron: Elizabeth Talbot 1527-1608, Countess of Shrewsbury, née Hardwick ('Bess of Hardwick').

Dates: 1591-9 new build.

Architect: thought to be Robert Smythson (*c*.1535-1614).

Bess of Hardwick bought the Hardwick estate, where she had grown up, in 1583. She started to build what became a 'prodigy' house before she had completed rebuilding Old Hardwick Hall nearby. The new house contained a correctly-oriented, two-storey, integral, assembly chapel spanning the ground and first floors of the NE end, and positioned on the low side of the house, close to service rooms. Seating in the main chapel comprised four forms, perhaps used in conjunction with unlisted fittings such as benches along the walls. The upper chapel contained three forms with decorative inlays, and a single chair and stool, presumably for the patron as at Chatsworth (*q.v.*). It was bounded on the W by an openwork screen which gave on to a landing furnished with five forms, perhaps allowing upper servants to follow services from this peripheral area. The chapel contained the only known examples of figurative hangings and moveable pictures in an Elizabethan chapel.

Sources/literature: *Of Household Stuff: the 1601 Inventories of Bess of Hardwick* (S.M. Levey and P. Thornton, editors)*, (London, 2001) pp. 51-2; Walpole, p. 29; A. Wells-Cole, *Art and Decoration in Elizabethan and Jacobean England* (New Haven and London, 1997), p. 295.

See also: main text and figs. 4.11, 4.12.

HARESTONE MANOR, BRIXHAM, DEVON (house and chapel, much restored, survive)

Patron: John Wood (d. 1537).

Dates: early to mid-Tudor alterations.

Wood extensively updated the small, essentially medieval house before his death in 1537. The linked, correctly-oriented chapel is at the E end of the N range, and at a slight angle to it, with an external entrance in the S wall. At first sight it looks like a detached chapel that was subsequently linked to an enlarged Tudor house, but close examination of the fabric seems to refute this. The fenestration was altered during the 19th century. An aumbry and piscina survive in the S wall. The position of the chapel is unusual: at ground-floor level it is next to the cellar, which has a squint providing a clear view of the entrance, but the solarium above has no visual or physical links to it.

Sources/literature: J. Lomas, 'Restoration of Higher Harestone Manor – Brixton (1972-1973)', *Devon*, 106 (1974), pp. 119-40.

HARRINGWORTH, NORTHAMPTONSHIRE (house largely rebuilt; chapel demolished)

Patrons: Zouche family.

Dates: 1550s event.

There was a 13th-century detached chapel near the medieval manor house. The Zouche family was buried there until *c.*1550.

Sources/literature: NA, Prob 11/134.

HARTLEY CASTLE, CUMBRIA (demolished)

Patrons: Musgrave family.

Dates: late Elizabethan conversion.

The medieval castle, rebuilt in the 14th century, was transformed into a large courtyard house during the reign of Elizabeth. The chapel gave onto the inner courtyard.

Sources/literature: Robinson, p. 271.

HARWOOD DALE, NORTH YORKSHIRE (a ruin)

Patron: Sir Thomas Hoby (d. 1640).

Dates: 1634 new build; 1636 event.

Hoby built the detached chapel to commemorate his wife, Lady Margaret Hoby (d. 1633) of Hackness Hall (*q.v.*), and to serve the tenants on the remote parts of the

Hackness Hall estate.

Hoby prevailed upon Richard Parr, The Bishop of Sodor and Man, to consecrate the chapel in 1636.

Sources/literature: A.T. Hart, *The Man in the Pew 1558-1660* (London, 1966), p. 170; *Diary of Lady Margaret Hoby* (J. Moody, editor), (Stroud, 1998), pp. 224-7.

See also: main text.

HATFIELD HOUSE, HERTFORDSHIRE (house and chapel survive, both somewhat altered)

Patrons: Robert Cecil (1563-1612), 1st Earl of Salisbury; William Cecil (1591-1668), 2nd Earl of Salisbury.

Dates: 1608-14 new build; 1644-6 events.

Architect: Robert Lemyinge (d. 1628).

The site was granted to Robert Cecil by James I in 1607 in exchange for Theobalds (*q.v.*). He built a compact, U-shaped, red brick house. The correctly-oriented, integral, two-storey, cross-range, colourfully decorated, high-church chapel was consecrated in 1614 (not, as Legg has it, in 1610-11). It occupies a site away from main circulation routes, and runs across the width of the original entrance (W) range. At the upper level it has galleries running along the N and S walls to the point where they join the upper chapel at the W end. The latter probably extended much further to the E than it does now and possessed a fireplace. The important Jacobean glass cycle has undergone alterations and it is clear that the work, by three hands, was not carefully co-ordinated: for instance, although most of the inscriptions are in Latin, one is in French. Today the order in which the scenes are arranged is puzzling, but this may be due to a later re-arrangement. Apart from the (incomplete) wall paintings, there were also six huge (the largest measuring 15ft across) paintings from the life of Christ on brightly coloured canvases by at least two hands. Although all are framed in the same way, they are of different sizes, and must have formed an irregular, but almost continuous, band of strident colour round the main body of the chapel. In addition, Rowland Bucket painted on cloth an Annunciation and a picture of herald angels appearing to shepherds. Overall, pre-Reformation ideas were used to help create a rich decorative scheme representing a complete reversal of Elizabethan ideas on chapel decoration. Fittings in the lower chapel comprised a pulpit and reading desk covered in black cloth embroidered with silver and gold thread. A red curtain hung behind the communion table, and the table itself was covered with a black velvet cloth embroidered with vine leaves. Worship was segregated, with women occupying the S. Maintaining this division would not have been simple since, in 1612, the household consisted of 56 males and five females. The upper chapel contained moveable furniture, probably richly upholstered (with black cloth embroidered with gold and tawny orange) and fashioned to a far higher (and more comfortable) standard, and colourful hangings.

By 1646, stained glass and paintings had been temporarily removed to save them from destruction during the Civil War, and the painted ceiling whitewashed.

Sources/literature: Hatfield House, Cecil MSS: Bills 216, Box A/5 f. 6r, Box A/7 f. 22r, Box A/9, Family Papers 5:41, Accounts 145/15 & 151/23; W. Butterfield, *Alterations in and about Hatfield House since 1868* (privately printed, 1908); Dowsing, pp. 358-60; C. Gapper, J. Newman and A. Ricketts, 'Hatfield: A House for a Lord Treasurer' in Croft, pp. 80, 85-6, 88-93; Legg, p. 318; Ricketts, *Cecil*; A.W. Wilkinson, 'The Great East Window of the Chapel of Hatfield House', *JBSMGP*, 12.4 (1959).

See also: main text and fig. 5.1; Plates IX, X, XIX, XX, XXI, XXII, XXIII.

HAWKSWORTH HALL, WEST YORKSHIRE (house, extended, survives; chapel does not)
Patrons: Hawksworth family.
Dates: late 16th/early 17th-century new build.
The late 16th/early 17th-century Hawksworth family house contained a chapel in a wing.
Sources/literature: Giles, pp. 18, 198-9.

HEATH OLD HALL, WAKEFIELD, WEST YORKSHIRE (house demolished; chapel does not survive)
Patron: John Kaye (a. late 16th century).
Dates: 1584-95 new build.
Kaye's house was said to be a fine example of Elizabethan architecture. His chapel was subsequently converted into stables.
Sources/literature: W. Cudworth, 'The Bradford family', *The Bradford Antiquary*, 2 (1895), pp. 127-30.

HENGRAVE HALL, SUFFOLK (house and chapel, much restored, survive)
Patron: Sir Thomas Kytson (d. 1540).
Dates: 1523-40 new build.
Kytson began building the moated, stone, courtyard house in 1523, later making much use of stone taken from dissolved abbeys. His integral, cross-range, two-storey chapel, oriented to the S, lies in the S range to the W of the main entrance, and is both secluded yet easy of access. No Tudor furnishings or decoration survive 18th and 19th-century alterations, although the much-reduced Victorian gallery may include some re-used Tudor parts. The double-height, liturgical E window contains the original glass that was imported from Antwerp in 1527 and installed in 1540. It was the last 16th century private chapel window to contain biblical images.
Sources/literature: Cambridge University Library, Hengrave, 81 & Hengrave MSS 27, no. 113; Airs, p. 29; J. Gage, *History and Antiquities of Hengrave in Suffolk* (London, 1822); D. MacCulloch, *Suffolk and the Tudors* (Oxford, 1986); H. Wayment, 'The Foreign Glass at Hengrave Hall and St James', Bury St Edmunds', *JBSMGP*, 18.2 (1987), pp. 166-79; *CL*, 16 Apr. 1910.
See also: main text and figs. 3.6, 3.7.

HERRINGSTON, DORSET (house, reduced and altered, survives; chapel does not)
Patron: Sir John Williams (d. 1617).
Dates: *c*.1569-1617 new build.
Williams rebuilt the house, bought by his grandfather in 1513, creating a courtyard house. It was entered through a gabled N range, and contained an integral chapel. The hall and great parlour were in the S range.
Sources/literature: Oswald, pp. 34-5.

HEYTESBURY HOUSE, WILTSHIRE (demolished)
Patrons: Lady Agnes Hungerford (d. 1523); Walter Hungerford (d. 1540), 1st Lord Hungerford.
Dates: 1523 event; 1540 event.
Nothing is known about the layout of the house, but an inventory following Lady

Agnes' execution for murder in 1523 lists numerous rich vestments and hangings in her chapel.

Her stepson, Walter, possessed a chaplain called William Bird who excoriated Henry VIII as a heretic, a factor contributing to his and his patron's execution in 1540.

Sources/literature: 'Inventory of the Goods of Dame Agnes Hungerford' (J.G. Nichols and J.E. Jackson, editors), *A*, 38 (1860), pp. 353-72.

See also: main text.

HIGH LEGH, CHESHIRE

East Hall (house demolished; chapel, extended and much restored, survives)

Patron: Thomas Legh (*c*.1513-89).

Dates: 1580-1 new build.

Legh built the large, much-ornamented house and detached chapel in 1580-1. The latter, an aisled structure originally measuring 48ft x 27ft, some hundred yards from the site of the house and possibly replacing an earlier chapel, is perhaps the only detached chapel to have been built under Elizabeth, and one of very few to have used stained glass. This was in the four-light E window, much damaged during the Civil War, and is now reset in the S window. It is difficult to determine how much of the interior is original. It has a tie-beam roof. Arcade piers are octagonal wooden posts. There is a W porch, dated 1581, that used to be at the E end, and a bell-turret. The easternmost of the (probably 19th-century) S clerestory windows are higher than others, perhaps indicative of some sort of differentiation for the earlier chancel. The chapel was not consecrated.

West Hall (house and chapel demolished)

Patrons: Legh family of West Hall.

Dates: mid 17th-century event.

The early 15th-century detached chapel fell into disuse in the mid-17th century, and was replaced in the 19th century.

Sources/literature: R. Richards, 'The Chapels of The Blessed Virgin Mary and St John at High Legh, Cheshire', *Transactions of the Historic Society of Lancashire and Cheshire*, 101 (1949), pp. 97-138.

See also: main text.

HIGHER MELCOMBE (also known as MELCOMBE HORSEY), DORSET

(house and chapel, partially rebuilt, survive)

Patron: Sir Thomas Freke (d. 1633).

Dates: by 1633 new build.

Originally a mid-16th-century courtyard house of banded flint and ashlar with a gatehouse, Freke added a linked, correctly-oriented, Gothic-style chapel as the N range. It consists of a single rectangular cell with an upper chapel, and has distinctive pointed windows in a mix of Decorated (S) and Perpendicular (N) styles. All appear to be 17th-century, and not transferred from a long-ruined medieval chapel nearby as previously surmised. It had one internal and three external entrances. Inside, there was a font and a pulpit. Now only the timber barrel-vault roof with moulded ribs and some heraldic roof bosses survive of the original fittings. The chapel was never consecrated. Later the main body was turned into a brewhouse and laundry, while the upper chapel was used for storing lumber.

Sources/literature: Hutchins, 4, p. 367; Oswald, pp. 23-4.

See also: main text and fig. 5.32.

HINCHINGBROOKE HOUSE, CAMBRIDGESHIRE (house, altered, survives; chapel does not)
Patron: Edward Montagu (1625–72), 1st Earl of Sandwich.
Date: 1672 event.
Sandwich inherited the former Augustinian nunnery from his father who had bought it from Sir Oliver Cromwell in 1627. In 1731, Loveday noted that 'in the Chappel are preserved the heart and bowels of Admiral Montague, as I remember'. This suggests that a chapel may have existed in the house at Sandwich's death (on the assumption that the 'Admiral' refers to Sandwich – who was blown up with his ship by the Dutch in 1672, and whose body was found near Harwich and buried at Westminster Abbey).
Sources/literature: Markham, p. 92.

HINTON HOUSE, SOMERSET (house, greatly altered, survives; chapel, altered, survives)
Patron: John Poulett (c.1586–1649), 1st Lord Poulett.
Dates: by 1636 additions.
Poulett inherited the early Tudor house in 1600, and added a new S wing containing staterooms. Presumably the chapel in the NE corner, next to the great stair, was created at this time. In 1736, Loveday was to note of it that 'the Altar-piece and Chimney front each other, they are each in a corner of the long sides'.
Sources/literature: Markham, pp. 238-9; C. Winn, *The Pouletts of Hinton St George* (London, 1976), pp. 129-58.

HOGHTON TOWER, LANCASHIRE (house, altered, survives; chapel does not)
Patron: Sir Richard Hoghton (1616–78).
Dates: post–1660 events.
The fortified, double-courtyard, Elizabethan (c.1561-5) house acquired at some stage a correctly-oriented chapel in the NE corner of the N range near the hall. The builder of the house, Thomas Hoghton, was a Roman Catholic, but his 17th-century successors were Puritans, notably Sir Richard. After the Restoration, he kept Puritan chaplains to tutor his family and service his chapel – which seems to have been able to accommodate a congregation of 180.
Sources/literature: Cliffe, pp. 68, 131-2, 195, 217; T. Garner and A. Stratton, *The Domestic Architecture of England during the Tudor Period*, 2 (London, 1908), pp. 145-8.

HOLDENBY HOUSE, NORTHAMPTONSHIRE (demolished)
Patron: Sir Christopher Hatton (1540-91).
Dates: c.1570-83 new build.
Hatton inherited the site from his father in 1546, and in due course built a huge, double-courtyard, 'prodigy' house that owed much in its inspiration to William Cecil's Theobalds (q.v.). Thorpe's plan shows that the integral, single-storey, assembly chapel was on the ground floor of the S end of the central range, and probably correctly-oriented. The main processional route from the hall to the great chamber on the floor above was separated from the main body of the chapel by an impressively detailed openwork screen that afforded a clear view into it from the passage. This, with other peripheral spaces off the W end and stairs, would have accommodated a significant number of people.
Sources/literature: T183-4; NA, Parliamentary Survey E317/35; M. Girouard, *Town and Country* (London, 1992), pp. 208-9; A. Hartshorne, 'Holdenby, Northamptonshire; its

Manors, Church and House', *AJ*, 65 (1908), pp. 89-120; E.S. Hartshorne, *Memorials of Holdenby* (London, 1868); *CL*, 18, 25 Oct. 1979.
See also: main text and figs. 4.1, 4.2.

HORHAM HALL, ESSEX (house, somewhat restored and reduced, survives; chapel does not)
Patrons: Sir John Cutte (d. 1520); Sir John Cutte (d. 1615).
Dates: early 16th-century rebuild; *c.*1600 event.
Cutte acquired the moated house in 1502, and started to rebuild it in brick with stone dressings. The chapel, which perhaps lay at the E end of the N wing, was unfinished at his death, but nonetheless, in 1509 before starting work on the chapel E window at Little Saxham Hall in Suffolk (*q.v.*), the glazier was required to inspect that at Horham Hall.
Cutte's great grandson, also Sir John, sold the house in *c.*1600, and transferred a stained glass window, depicting the story of the Passion, to his chapel at Childerley Hall (*q.v.*).
Sources/literature: Howard, pp. 12-14, 204.
See also: main text.

HORSEHEATH HALL, CAMBRIDGESHIRE (demolished)
Patrons: Sir Giles Alington (1572-1638); William Alington (1634-84), 3rd Lord of Killard and 1st Lord Alington of Wymondeley, known as 3rd Lord Alington.
Dates: 1591 event; 1663-5 new build.
Architect: Sir Roger Pratt (1620-85).
Nothing is known of the layout of the 16th-century Alington family house. The ceiling of the chapel there contained heraldic decoration.
Pratt built a compact house on the site for Lord Alington which contained an awkwardly placed integral chapel, oriented to the N. There was a (liturgical) W end gallery at mezzanine level supported by columns and accessed by a small stair.
Sources/literature: R. Pratt, *The Architecture of Sir Roger Pratt* (R.T. Gunther, editor), (Oxford, 1928), pp. 90, 125; C. Parsons, 'Horseheath Hall and its Owners', *Proceedings of the Cambridge Antiquarian Society,* 41 (1948), pp.1-51.
See also: main text and fig. 6.5.

HORTON MANOR, KENT (house, altered, survives; chapel, altered and knocked about, survives)
Patrons: Ballard family.
Dates: from 1530s event.
The detached, correctly-oriented, mainly 14th-century chapel stands about 100 ft from the then U-shaped, largely 15th-century Ballard family house. It probably began a new career as a barn shortly after the Reformation.
Sources/literature: Hussey, pp. 226-7; T. Tatton-Brown, 'The Topography and Buildings of Horton Manor near Canterbury', *AC*, 98 (1982), pp. 77-105.

HUNSTANTON HALL, NORFOLK (house rebuilt; chapel does not survive)
Patrons: Sir Thomas L'Estrange (a. 16th century) or Sir Hamon L'Estrange (a. 17th century).
Dates: 16th or 17th-century alterations.
The quadrangular, early Tudor, moated, L'Estrange family house was rebuilt in the 17th

century. According to a 19th-century description, the (assembly) chapel occupied the well of the great stair. The family sat in the chapel, while the household gathered on the stairs behind the balusters, and on the landing ('gallery') above. This was evidently a post-Reformation arrangement, and could well have been introduced under Elizabeth; alternatively, it might have been created by Sir Hamon, who carried out alterations 1623-1640s.

Sources/literature: D. Gurney, 'Extracts from the Household and Privy Purse Accounts of the Lestranges of Hunstanton', *A*, 25 (1834), p. 413.

See also: main text.

HYLTON CASTLE, COUNTY DURHAM (house and chapel, both much altered and restored, survive)

Patrons: Sir Thomas Hylton (d. 1558); William Hylton (a. mid-16th century); Sir William Hylton (d. 1600).

Dates: 1536 event; 1559 event; late 16th-century possible conversion.

The detached 12th-century chapel stands near the compact, rectangular, fortified block built by the Hyltons in the 15th century – which itself contained a small double-height chapel off the great hall. At the Dissolution of the Monasteries in 1536, the detached chapel was estimated to be worth £6 13s 8d.

The chapel was still in use in 1559, and may thereafter have been converted for secular use.

Sources/literature: W. Fordyce, *The History and Antiquities of the County Palatine of Durham*, 2 (Newcastle upon Tyne, 1855), pp. 543-7.

IGHTHAM MOAT, KENT (house survives, as do both chapels, their interiors somewhat altered)

Patrons: Sir William Selby (d. 1611); Selby family.

Dates: *c*.1600 alterations; 17th-century alterations and 1633 event.

Sir Richard Clement (*c*.1478-1538) modernised the moated, stone and timber, medieval house *c*.1521-9 to form a single-courtyard house. Selby, who bought it in 1591, created two bedrooms by inserting an extra floor that bisected the 'old' (14th-century), correctly-oriented, linked chapel in the E range.

It is not certain when the correctly-oriented, so-called 'Tudor' chapel on the first floor in the N range was created. The range itself was completed by Clement, but it is possible that the space was originally a long gallery, and not converted into a chapel until the 17th century by the Selby family which owned the house until the 19th century. It is presumably identical with the chapel that, according to Legg, was consecrated in 1633. It has a fine barrel-vaulted roof, decorated with boards possibly taken from the temporary pavilions erected in 1520 on the Field of the Cloth of Gold. The fittings are of many different dates.

Sources/literature: Howard, pp. 114, 208; D. Starkey, 'Ightham Moat: Politics and Architecture in early Tudor England', *A*, 107 (1982), pp. 153-63; Legg, p. 322.

INGATESTONE HALL, ESSEX (parts of house survive; chapel does not)

Patrons: Sir William Petre (1506-72); Petre family.

Dates: 1540-8 new build; by 1600 event.

Petre acquired the manor of the dissolved nunnery of Barking in 1539, and built a three-courtyard, brick house that was presumably finished by 1548 when he entertained the

Princess Mary there. The L-shaped, two-storey chapel in the E range of the inner court opposite the hall terminated the main access, and was isolated from main circulation routes. The entrance may have been in the N side of the chancel wall. There was provision for a fireplace in the NE wall. There was an upper chapel chamber or closet, accessible from the long gallery, from which the family could hear (and, after post-1600 alterations, possibly also see) the services.

By 1600 Ingatestone possessed a short, plain, wooden communion table on a frame. Priest holes still survive, Petre's wife being a Roman Catholic.

Sources/literature: Essex RO: 1566 survey (D/CP M186), 1600 inventory (D/CP F215), 1605 perspective map (D/CP P8A); Coope, p. 61; F.G. Emmison, *Tudor Secretary, Sir William Petre at Court and Home* (London, 1961); F.W. Steer and F.G. Emmison, *Ingatestone Hall in 1600* (Chelmsford, 1954).

KENNINGHALL, NORFOLK (largely demolished)
Patron: Thomas Howard (1473-1554), 3rd Duke of Norfolk.
Dates: 1524-40s new build.

Norfolk began building the large, brick, H-plan house, a rival to Cardinal Wolsey's Hampton Court, in 1524. The chapel was clearly large, since it contained six painted canvas hangings, depicting scenes from the Passion, each nine yards square. Painted glass also contained scenes from the Passion, and the great triptych on the altar displayed gilded scenes of the Birth, Passion and Resurrection. There were other rich ornaments and plate (most of which was melted down for coinage on the duke's attainder in 1547). Six chaplains served the chapel.

Sources/literature: R. Howlett, 'The Household Accounts of Kenninghall Park in the Year 1525', *Norfolk Archaeology*, 15 (1904), pp. 51-60; NA, LR 2/115 & 6.
See also: main text.

KEWE, CORNWALL (demolished)
Patron: Edward Courtenay (*c*.1526-1556), 1st Earl of Devon of 3rd creation.
Date: 1557 event.

An inventory taken after Devon's death shows that the chapel contained rich vestments, hangings depicting flowers and leaves, and three pictures on the altar.

Sources/literature: inventory quoted in *Royal Institution of Cornwall Journal*, 2 (1867), pp. 226-37.

KIMBERLEY, NORFOLK (demolished)
Patron: Sir Roger Woodhouse (d. 1588).
Date: 1588 event.

Woodhouse completed the moated, courtyard house, with round corner turrets and a keep or tower, prior to Queen Elizabeth's visit in 1574. The inventory taken on his death shows that the contents of the chapel were worth 2*s*.

Sources/literature: L.G. Bolingbroke, 'Two Elizabethan Inventories', *Norfolk Archaeology*, 15 (1904), pp. 93-107.

KIRBY HALL, NORTHAMPTONSHIRE (house survives as a shell, but no trace of chapel)
Patrons: Sir Humphrey Stafford (d. 1575); Sir Christopher Hatton (1540-91); Christopher Hatton (1605-70), 1st Lord Hatton; Christopher Hatton (1632-1706), 1st Viscount Hatton.

Dates: 1570–80 rebuild; 1638–40 modernisation; 1680–90 modernisation.
Architect: Nicholas Stone (1587–1647).
The early 16th-century manor house on the site belonged to Fineshade Priory until the Dissolution. In 1570, Stafford, who had inherited it from his father, began work on replacing it with a single-courtyard, stone house. Sir Christopher Hatton, who bought it in 1576, continued his work, transforming it into a 'prodigy' house. The chapel seems to have occupied part of the S range to the E of the great hall.
Extensive updating was carried out in 1638–40 to designs by Nicholas Stone, and in 1680–90. It was probably during the former alterations that the chapel was moved to a position over the main entrance in the N front.
Sources/literature: T137–40; G. H. Chettle, *Kirby Hall* (revised P. Leach), (London, 1989); J. Summerson, 'John Thorpe and the Thorpes of Kingscliffe', *AR,* 106 (1949), pp. 291–300.

KIRKOSWALD CASTLE, CUMBRIA (demolished)
Patrons: Thomas Dacre (1467–1525), 3rd Lord Dacre; William Howard (1563–1640), Lord Howard ('Belted Will') and/or Francis Dacre (d.1633), 9th Lord Dacre of the North.
Dates: early Tudor event; 1622 event; 1624 event.
A series of early Tudor, figurative pictures, the work presumably overseen by Thomas Dacre, decorated the ceilings of the great hall and the chapel of the early 13th-century castle.
In 1622, following the partial demolition of the castle, and perhaps taking advantage of prevalent doubts about the legitimacy of Francis Dacre's claim to Kirkoswald, Howard removed the ceiling paintings to the hall and chapel at Naworth Castle (*q.v.*).
In 1624, Howard installed at Naworth a stained glass Crucifixion and coats of arms which may also have come from Kirkoswald.
Sources/literature: Emery, 1, pp. 169, 233; T.H.B. Graham, 'Extinct Cumberland Castles', *Transactions of the Cumberland & Westmorland Antiquarian & Archaeological Society*, 12(NS), (1912), pp. 164–80.
See also: main text.

KIRTLING (OR CATLAGE) HALL, CAMBRIDGESHIRE (largely demolished)
Patron: William North (d. 1734), 6th Lord North.
Date: 1692 event.
North had the 16th-century house, built by his family in the 1530s, surveyed in 1692. At that point, it possessed a double-height chapel in the E wing.
Sources/literature: *VCH*, 10 (2002), pp. 61–8.

KNOLE, KENT (house and chapel survive, with alterations)
Patrons: Thomas Sackville (1536–1608), 1st Earl of Dorset; Richard Sackville (1589–1624), 3rd Earl of Dorset.
Dates: 1604–8 alterations; 1617 and 1619 events.
Queen Elizabeth granted Sackville the house in 1566. It had been built as a palace in the 1450s–60s by Thomas Bourchier, Cardinal Archbishop of Canterbury (*c.*1404–86), and bequeathed to the see of Canterbury. He, or one of his successors, built the linked, double-height, correctly-oriented chapel in the SE corner. Archbishop Cranmer subsequently

gave the house to Henry VIII. Thomas Sackville remodelled and redecorated the house and chapel from 1604, keeping the latter in its original position. The early 17th-century octagonal pulpit, placed against the N wall, survives, as do the stalls, which are arranged college-style.

In 1617 Lady Anne Clifford, then the wife of Richard Sackville, received communion at Knole, and in 1619 she recorded that the chaplain preached in the chapel there.

Sources/literature: Knyff, pl. 24; Clifford, pp. 57, 75; C.J. Phillips, *The History of the Sackville Family*, 2 (London, 1930), pp. 353-6; *CL*, 25 May, 1 Jun. 1912.

See also: main text.

LACOCK ABBEY, WILTSHIRE (house, altered, survives; chapel does not)

Patron: Sir William Sharington (*c*.1495-1553).

Dates: by 1553 conversion.

Sharington bought the suppressed Augustinian nunnery in 1539, and converted it into a double-courtyard house. The abbess' chapel seems to have survived in the S range until the early 18th century.

Sources/literature: Howard, pp. 155-62, 217; N. Pevsner, *The Buildings of England: Wiltshire* (Harmondsworth, 1963), pp. 254-8.

LAMER HOUSE, WHEATHAMPSTEAD, HERTFORDSHIRE (replaced)

Patron: Sir John Garrard, Bt (d. *c*.1637).

Dates: Jacobean event; 1631 event.

St Helen's parish church, Wheathampstead, contains a Jacobean pulpit taken, it is said, from the former chapel at Lamer House.

Benches dated 1631 are thought to have come from the same source.

Sources/literature: *VCH*, 2, pp. 297-309.

LANGLEY HALL, SHROPSHIRE (house demolished; chapel survives)

Patron: Fulk Lee (d. 1566).

ACTON BURNELL CASTLE, SHROPSHIRE (a ruin)

Patrons: Richard and George Hopton (a. late 16th/early 17th centuries).

Dates: 1564/1601 new build or reconstruction.

Langley Hall was a moated, L-shaped, stone and timber-framed, early 16th-century house whose site had passed to the Lee family in the 15th century. Langley chapel, a detached, correctly-oriented, single-cell building in the form of a simple rectangle, stands near the site of the Hall. It was probably built as a chapel of ease, and may have been a reconstruction of a chapel already on the site. The fittings are extremely simple and largely Jacobean, and there is no screen, but the space is divided into two very distinct liturgical areas.

The date 1564 appears outside, which indicates that the chapel was erected by Fulk Lee. However, the date 1601 appears on a roof beam which suggests that changes were effected by the Hopton brothers who were the patrons at that time (patronage having been temporarily transferred to the owners of Acton Burnell Castle – a fortified 13th-century manor house which itself contained a private chapel in the NE tower).

Sources/literature: Addleshaw, pp. 52, 111, 113; H. Davies, *Worship and Theology in England*, 2 (Princeton, 1975), pp. 26-7; *VCH*, 8 (1968), pp. 6-8, 142-6.

See also: main text and fig. 5.40.

LANGLEY PARK, BECKENHAM, KENT (replaced)
Patrons: Sir Humphrey Style (1499-1552); Edmund Style (1538-1616).
Dates: 1551 event; 1607 event.
Humphrey Style inherited the house from his father who had acquired it in 1501.
His Will of 1551 mentions among his goods and chattels, 'the seales and stores in the
Chappell'.
Edmund Style greatly extended the estate, and built a new chapel which was consecrated
in 1607 by William Barlow, Bishop of Rochester. The bishop's licence stated that there
had been a chapel or oratory at Langley 'from ancient times' which was 'well built and
properly furnished'. The new chapel may have possessed a clock and bell tower.
Sources/literature: R. Borrowman, *Beckenham Past and Present* (Beckenham, 1910),
pp. 205-14; Legg, pp. 1-8; G.W. Tookey, *The History of Langley Park, Beckenham, Kent*
(unpublished booklet, 1975), pp. 6-9.
See also: main text.

LANGLEY, BUCKINGHAMSHIRE (no trace survives)
Patron: John Pulteney (a. 1637).
Date: 1637 event.
The Arminian preacher and writer Oliver Whitbie praised the 'reverent conformity' of
Pulteney's private chapel in 1637.
Sources/literature: quoted in N. Tyacke, *Anti-Calvinists; the Rise of English Arminianism
c.1590-1640*, (Oxford, 1987), p. 219.

LASBOROUGH MANOR, GLOUCESTERSHIRE (replaced)
Patron: Lady Anne Fortescue (d. 1587).
Date: 1530 event.
Lady Anne inherited the house on the death of her first husband, Sir Giles Greville, in
1528 and subsequently married Sir Adrian Fortescue (*c.*1476-1539). Greville's daughter
and her husband William Nevill contested her right to the property, and occupied
the house in 1530. A detailed picture of the house emerged from the subsequent Star
Chamber proceedings, including the information that it contained a hall, galleries and
a chapel. It was eventually settled that the Fortescues would buy out the Nevills. Lady
Anne retained her title to the house after Fortescue was attainted and executed in
1539.
Sources/literature: *VCH*, 9 p. 288.

LATHOM HOUSE, LANCASHIRE (house demolished; chapel, somewhat restored,
survives)
Patron: Thomas Stanley (d. 1522), 2nd Earl of Derby.
Date: 1500 event.
Stanley built the detached chapel in the grounds of his extensive, moated, fortified, two-
courtyard, 1490s house with a multi-towered central block. It was consecrated in 1500.
Sources/literature: Emery, 1, p. 173; N. Pevsner, T*he Buildings of England: North Lancashire*
(Harmondsworth, 1979), p. 165.

LAUNDE ABBEY, LEICESTERSHIRE (house and chapel survive, much restored)
Patrons: Cromwell family.
Dates: mid–Tudor rebuild; 1551 event.

Thomas Cromwell (d. 1540), Earl of Essex, acquired the former Augustinian priory on its dissolution. The Cromwells created an H-shaped house.

The chapel contains a 1551 monument to Thomas' son, Gregory.

Sources/literature: N. Pevsner, T*he Buildings of England: Leicestershire and Rutland* (Harmondsworth, 1970), pp. 134–5.

LECKONFIELD CASTLE, EAST YORKSHIRE (a ruin)

Patron: Henry Percy (*c.*1532–85), 8th Earl of Northumberland ('Cruel Henry').

Date: 1574 event.

The Percy family acquired the manor in the 11th century. By the second half of the 15th century it had become a moated, brick and timber-framed, courtyard house, with three-storied towers at each angle. There was a chapel in the south range, near the family accommodation. Its presence is confirmed by a 1574 inventory taken following the release of the (Roman Catholic) 8th Earl of Northumberland from the Tower, by which time the house was already greatly decayed.

Sources/literature: *The Regulations and Establishment of the Household of Henry Algernon Percy, the Fifth Earl of Northumberland, at his Castles of Wresill and Lekinfield in Yorkshire* (T. Percy, editor; also known as *The Northumberland Household Book*), (London, 1827), p. 463.

LEDSTON HALL, WEST YORKSHIRE (rebuilt in the 17th and 18th centuries)

Patrons: Witham family.

Date: 1588 event.

The Withams acquired and rebuilt the former grange of Pontefract Priory after the Dissolution. In 1588, the family converted the integral medieval chapel into a parlour.

Sources/literature: Giles, p. 197.

See also: main text.

LEEZ PRIORY, ESSEX (house survives in part; chapel does not)

Patron: Charles Rich (1586-1658), 2nd Earl of Warwick.

Dates: from 1641 events.

The Rich family acquired the former Augustinian priory at the Dissolution, and converted it into a fashionable, red-brick house with an inner and outer quadrangle. Following her marriage to the future 4th Earl in 1641, Mary Rich (1625-78), née Boyle, moved in with her parents-in-law. There she was obliged to attend improving sermons in the Puritan 2nd Earl's chapel. Indeed, the earl required that sermons that he had heard in church be repeated to him in his private chapel.

Sources/literature: W. Gibson, A Social History of the Domestic Chaplain (London, 1997), p. 213 (note 51); Howard, pp. 149, 205; S.H. Mendelson, *The Mental World of Stuart Women* (Brighton, 1987), p. 81; *CL*, 4 Apr 1914.

LEIGHTON BROMSWOLD, CAMBRIDGESHIRE (demolished, or never built)

Patron: Gervase Clifton (d. 1618), Lord Clifton.

Dates: *c.*1608-16 possible new build.

Clifton prepared the site some time before 1608. Apart from the surviving gatehouse (built in 1616), it is not certain that any part of the symmetrical, U-shaped house shown on Thorpe's plan was actually built before Clifton committed suicide in the Tower, 'through *ennui*', in 1618. The chapel (orientation unclear) would have been isolated at the end of the right-hand arm of the 'U', with an apsidal three-bay window at the

liturgical E end, and a four-light window in the liturgical N and S walls. On plan, an ante-chapel, separated from the main chapel by an openwork screen, was lit from the liturgical S by a two-light window, while to the liturgical N it shared a four-light window with the main chapel. It gave on to a lobby at the bottom of a main stair. The balancing arm of the 'U' was to have housed the bake-house. It too had a three-bay apse, and those of its windows looking on to the entrance courtyard would have possessed the same external fenestration as the chapel.
Sources/literature: T65-6.

LEWESTON MANOR, DORSET (house replaced; chapel survives)
Patron: Sir John Fitzjames (a. 1616).
Date: 1616 new build.
The detached, correctly-oriented chapel in the grounds of the previous house is basically a single-cell rectangle, with a small W porch which serves as a narthex. Apart from crosses on the gables and a bellcote (all of which may well be later), the main cell of the chapel, including the E end, is extremely plain, while the entrance facade of the porch is highly decorated. Inside, there is perhaps the first surviving post-Reformation example of a conventional cross- (as opposed to college-style) pewing arrangement.
Sources/literature: none given.
See also: main text and figs. 5.12, 5.13, 5.14.

LITTLE CHARLTON (also known as CHARLTON COURT), EAST SUTTON, KENT (house survives in part; chapel does not)
Patrons: Robert Filmer (d. 1585) and/or Sir Edward Filmer (1566-1629).
Dates: c.1580s-1610 new build.
Summerson suspects that a Thorpe plan of a symmetrical, square, unnamed house with the hall in the centre is of Robert Filmer's newly-built Little Charlton. The chapel occupies a corner of the house, with an entrance from the great stair. In keeping with the symmetry of the fenestration of the house, the chapel both possessed an apsidal window, and contained an awkward triangular space created by a two-sided window. It is not clear whether the former was at the E end because the orientation of the chapel is uncertain, and an apsidal E end is otherwise unknown in the Elizabethan period. However, Summerson considers that the plan probably dates from c.1623. It may therefore include work undertaken under James I for Edward Filmer (who left the house, though he continued to own it, in 1609-10), by which time apsed chapels were once again acceptable.
Sources/literature: T171-2; J. Summerson, *The Book of Architecture of John Thorpe* (Glasgow, 1966), p. 25.

LITTLE MALVERN COURT, WORCESTERSHIRE (house, altered and restored, survives)
Patrons: Henry Russell (d. 1558); Milburgha Russell (d. c.1575), née Brockton.
Dates: 1560 event; 1575 event.
Russell bought the site of Little Malvern Priory for conversion into a country house in 1554. The inventory taken after his death lists a chapel chamber (containing bedding, a still, flagons, a lute etc.), but no chapel.
By 1575, on the death of Russell's wife, Milburgha, the still and lute had been removed from the chapel chamber.
Sources/literature: Wanklyn, pp. 32, 50.

LITTLE MORETON HALL, CHESHIRE (house and chapel survive)
Patrons: William Moreton (d. 1563); John Moreton (d. 1598).
Dates: *c*.1559-98 alterations.
The Moreton family had extended the moated, black and white, timber-framed, L-shaped, mid-15th-century house to the W in *c*.1480. The E wing was extended to the S in Elizabethan times, with the cross-range, correctly-oriented chapel installed at the E end. Further work completed the creation of a three-range courtyard house. The chancel, to the E of the main body of the chapel, was added in the late 16th century, is slightly off-centre and was painted with texts and decorative borders. It is separated from the main chapel by a simple, screened opening in the wall, with the hinged portion giving access to the chancel. No decoration survives in the main chapel, which was later used as a coal-hole. The chapel was originally floored with medieval tiles, possibly from a local monastery after the Dissolution. The prayer room above the main chapel probably contained a squint or window onto the chancel, and may have been used by the family when attending services.
Sources/literature: C.F. Stell, 'Little Moreton Hall', *Report of the Summer Meeting of the Royal Archaeological Institute at Keele* (1963), pp. 270-4; *CL*, 23 Apr. 1904, 30 Nov., 7 Dec. 1929.
See also: main text and figs. 4.7, 4.8.

LITTLE SAXHAM HALL, SUFFOLK (replaced)
Patron: Sir Thomas Lucas (d. 1531).
Date: 1505-14 new build.
Lucas built the moated, stone-dressed, red-brick, double-courtyard house with small projecting wings. The chapel was twice enlarged during the building programme. In 1509, before starting work on the E window, the glazier was required to inspect the equivalent window at Horham Hall (*q.v.*).
Sources/literature: Airs, p. 92; Howard, pp. 12-13, 37, 215.

LITTLE WENHAM HALL, SUFFOLK (house and chapel survive)
Patron: Lady Brewse (a.1644), née Peyton.
Date: 1644 event.
The 13th-century house of flint and brick with a square, linked chapel off the hall passed to Lady Brewse on the death of her husband Sir John in 1642. In February 1644, Dowsing notes that Lady Brewse promised to take down a picture of the Trinity. Despite his attentions, an undamaged three-quarter-length figure of Christ survives on the central roof boss. This chapel is the only private chapel mentioned by Dowsing that is still in existence.
Sources/literature: Dowsing, p. 238.
See also: main text.

LITTLECOTE HOUSE, WILTSHIRE (house, altered, survives; chapel survives)
Patron: Sir Alexander Popham (a. mid-17th century).
Dates: mid-17th-century alterations.
Popham inherited what was then probably an Elizabethan E-plan house, built of brick, and combined with parts of an older house. His long, thin, rectangular, correctly-oriented chapel runs along the NW wing and is relatively isolated from the heart of the house. It may incorporate part of a pre-Reformation chapel. Inside, the arrangement is typically

Puritan, with the pulpit dominating the E wall.
Sources/literature: *CL*, 25 Nov., 2 Dec. 1965.
See also: main text and figs. 5.35, 5.36.

LIVERSEDGE HALL, WEST YORKSHIRE (largely replaced; fragment of chapel survives)
Patrons: Nevill family.
Dates: late 15th/early 16th-century new build.
The house was built 'about the time of Henry VII', and comprised a central block and two wings. The chapel was said to be in the west wing. Now converted into living space, its blocked in E window survives with its trefoiled lights and quatrefoil being visible internally.
Sources/literature: Giles, p. 203.

LOCKO PARK, DERBYSHIRE (house replaced; chapel, much restored, survives)
Patron: Henry Gilbert (1659-1720).
Dates: 1669-73 new build.
Architect: possibly George Eaton (d. 1689).
Gilbert inherited a 'good stone house' of moderate size. It stood on or near the site of a Lazar hospital that was dissolved in 1539. He built the partially detached, stone, correctly-oriented chapel, and had it consecrated in 1673. Inside, the richly decorated, coffered, wooden ceiling has survived 19th-century restoration. The pulpit is said to be original. There is no upper chapel.
Sources/literature: *CL*, 5 Jun. 1969.
See also: main text and fig. 6.15; Plate XXVII.

LONGLEAT HOUSE, WILTSHIRE (house survives; chapel interior Gothicised)
Patrons: Sir John Thynne (d. 1580); Thomas Thynne (1640-1714), 1st Viscount Weymouth.
Dates: 1546-9 alterations; 1684 event.
Thynne bought the dissolved priory on the site in 1541. Over four programmes of building lasting nearly 40 years, and interrupted by a major fire in 1567, he converted it into a large courtyard house, the first of the Elizabethan 'prodigy' houses, with four uniform facades. His early building work (1546-9) concentrated on transforming the old monastic buildings into a single, two-storeyed range with buttery, hall and integral, L-shaped, NW (probably) -oriented chapel on the ground floor and the great chamber and other rooms above. This became the W wing.
The chapel was not consecrated until 1684.
Sources/literature: Knyff, pls. 39, 40; Longleat MSS, Inventory 1639; Airs, pp. 42-4; M. Girouard, 'Development of Longleat House between 1546 and 1572', *AJ*, 116 (1961), pp. 200-22; Legg, p. 325.
See also: main text.

LOSELEY PARK, SURREY (W wing, with chapel, demolished; rest of house survives)
Patrons: Sir William More (1520-1600); Sir George More (1553-1632); Sir William More, Bt (1643-84).
Dates: 1561-9 new build; *c.*1600-10 addition; 1668 event.

William More inherited the site from his father in 1549, and replaced the medieval manor house on the site with a substantial new house – using building materials from the dissolved Waverley Abbey. His account books contain a passing reference to a chapel.

More's son, George, added a W wing. According to Thorpe's plan, which Summerson considers probably dates from the first decade of the 17th century, this contained an L-shaped assembly chapel beneath the long gallery and separated from the great stair by an openwork screen with a central opening. If the site of the chapel was in truth transferred to the W wing as Thorpe's plan indicates, it would be an important example of the early revival of chapel building in the 17th century, for it was unusual to move the site of a chapel. Its impressive array of windows was evidently dictated by the need to adhere to the symmetry of the overall plan rather than the needs of the chapel.

In 1668, Sir William More obtained a licence from George Morley, Bishop of Winchester, for the celebration of divine service and administering of the sacraments. Contrary to earlier practice, the licence allowed the household to worship in the chapel on Sundays and feast days whenever it was inconvenient for them to attend their parish church in Guildford.

Sources/literature: T39-40; W. Bray, 'Observations on the Christmas Lord of Misrule, and on the King's Office of Revells and Tents', *A*, 18 (1817), pp. 317-18; Cliffe, *World*, p. 35; J. Evans, 'Extracts from the Private Account Book of Sir William More of Loseley in Surrey', *A*, 36 (1855), pp. 284-310; J. Summerson, *The Book of Architecture of John Thorpe* (Glasgow, 1966), pp. 23-4; *CL*, 25 May 1935.

LOW HAM, SOMERSET (house replaced, then demolished; chapel survives)
Patrons: Sir Edward Hext (d. 1624); George Stawell (1623-69); Ralph Stawell (*c*.1641-89), 1st Lord Stawell.
Dates: from 1623 new build; 1668-9 restoration; by 1689 event.
Hext built 'one of the best houses in the west of England' – probably in the late 16th-century. Below it, in 1623, he began to build a spectacular, detached, correctly-oriented chapel. The (1625) pulpit is on the S side of the nave, and just to the W of the screen.

It is thought that the chapel was badly damaged during the Civil War and was restored in 1668-9 by George Stawell (who had married Hext's only daughter and heiress). This included rebuilding the pointed E window. It was consecrated (or re-consecrated) in 1669.

By 1689, Ralph Stawell had appropriated two large pews and one ordinary pew in the body of the chapel, together with three in the S aisle and another on the N side. His son John, 2nd Lord Stawell (*c*.1669-92), later replaced Hext's house with a larger and more sumptuous edifice which he left unfinished and which quickly fell into ruin.

Sources/literature: 46th AGM, 'Low Ham Chapel and Manor', *Proceedings of the Somerset Archaeological Society*, 40.1 (1894), p. 33; J. Collinson, *History and Antiquities of the County of Somerset*, 3 (1791), p. 445; H. Colvin, 'Lord Stawell's Great House in Somerset', *AH*, 44 (2001), pp. 332-40; D.L. Hayward, 'Apportionment of Seats in Low Ham Church', *Somerset and Dorset Notes and Queries*, 4 (1895), p. 167; G.D. Stawell, *A Quantock Family* (Taunton, 1910), pp. 110-11, 470-5.

See also: main text and fig. 5.44; Plates XII, XVI.

LULWORTH CASTLE, DORSET (house, but not chapel, survives in a dilapidated state)
Patrons: Thomas Howard (1561-1626), 1st Earl of Suffolk; Humphrey Weld (d. 1685).

Dates: 1639 event; 1679 event.

A hunting lodge built as a square castle by Thomas Howard, 3rd Lord Bindon from 1605, Suffolk inherited it on the Bindon's death in 1611. An inventory of 1639 lists a chapel chamber – presumably installed during Suffolk's tenure. Its contents included a bed, bedding, a Bible and prayer books, implying that a number of people gathered there. The position of any chapel cannot be determined for certain.

The Roman Catholic Weld bought the house in c.1641, and renovated it after the Restoration. An inventory taken on his bankruptcy in 1679 lists a well-appointed chapel (that was probably a centre of worship for local Roman Catholics), and a closet looking into the chapel, but there is no mention of a chapel chamber. Weld's correctly-oriented chapel, in the N range, might well have occupied the same site as Suffolk's chapel – if there was one.

Sources/literature: Dorset RO, D/WLC/E96 & E99 (many thanks to David Greenhalf for these and other references, and for his generous help over the many problems connected with the chapel at Lulworth); Oswald, pp. 65-7.

LYME PARK, CHESHIRE (house, greatly altered, and chapel, altered and restored, survive)
Patron: Richard Legh (1634-87).
Dates: between 1643 and 1687 alterations.

The stone, mid-16th-century, E-plan or courtyard house incorporated parts of an earlier house. The correctly-oriented, integral, single-storey, apsed chapel was formed from the buttery and buttery parlour in the NE corner at some stage during Legh's tenure which started in 1643. Inside, the communion rail, raised on a single step, has openwork carved foliage. The apse is decorated with a frieze of cherubs and foliage. There is a raised family pew on the S side that is entered via a staircase and surrounded by pilasters and an openwork wooden parapet of carved foliage. On Legh's death, the chapel contained rich velvet furnishings. The screen and other fittings and decoration are 18th-century or later. The household entrance is at the W end of the S wall.

Sources/literature: Legh papers: largely uncatalogued papers in Lyme Park estate office; W. Beaumont, *History of the House of Lyme, in Cheshire, compiled from documents of the Legh family of that house, and from other sources* (Warrington, 1876); E. Legh, *The House of Lyme from its Foundation to the End of the Eighteenth Century* (London, 1917); *CL*, 5, 12, 19, 26 Dec. 1974.

LYNCH CHAPEL, SOMERSET (survives, the interior much restored)
Patrons: Sydenham family.
Dates: c.1530/40 new build.

The detached chapel was thought by Pevsner to have belonged to the manor house of the Sydenham family, though it may in fact have been built as a chapel of ease. The interior contains a piscina and two brackets built to support statues flanking the altar – if these are original they must predate the Commissioners and argue for a date in the early 1530s. Otherwise the interior, including the large three-light E window, has been much restored and renewed. There is disagreement over whether the wagon roof is original.

Sources/literature: N. Pevsner, *The Buildings of England: South and West Somerset* (Harmondsworth, 1985), p. 227.

LYPPIATT PARK, BISLEY, GLOUCESTERSHIRE (house, altered, survives; chapel survives)

Patron: Robert Wye (d. 1544).

Dates: early 16th-century alterations.

Wye extended the existing medieval house on acquiring it in *c*.1505, creating two irregular and incomplete courtyards, and encompassing the late 14th-century, W-oriented, detached chapel to the NW which stands next to the site of the gatehouse. He probably installed the arched light W and side windows of the chapel.

Sources/literature: N. Kingsley, *The Country Houses of Gloucestershire*, 1 (Cheltenham, 1989), pp. 128-9.

LYTES CARY, SOMERSET (house, much altered, and chapel survive)

Patrons: Sir John Lyte (d. 1568); Thomas Lyte (1568-1638).

Dates: 1520/30s alterations; 1631 restoration.

Sir John inherited a small medieval manor house in 1523, and enlarged and transformed it into a courtyard house. The addition of a S range linked the previously detached, correctly-oriented, 14th-century chapel to the main house, though the original external entrance in the N wall was retained, and no internal entrance created. A squint in the oriel of the great hall looked on to the chapel entrance.

The interior was restored in 1631 by Thomas, who had inherited the house in 1607. His work included the communion rail, screen, and various wall paintings. He also installed a painted frieze of coats of arms.

Sources/literature: E. Buckle, 'Lytescarey', *Proceedings of the Somersetshire Archaeological and Natural History Society*, 38 (1892) pp. 101-10; J. Collinson, *The History and Antiquities of the County of Somerset*, 3 (Bath, 1791); H.C. Maxwell Lyte, 'The Lytes of Lytescary', *Proceedings of the Somersetshire Archaeological and Natural History Society*, 38 (1892) pp. 1-100; *CL*, 18 Jul. 1947.

See also: main text and fig. 3.2; Plate XXVI.

MAPLEDURHAM HOUSE, OXFORDSHIRE (house, remodelled, survives; chapel replaced, but shell remains)

Patrons: Blount family.

Dates: possible 17th-century event.

In 1733, Loveday noted that the chapel in the Elizabethan H-plan house was above the great stair and had a painted altarpiece depicting the dead Christ by Paul Lorain. Markham suggests that Lorain could have been the 17th-century painter of churches, Nicolas Lorain. This would indicate that the chapel was in place during the 17th century – if so, it was probably in the S wing.

Sources/literature: Markham, p. 164.

MELCOMBE HORSEY see **HIGHER MELCOMBE**

MELTON CONSTABLE, NORFOLK (house survives as does chapel shell)

Patron: Sir Jacob Astley, Bt (1640-1729).

Dates: *c*.1664-70 new build.

Architect: predominantly Sir Jacob Astley.

Astley inherited an Elizabethan manor house which he largely demolished to erect a compact, triple-pile house with a large, single-storey, correctly-oriented, integral chapel occupying part of the central range. It was easily accessible but off main circulation routes. Inside, there was a mezzanine level upper chapel, and a link between the chapel and a side closet E of the little parlour (there may in fact have been two such closets, one for men and one for women).

Sources/literature: Knyff, pl. 51; H.A. Millon, *The Triumph of the Baroque* (London, 1999), pp. 498-501; R. North, *Of Building, Roger North's Writings on Architecture* (H. Colvin and J. Newman, editors), (Oxford, 1981) pp. 73-5.

See also: main text and fig. 6.6; Plate XXVIII.

MELWOOD, LINCOLNSHIRE (house not identified)

Patron: Sir George St Paul, Bt (1562-1613).

Dates: after 1611 new build.

Two Thorpe plans were produced for St Paul whom Summerson notes as being 'of Melwood (Owston) Lincs'. According to the plans, the chapel had a single, undifferentiated, four-light window, and was entered from the liturgical S via the screens passage.

Sources/literature: T55, 59.

MERSHAM-LE-HATCH, KENT (replaced)

Patron: Sir Norton Knatchbull, Bt (1602-85).

Date: 1632 event.

The private chapel was consecrated in 1632.

Sources/literature: Legg, pp. 139-145.

METHLEY HALL, WEST YORKSHIRE (demolished)

Patron: John Savile (d. *c*.1657).

Date: 1657 event.

A 1657 inventory of Savile's possessions indicates that there was a chapel in his 15th-century house that had been remodelled in the late 16th and early 17th centuries.

Sources/literature: Giles, pp. 18, 205.

MIDDLETON HALL, WARWICKSHIRE (house, remodelled and restored, survives; chapel does not)

Patron: Sir Henry Willoughby (d. 1549).

Date: 1550 event.

An inventory of the house, inherited by the Willoughby family in 1493, taken in 1550 after Willoughby's death mentions a chapel chamber (containing mattresses, blankets etc.), and its wording implies that there was also a well-equipped private chapel in or near the house.

Sources/literature: Nottingham University Library, Middleton MSS, Mi I 37.

MILTON HALL, PETERBOROUGH, CAMBRIDGESHIRE (house, altered, survives; chapel window survives)

Patron: Sir William Fitzwilliam I (1526-99) and/or Sir William Fitzwilliam II (d. 1618).

Dates: late 16th/early 17th-century rebuild.

The Fitzwilliam family bought the site in 1502, and Sir William I, who was formerly the governor of Fotheringay Castle (*q.v.*) and presided over the execution of Mary, Queen of Scots, carried out building works towards the end of the 16th century. His son, Sir William II, probably continued his work. The chapel was in the north wing next to the hall dais.

Sources/literature: N. Pevsner, *The Buildings of England: Bedfordshire and the County of Huntingdon and Peterborough* (Harmondsworth, 1974), pp. 291-3.

MINORIES (Sir Charles Lyttelton's House) (WHITECHAPEL), LONDON

Patron: Sir Charles Lyttleton, Bt (1628-1716).

Date: 1667 event.

Lady Anne Clifford recorded that in 1667 her granddaughter, Lady Cecilly Tufton (d. 1675), married Christopher Hatton (1632-1706; owner of Kirby Hall, *q.v.*), at the house of Sir Charles Littleton (*sic*) in the Minories – presumably in a private chapel there.

Sources/literature: Clifford, p. 193.

See also: main text.

MISTLEY HALL, ESSEX (demolished)

Patron: Paul Bayning (d. 1629), 1st Viscount Bayning.

Date: 1610 event.

In 1610, the unconsecrated status of the chapel of ease at Mistley was used to justify the argument that the chaplain was not obliged to wear a surplice while officiating there.

Sources/literature: T. W. Davids, *Annals of Evangelical Nonconformity in the County of Essex* (London, 1863), p.172; W. White, *History, Gazetteer and Directory of the County of Essex* (Sheffield, 1848), pp. 462-3.

See also: main text.

MOREHAMPTON PARK, HEREFORDSHIRE (no trace survives)

Patron: Sir John Hoskyns (1566-1638).

Dates: before 1638 event.

John Aubrey noted that the chapel in Hoskyns' house had two 'Hebrewe' words and two lines of verse over the altar.

Sources/literature: J. Aubrey, *Aubrey's Brief Lives* (O. Lawson Dick, editor), (London, 1958), p. 170.

MOTTISFONT ABBEY, HAMPSHIRE (house, remodelled, survives; chapel does not)

Patron: William Sandys (*c.*1470-1540), 1st Lord Sandys.

Dates: after 1536 conversion.

Sandys acquired the suppressed priory in 1536, and started to convert it into a double-courtyard house. The chapel was considered to be less richly decorated than that at Sandys' other main house, The Vyne (*q.v.*).

Sources/literature: Howard, pp. 151, 206.

NAWORTH CASTLE, CUMBRIA (house and oratory survive; chapel does not)

Patrons: Thomas Dacre (1467-1525), 3rd Lord Dacre; William Howard (1563-1640), Lord Howard ('Belted Will'); Charles Howard (1629-85), 1st Earl of Carlisle.

Dates: *c.*1515-25 alterations; 1618-33 alterations; 1640s events.

The integral chapel in the 14th-century castle, which was partially rebuilt by Dacre, was oriented to the N, lay on the main floor and ran along the E range. The entrance to the main chapel was at the liturgical W end. The chapel was lit by two great rectangular windows, with close panel tracery, on the liturgical N side. Only the windows at the dais end of the hall are larger.

Lord William Howard, a Roman Catholic convert, came to Naworth shortly after his release from the Tower in 1601, having earlier married a Dacre heiress. He extensively restored the chapel. In 1622, he installed a ceiling of 58 early Tudor painted panels, depicting patriarchs, kings of Judah and others, removed from Kirkoswald Castle (q.v.), and in 1624, a stained glass Crucifixion and coats of arms – possibly also from Kirkoswald. He probably attended mass in his private chapel or oratory. This was richly ornamented, and contained a retable of 1514 comprising three ogee-arched compartments depicting the Scourging, Crucifixion and Resurrection.

The Protestant Sir Charles Howard (later 1st Earl of Carlisle), William's great grandson, inherited Naworth in 1644. In 1649, Anne, Lady Halkett recorded that she attended services in the chapel.

Sources/literature: *The Memoirs of Anne, Lady Halkett and Ann, Lady Fanshawe* (J. Loftis, editor), (Oxford, 1979), pp. 32, 35, 41-2; 'Naworth Estate and Household Accounts, 1648-1660' (C.R. Hudleston, editor), (Durham and London, 1958); *Household Books of the Lord William Howard of Naworth* (G. Ornsby, editor), (Durham, 1878), pp. xlii-lxxi, 132-3, 194; E. Croft-Murray, *Decorative Painting in England*, 1 (London, 1962), pp. 16, 158b, 173a, pl. 28; W. Hutchinson, *The History of the County of Cumberland*, 1 (Carlisle, 1794), pp. 134-7; D. and S. Lysons, *Magna Britannia*, 4 (London, 1816), p. cciv-v.

See also: main text and figs. 3.11, 3.12; Plates V, VI.

NETHERTON HALL, FARWAY, DEVON (house, restored, survives; chapel does not)

Patron: Sir Edmund Prideaux, Bt (c.1555-1629).

Date: c.1607 rebuild.

Prideaux bought the property, which had belonged before the Dissolution to the nearby Canonsleigh nunnery, and rebuilt it in c.1607. There was a chapel in a projecting S wing.

Sources/literature: 'The Prideaux Collection of Topographical Drawings' (J. Harris, editor), *AH*, 7 (1964), pp. 32-3, 81; W.G. Hoskins, *Devon* (London, 1954), p. 397.

NEW HALL, ESSEX (house, restored, survives; chapel does not)

Patron: George Villiers (1592-1628), 1st Duke of Buckingham.

Dates: 1620-3 event.

Henry VIII's red-brick, courtyard house of Beaulieu, built in 1517-21, and which contained a chapel in its W range, was granted to Thomas Radcliffe, 3rd Earl of Sussex, in 1573 and partially rebuilt by him. Buckingham bought it in 1622, by which time it was known as New Hall. A contemporary Inigo Jones design for one bay of a coffered wooden ceiling, supposedly for a *trompe l'oeil* modification of an existing, Tudor, panelled roof, is thought likely to have been for Buckingham's closet in his chapel there. Certainly Jones' estimates for Buckingham's chapel included fitted paintings (there is no clue to the subject matter), and indicated that a beamed ceiling may have been intended.

Sources/literature: J. Harris and G. Higgott, *Inigo Jones: Complete Architectural Drawings* (London, 1989), pp. 178-9.

See also: main text and Plate XXV.

NEWNHAM PADDOX, WARWICKSHIRE (demolished)

Patron: Basil Feilding, 2nd Earl of Denbigh (1608-75).

Date: 1668 new build.

In 1688, Denbigh installed a chapel, perhaps in one of the wings of the large, but architecturally modest, U-shaped house that had been built or enlarged by the Feilding family in the late 16th and early 17th centuries.

Sources/literature: Tyack, pp. 148-51.

NEWSTEAD ABBEY, NOTTINGHAMSHIRE (house and chapel, altered, survive)

Patron: Sir John ('Little John') Byron (1487-1567).

Dates: 1540s alterations.

Byron bought the dissolved 12th/13th-century Augustinian priory in 1540. Though a Commissioner for Nottingham and playing a part in suppressing the Pilgrimage of Grace, he was not wholly sympathetic to the Reformation. He transformed the cloister complex into a courtyard-style house, and created a correctly-oriented, single-storey chapel out of the former chapter house in the E range. Although the family rooms were above, they and their household (thought to number about 80) shared the only entrance in the W wall. The chapel is surprisingly small in relation to the size of the household, and inside there is no apparent means of separating family from retainers. An 18th-century sketch shows the chapel equipped with fairly rudimentary, perhaps 17th-century, stalls, but it is not known how it was furnished in Byron's day.

Sources/literature: *Papers and Discussion from a Day Symposium organised by the Society of the Architectural Historians of Great Britain in association with the Thoroton Society* (4 Apr. 1992); Howard, pp. 151-6, 213; V.W. Walker, *The House of Byron* (London, 1988).

NORTH WYKE, DEVON (house and chapel, much restored, survive)

Patron: John ('Warrior') Wykes (1524-91).

Dates: mid to late Tudor alterations.

Wykes turned his modest, medieval house into a more substantial courtyard house. In doing so, he appears to have extended the correctly-oriented, medieval chapel, originally part of an independent gatehouse (S) range, and linked it to the fabric of his expanding courtyard house at both ground and first floor levels. The main entrance is by means of an external door in the N wall leading to the main courtyard. The double-height chancel has a Tudor E window decorated with the arms of Wykes and his wife, Mary Giffard. No interior detailing survives, but there are signs that a screen may have been intended. There is some evidence that the E window was left unglazed and the chapel never fully finished.

Sources/literature: E. Lega-Weekes: unpublished notes taken during excavations.

See also: main text.

NOSELEY HALL, LEICESTERSHIRE (house replaced; chapel, restored, survives)

Patrons: Thomas Hazelrig (d. 1600); Sir Arthur Hazelrig, Bt (d. 1661).

Dates: 1578-84 events; 1633 event.

The detached, medieval chapel stands near the house. Originally a private chapel to the Hall, it later became collegiate in character. After the dissolution of the college in 1547, the Hazelrig family asserted control over appointments. By this time the parish church had long fallen into disuse and was shortly to be demolished by the Hazelrigs. Control over the chapel was subsequently contested by the Crown and a legal tussle ensued 1578-84 with the then patron, Sir Thomas, judgement being given in favour of the former.

The Hazelrig family were subsequently appointed as lay rectors with powers of appointment to the curacy. In 1633, the fiercely Puritan Sir Arthur did not appoint a curate, retaining the tithes and keeping a chaplain in his house.
Sources/literature: *VCH*, 5 (1964), pp. 264-70.

OFFCHURCH BURY, WARWICKSHIRE (house, much altered, survives; chapel does not)
Patron: Sir Valentine Knightley (a. 1560s).
Dates: 1560s modernisation.
Knightley probably remodelled and modernised the early 16th-century manor house, formerly the property of Coventry Priory, in the 1560s. It had contained a hall, chapel and vaulted gatehouse.
Sources/literature: *VCH*, 6, pp. 195-6.

OLD THORNDON HALL, ESSEX (replaced)
Patron: John Petre (d. 1613), 1st Lord Petre.
Dates: 1593-*c*.1595 alterations.
In 1573, John Petre bought the brick mansion of *c*.1415, and remodelled it to form a rambling house. The chapel was on the first floor to the W of the house, and probably fairly large since it was later converted into a bedroom for 4th Lord Petre. The glass was set in the chapel windows in 1594. The ceiling was of fretted plaster. John Petre's wife and descendants were Roman Catholic (William Byrd is thought to have composed music for the chapel).
Sources/literature: Essex RO, D/DP A22; J. Ward, *Old Thorndon Hall, Essex* (Chelmsford and London, 1972).

OLD WOLLATON HALL, NOTTINGHAMSHIRE (demolished)
Patrons: Sir Henry Willoughby (d. 1549); Sir Francis Willoughby (1546-96).
Dates: 1550 and 1585 events.
An inventory taken on Sir Henry's death in 1549 lists a chapel within the late 15th-century manor and farm buildings grouped round a courtyard. The chapel contained a hanging of green and red 'saye', two candlesticks and two cruets, as well as vestments for priest, deacon and sub-deacon.
A 1585 inventory makes no mention of the chapel.
Sources/literature: A.T. Friedman, *House and Household in Elizabethan England, Wollaton Hall and the Willoughby Family*, (Chicago and London, 1989), pp. 38-41; J. Hodson, 'The First Wollaton', *Transactions of the Thoroton Society of Nottinghamshire*, 72 (1968), pp. 59ff.

OSTERLEY PARK, MIDDLESEX (house comprehensively remodelled; chapel does not survive)
Patron: Sir William 'The Conqueror' Waller (*c*.1597-1668).
Date: 1668 event.
Waller bought the Elizabethan courtyard house, built of brick with four corner towers, in 1655. The inventory taken on Waller's death in 1668 lists a chapel containing chairs, forms and a pulpit. A chamber was set aside for the chaplain.
Sources/literature: Cliffe, p. 226; *CL*, 14 Sep. 1988.

OXHEY PLACE HALL, HERTFORDSHIRE (house demolished; chapel, somewhat altered, survives)
Patrons: Sir James Altham (d. 1617); Sir John Bucknall (c.1650-1711).
Dates: 1612 new build; c.1690 alterations.
Altham bought the estate, a pre-Reformation property of St Albans Abbey, in 1604 and built a large house there. In 1612, he erected and had consecrated a correctly-oriented, flint and brick, household chapel nearby − where he was to be buried, and whose interior later suffered from use as a storeroom and barracks by Parliamentary troops.
Bucknall inherited the estate from his father William (1629-76) who had bought it in 1668. He, or possibly his father, replaced Altham's house with a square, brick, courtyard house with flanking bays known simply as Oxhey Place. In c.1690 he repaired and restored the chapel and installed a large wooden reredos with twisted columns supporting a broken pediment which all but obscures the E window. Further restoration took place in the 18th, 19th and 20th centuries.
Sources/literature: H. Chauncy, *The Historical Antiquities of Hertfordshire*, (London, 1700), p. 485b; E.J. Chapman, 'Sir William Bucknall of Oxhey Place, Watford, 1629-1676', *Hertfordshire's Past*, 21 (1986), pp. 12-15; P.M. Hunneyball, 'Country Retreats in Seventeenth-Century Hertfordshire', *The Renaissance Villa in Britain, 1500-1700* (M. Airs and G. Tyack, editors), (Reading, 2007), pp. 192-205; Legg, p. 318; Smith, p. 206; *VCH*, 2 (1908), pp. 456-7.

PEARTREE HOUSE, SOUTHAMPTON, HAMPSHIRE (house, altered, survives; chapel largely replaced)
Patron: Richard Smith (d. c.1630).
Date: 1620 new build.
Smith built the detached Jesus Chapel near his Jacobean house. It measured some 50ft x 20ft, and possessed a wooden chancel screen and a gallery. It was probably a chapel of ease. It was consecrated in 1620.
Sources/literature: Legg, pp. 47-80.

PETWORTH HOUSE, WEST SUSSEX (house and 'great chapel' survive, largely intact)
Patrons: Henry Percy (c.1532-85), 8th Earl of Northumberland ('Cruel Henry'); Henry Percy (1564-1632), 9th Earl of Northumberland ('the Wizard Earl'); Charles Seymour (1662-1748), 6th Duke of Somerset ('the Proud Duke').
Dates: 1574 event; 1582-3 alterations; 1633 event; 1685-1702 alterations.
The 8th Earl of Northumberland, newly released from the Tower, took possession of the largely medieval Petworth, built of brick and stone, in 1574 following the execution of his elder brother, the 7th Earl ('Simple Tom'; 1528-72). It contained two chapels: the 'little chapel' was at the upper end of the parlour and contained one window and a marble altar (the 7th and 8th Earls were Roman Catholic); the surviving 13th/14th-century, correctly-oriented, 'great chapel' measured 48ft x 24ft, and had ten glass windows, some in poor repair. At the upper end of the latter was a former vestry, then in use as a kitchen, while a mezzanine level closet near the great chamber looked into the chapel.
In 1582-3, as part of a programme of improvements to the house, the 8th Earl renovated the 'great chapel', removing the old stalls and seats.
The (Protestant) 9th Earl modestly extended the house − to which he was confined on his release from the Tower in 1621. An inventory taken in 1633 after his death gave the

value of the contents of the chapel as £14.3s, compared with £125 for 'his lordship's chamber'. Its contents included nine forms to kneel on covered in 'matt'. A chaplain had been appointed in 1626, before which there had been no clergy in the house.

The 'Proud Duke' acquired the house, which had been further extended by the 10th Earl, on marrying the daughter of the last (11th) Percy Earl in 1682. He rebuilt Petworth in Franco-Dutch style as a single-range, double-pile house. He reduced the size of the chapel to the W by some eight feet, but retained it as a double-height, relatively isolated, linked space of medieval character at the N end of the range. Original medieval windows in the S walls, spared by the 8th Earl, were retained, as was the large E window with its heraldic glass. The main chapel was accessed by a passage linking it to the low end of the house. There was a probably a separate entrance to the extravagantly carved, W end family gallery above. This dominates the mixed-media chapel interior which has a largely secular feel. Existing heraldic glass was supplemented by the manufacture of new similar glass. The relatively plain plaster ceiling is by Edward Goudge. Seating is college style. (In 1702, *trompe l'oeil* Gothic windows with painted heraldry replaced blocked up windows along the N wall.)

Sources/literature: G.R. Batho, 'The Percies at Petworth, 1574-1632', *SAC,* 95 (1957), pp. 1-27; *The Household Papers of Henry Percy, 9th Earl of Northumberland (1564-1632)* (G.R. Batho, editor), (London, 1962).

See also: main text and figs. 6.26, 6.27.

PIRTON COURT, WORCESTERSHIRE (house, altered, survives; chapel does not)

Patron: Thomas Folliott (d. 1618).

Date: 1618 event.

Folliott inherited the moated, timber-framed house from his father in *c.*1579, and was presumably responsible for its updating. An inventory taken on his death lists a chapel containing a clocke, a bell, a square (presumably altar) table, a carpet, two cushions and two 'formes'. This contrasts with a 1579 inventory (taken on the death of Folliott's father, John d. *c.*1579) in which no chapel is listed (but see The Hermitage below).

Sources/literature: Wanklyn, pp. 54–8, 136.

POOLEY HALL, WARWICKSHIRE (house survives as three separate ranges; chapel does not)

Patron: Sir Thomas Cokayne (d. 1537).

Dates: after 1509 alterations.

Cokayne, who possessed a number of chaplains, appears to have rebuilt a decayed 13th-century chapel, creating a detached, correctly-oriented chapel set at an angle to his red-brick, early Tudor house that could once have enclosed a courtyard. It may have been connected to the house by a vaulted passage.

Sources/literature: A.E. Cockayne, *Cockayne Memoranda*, (Congleton, 1873), p. 86; W. Dugdale, *The Antiquities of Warwickshire* (London, 1730), p. 1121; W. Niven, *Illustrations of Old Warwickshire Houses* (London, 1878), p. 12; W. Smith, *A New and Compendious History of the County of Warwickshire* (Birmingham, 1830), p. 371.

PRINKNASH PARK, GLOUCESTERSHIRE (house and chapel, both much altered and restored, survive)

Patron: Sir John Bridgeman (d. 1638).

Dates: 1628-9 alterations.

Bridgeman and his son, George, bought the largely early 16th-century house – which had belonged to the bishops of Gloucester before the Reformation - in 1628. They transformed it into an H-plan house by the addition of a NE wing. This included a correctly-oriented, integral chapel which was consecrated in 1629. The nave windows contain restored 16th-century glass, perhaps that remarked on by Walpole some 150 years later when he described 'painted glass with many angels in their coronation robes' in the 'small and low' chapel.

Sources/literature: W. Bazeley, 'History of Prinknash Park', *Transactions of the Bristol & Gloucester Archaeological Society*, 7 (1882-3), pp. 267-306; J. Brewer, *Delineations of Gloucestershire* (London, 1825), p. 149; Walpole, p. 75; *CL*, 22 Sep. 1906.

RAGLAN CASTLE, MONMOUTHSHIRE (survives as a ruin)

Patron: Edward Somerset (1601-67), 2nd Marquis of Worcester.

Dates: 1640s event.

The magnificent 15th-century castle-palace was restored and enhanced over the next 100 years, notably by William Herbert (d. 1469), Earl of Pembroke – who built the chapel – and William Somerset (1529-89), 3rd Earl of Worcester - who was responsible for the long gallery. The correctly-oriented (just) chapel was back to back with the great hall, and lay in the central range that bisected two courts. It appears that, in the 1640s, non-denominational worship took place there, and the Roman Catholic Somerset heard mass privately elsewhere. The latter's chaplain, Thomas Bayly, who served him for three years during the Civil War, and lived through the 1646 siege by Parliamentary troops, noted that half the servants were Roman Catholic and half Protestant.

Sources/literature: T. Bayly, *Certamen Religiosum: or, a Conference between His late Majestie Charles King of England, and Henry, late Marquis and Earl of Worcester, concerning religion* (London, 1649); T. Bayly, *The Golden Apophthegms of His Royall Majesty King Charles I, and Henry Marquis of Worcester* (London, 1660); *CL*, 9 Nov. 1989.

See also: main text.

RAGLEY HALL, WARWICKSHIRE (house, remodelled, survives; chapel now a library)

Patron: Edward Conway (*c.*1623-1683), 1st Earl of Conway.

Dates: 1679-83 new build.

Architects: William Hurlbutt (d. *c.*1698) and Robert Hooke (1635-1703).

The Conway family bought the site, once the property of Evesham Abbey, in 1595. Edward Conway's new house, which he died before completing, comprised a central block with four corner pavilions. Unlike many (perhaps all) other Restoration H-plan houses, an 18th-century plan shows that the single-storey, integrated chapel, oriented to the S, was not housed in a pavilion but within the central block.

Sources/literature: Knyff, pl. 71; P. Leach, 'Ragley Hall Reconsidered', *AJ*, 136 (1979), pp. 265-8.

See also: main text.

RAYNHAM HALL, NORFOLK (house, somewhat altered, survives; chapel now a saloon)

Patron: Sir Roger Townshend (d. 1637).

Dates: *c.*1618-35 new build.

Architect: Sir Roger Townshend with William Edge (*c*.1584-1643).

Over several years, and probably influenced by the work of Inigo Jones, Townshend designed and built a pioneering, early Classical, compact, double-pile house. The evidence for the existence of an integral, single-storey, correctly-oriented chapel rests on a 1671 plan of the ground floor on which the large central room of the E front is inscribed 'chapel'. It was evidently a formative element. The three windows at the E end may have received a distinctive treatment.

Sources/literature: RIBA drawings collection, 1671 plan and elevation; L. Campbell, 'Documentary Evidence for the Building of Raynham Hall', *AH*, 32 (1989), pp. 52-67; J. Harris, 'Raynham Hall, Norfolk', *AJ*, 118 (1961), pp. 180-7.

See also: main text and fig. 5.24.

RED HOUSE, MOOR MONKTON, NORTH YORKSHIRE (house reduced and rebuilt; chapel, now detached, survives)

Patrons: Sir Henry Slingsby I (1583-1634); Sir Henry Slingsby II, Bt (1601-1658); Sir Thomas Slingsby, Bt (1636-88).

Dates: *c*.1600-22 new build; 1630s event; post-1660 event.

Sir Henry Slingsby I started work on a new house in 1607, but may have begun the correctly-oriented chapel, which occupied a wing of the house, as early as 1600. The date of its completion is unclear. Slingsby's son, Sir Henry Slingsby II, described in his diaries how the chapel was used, but it is not always clear whether he is referring to the chapel as built or as subsequently altered. Inside, the layout resembles the pre-Reformation two-cell model.

In the early 1630s, Slingsby II asked the Archbishop of York, Richard Neile, to consecrate the chapel, but permission was refused lest the privilege be abused by the irregular celebration of the sacraments (it was probably consecrated by 1641).

After the Restoration, altar rails were installed at the E end.

Sources/literature: *The Diary of Sir Henry Slingsby of Scriven, Bart* (D. Parsons, editor), (London, 1836), pp. 3-4, 7-8, 18-21; *CL*, 27 Oct. 1944.

See also: main text and figs. 5.7, 5.8, 5.9.

REPTON MANOR, ASHFORD, KENT (disappeared)

Patron: Sir John Fogge (d. 1490).

Date: 1490 event.

Fogge left most of the contents of his chapel to his son in his will, while giving his wife a life interest in a vestment, a 'Massebooke', two silver basins, a silver gilt cross, two silver gilt cruets and a gilt 'sakering' bell.

Sources/literature: Hussey, p. 219.

RIPLEY CASTLE, NORTH YORKSHIRE (house, altered, survives; chapel does not)

Patron: Sir William Ingleby (d. 1617).

Date: 1617 event.

An inventory on Ingleby's death of the fortified house, that had been rebuilt in 1548-55, lists the chapel contents as a table, bedsteads and lumber, while the chapel chamber contained bedroom furniture.

Sources/literature: Crossley, pp. 170-1, 182-98.

See also: main text.

RISLEY HALL, DERBYSHIRE (house demolished; chapel, altered, survives)
Patrons: Michael (d. 1591) and Katherine (d. 1595, née Talocke or Totlock) Willoughby;
Sir Henry Willoughby, Bt (d. 1649).
Dates: by 1593 new build; 1632 event.
By 1593, the Willoughbys had built the detached, correctly-oriented chapel of All Saints
as a chapel of ease near their large, U-shaped, early Tudor house. It has a largely Gothic
doorway, four-centred with a hood mould. The S windows are round-headed but with
intersecting tracery. Inside, the chapel contains one of the few surviving Elizabethan
screens – functional and plain, except for two small, carved heads incorporated into the
fabric.
Sir Henry Willoughby arranged to have the chapel consecrated in 1632, citing the
difficulty experienced by local people in travelling to the parish church in winter. The
chalice, paten cover and two patens are from that date.
Sources/literature: Legg, pp. 130–8.
See also: main text.

ROEHAMPTON HOUSE (also known as ROEHAMPTON GROVE or GROVE HOUSE), LONDON (replaced)
Patron: Richard Weston (1577–1635), 1st Earl of Portland.
Date: 1632 event.
The chapel in the then Lord Weston's early 17th-century house was consecrated by
Laud, then Bishop of London, in 1632.
Sources/literature: Lambeth Palace Library, Register of Archbishop Abbot, ff. 126b, 127b;
Legg, p. 321; D. and S. Lysons, *Magna Britannia,* 1.1 (London, 1810), p. 315; H. Walpole,
Anecdotes of Painting in England, 1 (Strawberry Hill, 1765), p. 142; *VCH*, 4 (1912), pp.
79–80.
See also: main text.

ROYTON MANOR, LENHAM, KENT (house, much reduced, survives; chapel
demolished)
Patrons: Robert Atwater (d. 1522); Thomas Atwater (c.1500–47).
Dates: 1520–40 event.
Robert Atwater bought the house in the early 16th century. He, or just possibly Thomas
Atwater, installed carved wainscoting in the 'free' 14th-century chapel which stood
nearby, three lengths of which are believed to be identical with wooden panelling
brought from Royton to the neighbouring Chilston Park in c.1900. The panels
comprise bust reliefs, emblems of the Passion and arabesques, all framed within French-
style Renaissance arches, and are considered to be striking examples of early English
Renaissance craftsmanship.
Sources/literature: Hussey, p. 241; *CL*, 19 Dec 1952.
See also: main text.

RUG, DENBIGHSHIRE (house replaced; chapel survives, somewhat restored)
Patron: Sir William ('Old Blue Stockings') Salesbury (1580–1660).
Date: 1637 new build.
Salesbury (or Salisbury) inherited the Rug estate, with its fair-sized, 16th-century house,
in 1611. In 1637, he built a detached, correctly-oriented chapel of ease in the grounds
half a mile away. It is a plain, stone, single-cell building. Inside, the rich decorative

scheme relies on texts and medieval symbols, rather than biblical images, to convey its message. The beams of the open timber roof are painted with arabesques of trailing roses interspersed with bunches of grapes. Between them, the panels of the nave ceiling are painted in a swirling pattern of blues, presumably to represent rich fabric, while the E end is emphasised by stars and winged cherubs against a plain blue background. Roof bosses with a mixture of Christian and secular symbols mark the terminations and intersections of the main timbers. Simple, somewhat crudely modelled angels project from the base of the more important trusses, while winged and crowned cherub heads terminate the lesser timbers. Although there is a medieval-style E window with tracery, there is no evidence that painted glass was designed for it. Below the roof runs an elaborate and highly coloured frieze with panels depicting Christian symbols set amongst stylised foliage. Below that, the walls now consist largely of white plaster, but wall paintings have been preserved on the N wall to the E and W of the 19th-century screen. These are restrained: a Welsh biblical text in a strapwork frame and a sombre *memento mori* using symbols and texts to emphasise the inevitability of death. The decoration of the fittings, especially the pews, although not free from 19th-century interference, continues the general scheme. E of the screen, the family pew combines texts, arabesque patterns and a decorative frieze with flowers and symbolic beasts. The benches of the W part of the chapel are decorated with various beasts carved on the ends above a continuous frieze of thistles, foliage and grapes. There is an upper chapel at the W end. It seems that the chapel was never consecrated.

Sources/literature: C.M. Griffith, 'A Report on the Deanery of Penllyn and Edeirnion, by the Rev. John Wynn, 1730', *MHRS, Extra Publications*, 1.3 (1955), pp. 38-44; D.B. Hague, 'Rug Chapel, Corwen', *MHRS*, 3 (1957-60), pp. 167-83; W.F. Irvine, 'Notes on the History of Rug', *MHRS*, 1 (1949-51), pp. 77-82; 'Llangollen Report', *Archaeologia Cambriensis*, 90 (1935), pp. 343-5; B.G. Owens, 'Rug and Its Muniments', *MHRS*, 1 (1949-51), pp. 83-8; W.N. Yates, 'Rug Chapel, Llangar Church, Gwydir Uchaf Chapel' (D.M. Robinson and R. Avent, editors), (Cardiff, 1993); *CL*, 6 Oct. 1983.
See also: main text and Plate XXIV.

RUSHBROOKE HALL, SUFFOLK (demolished)
Patron: Sir Robert Jermyn (d. 1552).
Dates: 1552 event.
On attending Jermyn's funeral, the merchant Henry Machyn recorded in his diary that he possessed a 'godly chapel of syngyng men' at Rushbrooke.
Sources/literature: H. Machyn, 'Diary of Henry Machyn, Citizen and Merchant-Taylor of London from AD 1550 to AD 1563' (J. Nichols, editor), (London, 1848), pp. 27, 397.
See also: main text.

RYCOTE PARK, OXFORDSHIRE (house demolished; chapel survives)
Patrons: John Williams (d. 1559), Lord Williams; Francis Norreys (1578-c.1622), 1st Earl of Berkshire; Elizabeth Norreys (c.1602-1645), Lady Rycote and Edward Wray (c.1600-1658); James Bertie (1653-99), 1st Earl of Abingdon.
Dates: by 1559 event; c.1610-25 refit; 1680s alteration.
Williams bought the property from the Heron family, and is believed to have created a moated, brick, courtyard house. The detached, correctly-oriented, 15th century chapel stands near its site, and comprises a continuous nave and chancel, with a wagon roof. It was originally attached to a chantry. An elaborate Tudor doorway was installed (perhaps

by Williams before his death in 1559) towards the W end of the N wall to form the entrance from the house. There is a simpler entrance on the S side.

The chapel interior uses a mix of re-used medieval fittings with additions of *c*.1610-25 and *c*.1682, and is divided into two unequal cells by a screen whose central opening is arched and crested. The earlier alterations were presumably carried out by Berkshire, who inherited the house in 1601, and his daughter Elizabeth and son-in-law Wray. At this stage, the communion table was probably in the body of the E cell, and communicants sat round it. Above it and below the E window was a commandment board, now in the tower. The ceiling was painted blue with superimposed paper stars painted silver. Writing in 1735, Loveday noted that the house contained a 'popish' chapel or closet, complete with a wooden chalice of 1624. Mass may have been celebrated in this private closet, with Protestant services being held in the main chapel.

Abingdon inherited the house via his mother, Bridget, née Wray. His alterations to the E end in the 1680s ensured that the communion table could not be moved into the centre of the E cell, and included steps up to the E cell, and perhaps a marble floor. Here the family sat, while the servants sat or stood in the lower W cell.

Sources/literature: Knyff, pl. 34; Markham, pp. 216-7; J. Salmon, *Rycote Chapel* (London, 1996); *CL*, 27 Oct. 1928.

See also: main text and figs. 5.42, 6.28.

ST CLERE, KEMSING, KENT (house, somewhat altered, survives; chapel does not)

Patron: Sir John Sedley, Bt (*c*.1600-73).

Date: 1633 event.

Sedley had the chapel in his newly built, double-pile house consecrated in 1633.

Sources/literature: J. Newman, *The Buildings of England: West Kent and the Weald* (Harmondsworth, 1969), pp. 336-7.

ST MICHAEL'S MOUNT, CORNWALL (house and chapel, much restored, survive)

Patron: John St Aubyn (d. 1684).

Dates: post-1660 conversion.

The Mount had been a priory of Syon Abbey until the Dissolution. It then belonged to the Crown until its sale to Robert Cecil, later 1st Earl of Salisbury, in 1599. St Aubyn bought it in 1659, and subsequently converted the monastic church into a private chapel.

Sources/literature: J. St Aubyn, *St Michael's Mount* (St Ives, 1978).

ST PAUL'S COVENT GARDEN, LONDON (house demolished; chapel, altered, survives)

Patron: Francis Russell (1593-1641), 4th Earl of Bedford.

Dates: 1630s new build and events.

Architect: Inigo Jones (1573-1652).

A detached, single-cell chapel of brick 'sparingly dressed with stone, stucco and wood', it stands to the NE of the site of the demolished Bedford House, and was the most Classical ecclesiastical building of the Caroline period. It was financed and largely furnished by Bedford, and dominated Jones' piazza from its position at the centre of the W side. The roof sported a wooden cross at either end, but inside, the most expensive fittings were the pulpit and reading desk. The chapel was designed to be oriented to the W, with the grand E portico forming the entrance but, presumably following pressure by Laud, then bishop of London, a chancel was created at the E end and the communion table, set on black and white marble against the E wall, raised by one step and possibly railed. Bedford intended St Paul's as a parish church serving his residential development and Bedford house, but this was held to require an Act of Parliament (tricky during the '11 Years Tyranny'), and in 1638 it was consecrated as a chapel of ease to St Martin-in-the-Fields, only achieving parish status in 1646 (in *c*.1649, the marble floor was to be taken up and the altar table moved temporarily to the N wall).

Sources/literature: NA, PC 2/49, pp. 71, 145-8; D. Duggan, 'The Architectural Patronage of the 4th Earl of Bedford, 1587-1641' (unpublished Ph.D thesis, Courtauld Institute, University of London, 2002), pp.159-163; D. Duggan, '"London the Ring, Covent Garden the Jewell of that Ring": New Light on Covent Garden', *AH*, 43 (2000), pp. 152-4; 'The Parish of St Paul Covent Garden' *Survey of London*, 36 (London, 1970), pp. 64-122.

See also: main text.

SALISBURY HOUSE (THE STRAND), LONDON (demolished)

Patrons: Robert Cecil (1563-1612), 1st Earl of Salisbury; William Cecil (1591-1668), 2nd Earl of Salisbury.

Dates: 1602-10 rebuild; 1629-46 events.

Architect: perhaps Simon Basil (d. 1615).

Cecil bought Worcester House in the Strand in 1599, and rebuilt it from 1602 as Salisbury House. Building accounts show that Rowland Bucket designed and painted windows for the chapel. Some of the painted glass was installed by Richard Butler.

Subsequent inventories covering 1629-46 indicate that the upper chapel possessed a fireplace. It was richly decorated with crimson hangings embroidered with the Salisbury arms, and matching window cloths, while the furniture was covered with crimson damask, suggesting that upholstery and hangings followed a co-ordinated decorative scheme. It also contained two organs and (unusually) a pulpit. The communion table in the lower chapel was covered with a green cloth. No hangings were listed for the lower chapel, and it contained a motley collection of carpets and cushions. The impression remains that the lower chapel was virtually unused, that the family worshipped in the upper chapel, and that a so-called 'prayer house' was used for household religious gatherings.

Sources/literature: Hatfield House, Cecil MSS: Box C/8, Family Papers III, Bills A160/1 115v; M. Archer, 'Richard Butler, Glass-painter', 132, *Burlington Magazine* (1990), p. 310; Ricketts, *Cecil*.

See also: main text.

SHARLSTON HALL, WEST YORKSHIRE (house, altered, survives; chapel does not)

Patrons: Stringer family.

Dates: 16th-century addition.

A timber-framed wing built on to the 15th-century house in the 16th century may have been designed to house a chapel.

Sources/literature: Giles, pp. 20, 212.

SHEFFIELD CASTLE, SOUTH YORKSHIRE (demolished)
Patron: George Talbot (*c.*1528-90), 6th Earl of Shrewsbury.
Date: 1582 event.
Mary Queen of Scots was held prisoner for fourteen years in the stone-built, 13th-century castle under Shrewsbury's supervision. An inventory taken in 1582 mentions that the chapel contained wooden pulpits.
Sources/literature: S.L. Ticker, 'Descent of the Manor of Sheffield', *Journal of the British Archaeological Association*, 30 (1874), pp. 251-60.
See also: main text.

SHELTON HALL, NORFOLK (demolished)
Patron: Sir Ralph Shelton (d. 1498).
Dates: *c.*1480s new build.
Shelton built the moated, multi-courtyard, brick house and surrounded it with a battlemented wall. The two-storey, correctly-oriented, integral chapel to the S of the gatehouse in the E range possessed a large distinctive E window.
Sources/literature: J. Armstrong, 'Notes on the Church and Family of Shelton,' *Norfolk Archaeology*, 12 (1895), pp, 234-42; Emery, 2, pp. 149-51.
See also: main text and fig. 3.15.

SHERIFF HUTTON PARK, NORTH YORKSHIRE (house, remodelled, survives; chapel does not)
Patron: Sir Arthur Ingram (d. 1642).
Dates: by 1635 events.
This was Ingram's first country house, often described as a lodge. U-shaped and built of brick and building material removed from Sheriff Hutton Castle, it was finished in about 1624. The chapel was in one of the wings. By 1635, the organ and coloured glass had been removed for installation in Ingram's new chapel at Temple Newsam (*q.v.*).
Sources/literature: *CL,* 8, 15 Sep. 1966.

SHINGAY, CAMBRIDGESHIRE (demolished)
Patron: John Russell (d. 1681).
Date: 1644 event.
In March 1644, Dowsing noted that the chapel contained a crucifix and pictures. Russell was the third child of Francis Russell, 4th Earl of Bedford (*q.v.* St Paul's Covent Garden and Woburn).
Sources/literature: Dowsing, p. 270.

SHURLAND, ISLE OF SHEPPEY, KENT (a ruin)
Patron: Sir Thomas Cheyney (d. *c.*1556).
Dates: 1520s new build.
Cheyney presumably finished building his large, brick and stone, multi-courtyard house, which commanded an important defensive position near the E Kent coast, in time for Henry VIII's visit in 1532. The layout, with numerous secondary courts in addition to the familiar base court, was perhaps conditioned by the need to house the large number of Cheyney's retainers (at least 400). The chapel, too, was unusually large. It was correctly-oriented and positioned at right angles to the two-storey E range. Retainers would probably have entered the chapel at the W end via the open *loggia* in the E range,

while the family would have used the long gallery above.
Sources/literature: NA, Royal Sequestration Order, SP 12/75 and 87; J. Cave-Brown, 'Shurland House', *AC,* 23 (1898) pp. 86–93.
See also: main text and Plate I.

SISSINGHURST CASTLE, KENT (house, much reduced, survives; chapel does not)
Patron: Sir John Baker (1608–53).
Dates: post–1623 addition; 1637 or 1639 event.
Baker inherited the magnificent, largely Elizabethan, tower and courtyard house – which may well have had a chapel in its early Tudor form - from his father in 1623. He added a chapel, pleading that it was not possible for him and his family to attend the parish church at Cranbrook 'without much trouble and danger'. All that is known of its position is that it was 'apart from the ordinary part of the house'.
The chapel was consecrated in 1637 or 1639.
Sources/literature: Legg, p. 322; N. Nicholson, *Sissinghurst Castle* (1964), pp. 23, 27–8.

SLAUGHAM PLACE, EAST SUSSEX (a ruin)
Patrons: Richard Covert (d. 1579); Sir Walter Covert (1543–1631).
Dates: Elizabethan new build; late Elizabethan alterations.
The single-courtyard house was probably built by Richard Covert. A survey by Thorpe shows that the small, probably incorrectly-oriented, single-storey chapel was situated across a side range on the ground floor between a wine cellar and a bedchamber. Separated by an openwork screen from a passage leading to the great stair, it appears to have been one of the earliest examples of an assembly chapel.
Thorpe prepared proposals for alterations on Walter Covert inheriting the house in 1579. They included moving the chapel to a position formerly occupied by the great stair. Slightly larger than its predecessor, it too was to be incorrectly-oriented and, separated from the parlour on two sides by an openwork screen, to retain the character of an assembly chapel. The liturgical E window was shown well off-centre to match the overall symmetry of the facade.
Sources/literature: T239–40; T239–40 Insets A & B.
See also: main text and fig. 4.4.

SMALLBRIDGE HALL, SUFFOLK (house, reduced, survives; chapel does not)
Patrons: Waldegrave family.
Date: 1644 event.
In February 1644, Dowsing visited the substantial, brick, 16th-century house and ordered the destruction of pictures in the integral household chapel. He had been unable to carry out the instruction himself because no one could find the chapel key.
Sources/literature: Dowsing, p. 248.
See also: main text.

SMITHILLS HALL, LANCASHIRE (house, restored and extended, survives; chapel survives with internal restoration)
Patron: Andrew Barton (a. early 16th century).
Dates: early 16th-century alterations.
In extending his half-timbered, 15th-century, courtyard house Barton concentrated on

the E wing, incorporating a correctly-oriented, integral, double-height, stone chapel and adjacent vestry and withdrawing room. Tudor heraldic glass survives in the E window (containing Archbishop Cranmer's arms). There is what appears to be a 17th-century corridor leading W from the withdrawing room to the chapel.

Sources/literature: *VCH*, 5 (1991), pp. 11-14; J.T. Smith, 'Lancashire and Cheshire Houses: Some Problems of Architecture and Social History', *AJ*, 127 (1970), pp. 163-5; Westfall, pp. 23-4; *CL*, 8 Nov. 1902, 2 Oct. 1929.

SNAPE CASTLE, NORTH YORKSHIRE (house largely a ruin; chapel survives as a parish church)

Patrons: Thomas Cecil (1542-1623), 1st Earl of Exeter; John Cecil (1648-1700), 5th Earl of Exeter.

Dates: 1580s event; late 1680s event.

Thomas Cecil acquired the large, 15th-century, courtyard house, formerly the marital home of Catherine Parr, in 1577 on the death of his father-in-law, the 4th Lord Latimer. He transformed it into a castellated manor house. While he probably adapted the interior of the (initially detached) chapel in the S range to Protestant worship, he left its splendid pre-Reformation windows intact.

John Cecil commissioned illusionistic paintings for the chapel from Verrio in the late 1680s. His coved ceiling survives – in poor condition, doubtless due to the chapel's use as a 19th-century grain store.

Sources/literature: T. Horsfall, *The Manor of Well and Snape* (Leeds, 1912); Ricketts, *Cecil*; *CL*, 6 Mar. 1986.

See also: main text.

SOUTHAMPTON HOUSE (later BEDFORD HOUSE), BLOOMSBURY, LONDON (demolished)

Patrons: Thomas Wriothesley (1607-67), 4th Earl of Southampton; Lady Rachel Russell (1637-1723), née Wriothesley.

Dates: 1665 event; 1670 event.

Southampton built the house 1657-60 as part of his Bloomsbury Square development. Evelyn dined there in 1665, and noted that it contained 'a pretty Cedar Chapell'.

In 1670, Evelyn attended the wedding of his niece in the chapel. By that time Rachel Russell had inherited it from her father. A year earlier she had married William, Lord Russell, the eldest son of the 5th Earl (subsequently 1st Duke) of Bedford, and the house later became known as Bedford House.

Sources/literature: Evelyn, 3, pp. 398, 551.

STANTON HARCOURT MANOR, OXFORDSHIRE (tower containing chapel survives, but little else)

Patrons: Harcourt family.

Dates: late Tudor addition.

The medieval, Harcourt family house comprised buildings irregularly grouped around a courtyard. The chapel is in a *c.*1470-80 four-storey tower – Pope later worked on his translation of *The Iliad* on an upper floor. A family room upstairs had a squint above the chancel arch giving on to the altar, while the servants congregated in the nave. The chapel doorway is probably Elizabethan.

Sources/literature: J. Sherwood and N. Pevsner, *The Buildings of England: Oxfordshire* (Harmondsworth, 1975), pp. 781-3.

STAUNTON HAROLD HALL, LEICESTERSHIRE (house replaced; chapel survives)
Patrons: Sir Robert Shirley, Bt (1629-56); Sir Seymour Shirley, Bt (b.1647).
Dates: 1653-65 new build.
Robert Shirley started building a detached, correctly-oriented chapel near his medieval and 16th-century castellated house that had been updated in the early 17th century, and already contained a chapel. Begun as an act of defiance towards the Commonwealth, the new chapel was finished by the guardians of his son, Seymour, after the Restoration. It resembles a richly decorated, Gothic, parish church, but with some Classical motifs. Inside, it both contains a narthex and follows a liturgical two-cell arrangement. It is not clear whether there were moveable kneeling forms in front of the altar table. A commandment board was set up over the altar, and textiles also focused attention on the E end.
Sources/literature: Dowsing, pp. 337–50; Knyff, pl. 43; G. Jackson Stops and J. Pipkin, *The English Country House, a Grand Tour* (London, 1985*)*, p. 212; J. Simmons and H. Colvin, 'Staunton Harold Church', *AJ,* 112, (1955), pp 173-4; *CL*, 5, 12 Apr. 1913.
See also: main text and figs. 5.28, 5.29, 5.30, 5.31.

STEANE PARK, NORTHAMPTONSHIRE (fragments of original house survive; chapel survives)
Patrons: Sir Thomas Crewe (1565-1634); John Crewe (1598-1679), 1st Lord Crewe.
Dates: 1620-2 new build; post-1634 alterations.
Sir Thomas Crewe, a leading Puritan, acquired the largely medieval, U-shaped house on marrying one of the five daughters of the former owner, Reginald Bray, and buying the shares of the other four. He built the detached, correctly-oriented, complex, Gothic-style chapel at right angles to the N of the house to replace the medieval parish church of the deserted local village. He may have re-used its windows in his new chapel. Inside, the ecclesiastical standards of high nave with low aisles combine with the architectural articulation to create a very original Puritan interior.
An ornate, Ionic door was inserted into the S wall, perhaps by Crewe's son John, after he inherited the house in 1634, to provide more direct access for the household.
Sources/literature: R. Sibbes, *The Brides Longing for her Bridegroomes Second Coming* (London, 1638); *CL*, 2 Jul. 1938.
See also: main text and Plates XIV, XV.

STOCKELD PARK, NORTH YORKSHIRE (house replaced)
Patron: William Middleton (d. 1614).
Date: 1614 event.
An inventory taken on Middleton's death refers to a chapel chamber containing a bedstead, and a chapel parlour that contained bedding.
Sources/literature: Crossley, pp. 170-81.

STOCKTON HOUSE, WILTSHIRE (house and shell of possible chapel survive)
Patrons: Topp family.
Dates: mid-17th-century new build.
John Topp (d. 1640) built a compact, gabled, rectangular, late Elizabethan manor house of banded flint and stone. Linked to the W front at right-angles, and running E/W, is a later rectangular building that may have been intended as a (roughly correctly-oriented) linked chapel. It is faced with chequered flint and stone, and perhaps dates from the

Commonwealth. The S facade has three distinctive windows below a string-course. The W wall has an oval window. Nothing survives of the original interior fittings. There is a large, supposedly Tudor, fireplace at the E end, flanked by two doorways, one leading to an annex with a gabled roof that is said to have been the minister's quarters, the other to a possible vestry.

Sources/literature: *CL*, 9 Feb. 1984.

See also: main text.

STOKE BRUERNE PARK, NORTHAMPTONSHIRE (central block destroyed; shell of possible chapel, somewhat altered, survives)

Patron: Sir Francis Crane (d. 1636).

Dates: *c*.1629-35 new build.

Architect: attributed to Inigo Jones (1573-1652).

Crane built his new, Palladian-style house on land granted to him in 1627 by Charles I, possibly utilising lead purloined from the neighbouring Collyweston (*q.v.*). Colen Campbell attributed the design to Inigo Jones. Campbell's plan shows what seems to be a correctly-oriented, single-cell, double-height chapel occupying the E pavilion. It is not known how the interior was fitted out and decorated.

Sources/literature: *VB*, 3 (London, 1725), pl. 9.

See also: main text and figs. 5.16, 5.17, 5.18.

STOKE NEWINGTON (Sir Thomas Kytson's house), LONDON (demolished)

Patron: Sir Thomas Kytson (d. 1540).

Dates: pre 1540 event.

The chapel contained a hanging depicting St Jerome.

Sources/literature: none given.

STOKE PARK, SUFFOLK (demolished)

Patron: Thomas Howard (1473-1554), 3rd Duke of Norfolk.

Dates: 1531-2 event.

A cross and two images were taken out of the detached chapel in the park and thrown into nearby water after Norfolk had removed to Kenninghall (*q.v.*). See also Tendring Hall below.

Sources/literature: J. Foxe, *Acts and Monuments* (J. Pratt, editor) 4, (1870), p. 707; *The Register or Chronicle of Butley Priory, Suffolk* (A.G. Dickens editor), (Winchester, 1951).

STOW, CORNWALL (demolished)

Patron: John Grenville (1628-1701), 1st Earl of Bath.

Date: *c*.1680 new build.

Grenville inherited the site and built an H-plan house modelled on Clarendon House (*q.v.*). On its demolition some 50 years later, panelling and the pulpit from the chapel (location unknown) were removed to the new chapel at Stowe in Buckinghamshire, and from there to the new (1927-8) chapel at Stowe School.

Sources/literature: 'The Prideaux Collection of Topographical Drawings' (J. Harris, editor), *AH*, 7 (1964), pp. 37, 104.

STRATTON HOUSE, HAMPSHIRE (replaced)

Patron: Lady Rachel Russell (1637-1723), née Wriothesley.

Date: 1684 event.

Lady Russell was given the substantial three-storey stone house by her father, Thomas Wriothesley, 4th Earl of Southampton. In 1684, after the death of her husband, William, Lord Russell (executed in 1683 on being found guilty of complicity in the Rye House plot), she consulted a spiritual counsellor about finding a chaplain for her chapel in the house.

Sources/literature: *The Letters of Lady Rachel Russell* (Thomas Selwood, editor), 1 (London, 1792), pp. 256, 285-6.

STUBLEY (OLD) HALL, LANCASHIRE (house, reconstructed and reduced, survives; chapel does not)

Patron: Robert Holt (d. 1560).

Date: 1561 event.

Holt inherited the *c*.1529 U-shaped house of brick and stone in 1556. An inventory taken on his death mentions a 'chappel chamber' but no chapel. However, *VCH* states that there was originally a chapel in the house, probably at the E end of the W wing.

Sources/literature: *VCH*, 5 (1991), pp. 223-4.

SYON HOUSE, MIDDLESEX (house, restored, survives; chapel does not)

Patron: Henry Percy (1564-1632), 9th Earl of Northumberland ('the Wizard Earl').

Date: 1633 event.

The original house was built from 1547 by Edward Seymour, Duke of Somerset ('Protector Somerset'; *c*.1506-52) on the site of the dissolved Syon Abbey. Northumberland was granted the lease in 1597 by Elizabeth I, and full possession by James I soon after. Retaining the shell of Somerset's house, and despite his imprisonment in the Tower 1605-22, he comprehensively rebuilt it from 1603, creating a square, battlemented, courtyard house with four corner towers. An inventory following his death refers to an upper chamber 'used for a chapel' on the S side of the house whose furnishings included a table, hangings, carpets, cushions and forms. It also mentions a chamber next to the 'oulde' chapel, and a 'chamber next to the chappell chamber', as well as 'a chamber where prayers were said'.

Sources/literature: *The Household Papers of Henry Percy, 9th Earl of Northumberland (1564-1632)*, (G.R. Batho, editor), (London, 1962), p. 127.

TABLEY HALL, CHESHIRE (house a ruin; chapel, somewhat altered, survives on a new site)

Patron: Sir Peter Leycester, Bt (1614-78).

Dates: 1674-8 new build.

The chapel was detached and stood on an island next to the medieval house that had been updated in the 16th and early 17th centuries. Leycester carried out further alterations to the house in the 1670s before erecting the chapel. It replaced a medieval chapel nearby that was shared by the Leycester and Daniell families. Moved in the early 20th century, its original orientation is not known. Built of red brick in the shape of a rectangle with curved gables at either end, it uses a not particularly skilful mix of Classical and earlier forms. Inside, the vault over the nave area may have been clouded, with stars towards the E end. Simple, almost Jacobean, perspective panelling runs round the walls, each panel being flanked by Ionic pilasters which may have been picked out in gilt. The cornice above the pilasters contains a frieze with winged cherub heads. The pulpit, with painted sounding board and a reading pew next to it, is on the S side: although clearly an important part of the fittings, it does not outrank the communion table, which is raised and protected by an altar rail. A W screen − the last to feature in a private chapel in the 17th century − separates the main chapel from an ante-chapel. It has a central open pediment on columns surmounted by a statue of St Peter. Two distinctive family pews stand at the W end beneath the singers' gallery. The entrance, also beneath the gallery, is at the W end of the S wall.

Sources/literature: Leycester's uncatalogued documents in the John Rylands Library, Manchester; *CL*, 14, 28 Jul. 1923.
See also: main text and figs. 6.24, 6.25.

TEDDINGTON, LONDON (demolished)
Patron: Thomas Wentworth (1591-1667), 1st Earl of Cleveland.
Date: 1631 event.
The household chapel was consecrated in 1631.
Sources/literature: Legg, p. 321.

TEMPLE NEWSAM, WEST YORKSHIRE (house, remodelled, survives: chapel shell survives)
Patrons: Thomas Darcy (1467-1537), Lord Darcy; Matthew Stewart (1516-71), 4th Earl of Lennox; Sir Arthur Ingram I (d. 1642); Sir Arthur Ingram II (1596-1655); Thomas Ingram (1632-60); Henry Ingram (1641-66), 1st Viscount Irwin.
Dates: 1521 event; 1565 event; 1622-38 rebuild; 1644 event; 1660s events.
Darcy built the large, early Tudor, one or two-courtyard, brick house between 1489 and 1535 on a site that had been granted to the family by Edward III after the suppression of the Knights Templar − from whom it derived its name. An Inventory of 1521 lists a chapel, apparently on the first floor in the W or S wing.
The house passed to Lennox on Darcy's execution in 1537 for his part in the Pilgrimage of Grace (Lennox's son, Earl of Darnley, husband of Mary Queen of Scots, was born there in 1545). A 1565 inventory, taken when the house was confiscated by the Crown, indicates that the chapel was no longer in use, and lists two related rooms: a 'Chambre within the Chapell' containing a bedstead, and a 'chapell chambre' containing bedsteads, a lute, a crossbow, quivers of bolts and arrows, a curtain, cloths and other articles. Judging by the position of these rooms, it is possible that the chapel was on the W side of the N range, near the great chamber and main apartments in the W range, and away from the great hall in the S range.
Sir Arthur Ingram I bought the house in 1622, and created an essentially Jacobean U-shaped house of brick with stone dressings by demolishing the E wing, and rebuilding the S and N wings. His integral, correctly-oriented, double-height chapel was at the E end of the N wing, possibly replacing its 16th-century predecessor. In 1631, an organ was transferred from the chapel at Ingram's earlier country house, Sheriff Hutton Park (*q.v.*), which later also lost its coloured glass to the new chapel. A pulpit was installed by 1636. In the same year, the pews were painted and gilded, a start was made on the plasterwork, and John Carleton began work on the painted decoration comprising fixed panels and canvases.
In 1644, 140ft of 'new glass' was ordered for the chapel, perhaps indicating that Sir Arthur Ingram II removed papist imagery following his father's death.
Inventories of 1660 and 1666 indicate that the chapel was in use, though sparsely furnished.

Sources/literature: Knyff, pl. 42; Leeds City Art Galleries Collection, 38.1/79; West Yorkshire Archive Service, Leeds: WYL 150 TN EA3, 3/10, 13/18 (i) & WYL (Pawson MSS) 178/1, 2, 14; E.W. Crossley, 'A Temple Newsam Inventory, 1565', *YAJ*, 25 (1918-19), pp. 91-100; R. Fawcett, 'The Early Tudor House in the Light of Recent Excavations', *LAC*, 70 (1972), pp. 5-11; C. Gilbert, 'Light on Sir Arthur Ingram's Reconstruction of Temple Newsam 1622-38', *LAC*, 51 (1963), pp. 6-12; D. Hill, 'Archives and Archaeology at Temple Newsam House', *LAC*, 89 (1981), pp. 22-30; A. Robertson, 'The Jacobean Chapel at Temple Newsam', *LAC*, 76 (1975), pp. 21-3; A. Wells-Cole 'The Dining Room at Temple Newsam', *LAC*, 110 (1992), pp.16-24.
See also: main text and fig. 5.15.

TENDRING HALL, SUFFOLK (demolished)
Patrons: Thomas Windsor (*c.*1627-87), 7th Lord Windsor and 1st Earl of Plymouth.
Date: 1644 event.
Windsor presumably inherited the house on the death of his uncle, Thomas, 6th Lord Windsor (d. 1641). In February 1644, Dowsing destroyed pictures and a crucifix in the detached chapel in the park. It also contained a window showing a kneeling figure of a Howard wearing a heraldic tabard over his armour. This chapel had been an earlier victim of iconoclasm when part of the 3rd Duke of Norfolk's estate of Stoke Park (*q.v.*).
Sources/literature: Dowsing, p. 248.
See also: main text.

THANET HOUSE, ALDERSGATE STREET, LONDON (demolished)
Patron: Nicholas Tufton (1631-79), 3rd Earl of Thanet.
Date: 1665 event.
Lady Anne Clifford recorded that her granddaughter, Lady Francis Tufton, married Henry Drax in the chapel at Thanet House in 1665.
Sources/literature: Clifford, p. 180.
See also: main text.

THE HERMITAGE, WORCESTERSHIRE (disappeared)
Patron: John Folliott (d. *c.*1579).
Date: 1579 event.
The house was near the Folliott estate of Pirton Court (*q.v.*). An inventory taken after Folliott's death lists a chapel (contents not shown) and a 'chamber over the chappele' containing bedding.
Sources/literature: Wanklyn, pp. 59-60.

THE VYNE, HAMPSHIRE (house largely demolished; chapel, much altered, survives)
Patrons: William Sandys (*c.*1470-1540), 1st Lord Sandys; Chaloner Chute (*c.*1595-1659).
Dates: early 16th-century alterations; by 1653 event.
The original chapel was created in the 12th century because the house was so far from the parish church at what is now Sherborne St John. Sandys inherited what was a small manor house with other freestanding buildings in 1496, and created a huge, red-brick house with three courtyards in the first years of the new century - most

of which was pulled down in the mid–17th century. It seems that Sandys' correctly-oriented, double-height chapel may have occupied part of the gatehouse (E) range. On the ground floor, there was a vestry on the S side, with a separate entrance to the main chapel. The flooring may have consisted of majolica tiles. The 1542 inventory shows that the chapel was richly endowed with silver and gilt plate, and contained colourful and costly tapestries, canopies, hangings and altar cloths, all with a mix of biblical and floral motifs, and designed to emphasise the E end. Tapestries on the walls of the Sandys' first floor closets contained floral and heraldic motifs.

Chute bought the house in 1653, and partially rebuilt it. By that time, a Crucifixion in stained glass, probably from the ruined Chapel of the Holy Ghost, Basingstoke (*q.v.*), may have already been installed in the chapel E window.

Sources/literature: M. Howard, *The Vyne* (London, 1998); M. Howard and E. Wilson, *The Vyne, a Tudor House Revealed* (London, 2003); H. Wayment 'The Stained Glass of the Chapel of the Vyne and the Chapel of the Holy Ghost, Basingstoke', *A*, 107 (1982), pp. 141–52; *CL*, 10, 17 Apr. 2003.

See also: main text and figs. 3.17, 3.18; Plates III, IV.

THEOBALDS, HERTFORDSHIRE (house largely demolished; chapel does not survive)

Patron: William Cecil (1520-98), Lord Burghley.

Dates: from 1564 new build.

Building on the site of an old manor house, Burghley created over the years a large house, in his own words 'glorious and elegant to be seen', with three main courtyards. It was surveyed by Thorpe, probably in 1606 and shortly before ownership passed to James I. The two-storey chapel ran along the S range of the ground floor of the middle court, and was probably correctly-oriented. There was no E window because the E end was an internal wall. There was one external entrance in the NW corner, and an internal entrance in the W wall leading to an upper chapel or raised pew, presumably for the family. Four steps led down from this raised area to the main chapel.

Sources/literature: T245; J. Nichols, *Progresses and Public Processions of Queen Elizabeth*, 1 (1823), p. 201; Ricketts, *Cecil*; J. Summerson, 'The Building of Theobalds 1564–85', *A*, 97 (1959), pp. 107–26.

See also: main text.

THORESBY HOUSE, NOTTINGHAMSHIRE (destroyed)

Patrons: William Pierrepoint (1662-90), 4th Earl of Kingston; Evelyn Pierrepoint (*c.*1665-1726), 1st Duke of Kingston.

Dates: 1683-7 alterations; 1695-6 refit.

Architect: possibly William Talman (1650-1719).

The 4th Earl inherited the existing early to mid–17th-century house in 1682, and remodelled it into a square, brick, courtyard house with stone dressings, possibly to a design by William Talman. The integral, correctly-oriented, rectangular chapel was to the NW of the courtyard, and evidently exerted an important influence on the overall plan. Particular care was taken in planning a processional route to the upper chapel. The W and S walls of the chapel were lit by two windows each, none of which were probably distinctive. The E wall and N walls were internal. The chapel contained paintings by Laguerre.

The chapel was refitted in 1695-6 after a fire that broke out soon after the earlier work on the house was completed. Four columns supported the gallery.

Sources/literature: BL, Egerton MSS 3256; *VB*, I (London, 1715), pp. 90–91; G. Vertue, *Note Books*, 6 (Oxford, 1955), pp. 24, 73; J. Harris, 'Thoresby House, Nottinghamshire', *AH*, 4 (1961), pp. 10–21; J. Harris, 'Thoresby Concluded', *AH*, 6 (1963), pp. 103–5; G.F. Webb, 'Letters and Drawings of N. Hawksmoor', *WS*, 19 (1931), p. 126.

See also: main text and fig. 6.11.

THORNBURY CASTLE, GLOUCESTERSHIRE (house, restored, survives; chapel does not)

Patron: Edward Stafford (1478–1521), 3rd Duke of Buckingham.

Dates: *c*.1511–21 alterations.

Buckingham acquired the medieval house, consisting of a hall (*c*.1330), chapel (1435), and other rooms and lodgings set round an inner court, along with subsidiary ranges and courts, in *c*.1498. Though unfinished at the time of his execution in 1521, he had nonetheless transformed it into a magnificent, stone, double-courtyard mansion in which Mary I subsequently spent her childhood and Henry VIII lived later with Anne Boleyn. The chapel, which was E of the great hall, was divided into an inner and outer chapel, with the latter consisting of a lower area where members of the household stood, and a higher level with two pews or closets for the duke and duchess. The inner chapel contained benches facing each other across the chancel for priests, clerks and other chapel staff, who numbered about 30, including 18 singing men and 9 boys. The new build included a gallery leading from the principal lodgings both to the chapel, and from the castle to a pew constructed beside the N chancel window of the parish church.

Sources/literature: BL, Stowe MSS 795, f. 59 ff (1583 survey); Staffordshire RO, D641 (accounts); J. Gage, 'The Household Book of Edward Stafford, Duke of Buckingham', *A*, 25 (1834), pp. 311–27; A.D.K. Hawkyard, 'Thornbury Castle', *Transactions of the Bristol and Gloucestershire Archaeological Society*, 95 (1977) pp. 51–8; Leland, pt. 5.10, pp. 99–100.

See also: main text.

THORNTON COLLEGE, LINCOLNSHIRE (house demolished; ruins of abbey/college survive)

Patron: Sir Vincent Skinner (d. *c*.1615).

Dates: 1602–15 new build.

Skinner bought the site of the dissolved Thornton Abbey, which had been transformed into a college by Henry VIII and suppressed under Edward VI, in 1602. His first house collapsed and had to be replaced. Thorpe's plan shows a rectangular narthex type chapel with a four-light window at the liturgical E end, and separated from the ante-chapel, also with a four-light window, by an openwork screen.

Sources/literature: T67–9.

See also: main text.

TITCHFIELD ABBEY (PLACE HOUSE), HAMPSHIRE (a ruin)

Patron: Thomas Wriothesley (1505–50), 1st Earl of Southampton.

Date: 1538 event.

Southampton acquired the dissolved 13th-century abbey in 1537 and converted it into a house. In writing to him in 1538 about pulling down the abbey church, the Royal Commissioners implied that he would be building a chapel there.

Sources/literature: *Letters & Papers Foreign and Domestic of the Reign of Henry VIII 1509-*

47 (J.S. Brewer, J. Gairdner and R.H. Brodie, editors), 13.1 (London, 1892), pp. 6-7; W.H. St J. Hope, 'The Making of Place House at Titchfield near Southampton', *AJ*, 63 (1906), pp. 231-43; Howard, pp. 139-42, 149-51, 206.

TODDINGTON MANOR, BEDFORDSHIRE (demolished)

Patrons: Henry Cheney (d. 1587), Lord Cheney; Thomas Wentworth (1591-1667), 1st Earl of Cleveland.

Dates: from *c*.1559 new build; 1644 event.

Cheney inherited the site from his father in 1559, and built a large, courtyard house of three storeys, entered through an arch in the S range. The hall was in the N range with the high end to the W, and possessed a magnificent central bay window also lighting the parlour and great chamber above. The E range contained offices and the chapel, which appeared to flank the inner wall of the tennis court.

Cleveland inherited the estate from Cheney's widow, in 1614. An inventory taken in 1644 lists the contents of the chapel as a Bible, two desks and a cushion for the pulpit.

Sources/literature: T234; BL, Survey by Ralph Agas (1581), Add MS 38065H; R. Lee, *Law and Local Society in the time of Charles I: Bedfordshire and the Civil War*, (Bedford, 1986), pp. 144-9; *CL*, 23 Mar. 1961.

TOFT HALL, CHESHIRE (house, much altered, survives; chapel does not)

Patrons: Leycester family, (possibly George Leycester (a. late 17th century).

Date: 1669 event.

Peter Leycester of Tabley Hall noted that, by 1669, the chapel had been converted to secular use. A brick H-plan house was built on the site, probably by George Leycester, in the late 17th century. It is not clear whether it was this or its predecessor which contained the converted chapel.

Sources/literature: P. Leycester, *Historical Antiquities* (London, 1674), pp. 193-7, quoted in Cliffe, *World*, p. 34.

TONG, SITTINGBOURNE, KENT (disappeared)

Patron: Henry Fitzroy (1519-36), Duke of Richmond.

Date: 1526 event; 1536 event.

An inventory of 1526 indicates that a proportion of Fitzroy's 'chapelle stuff', including altar cloths and vestments, was at his manor of Tong.

Nichols asserts that, at the time of Fitzroy's death in 1536, and notwithstanding the fact that Collyweston (*q.v.*) was his main residence, the principal furniture of his chapel was at Tong which, he suggests, was near Sittingbourne in Kent.

Sources/literature: J.G. Nichols, 'Memoir of Henry Fitzroy, Duke of Richmond and Somerset', *Camden Miscellany,* 3 (1855), p. vi; J.G. Nichols (editor), 'Inventory of the Goods of Henry Fitzroy, Duke of Richmond', *Camden Miscellany,* 3 (1855), pp. 13-14.

TOWNELEY HALL, LANCASHIRE (house, much altered, and chapel, moved and enlarged, survive)

Patron: Sir John Towneley (1473-1541).

Date: *c*.1515 new build.

Towneley built a chapel in the (possibly detached) E range of his medieval courtyard house whose great hall occupied the W range. The chapel was next to a sacristy, and below the nursery, Towneley's chamber and the library, from which there was said to be

access to a family upper chapel. The E range was demolished in 1712, and the chapel moved, with some of its furnishings, to the first floor of the NW corner. It is divided into a nave and chancel. There are three windows and a door leading to a small priest's chamber on the W side, and a four-light window in the liturgical E wall. The chancel has blind Gothic tracery with a running vine border. The original altar rail is in the Towneley Chapel in St Peter's church, Burnley. The ceiling is panelled and perhaps dates from Towneley's time, but the rest probably dates from the early 17th century (the Towneley family remained Roman Catholic throughout their tenure).
Sources/literature: S. Bourne, *An Introduction to the Architectural History of Towneley Hall* (Burnley, 1979); *VCH*, 4 (1990), pp. 457–63.

TRELOWARREN, CORNWALL (house, much altered, survives; chapel, lengthened and Gothicised, survives)
Patrons: Francis Vyvyan (d. 1635); Sir Richard Vyvyan, Bt (d. 1662).
Dates: 1622-38 new build.
The Vyvyans acquired the house by marriage in the 15th century. From 1622, consideration was given to building a chapel, either as a detached building or one that formed a projecting wing of the existing W facing, mid-15th-century house. It was to have a large E window containing plain glass, five windows in both N and S walls and a painted boarded roof. In 1637, Richard Vyvyan agreed that construction should start. The end result was a U-shaped house, of which the linked, five bay chapel formed the S wing. The accounts mention four pews with partitions, a communion table and desk. There was also a pulpit.
Sources/literature: Cornwall RO, V/EC/4/2, 8-9; *CL*, 8 Apr. 1916, 22 July 1999.
See also: main text.

TYTTENHANGER, HERTFORDSHIRE (house and chapel, somewhat altered, survive)
Patron: Sir Henry Blount (1602-82).
Dates: from 1655-60 new build.
Architect: possibly Peter Mills (1598-1670).
Blount inherited the site in 1654, and built a relatively unambitious, double- pile, brick house with a simple, integral chapel (about 18ft x 24ft), on the second floor.
Sources/literature: Hertfordshire RO, D/EC/P2; *CL*, 11 Oct. 1919.
See also: main text and figs. 5.25, 5.26.

UGBROOKE PARK, DEVON (house, rebuilt, survives; chapel, greatly altered, survives)
Patron: Thomas Clifford (1630-1673), 1st Lord Clifford.
Date: 1671 event.
The chapel in the house built by Clifford (and where the (Roman Catholic) poet and dramatist John Dryden is said to have stayed) was consecrated according to Protestant rites in 1671. Clifford declared himself to be Roman Catholic in 1672.
Sources/literature: *CL*, 20, 27 Jul., 3 Aug. 1967.

UMBERLEIGH HOUSE, DEVON (house, remodelled, survives; chapel demolished)
Patrons: Bassett family.

Dates: early Tudor event.

An early Tudor chancel screen was installed in the private chapel. Now at Atherington parish church, it has hinged central doors and a solid lower level above which are cusped openings and delicate filigree cresting.

Sources/literature: Cherry, pp. 139-40.

See also: main text and fig. 3.19.

UTKINTON HALL, CHESHIRE (house, reduced, survives; chapel does not)

Patrons: Sir John Crewe I (d. 1670); Sir John Crewe II (1641-1711).

Dates: 1635 event; 1644 event; 1672 and 1690 events.

Sir John Crewe I's wife Mary inherited the Elizabethan courtyard house on the death of her father, Sir John Done, in 1629. Crewe, who was the second son of Sir Ranulph Crewe of Crewe Hall (*q.v.*), had the chapel consecrated by bishop John Bridgeman of Chester in 1635.

In 1672 and 1690 Sir John Crewe II had the chapel licensed for nonconformist worship. Cliffe believes that this could be a different chapel from that consecrated in 1635.

Sources/literature: Cliffe, pp. 193, 211; Ormerod, 2, pp. 249, 251.

WAKERLEY, NORTHAMPTONSHIRE (demolished)

Patron: Sir Richard Cecil (1570-1633).

Dates: by 1633 new build.

There was a chapel in the large house built by Cecil. He was the second son of Thomas Cecil, 1st Earl of Exeter, and the father of the 3rd Earl.

Sources/literature: Burghley House, Exeter MS 28/56.

WALTONS, ESSEX (house, much altered, survives; chapel does not)

Patron: William Maynard (1586-1640), 1st Lord Maynard.

Date: 1636 event.

Maynard had the chapel in his U-plan Elizabethan house consecrated in 1636.

Sources/literature: NA, Prob 11/85, ff. 185, 190v., 194.

WARE PARK, HERTFORDSHIRE (house replaced)

Patron: Thomas Fanshawe (1596-1665), 1st Viscount Fanshawe.

Dates: by 1661 event.

Fanshawe inherited the house, built by his grandfather in 1570-5, from his father in 1616. Bishop Cosin of Durham consecrated his chapel in 1660 or 1661.

Sources/literature: Legg, pp. 218-223; Smith, p. 201.

WARWICK CASTLE, WARWICKSHIRE (house, somewhat altered, survives; chapel, remodelled, survives)

Patron: Fulke Greville (1554-1628), 1st Lord Brooke.

Dates: by 1617 rebuild.

James I conveyed the house, then a fortified medieval ruin, to Greville in 1604. The latter had thoroughly restored much of the S range by 1617. His work is thought to have included rebuilding the existing, correctly-oriented, integral chapel — which had an external entrance at the W end, and an internal entrance in its south wall which opened on to a passage to the great hall.

Sources/literature: Tyack, pp. 200-8.

WATER EATON, OXFORDSHIRE (house and chapel survive)
Patrons: Frere family.
Dates: *c*.1610 new build.
The detached, correctly-oriented, double-cell chapel, built of stone in the grounds of the Elizabethan house, may have served as a chapel of ease as well as a family chapel. The usually quoted date of 1610 has no particular provenance. Externally, the two cells are clearly distinguished by a variation in the roofline. The fenestration is regular, and the chapel is lit from the S and E. It uses pre-Reformation window types with depressed, four-centred arches with hood moulds. It has one external entrance (a standard four-centred arch with stone surround) in the S wall. Inside, all plaster has been removed and no decorative/sculptural features survive. In the W cell, the pews are arranged conventionally. The octagonal pulpit, with tester and reading shelf, is on the N wall, close to the (tidied up) chancel arch. The screen is largely original, of a standard Jacobean type, and is the most decorated item in the church. It is arcaded above and panelled below, with a central door.
Sources/literature: *CL*, 9 Nov. 1907.
See also: main text.

WELBECK ABBEY, NOTTINGHAMSHIRE (house remodelled; chapel does not survive)
Patron: William Cavendish (1593-1676), 1st Duke of Newcastle.
Date: 1636 event.
Architect: John Smythson (d. 1634).
Formerly the English headquarters of the Premonstratensian Order, the complex was eventually bought (in 1607) by Sir Charles Cavendish, son of Bess of Hardwick. The house his son William inherited in 1617 had been partially rebuilt by Robert Smythson, and he employed the latter's son John to undertake further building work there. In 1636, there was a chapel containing an organ somewhere within what may still have been a jumble of monastic and lay buildings. It could well have been in the former monastic frater in the S range.
Sources/literature: L. Worsley, 'The Architectural Patronage of William Cavendish, 1st Duke of Newcastle, 1593-1676' (unpublished Ph.D thesis, University of Sussex, 2001).

WENTWORTH WOODHOUSE, SOUTH YORKSHIRE (house, greatly extended and largely rebuilt, survives; chapel replaced)
Patron: Thomas Wentworth (1593-1641), 1st Earl of Strafford.
Dates: by 1633 rebuild.
Strafford inherited the stone, mid–Tudor, courtyard house, that had probably been somewhat updated by his father and may have already contained a chapel, in 1614, and transformed it into an E-plan house with many outbuildings. It is likely that Strafford's chapel possessed a clock tower and was to the W of the main house − either detached or at the end of a range.
Sources/literature: *CL*, 20, 27 Sep., 4, 11 Oct. 1924; 17, 24 Mar. 1983.

WESTENHANGER CASTLE, HYTHE, KENT (a ruin)
Patrons: Scott family; Sir Edward Poyning (d. 1521).
Dates: 1486 event; by 1521 rebuild/restoration.
The moated, 14th-century, fortified house possessed a chapel measuring 33ft x 17ft. In

1486 various members of the Scott family were granted a licence allowing their chapels to be served by an 'efficient' chaplain for themselves and their families.

Poyning succeeded to the house in 1503 (his wife was a Scott), and carried out rebuilding and restoration work, possibly including the chapel.

Sources/literature: Hussey, p. 257.

WESTWOOD HOUSE, WORCESTERSHIRE (house, somewhat altered, survives; chapel – if there was one – does not)

Patrons: Sir John ('Lusty') Packington (c.1549-1625); Sir John Packington, Bt (d. 1688).

Dates: by 1618 addition; 1689 event.

'Lusty' Packington built a large, square tower block in the 1590s on former monastic land that he had inherited, perhaps from his great uncle, also Sir John (d. 1560). By 1618 he had added four red sandstone wings, each extending diagonally from a corner of the tower. According to a 17th-century plan, the NE wing was given over to a large (45ft x 25ft) chapel, oriented to the N with a four-light window set into an apsidal liturgical E end. It was relatively isolated, being entered from the liturgical NW from an indeterminate area off the great stair and across from the hall. However, *VCH* notes that this room was only referred to as the chapel 'to bring it more into accord with the notions of ecclesiastical propriety then prevalent'.

An inventory of 1689 taken on the death of Packington's great grandson, also John, lists a chaplain's chamber (containing a bed and other domestic furniture) but no chapel.

Sources: Knyff, pl. 65; F.B. Andrews, 'Westwood (Worcestershire)', *Transactions and Proceedings of the Birmingham Archaeological Society*, 43 (1917), pp. 63-72; E.A.B. Barnard, 'The Pakingtons of Westwood', *Transactions of the Worcestershire Archaeological Society*, n.s., 13 (1936), pp. 28-49; A. Gomme, 'Re-dating Westwood', *AH*, 44 (2001), pp. 310-21; *VCH*, 3 (1913), pp. 234-6; Wanklyn, p. 252.

WILLINGTON MANOR, BEDFORDSHIRE (demolished)

Patrons: Sir John Gostwick (d. 1545); Sir Edward Gostwick Bt (1620-71).

Dates: 1541 event; by 1637 event.

Sir John Gostwick bought the site in 1529, and built a large house of wood and brick there. He sometimes lent chapel plate and vestments for use in Willington parish church and other churches nearby. This, and the fact that Henry VIII was said to have slept in a chamber 'near the chapel' in 1541, indicates that Gostwick had a private chapel in his house. However, it has been suggested that the chapel referred to was one built by him, and still in existence, within the parish church, and that the plate was locked up with other household plate when not out on loan. On balance, there was probably no private chapel in the house at this time.

Sir Edward Gostwick, a deaf mute, succeeded his father in 1630. He had a household chapel consecrated by Bishop John Williams of Lincoln between 1631 and 1637.

Sources/literature: E. Duffy, *The Stripping of the Altars* (New Haven and London, 1992), p. 489; H.P.R. Finberg, 'The Gostwicks of Willington', *The Bedfordshire Historical Record Society*, 36 (1956), pp. 59-60, 69, 71, 79, 103; F. Heal and C. Holmes, *The Gentry in England 1500-1700* (London, 1994), pp. 340-1; A. Spicer '"God Will Have a House": Defining Sacred Space and Rites of Consecration in Early Seventeenth-Century England' in *Defining the Holy: Sacred Space in Medieval and Early Modern Europe* (A. Spicer and S. Hamilton, editors), (Aldershot, 2005), p. 229; *VCH*, 3 (1912), pp. 262-6.

WILTON HOUSE, WILTSHIRE (house, altered, survives; chapel does not)
Patrons: William Herbert (1506-70), 1st Earl of Pembroke; Philip Herbert (1584-1649), 4th Earl of Pembroke.
Dates: 1543-63 rebuild; late 1630s remodelling.
Architect: Isaac de Caus (*fl.* 1620s-40s).
The house, built by the 1st Earl of Pembroke on the site of the dissolved Benedictine abbey, comprised four stone ranges surrounding a courtyard, and incorporated substantial parts of the claustral buildings. The chapel was probably in the W range. A 1561 inventory lists a table for the altar with a silver and gilt picture of Christ and the Apostles. Of exceptional quality were the wall hangings, each nine yards square and probably dating from before the Reformation. They were embroidered with gold thread, and decorated with scenes from the Passion.
The 4th Earl inherited Wilton in 1630, and partially remodelled it in the new Classical style. Isaac de Caus designed a new chapel for the W (garden) wing. It was not built precisely to de Caus's design, and its exact position is not known, but it probably occupied the same general area as its 16th-century predecessor. Inside, there was probably an upper chapel, lit by a window overlooking the court, and containing a fireplace. It was entered by doors at the E and N ends.
Sources/literature: BL, Add. MS 33767B, f. 24; Lieutenant Hammond, 'Relation of a Short Journey of the Western Counties', *Camden Miscellany*, 16 (1936), pp. 66-8; J. Rocque: 1746 plan (Courtauld Institute, BF 2639/1); *Survey of the Lands of William, 1st Earl of Pembroke* (C.R. Stratton, editor), (London, 1909); *VB*, 3 (London, 1725), p. 18; Victoria and Albert Museum Library, 1561 inventory, NAL KRP.D.30; J.J. Bold, *Wilton House and English Palladianism*, (London, 1988), pp. 40-3, 64; H.M. Colvin, 'The South Front of Wilton House', *AJ*, 111 (1954), p. 181-90; J. Harris and A.A. Tait, *Catalogue of Drawings by Inigo Jones, John Webb and Isaac de Caus at Worcester College, Oxford* (Oxford, 1979), p. 48 (no. 111), pl. 92; J. Heward, 'The Restoration of the South Front of Wilton House', *AH*, 35 (1992), pp. 78ff.
See also: main text and figs. 5.22, 5.23.

WIMBLEDON HOUSE, LONDON (demolished)
Patrons: Thomas Cecil (1542-1623), 1st Earl of Exeter; Queen Henrietta Maria (1609-69).
Dates: from 1588 new build; 1623 event; from 1638 alterations.
According to a plan by Thorpe, Cecil created one of the first assembly chapels in his innovative, substantial, U-shaped, single-pile, brick house with stone dressings. It was correctly-oriented, comprised a single-storey and occupied a cross-range position in the centre of the E range.
In 1623, Joseph Hall, the future bishop of Exeter and Norwich, praised the 'comely whiteness and well contrived coarctation' of the chapel.
In 1638, the house was acquired for (the Roman Catholic) Queen Henrietta Maria, the chapel moved to the SE corner, and a liturgical E window installed. In 1649, shortly before she was deprived of the house, the chapel contained a pulpit and pews. The floor was of black and white marble, and the arched roof and walls were painted with 'landskips'.
Sources/literature: T113-14; BL, Lansdowne MS 118, App. 2/8; BL, H. Winstanley engravings 1678; BL, King's Maps; RIBA, Smythson, I/24; 'A Survey of the Manor of Wymbledon, alias Wimbleton, 1649' (J. Caley, transcriber), *A*, 10 (1792), pp. 399-448;

'The Parliamentary Survey of Richmond, Wimbledon and Nonsuch in the County of Surrey, AD 1649' (W. Hart, editor), *Surrey Archaeological Collections*, 5 (1871), pp. 104–11; 'Miscellaneous Designs and Drawings by Sir Christopher Wren and Others' (A.T. Bolton and H.D. Hendry, editors), (Oxford, 1935), pp. 15–16, pl. II; C. Knight, 'The Cecils at Wimbledon' in Croft, pp. 47–66; D. L. Lysons, *Environs of London*, 1 (London, 1792), pp. 521ff; J.F. Merritt, 'Puritans, Laudians, and the Phenomenon of Church-Building in Jacobean London', *Historical Journal*, 41.4 (1998), p. 956; Ricketts, *Cecil*.
See also: main text and fig. 4.3.

WIMBLEDON PARSONAGE, LONDON (house, much restored, survives, as does supposed chapel)
Patron: William Cecil (1520-98), Lord Burghley.
Dates: 1550s events.
The house, acquired by Cecil in 1549, dates mainly from the early 16th century. It contains an earlier, possibly 13th-century, room which may have been the chapel where prayers were read in 1550-3. In 1556, after Mary's accession, Cecil and his second wife Mildred confessed and received communion there.
Sources/literature: NA, State Papers Domestic: Mary 11/8/1; C.S. Higham, *Wimbledon Manor House under the Cecils* (London, 1962), p. 8; C. Knight, 'The Cecils at Wimbledon' in Croft, pp. 48-52.

WITHCOTE MANOR, LEICESTERSHIRE (house replaced; chapel, its interior remodelled, survives)
Patrons: William Smith (d. 1506); Catherine Smith/Radcliffe (a. early 16th century), née Ashby; Roger Radcliffe (d. *c*.1537).
Dates: *c*.1506-37 new build.
Smith acquired the property in 1506 on the death of his father-in-law, William Ashby, and began to build a detached, rectangular, single-cell, correctly-oriented, chapel. It was completed by his widow, Catherine, and her second husband, Roger Ratcliffe. The N and S walls have four rectangular, square-headed windows with three arched lights containing 1530s stained glass (thought to be by Galyon Hone who also installed much of the painted glass in the chapel at King's College, Cambridge) depicting biblical figures and heraldic devices – including the arms of Jane Seymour. Small scenes below include a Crucifixion and heraldic devices. There are entrances (with depressed arches) in the N and S walls, the former being the more elaborate and probably intended for the household. There is a blocked up entrance in the W wall. The interior was greatly restored in the 18th century.
Sources/literature: A.R. Dufy, 'Withcote Chapel', *AJ*, 112 (1955), pp. 178-81; J. Nichols, *History and Antiquities of the County of Leicester*, 2.1 (London, 1795) pp. 387-92; C. Woodforde, 'The Painted Glass in Withcote Church, *Burlington Magazine*, 75 (Jul. 1939), pp. 17-22.
See also: main text.

WOBURN ABBEY, BEDFORDSHIRE (house, altered, survives; chapel does not)
Patron: Francis Russell (1593-1641), 4th Earl of Bedford.
Date: *c*.1630 alterations.
Architect: possibly Nicholas Stone (1587-1647).
Henry VIII granted the former Cistercian abbey to the Russell family in 1547, but no

major work appears to have been carried out there until after the 4th Earl inherited the house in 1627. The hall and integral, single-storey chapel (orientation unclear) were created from the lay brothers' frater on the entrance (W) facade.

Sources/literature: Woburn Archive (uncatalogued); D. Duggan, 'The Architectural Patronage of the 4th Earl of Bedford, 1587-1641' (unpublished Ph.D thesis, University of London, 2002), pp. 25-68; D. Duggan, 'Woburn Abbey: the first episode of a great country house', *AH*, 46 (2003), pp. 57-80.

See also: main text and figs. 5.19, 5.20.

WOLFETON HOUSE, DORSET (much of house, including chapel, demolished)
Patrons: Sir Thomas Trenchard (d. 1550); Sir George Trenchard (d. 1630).
Dates: 1530s and/or post-1557 rebuild.

Thomas Trenchard inherited the medieval house from his father in 1495, and rebuilt it to form a compact, stone, courtyard house, with the gatehouse in the E range. George Trenchard inherited the house in 1557, and rebuilt and extended it, creating a second courtyard to the W. The date of the (possibly free-standing and probably correctly-oriented) chapel, that formed part of the N side of the gatehouse courtyard, is uncertain. It could have been created and/or adapted during either or both of the rebuilding programmes.

Sources/literature: Hutchins, 1, p. 547; Oswald, pp. 14-17.

WOLLATON HALL, NOTTINGHAMSHIRE (house survives; chapel does not)
Patron: Sir Francis Willoughby (1546-96).
Dates: 1580-8 new build.
Architect: Robert Smythson (*c*.1535-1614).

A flamboyant, rectangular, stone-built house with a high central hall and four corner turrets, it replaced Old Wollaton Hall (*q.v.*), the former seat of the Willoughby family. It seems likely that Willoughby, a coal magnate with aristocratic connections and an evident love of display, would have had a chapel. Moreover, he was said to have composed sermons for his chaplains to preach to him. But its position is hard to determine. The favoured candidate is an inner chamber that had no fireplace, faced E and was entered from the NW via a so-called chapel chamber in the SE corner of the house. But the chapel chamber was always furnished as a bedchamber, and by 1596 the inner chamber too was furnished as a bedroom.

Sources/literature: Knyff, pl. 68; RIBA, Smythson I/25; T29, T49; D.N. Durant, 'Wollaton Hall – a Rejected Plan', *Transactions of the Thoroton Society of Nottinghamshire*, 76 (1972), pp. 13-16; A.T. Friedman, *House and Household in Elizabethan England, Wollaton Hall and the Willoughby Family* (Chicago and London, 1989), *passim*; M. Girouard, *Robert Smythson & the Elizabethan Country House* (New Haven and London, 1983), esp. pp. 82-108.

WOODCOTE PARK, SURREY (house rebuilt; chapel does not survive)
Patrons: Evelyn family.
Dates: after 1672 event.
Verrio was commissioned to produce an illusionistic ceiling for the chapel.

Sources/literature: E. Croft-Murray, *Decorative Painting in England, 1537-1837*, 1 (London, 1962), p. 242.

See also: main text.

WOOD HALL, WORCESTERSHIRE (demolished)
Patron: William Gower (d. 1566).
Date: 1566 event.
The contents of the chapel, listed in an inventory taken on Gower's death in 1556, indicate that it had been converted into a still.
Sources/literature: Wanklyn, p. 40.
See also: main text.

WOODHEY HALL, CHESHIRE (house demolished, chapel survives)
Patrons: William Wilbraham (d. *c*.1534); Elizabeth, Lady Wilbraham (a. 1692 and 1699), née Mitton (widow of Sir Thomas (d.1692)).
Dates: 1534 event; *c*.1697–9 new build.
William Wilbraham left money in his will for services to be conducted in his chapel at Woodhey.
By 1692, the formidable, low-church Lady Wilbraham had replaced a house of *c*.1600 with a brick house of some grandeur with tall windows and a hipped roof behind a parapet. Her rectangular, brick, linked, correctly-oriented, single-cell chapel, begun in 1697 and now fully detached, is a good example of a late 17th-century preaching box. The W end family gallery was entered from the first floor of the house. The entrance to the main chapel is from the N opposite a false door in the S. Inside, the floor was of stone flags, and seating is college style. The walls are panelled. In 1699 a Commandment board was installed in a central E end position above the pulpit.
Sources/literature: Cliffe, p. 227.
See also: main text and figs. 6.13, 6.14.

WOODLANDS MANOR, WILTSHIRE (house survives; chapel does not)
Patrons: Doddington family.
Date: *c*.1570 event.
The 14th-century, correctly-oriented, single-storey, linked chapel was on the first floor at the NW end of the single-range, U-shaped house. It was next to the hall, and entered via a staircase to the SE. In *c*.1570 it was converted into family accommodation.
Sources/literature: Westfall, pp. 23–4.

WOODLANDS PARK, DORSET (traces survive)
Patron: Henry Hastings (1551–1650).
Date: pre 1650 event.
Hastings, a nephew and sometime protégé of the Puritan Henry Hastings, 3rd Earl of Huntingdon, inherited the red-brick, Tudor house on the death of his wife, Dorothy née Willoughby (daughter of Sir Francis Willoughby of Wollaton Hall, *q.v.*). A disused chapel lay next to the parlour. Apparently spurning the pious example of his uncle, being 'indifferent to either morality or religion', Hastings used the pulpit as a larder containing beef, venison, bacon and apple pie. His proclivities anticipated by some years those of Arthur St Leger, 3rd Lord Doneraile, who converted his chapel at the Manor of Groves in Hertfordshire into a kitchen in the 1740s. His achievement was celebrated in a poem of eleven verses by Paul Whitehead (1710–74), including:

> The lord of the mansion most rightly conceiting,
> His guests lov'd good prayers much less than good eating;

And possess'd by the devil, as some folks will tell ye,
What was meant for the soul, be assign'd to the belly.

The bell's solemn sound, that was heard far and near,
And oft rous'd the chaplain unwilling to pray'r,
No more to good sermons now summons the sinner,
But blasphemous rings in – the country to dinner.

Sources/literature: A. Chalmers, *The Works of the English Poets from Chaucer to Cowper*, 16 (London, 1810), p. 228; C. Cross, *The Puritan Earl: The Life of Henry Hastings Third Earl of Huntingdon, 1536 – 1595* (London, 1966), p. 54; A. T. Hart, *The Man in the Pew 1558-1660* (London, 1966), p. 45.
[Editor's note: thanks to Nicholas Cooper for telling me about Whitehead's poem.]

WOODSOME HALL, WEST YORKSHIRE (house, updated in the 17th century, survives; chapel does not)
Patron: Arthur Kay (d. 1582).
Date: 1580 event.
Little is known about the chapel in the early 16th-century, timber-framed house, but it may have occupied a block projecting forward from the parlour wing. It was transformed into two parlours in 1580.
Sources/literature: Giles, pp. 18, 20, 197.

WRESSLE CASTLE, EAST YORKSHIRE (ruined S range, with chapel shell, survives)
Patron: Henry Percy (1478-1527), 5th Earl of Northumberland.
Dates: early 16th-century event.
The 14th-century house was transformed in the 1390s by the Percys into an impressive castle built round a courtyard, and updated by the 5th earl. *The Northumberland Household Book* records the daily arrangements in his household, including his chapels, during the first decades of the 16th century. The double-height, double-cell, correctly-oriented chapel ran along the E end of the S range and effectively terminated the main sequence of rooms. There were five entrances catering for different sections of the household, and the upper chapel consisted of a variety of linked peripheral spaces, including a pew for the patron – who on occasion attended mass in his private closet which had its own altar, and was probably a small room off his chamber.
Sources/literature: West Sussex RO, PHA 3538-47 (cited by kind permission of Lord Egremont, the owner of those documents); Leland, pt. 1.1, p. 53; *The Regulations and Establishment of the Household of Henry Algernon Percy, the Fifth Earl of Northumberland, at his Castles of Wresill and Lekinfield in Yorkshire* (T. Percy, editor; also known as *The Northumberland Household Book*), (London, 1827), p. 332; Howard, p. 207; Westfall, pp. 18-23.
See also: main text and figs. 3.13, 3.14.

WROXTON ABBEY, OXFORDSHIRE (house, restored and augmented, survives; 18th-century chapel survives)
Patron: William Pope (1573-1631), 1st Earl of Downe.

Dates: possible *c*.1610–31 rebuild.

Pope leased the former Augustinian priory from Trinity College, Oxford and started to rebuild it. It was left unfinished at his death, and completed/altered by the North family over the next 200 years. There is no direct evidence for a 17th-century chapel. However, the present (1747) chapel has a door dated 1618, and it is thought that stained glass of 1622/3 or 1632 by Bernard and/or Abraham Van Linge in the present chapel, resembling that of 1622 by Bernard Van Linge at Wadham College, Oxford, may have been intended for an earlier chapel on the site.

Sources/literature: H.T. Kirby, 'The Van Linge Window at Wroxton Abbey, Oxfordshire', *JBSMGP*, 14.2 (1965), pp. 117–21; G.Vertue, *Note Books*, 4 (Oxford, 1936), p. 192; *VCH*, 9 (1969), pp. 172–3; *CL*, 3, 10, 24 Sep. 1981.

WYTHENSHAWE HALL, CHESHIRE (house, much altered, survives; chapel does not)

Patron: Robert Tatton (1606–69).

Date: 1643 event.

Tatton inherited the timber-framed, H-plan house, which had been rebuilt after a fire by a forebear before 1579. An inventory taken in 1643 after the house was captured by Parliamentary troops shows that there was a chapel on the site below a bedroom.

Sources/literature: Manchester Archives and Local Studies (GB127), MISC/208.

A SELECTION OF OTHER CHAPELS
WHERE ANNABEL RICKETTS NOTED
THE OCCURRENCE OF CONTEMPORARY
CHANGES

SOME EPISCOPAL CHAPELS
Bishop Auckland Palace, Co. Durham (bishops of Durham); Bishopsthorpe, York (archbishops of York); Buckden Palace, Cambridgeshire (bishops of Lincoln); Cuddesdon Palace, Oxfordshire (bishops of Oxford); Durham Castle (bishops of Durham); Farnham Castle, Surrey (bishops of Winchester); Gloucester (Bishop's Palace), Gloucestershire (bishops of Gloucester); Hartlebury Castle, Worcestershire (bishops of Worcester); Lambeth Palace, London (archbishops of Canterbury); Lichfield Old Palace, Staffordshire (bishops of Lichfield); Ludham House, Norfolk (bishops of Norwich); Norwich (Bishop's Palace), Norfolk (bishops of Norwich); Otford Palace, Kent (archbishops of Canterbury); Rose Castle, Cumbria (bishops of Carlisle); Winchester (Bishop's Palace), Hampshire (bishops of Winchester)

SOME COLLEGE CHAPELS
Oxford: All Souls; Brasenose; Corpus Christi; Jesus; Lincoln; Magdalen; New; Oriel; Trinity; University; Wadham
Cambridge: Christ's; Emmanuel; Gonville & Caius; King's; Pembroke; Peterhouse; St Catharine's; St John's

SOME HOSPITAL CHAPELS
Abbot's Hospital, Guildford, Surrey; Appleby (St Anne's), Cumbria; Bootham Hospital, York; Sexey's Hospital, Bruton, Somerset; Trinity Hospital, Greenwich, London; Whitgift's Hospital, Croydon, London

SOME POST-MARIAN ROMAN CATHOLIC CHAPELS
Baddesley Clinton Hall, Warwickshire; Basing House, Hampshire; Battle Abbey, East Sussex; Birchley Hall, Billinge, Lancashire; Burton Constable Hall, East Yorkshire; Carlton Hall, West Yorkshire; Coldham Hall, Suffolk; Corby Castle, Cumbria; Coughton Court, Warwickshire; Deene Park, Northamptonshire; Dilston Hall, Northumberland; Dingley Hall, Northamptonshire; Dunsland House, Devon; Gawsworth Hall, Cheshire; Grafton Manor, Worcestershire; Harrowden, Northamptonshire; Harvington Hall, Worcestershire; Hazelwood Castle, North Yorkshire; Hendred House, Oxfordshire; Kirkby Hall (formerly Cross House), Furness, Cumbria; Lulworth Castle, Dorset (see also main Gazetteer above); Madeley Court, Shropshire; Milk Street (Sir Thomas Kytson II's house), London; Moseley Old Hall, Staffordshire; Mowbreck Hall, Lancashire; Plowden Hall, Shropshire; Quendon Hall, Essex; Samlesbury Hall, Lancashire; Sawston Hall, Cambridgeshire; Sizergh Castle, Cumbria; Speke Hall, Liverpool; Stoneyhurst, Lancashire; Stonor Park, Oxfordshire; Sutton Hall, Cheshire; Tichborne Park, Hampshire; Towneley Hall, Lancashire (see also main Gazetteer above); Ufton Court, Berkshire; Wardley Hall, Lancashire; Wardour Castle, Wiltshire; Wimbledon House, London (see also main Gazetteer above); Woolas Hall, Worcestershire

SELECT BIBLIOGRAPHY

[There follows a selection of the published works, largely of general and/or thematic interest, which Annabel Ricketts consulted when preparing her thesis (with a few more recent works inserted by the Editor). Publications relating solely to individual houses will be found in the **Gazetteer.**]

PRIMARY SOURCES

ADDISON, L., *An Introduction to the Sacrament* (London, 1686)

AUBREY, J., *Aubrey's Brief Lives* (O.L. Dick, editor), (London, 1958)

_____, *Perambulation of Half the County of Surrey in The Natural History and Antiquities of the County of Surrey, begun in the year 1673, by John Aubrey … and continued to the present time* (R. Rawlinson, editor), (London, 1719)

BACON, F., *Of Building and Gardens* (London, 1597)

_____, 'On Building', *The Works of Francis Bacon*, 6 (J. Spedding, editor), (London, 1858)

BATHO, G.R., (editor), *The Household Papers of Henry Percy, 9th Earl of Northumberland* (London, 1962)

BAYLY, T., *Certamen Religiosum: or, a Conference between His late Majestie Charles King of England, and Henry late Marquess and Earl of Worcester, concerning religion* (London, 1649)

_____, *The Golden Apophthegms of His Royall Majesty King Charles I, and Henry Marquis of Worcester* (London, 1660)

BLOME, R., *The Gentleman's Recreation* (London, 1686)

BOLINGBROKE, L.G., 'Two Elizabethan Inventories', *Norfolk Archaeology*, 15 (1904)

BOORDE, A., *A Compendyous Regyment or a Dyetary of Health (1542)* (F.J. Furnivall, editor), (London, 1870)

BOWLE, J., *A Sermon Preached at Flitton in the Co. of Bedford at the Funeral of the Rt. Hon. Earle of Kent* (London, 1614)

BRATHWAITE, R., *Some Rules and Orders for the Government of the House of an Earle* (London, 1821)

BRAY, G. (editor), *The Anglican Canons 1529-1947* (Reading, 1998)

BRERETON, W., *Travels in Holland, The United Provinces, England, Scotland and Ireland, 1634-1635* (E. Hawkins, editor), (Manchester, 1844)

CAMPBELL, C., *Vitruvius Britannicus*, 1-3, (London, 1717-25)

CHOLMEY, H., *The Memoirs of Sir Hugh Cholmey* (Malton, 1870)

CLIFFORD, D. (editor), *Diary of Lady Anne Clifford* (Stroud, 1992)

COLLIER, J.P. (editor), *The Household Books of John, Duke of Norfolk, and Thomas, Earl of Surrey; temp. 1481-1490* (London, 1844)

COLLINSON, P. (editor), 'Letters of Thomas Wood, Puritan, 1566–1577', *Bulletin of the Institute of Historical Research, Special Supplement No. 5* (1960)

COSIN, J., *The Correspondence of John Cosin DD, Lord Bishop of Durham* (Durham, 1872)

COX, C. J., 'The Household Books of Sir Miles Stapleton, Bt.', *The Ancestor*, 2 (July 1902)

CROSSLEY, E. W., 'Two Seventeenth Century Inventories', *Yorkshire Archaeological Journal*, 34 (1939)

DARRELL, W., *A Gentleman instructed in the Conduct of a Virtuous and Happy Life. Written for the Instruction of a Young Nobleman*, 2nd edn. (London, 1704)

DE LA PRYME, A., *The Diary of Abraham De la Pryme, the Yorkshire Antiquary* (C. Jackson, editor), (Durham, 1870)

DEFOE, D., *A Tour through the Whole Island of Great Britain*, 1-2 (London and New York, 1985)

DONNE, J., *Sermons* (E. Simpson and G. Potter, editors), 1-10 (Berkeley, 1954)

DOWSING, W., *The Journal of William Dowsing* (T. Cooper, editor), (Woodbridge, 2001)

ELLIS, H. (editor), 'Inventories of Goods etc in the Manor of Chesworth, Sedgewick and Other Parks', *Sussex Archaeological Collections*, 13 (1861)

EMMISON, F. G. (editor), 'Elizabethan Life: Wills of Essex Gentry and Merchants proved in the Prerogative Court of Canterbury', *Essex Record Office*, 71 (Chelmsford, 1978)

EVELYN, J., *The Diary of John Evelyn*, 1-6 (E.S. de Beer, editor), (Oxford, 1955)

FAIRCLOUGH, S., *The Saints Worthinesse and the Worlds Worthlessnesse* (London, 1653)

FIENNES, C., *The Journeys of Celia Fiennes* (C. Morris, editor), (London, 1949)

FINCHAM, K. (editor), *Visitation Articles and Injunctions of the Early Stuart Church*, 1-2 (Woodbridge and Rochester, 1994 and 1998)

FLORIO, J., *Worlde of Wordes or Most copious and exact Dictionarie in Italian and English* (London, 1598)

_____ *Queen Anne's New World of Words or Dictionarie of the Italian and English Tongues* (London, 1611)

FOXE, J., *The Acts and Monuments of John Foxe* (J. Pratt, Editor), 1–4 (London, 1870)

FRERE, W.H. AND KENNEDY, W.M. (editors), *Visitation Articles and Injunctions of the Period of the Reformation*, 1–3 (London, 1910)

GAGE, J., 'The Household Book of Edward Stafford, Duke of Buckingham' *Archaeologia,* 25 (1834)

GEE, H. AND HARDY, W. (editors), *Documents Illustrative of English Church History* (London, 1896)

HALL, J., *Works* (P. Wynter, editor), 1–10 (Oxford, 1863)

HALSTEAD, R., *Succinct Genealogies* (London, 1685)

HAMMOND, LIEUTENANT, *A Relation of a Short Survey of the Western Counties … in 1635* (L.G. Wickham Legg, editor), (London, 1936)

HARRISON, W., *The Description of England* (G. Edelen, editor), (Ithaca, 1968)

HENTZNER, P., *A Journey into England in the year 1598* (H. Walpole, editor), (Edinburgh, 1881)

HEYWOOD, O., *Oliver Heywood, His Diaries, Anecdote and Event Books*, 1–3 (J. Horsfall Turner, editor), (Brighouse, 1882)

HOBY, LADY M., *The Diary of Lady Margaret Hoby* (J. Moody, editor), (Stroud, 1998)

HOOKER, R., *Of the Lawes of Ecclesiasticall Politie* (London, 1594 and 1597)

HOPE, W.H.ST.J. (editor), 'The Last Testament and Inventory of John de Vere, Thirteenth Earl of Oxford', *Archaeologia*, 66 (1915)

HUYGENS, L., *The English Journal 1651-1652* (A.G.H. Bachrach and R.G. Collmer, editors) (Leiden, 1982)

IRVINE, W.F. (editor), 'A Collection of Lancashire and Cheshire Wills', *Record Society for the Publication of Original Documents Relating to Lancashire and Cheshire*, 30 (1896)

JULIUS, P., 'Diary of the Journey of Philip Julius, Duke of Stettin–Pomerania, through England in the year 1602' (G. von Bulow and W. Powell, editors), *Transactions of the Royal Historical Society*, n.s. 6, (London, 1892)

KENNETT, W., *A Sermon Preach'd at the Funeral of the … Duke of Devonshire* (London, 1708)

————————, *Memoirs of the Cavendish Family* (London, 1708)

KEYSER, C.E., *List of Buildings in Great Britain and Ireland having Mural and other painted Decorations: of dates prior to the latter part of the sixteenth century* (London, 1883)

KNOX, J., *The Works of John Knox,* 1-6 (D. Laing, editor), (Edinburgh, 1846-64)

KNYFF, L. AND KIP, J., *Britannia Illustrata* (J. Harris and G. Jackson-Stops, editors), (Bungay, 1984)

LAUD, W., *The Works,* 1-2 (W. Scott, editor), (1847-9); 3-7 (J. Bliss, editor), (1853-60); (facs. edn., Hildesheim and New York, 1977)

LELAND, J., *The Itinerary of John Leland in or about the Years 1535-1543* (L.T. Smith, editor), 1-5 (London, 1906-10)

LEVEY, S.M. AND THORNTON, P.K. (editors), *Of Household Stuff: the 1601 Inventories of Bess of Hardwick* (London, 2001)

LEYCESTER, P., *Historical Antiquities,* 1-2 (London, 1673)

LISLE, A.P., *The Lisle Letters* (M.St C. Byrne, editor), (Chicago, 1981)

LOFTIS, J. (editor), *The Memoirs of Anne, Lady Halkett and Ann, Lady Fanshawe* (Oxford, 1979)

LONGSTAFFE, W.H.D. (editor), *The Acts of the High Commission Court within the Diocese of Durham* (Durham, 1858)

LOVEDAY, J., *Diary of a Tour in 1732 through parts of England, Wales, Ireland and Scotland, made by John Loveday of Caversham* (J.E.T. Loveday, editor), (Edinburgh, 1890)

MACHYN, H., *The Diary of Henry Machyn, Citizen and Merchant Taylor of London, from A.D. 1550 to A.D. 1563* (J. G. Nichols, editor), (London, 1848)

MARKHAM, G.M., *Country Contentments: or, The Husbandsmans Recreations* (London, 1633-7)

MUNDY, P., *The Travels of Peter Mundy in Europe and Asia, 1608-67,* 4 (R.C. Temple, editor), (London, 1924)

NICHOLS, J.G. (editor), 'Inventory of the Goods of Henry Fitzroy, Duke of Richmond', *Camden Miscellany,* 3 (1855)

NICHOLS, N., *Memoirs of the Life and Times of Sir Christopher Hatton* (London, 1847)

NORDEN, J., *Speculum Britanniae* (London, 1593)

NORTH, R., *Of Building, Roger North's Writings on Architecture* (H. Colvin and J. Newman, editors), (Oxford, 1981)

NOTT, G.F. (editor), *The Works of Henry Howard and of Sir Thomas Wyatt the Elder* (London, 1815-16)

ORNSBY, G. (editor), *Household Books of the Lord William Howard of Naworth,* (Durham, 1878)

PEACHAM, H., *The Art of Drawing with the Pen* (London, 1606)

_____, *The Complete Gentleman* (London, 1622)

_____, *The Gentleman's Exercise or Graphice* (London, 1612)

PECK, F., *Desiderata Curiosa*, 1–2 (London, 1732)

PEPYS, S., *The Diary of Samuel Pepys* (R. Latham and W. Matthews, editors), (London, 1970)

PERCY, T. (editor), *The Regulations and Establishment of the Household of Henry Algernon Percy, the Fifth Earl of Northumberland, at his Castles of Wresill and Lekinfield in Yorkshire* (London, 1827)

PILKINGTON, J., *The Works of James Pilkington* (J. Scholefield, editor), (Cambridge, 1842)

PLATTER, T., *Thomas Platter's Travels in England, 1599* (C. Williams, editor), (London, 1937)

POCKLINGTON, J., *Altare Christianum: or The Dead Vicar's Plea* (London, 1637)

PRATT, R., *The Architecture of Sir Roger Pratt* (R.T. Gunther, editor), (Oxford, 1928)

PRYNNE, W., *Brief Survey and Censure of Mr Cozens* (London, 1628)

_____, *Canterburies Doome, or the First Part of a Compleat History of the Commitment, Charge, Tryall, Condemnation and Execution of William Laud, late Archbishop of Canterbury* (London, 1646)

RIPA, C., *Iconologia* (facs. edn., New York and London, 1976)

SCHELLINKS, W., 'Journal of Travels in England 1661-1663' (M. Exwood and H.L. Lehmann, editors), (London, 1993)

SCOTT, S.D. (editor), 'A Book of Orders and Rules of Anthony Viscount Montagu in 1595', *Sussex Archaeological Collections*, 7 (1854)

SEARLE, A. (editor), *Barrington Family Letters 1628-1632* (London, 1983)

Seconde Tome of Homilies (London, 1562/3)

SELWOOD, T. (editor), *The Letters of Lady Rachel Russell* (London, 1792)

SHUTE, J, *The First and Chief Groundes of Architecture* (facs. edn., London, 1912)

SIBBES, R., *The Brides Longing for her Bridegroomes Second Coming* (London, 1638)

SLINGSBY, SIR HENRY OF SCRIVEN, *The Diary of Sir Henry Slingsby of Scriven, Bart.* (D. Parsons, editor), (London, 1836)

SMITH, R., *The Life of the Most Honourable and Vertuous Lady, the Lady Magdalen, Viscountesse Montague* (St Omer, 1627)

ST CLARE BYRNE, M., *The Lisle Letters* (Chicago, 1981)

STARKEY, D. (editor*), The Inventory of King Henry VIII* (London, 1998)

SUMMERSON, J. (editor), *The Book of Architecture of John Thorpe* (Glasgow, 1966)

THORESBY, R., *The Diary of Ralph Thoresby FRS (1677-1724)* (J. Hunter, editor), (London, 1830)

VERTUE, G., 'Notebooks', 5 (Oxford, 1938)

————, 'Notebooks', 6 (Oxford, 1955)

WALDSTEIN, BARON ZDENKONIUS BRTNICENCIS, *The Diary of Baron Waldstein: A Traveller in Elizabethan England* (G.W. Groos, editor/translator), (London, 1981)

WANKLYN, M. (editor), *Inventories of Worcestershire Landed Gentry, 1537-1786* (Worcester, 1998)

WEDEL, VON L., 'Journey through England and Scotland made by Lupold von Wedel, 1584-5', (G. von Bulow, editor/translator), *Transactions of the Royal Historical Society*, New Series, 9 (1895)

WHARTON, H. (editor), *The History of the Troubles and Tryal of the Most Reverend Father in God, and Blessed Martyr, William Laud, Lord Archbishop of Canterbury* (London, 1695)

WHELER, G., *Account of the Churches, or Places of Assembly, of the Primitive Christians* (London, 1689)

———— *The Protestant Monastery: or Christian Oeconomicks, Containing Directions for the Religious Conduct of a Family* (London, 1698)

WILLET, A., *Synopsis Papismi* (London, 1613)

WILLIAMSON, J., *A Modest Essay upon the Character of her Late Grace the Duchess-Dowager of Devonshire* (London, 1710)

WOTTON, H., *The Elements of Architecture* (C.F. Hard, editor), (facs. edn., Charlottesville, 1968)

WRIOTHESLEY, C., *Chronicle of England During the Reigns of the Tudors from AD 1485-1559* (W. Douglas Hamilton, editor), 1 (London, 1875), 2 (London, 1877)

SECONDARY SOURCES

A GENTLEMAN OF OXFORD, *The New Oxford Guide; or, Companion through the University* (Oxford, 1759)

ADDLESHAW, G. AND ETCHELLS, F., *The Architectural Setting of Anglican Worship* (London, 1948)

AIRS, M., *The Tudor and Jacobean Country House: a Building History* (Stroud, 1995)

ANDERSON, M.D., *History and Imagery in British Churches* (London, 1995)

ANSTRUTHER, G., *Vaux of Harroden* (Monmouth, 1953)

ARCHER, M., 'Richard Butler, Glass Painter', *Burlington Magazine*, 132 (1990)

ASTON, M., *England's Iconoclasts* (Oxford, 1988)

————, 'Segregation in Church', *Women in the Church* (W.J. Sheils and D. Wood, editors), (Oxford 1990)

BAKER, C.H.C. AND BAKER, M., *The Life and Circumstances of James Bridges, First Duke of Chandos, Patron of the Liberal Arts* (Oxford, 1949)

BALDWIN, D., *The Chapel Royal, Ancient and Modern* (London, 1990)

BEARD, G., *Craftsmen and Interior Decoration in England, 1660-1820* (London, 1986)

BOLD, J., *John Webb: Architectural Theory and Practice in the Seventeenth Century* (Oxford, 1989)

————, and Chaney, E. (editors), *English Architecture Public and Private − Essays for Kerry Downes* (London and Rio Grande, 1993)

————, with Reeves, J., *Wilton House and English Palladianism, Some Wiltshire Houses* (London, 1988)

BOLTON, A.T. AND HENDRY, H.D. (editors), *Miscellaneous Designs and drawings by Sir Christopher Wren and Others* (Oxford, 1935)

BOND, F., *Screens and Galleries in English Churches* (London, New York and Toronto, 1908)

BOWYER, J., *The Evolution of Church Building* (St Albans, 1977)

BRAY, W., 'Observations on the Christmas Lord of Misrule, and on the King's Office of Revells and Tents', *Archaeologia*, 18 (1817)

BREWER, J.N., *Delineations of Gloucestershire* (London, 1825)

BRIDGES, J., *The History and Antiquities of Northamptonshire* (P. Whalley, editor), 1-2 (Oxford, 1791)

BRISTOW, I.C., *Architectural Colour in British Interiors 1615-1840* (New Haven and London, 1996)

BUCKLER, J., *Observations on the original architecture of Saint Mary Magdalen College, Oxford; and on the innovations anciently or recently attempted* (London, 1823)

BURKE, J.B., *A Visitation of The Seats and Arms of the Noblemen and Gentlemen of Great Britain*, 1-2 (London, 1852-3)

CHAMBERS, J., *The English House* (London, 1985)

CHANEY, E., *The Grand Tour and the Great Rebellion* (Geneva, 1985)

CLAPHAM, A.W. AND GODFREY, W.H., *Some Famous Buildings and Their Story* (London, 1913)

CLIFFE, J.T., *Puritans in Conflict – the Puritan Gentry during and after the Civil Wars* (London and New York, 1988)

_____, *The Puritan Gentry Besieged 1650-1700* (London and New York, 1993)

_____, *The Puritan Gentry: Great Puritan Families of Early Stuart England* (London, Boston, Melbourne and Henley, 1984)

_____, *The World of the Country House in Seventeenth-Century England* (New Haven and London, 1999)

COLLINSON, J., *The History and Antiquities of the County of Somerset*, 1-3 (Bath, 1791)

COLVIN, H., *A Biographical Dictionary of British Architects 1600-1840* (New Haven and London, 1995)

_____, *Essays in English Architectural History* (New Haven and London, 1999)

_____ (editor), *The History of the King's Works,* 4-5 (London, 1982, 1976)

COOK, G.H., *Letters to Cromwell and Others on the Suppression of the Monasteries* (London, 1965)

COOPE, R., 'The 'Long Gallery': Its Origins, Development, Use and Decoration', *Architectural History,* 29 (1986)

COOPER, N., *Houses of the Gentry 1480-1680* (New Haven and London, 1999)

CRAVEN, M. AND STANLEY, M., *The Derbyshire Country House* (Derby, 1991)

CROFT, P. (editor), *Patronage, Culture and Power, The Early Cecils 1558-1612* (London, 2002)

CROFT-MURRAY, E., *Decorative Painting in England, 1537-1837,* 1 (London, 1962)

CROSS, C., *The Puritan Earl: The Life of Henry Hastings Third Earl of Huntingdon, 1536 – 1595* (London, 1966)

_____, (editor), *Patronage and Recruitment in the Tudor and Early Stuart Church* (York, 1996)

CUNNINGHAM, C., *Stones of Witness: Church Architecture and Function* (Stroud, 1999)

DAVIDS, J.W., *Annals of Evangelical Nonconformity in the County of Essex* (London, 1863)

DAVIES, H., *Worship and Theology in England,* 2 (Princeton, 1975)

DAVIES, J.H., *The Life and Opinions of Robert Roberts as Told by Himself* (Cardiff, 1923)

DE FIGUEIREDO, P. AND TREUHERZ, J., *Cheshire Country Houses* (Chichester, 1988)

DIRSZTAY, P., *Church Furnishings, a NADFAS Guide* (London and Henley, 1978)

DOVEY, Z., *An Elizabethan Progress* (Stroud, 1999)

DOWNES, K., *The Architecture of Wren* (St Albans, 1982)

_____, *English Baroque Architecture* (London, 1966)

DUFFY, E., *The Stripping of the Altars, Traditional Religion in England 1400-1580* (New Haven and London, 1992)

DUGDALE, W., *The Antiquities of Warwickshire* (London, 1730)

DUGGAN, D., 'The Architectural Patronage of the 4th Earl of Bedford, 1587-1641' (unpublished Ph.D thesis, University of London, 2002)

DUNBAR, J. G., 'The Building Activities of the Duke and Duchess of Lauderdale, 1670-82', *Archaeological Journal,* 132 (1975)

DURANT, D.N., *Bess of Hardwick, Portrait of an Elizabethan Dynast* (Newark, 1988)

DUTTON, R., *The Age of Wren* (London, New York, Toronto and Sydney, 1951)

EMERY, A., *Greater Medieval Houses of England and Wales, 1300-1500,* 1-3 (Cambridge, 1996-2006)

EMMISON. F.G., *Elizabethan Life,* 1-5 (Chelmsford, 1970-80)

_____, *Tudor Secretary. Sir William Petre at Court and Home* (London, 1961)

ESTERLY, D., *Grinling Gibbons and the Art of Carving* (London, 1998)

FINCHAM, K. AND LAKE, P., 'Ecclesiastical Policy of James I', *Journal of British Studies,* 24.2 (1985)

FORDYCE, W., *The History and Antiquities of the County Palatine of Durham,* 1-2 (Newcastle upon Tyne, 1855)

GAIMSTER, D. AND GILCHRIST, R. (editors), *The Archaeology of Reformation 1480-1580* (Leeds, 2003)

GAIRDNER, J., *The English Church in the Sixteenth century from the Accession of Henry VIII to the Death of Mary* (London, 1904)

GARNER, T. AND STRATTON, A., *The Domestic Architecture of England during the Tudor Period,* 1-2 (London, 1908-11)

GENT, L. (editor), *Albion's Classicism: the Visual Arts in Britain 1550-1660* (New Haven and London, 1995)

GIBSON, K., 'The Decoration of St George's Hall, Windsor, for Charles II', *Apollo,* 147 (May 1998)

GIBSON, W., *The Social History of the Domestic Chaplain 1530-1840* (Leicester, 1997)

GILES, C., *Rural Houses of West Yorkshire, 1400-1830* (London, 1986)

GIROUARD, M., *Life in the English Country House, A Social and Architectural History* (New Haven and London 1978)

_____, *Robert Smythson & The Elizabethan Country House* (New Haven and London 1983)

_____, *Town and Country* (London, 1992)

GOTCH, J.A., 'The Renaissance in Northamptonshire', *Journal of the Proceedings of RIBA*, n.s., 6 (1890)

GROVE, J., *Lives of all the Earls and Dukes of Devonshire* (London, 1764)

GUILLERY, P., 'Broadway Chapel, Westminster: a forgotten exemplar', *London Topographical Record*, 26 (1990)

HAIGH, C., *Reformation and Resistance in Tudor Lancashire* (London, 1975)

_____ (editor), *The English Reformation Revised* (Cambridge, 1987)

HALL, M. (editor), *Gothic Architecture and Its Meanings 1550-1830* (Reading, 2002)

HARRIS, J., *The Architect and the British Country House* 1620–1920 (Washington DC, 1985)

_____, *The Artist and the Country House* (London, 1979)

_____, 'The Duchess of Beaufort's Observations on Places', *Georgian Group Journal*, 10 (2000)

_____, *The Palladians* (London 1981)

_____ (editor), 'The Prideaux Collection of Topographical Drawings' *Architectural History*, 7 (1964)

_____, *William Talman, Maverick Architect* (London, 1982)

_____ and HIGGOT, G., *Inigo Jones: Complete Architectural Drawings* (London, 1989)

_____ and TAIT, A.A., *Catalogue of Drawings by Inigo Jones, John Webb and Isaac de Caus at Worcester College, Oxford* (Oxford, 1979)

HART, A.T., *The Man in the Pew 1558-1660* (London, 1966)

HASTED, E., *History of Kent,* 1-12 (Canterbury, 1797-1801)

HEAL, F. AND HOLMES, C., *The Gentry in England and Wales, 1500-1700* (Basingstoke, 1994)

HEWARD, J. AND TAYLOR, R., *The Country Houses of Northamptonshire* (Swindon, 1996)

HILL, O. AND CORNFORTH, J., *English Country Houses, Caroline, 1625-1685* (London, 1966)

HOLMES, M., *The Country House Described, an Index to the Country Houses of Great Britain and Ireland* (Winchester, 1986)

HOOK, J., *The Baroque Age in England* (London, 1976)

HORSFIELD, T.W., *The History, Antiquities and Topography of the County of Sussex*, 1-2 (Lewes, 1835)

HOSKINS, W.G., *Devon* (London, 1954)

HOWARD, M., *The Domestic Building Patronage of the Courtiers of Henry VIII* (unpublished Ph.D thesis, University of London, 1985)

_____, *The Early Tudor Country House: Architecture and Politics 1490-1550* (London, 1987)

_____, *The Vyne* (London, 1998)

_____ and WILSON, E., *The Vyne, a Tudor house Revealed* (London, 2003)

HOWARTH, D., *Images of Rule, Art and Politics in the English Renaissance, 1485-1649* (Basingstoke and London 1997)

_____ (editor), *Art and Patronage in the Caroline Courts: essays in honour of Sir Oliver Millar* (Cambridge, 1993)

HUGHES, P., *The Reformation in England*, 1-3 (London 1950-4)

HUSSELBY, J., 'Architecture at Burghley House; The Patronage of William Cecil 1553-1598' (unpublished Ph.D thesis, University of Warwick, 1996)

HUTCHINS, J., *History and Antiquities of the County of Dorset*, 1-4 (London 1870)

_____, *Vitruvius Dorsettienses* (London, 1816)

HUTCHINSON, W., *The History of the County of Cumberland*, 1-2 (Carlisle, 1794)

JACKSON STOPS G. AND PIPKIN, J., *The English Country House, a Grand Tour* (London, 1985)

JACKSON STOPS G., SCHOCHET, G.J., ORLIN, L.C. AND MACDOUGALL, E.B. (editors), *The Fashioning and Functioning of the British Country House* (Washington DC, 1989)

JONES, P. VAN B., *The Household of a Tudor Nobleman* (Urbana, 1917)

KAPLAN, B.J., 'Fictions of Privacy: House Chapels and the Spatial Accommodation of Religious Dissent in Early Modern Europe', *American Historical Review*, 107.4 (2002)

KELLER, F-E., 'Christian Eltester's drawings of Roger Pratt's Clarendon House and Robert Hooke's Montagu House', *Burlington Magazine,* 128 (Oct. 1986)

KINGSLEY, N., *The Country Houses of Gloucestershire*, 1 (*1500-1600*) (Cheltenham, 1989); 2 (*1660-1830*) (Chichester, 1992)

LAMBARDE, W., *A Perambulation of Kent* (London 1826)

LEE, R., *Law and Local Society in the time of Charles I: Bedfordshire and the Civil War* (Bedford, 1986)

LEES-MILNE, J., *English Country Houses, Baroque 1685-1715* (London, 1970)

LEGG, J. WICKHAM (editor), *English Orders for Consecrating Churches in the Seventeenth Century* (London, 1911)

LIVERSIDGE, M.J.H., 'Prelude to the Baroque: Isaac Fuller at Oxford', *Oxoniensia*, 57 (1993)

LODGE, E., *Illustrations of British History,* 1–3 (London, 1791)

LYSONS, D.L., The Environs of London, 1–4 (London, 1792-6)

LYSONS, D. AND S., *Magna Britannia,* 1-6 (London, 1806–22)

MACCULLOCH, D., *Suffolk and the Tudors* (Oxford, 1986)

MCCULLOUGH, P.E., *Sermons at Court, Politics and Religion in Elizabethan and Jacobean Preaching* (Cambridge, 1998)

MAGUIRE, A., 'Country House Planning in England from 1660–1700' (unpublished Ph.D thesis, University of London, 1989)

MARKHAM, S., *John Loveday of Caversham* (London, 1984)

MARKS, R., *Stained Glass in England during the Middle Ages* (London, 1993)

MARKS, R. AND WILLIAMSON, P. (editors), *Gothic Art for England 1400-1547* (London, 2003)

MENDELSON, S.H., *The Mental World of Stuart Women* (Brighton, 1987)

MERRITT, J., 'Puritans, Laudians, and the Phenomenon of Church-Building in Jacobean London', *Historical Journal*, 41. 4 (1998)

MERTES, K., *The English Noble Household, 1250-1600* (Oxford, 1988)

MILLON, H.A., *The Triumph of the Baroque* (London, 1999)

MOORMAN, J.R.H., *A History of the Church in England* (London, 1986)

MORANT, P., *History of the Antiquities of the County of Essex*, 1-2 (London, 1768)

MOWL, T., *Elizabethan Jacobean Style* (London, 1993)

_____ and EARNSHAW, B., *Architecture without Kings, The Rise of Puritan Classicism under Cromwell* (Manchester and New York, 1995)

MOYNAHAN, B., *William Tyndale: If God Spare My Life* (London, 2003)

NEWDIGATE, R., *Cavalier and Puritan in the Days of the Stuarts* (A.E. Newdigate, editor), (London, 1901)

NEWMAN J., 'The Architectural Setting', *The History of the University of Oxford*, 4 (N. Tyacke, editor), (Oxford, 1997)

_____, 'The Elizabethan and Jacobean Great House: a Review of Recent Research', *Archaeological Journal*, 145 (1988)

_____, 'Hugh May, Clarendon and Cornbury', *English Architecture Public and Private* (J. Bold and E. Chaney, editors), (London, 1993)

NICHOLS, J., *History and Antiquities of the County of Leicester*, 1-4 (London, 1795-1811)

_____, *Progresses and Public Processions of Queen Elizabeth*, 1-3 (London, 1823)

NICHOLS, J.G., 'Memoir of Henry Fitzroy, Duke of Richmond and Somerset', *Camden Miscellany,* 3 (1855)

NIVEN, W., *Illustrations of Old Warwickshire Houses* (London, 1878)

ORMEROD, G., *History of the County Palatine and City of Cheshire* (T. Helsby, editor), 1-3 (London, 1875-82).

OSBORNE, J., *Stained Glass in England* (London, 1981)

OSWALD, A., *Country Houses of Dorset* (London, 1935)

_____, *Country Houses of Kent* (London, 1933)

'Parish Church of St. James, Westminster, Part 2, North of Piccadilly', *Survey of London*, 32 (London, 1963)

PARRY, G., *The Golden Age Restor'd, The Culture of the Stuart Court, 1603-42* (Manchester, 1981)

PEVSNER, N., 'Old Somerset House', *Architectural Review*, 16 (1954)

_____, *The Buildings of England*: series (with various co-authors)

RICHARDSON, C.J., *Architectural Remains of the Reigns of Elizabeth and James I* (London, 1840)

_____, *Observations on the Architecture of England during the Reigns of Queen Elizabeth and King James I* (London, 1836)

_____, *Studies from Old English Mansions, their furniture, gold and silver plate, &c*, 1-4 (London, 1841-48)

RICKETTS, A., 'The Country House Chapel in the Seventeenth Century', *The Seventeenth Century Great House* (M. Airs, editor), (Oxford, 1995)

_____, 'The Evolution of the Protestant Country House Chapel *c*.1500 – *c*.1700' (unpublished Ph.D thesis, University of London, 2003)

ROBINSON, J.M., *A Guide to the Country Houses of the North-West* (London, 1991)

Royal Commission on the Historical Monuments of England, *An Inventory of the Historical Monuments in the County of Cambridge*, 1-2 (London, 1968)

RYE, W.B., *England as seen by Foreigners in the days of Elizabeth and James I* (London 1865)

SANDON, E., *Suffolk Houses, A Study of Domestic Architecture* (Woodbridge, 1993)

SCOTT THOMSON, G., *Life in a Noble Household 1641-1700* (London, 1937)

SEKLER, E.F., *Wren and his Place in European Architecture* (London, 1956)

SHIRLEY, E.P., *Stemmata Shirleiana* (London, 1841)

SMITH, J.T., *Hertfordshire Houses, Selective Inventory* (London, 1993)

_____, 'Lancashire and Cheshire Houses: Some Problems of Architecture and Social History', *Archaeological Journal*, 127 (1970)

SMITH, W., *A New and Compendious History of the County of Warwickshire* (Birmingham, 1830)

SNODIN, M., AND STYLES, J., *Design and the Decorative Arts* 1500–1900 (London, 2001)

SODEN SMITH, R.H., *A First List of Buildings having Mural and other Painted Decoration, of Dates previous to the Middle of the 16th Century* (C.E. Keyser, editor), (London, 1883)

SPICER, A. AND HAMILTON, S. (editors), *Defining the Holy: Sacred Space in Medieval and Early Modern Europe* (Aldershot, 2005)

SPOTTISWOODE, J., *History of the Church of Scotland*, 1-3, (Edinburgh, 1851)

SPRAGGON, J., *Puritan Iconoclasm during the English Civil War* (Woodbridge, 2003)

STAWELL, G.D., *A Quantock Family. The Stawells of Cothelstone and their descendants* (Taunton, 1910)

STELL, C.F., *Nonconformist Chapels and Meeting-Houses in the North of England* (London, 1994)

SUMMERSON, J., *Architecture in Britain, 1530 to 1830* (Harmondsworth, 1977)

_____, *Inigo Jones* (New Haven and London, 2000)

_____, 'John Thorpe and the Thorpes of Kingscliffe', *Architectural Review,* 106 (1949)

THORNTON, P., *Authentic Decor, The Domestic Interior 1620-1920* (London, 1984)

_____, *Seventeenth-Century Interior Decoration in England, France & Holland* (New Haven and London, 1983)

THURLEY, S., *The Royal Palaces of Tudor England* (Newhaven and London, 1993)

_____, 'The Stuart Kings, Oliver Cromwell and the Chapel Royal, 1618-1685', *Architectural History,* 45 (2002)

TIPPING, H.A., *English Homes: Early Tudor 1485-1558* (London and New York, 1924); *Late Tudor and Early Stuart 1558-1649* (London and New York, 1929); *Late Stuart 1649-1714* (London and New York, 1929)

TWIGG, J., *The University of Cambridge and the English Revolution, 1625-1688* (Woodbridge, 1990)

TWYCROSS, E., *The Mansions of the County Palatine of Cheshire,* 1-2 (London, 1850)

_____, *The Mansions of England and Wales,* 1-5 (London, 1847-50)

TYACK, G., *Warwickshire Country Houses* (Chichester, 1994)

TYACKE, N., *Anti-Calvinists: The Rise of English Arminianism c.1590-1640* (Oxford, 1987)

Victoria County History series

WALPOLE, H., *Anecdotes of Painting in England,* 1-4 (Strawberry Hill, 1765)

_____, *Journals of Visits to Country Seats, etc.* (P.J. Toynbee, editor), (Glasgow, 1928)

WELLS-COLE, A., *Art and Decoration in Elizabethan and Jacobean England* (New Haven and London, 1997)

WESTFALL, S.R., *Patrons and Performance: Early Tudor Household Revels* (Oxford, 1990)

WHITE, W., *History, Gazetteer and Directory of the County of Essex* (Sheffield, 1848)

WILLIAMS, N.J., *Thomas Howard, 4th Duke of Norfolk* (London, 1964)

WINCHESTER, B., *Tudor Family Portrait* (London, 1955)

WITTKOWER, R., *Palladio and English Palladianism* (London, 1983)

WOOD, D. (editor), *The Church and the Arts* (Oxford, 1995)

WORSLEY, G., *Classical Architecture in Britain, The Heroic Age* (New Haven and London 1995)

WORSLEY, L., 'The Architectural Patronage of William Cavendish, 1st Duke of Newcastle, 1593–1676' (unpublished Ph.D thesis, University of Sussex, 2001)

WORSLEY, R., *History of the Isle of Wight* (London, 1791)

YATES, N., *Buildings, Faith and Worship: The Liturgical Arrangement of Anglican Churches 1600-1900* (Oxford, 1991)

INDEX

Bold type refers to illustrations. Roman numerals indicate plate numbers in the colour section.

Middleton Hall, Warwickshire 278
Middleton, William (d. 1614) 294
Middleton, Sir William (*c*.1636-90) 223
Mildmay, Sir Walter (*c*.1520-89) 218
Milk Street (Sir Thomas Kytson II's house), London 312
Mills, Peter (1598-1670) **106**, 302
Milne family 254
Milton Hall, Peterborough, Cambridgeshire 278-9
Minories (Sir Charles Lyttelton's house), London 28, 279
Mistley Hall, Essex 27, 279
Montacute House, Somerset 18, 197n
Montagu, Edward (1562-1644), 1st Lord Montagu 227
Montagu, Edward (1625-72), 1st Earl of Sandwich 264
Montagu, Ralph (*c*.1638-1709), 1st Duke of Montagu 227
Montagu, Richard (1577-1641), Bishop of Durham 198 n.17
Montague, Viscountess Magdalen (1538-1608) 78
Moore, Gabriel (*fl*. early 17th C) 237
Mordaunt, Henry (1623-97), 2nd Earl of Peterborough 248
More, Sir George (1553-1632) 274-5
More, Sir Thomas (1478-1535) 254
More, Sir William (1520-1600) 274-5
More, Sir William, Bt (1643-84) 274-5
Morehampton Park, Herefordshire 279
Moreton family 81, 273
Moreton, John (d. 1598) 273
Moreton, William (d. 1563) 273
Morley, George (1598-1684), Bishop of Winchester 223, 275
Morrison family 235
Morton, Thomas (1564-1659), Bishop of Durham 198 n.17, 199 n.34
Moseley Old Hall, Staffordshire 312
Mottisfont Abbey, Hampshire 279
Mottisfont parish church, Hampshire 223
Moulton parish church, Lincolnshire 187-9
Mowbreck Hall, Lancashire 312
Musgrave family 260
Mytton family 258
Mytton, Edward (1553-83) 258

Naworth Castle, Cumbria 35, **36**, **37**, 39, 40, 41, 57, 123, 129-30, 135, 141, 196 n.9, 202 n.48, 208 n.72, 209.n.78, 268, 279-

80, **V**, **VI**
Neile, Richard (1562-1640), Bishop of Durham and Archbishop of York 27, 28, 137, 198 n.17, 286
Netherton Hall, Farway, Devon 252, 280
Nevill family 68, 274
Nevill, John (d. 1577), 4th Lord Latimer 293
Nevill, Richard (1468-1530), 2nd Lord Latimer 16, 196 n.1
Nevill, William (a. 1530s) 270
New College, Oxford 312
New Hall, Essex 139, 280, **XXV**
Newcastle, 1st Duke of, *see* Cavendish, William
Newdigate, Sir John (1571-1610) 219
Newdigate, Sir John, Bt (1719-1806) 82, **83**
Newdigate, Sir Richard, Bt (1602-78) 219
Newdigate, Sir Richard, Bt (1644-1710) 219
Newnham Paddox, Warwickshire 280-1
Newstead Abbey, Nottinghamshire 281
Newton, Sir Adam (d. 1630) 237-8
Newton, Sir John, Bt (1626-99) 167, 247
Nonconformism, *see* Puritans/Puritanism
Nonsuch Palace, Surrey 249
Norden, John (1548-*c*.1625) 202 n.7
Norfolk, Dukes of, *see* Howard
Norreys family 207 n.48
Norreys, Elizabeth, Lady Rycote (*c*.1602-1645) 288-9
Norreys, Francis (1578-*c*.1622), 1st Earl of Berkshire 288-9
North family 268, 311
North, Edward (d. 1564), 1st Lord North 238
North, William (d. 1734), 6th Lord North 268
North Wyke, Devon 30-1, 281
Northampton, Earls of, *see* Compton
Northumberland Household Book 29, 35, 49, 51, 199 n.1, 310
Northumberland, Earls of, *see* Percy
Noseley Hall, Leicestershire 281-2
Nottingham, 2nd Earl of, *see* Finch, Daniel
Norwich (Bishop's Palace) 312

Offchurch Bury, Warwickshire 282
Offley, Sir Thomas (*c*.1505-82) 247
Old Hardwick Hall, Derbyshire 259
Old Thorndon Hall, Essex 282
Old Wollaton Hall, Nottinghamshire 282, 308
Oratories 13, 22, 123, 189, 196 n.9, 202 n.7,